THE HOUSE OF
SAULX-TAVANES

Robert Forster

The House
of Saulx-Tavanes

Versailles and Burgundy
1700–1830

THE JOHNS HOPKINS PRESS: BALTIMORE AND LONDON

NOTE: Two variations of the family name appear in the documents, "Tavanes" and "Tavannes." I have adopted the spelling used in the Royal Letter Patent of 1786 (*see* Document I).

R.F.

The Johns Hopkins Press, Baltimore, Maryland 21218
The Johns Hopkins Press Ltd., London

Library of Congress Catalog Card Number 75-150041
International Standard Book Number 0-8018-1247-X

CONTENTS

To

FREDERIC CHAPIN LANE

PREFACE

This is a history of the last century in the life of a great noble family. As such, it necessarily discusses only the final stage in a much longer history, one that had its beginning in the chancellery of the Burgundian dukes in the early fifteenth century and reached a peak of political importance during the Wars of Religion a hundred years later.

It would be most revealing to follow more closely the rise of the Saulx-Tavanes in these years, for it would tell us much about the so-called *grands*, their levers of power, their values and skills as councillors, captains, and seigneurs. It would help us to clarify the gradual transition of the French aristocracy from local provincial independence to Royal Court dependence and, hopefully, to capture the ambiguities and ambivalences of a ruling class in the process of domestication. Unfortunately, this cannot be done. The sources are not sufficient for more than a sketch of these earlier centuries. Adequate documentary materials become available only when the family gravitated to Paris at the turn of the eighteenth century. Moreover, hindsight makes it almost impossible to ignore the coming of the Revolution and the eclipse of the old Court. The entire narrative, as well as the analytical questions emerging from it, are necessarily influenced by our own awareness of the impending crisis, not to say doom. I have tried to avoid the worst blemishes that mark history written à la Cassandra. On the other hand, it would be a mistake not to investigate the reasons for the decline of a great noble house.

Why study one noble family? What can the social historian learn from a single case? Abandoning all claims to the typicality of the family in any statistical sense does not mean retreating to antiquitarianism and the quaintness of the particular. The actions and attitudes of more than four generations of noble courtiers such as the Saulx-Tavanes can tell us a great deal about the society in which they lived, about that society's working assumptions and its formal structure. The study of a family can thus become one of the most effective ways of establishing a continuous relation with a manageable group of individuals. This group does not need to be limited to the members of the family proper; it can include individuals with whom the family had most regular contacts—other nobles and "notables," officials at various levels of the royal administration, creditors, estate agents, tenants, and even a certain number of ordinary country people. If the sources do not permit a rigorous psychological analysis of this "extended family," they do furnish individual portraits with specific characteristics that would be difficult to attain in a more general study of a social group. Such distinct contours can provide some insight into the attitudes and values, not only of a *grand seigneur* but also of a whole cross-section of eighteenth-century society, both urban and rural, representing various tiers of the social hierarchy. A number of specific questions must be asked about these two worlds of Versailles and Burgundy.

First, how did an old military family promote its fortune at court? This question involves family discipline, marriage policy, and debt management, as well as the more obvious maneuvers for pensions and favors in the daily performance of court functions. Second, there is the question of how the Saulx-Tavanes managed their estates from Paris. The relationship of court nobles to landed society is perhaps the most important part of this book. The most crucial issues here are the role of the noble landlord in agricultural improvement and the effects—psychological as well as economic—of his managerial methods on the local rural community. Third, it is important to know how the family spent its money. The budgetary priorities of the Saulx-Tavanes tell us much about the style of life of a noble family at Paris and about its changing relations to creditors. And fourth, what form did the Revolution take and what were its effects on the family's estate in Burgundy? Looking at this circumscribed area, one can debate who "won" and who "lost" the Revolution in the provinces. For the Saulx-Tavanes, as for many other *emigré* nobles, survival was a matter of preserving not only life and revenues, but also name, rank, and esteem. How did they meet the challenge of a new century?

This study, then, treats a number of general questions about French society in the century between the reign of Louis XIV and the Restoration, as reflected in the fate of a single family and a single rural estate. If it does not claim "statistical typicality," it makes a case for "plausible typicality." I remain convinced that the Saulx-Tavanes did not act very differently from other court nobles. The pressures and norms that guided or limited their actions were those of their *milieu*. Understanding this in sufficient depth, one does not need excessive determinism to conclude that there must have been other Saulx-Tavanes.

Finally, this book is not only a "study"; it is also a story. I hope that, despite digressions on various special problems in the social and economic history of France in this period, the central theme remains intact and visible. My purpose has been to blend narrative and analysis. The reader will be the judge of whether this goal has been achieved.

ACKNOWLEDGMENTS

I wish to thank the Social Science Research Council and Dartmouth College for providing me with both the resources and the time to pursue research in Dijon, France, in 1964. The *archiviste-adjointe* of the departmental archives, Mlle Françoise Vignier, was especially helpful during my stay in Dijon. I also want to express appreciation to the librarians of Baker Library, Dartmouth College, for their generous assistance over several summers. Finally, I wish to thank James C. Davis, Elborg H. Forster, Frederic C. Lane, R. Burr Litchfield, Marc Raeff, Orest Ranum, David Spring, Lawrence Stone, Perry Viles, Sasha Weitman, and Martin Wolfe for their helpful criticism while this study was in preparation. All documents included in this book have been translated by Elborg H. Forster. A special acknowledgment is due to Linda Vlasak of The Johns Hopkins Press for numerous improvements in the manuscript.

ABBREVIATIONS

A. D. for *Archives Départmentales, Côte d' Or*; series letter and bundle number to follow (e.g., *A. D.*, E–1748).

Other departmental archives will be cited as *A. D.*, followed by the name of the department and the bundle number.

A. N. for *Archives Nationales*, Paris.

TABLE OF MEASURES
Used in Northern Burgundy in Eighteenth Century

SQUARE MEASURE:

perche	9.52 sq. meters	11.4 square yards
petit journal	22.85 *ares*	0.57 acres
(240 *perches*)		
grand journal	34.28 *ares*	0.85 acres
(360 *perches*)		
soiture	34.28 *ares*	0.85 acres
(for meadow)		
arpent coutumier	41.90 *ares*	1.03 acres
(for wood)		
arpent royal	51.07 *ares*	1.26 acres
ouvrée	4.28 *ares*	0.11 acres

CAPACITY MEASURE:

livre	489 grams	17.12 ozs.
quintal	48.9 kg.	107.56 lbs.
(100 *livres*)		
mesure	19.56 kg.	43.03 lbs.
(about 40 *livres*)		
quarteau	57 *litres*	1.62 American bushels
emine	512 *litres*	14.55 American bushels
(for grain)		
moule de Dijon	1.47 *stère*	52.11 cubic feet
(for wood)		
muid or *pièce*	228 *litres* at Dijon	60.16 gallons
(for wine)	257 *litres* at Beaune	67.81 gallons

LONG MEASURE:

perche	3.08 meters	10.0 feet
aune de Dijon	0.81 meters	2.6 feet
toise de Bourgogne	2.43 meters	7.9 feet

SOURCE: P. de Saint-Jacob, *Les paysans de la Bourgogne du Nord au dernier siècle de l'Ancien Régime* (Dijon, 1960), p. xxxvii.

THE HOUSE OF
SAULX-TAVANES

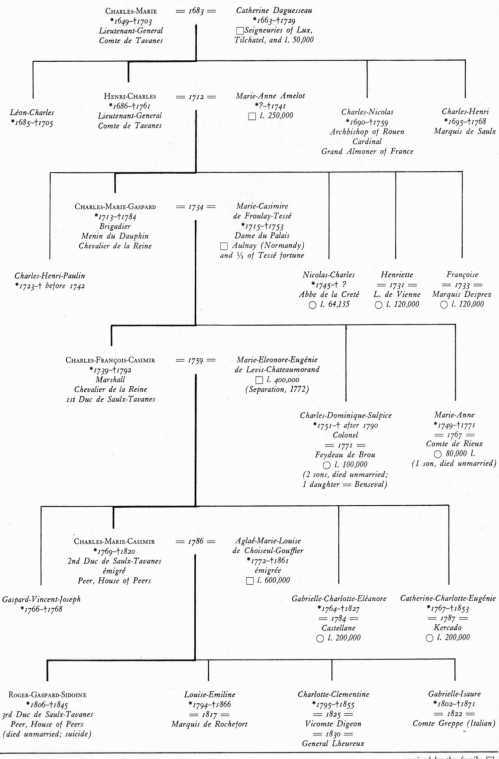

CHARLES-MARIE
*1649–†1703
Lieutenant-General
Comte de Tavanes
= 1683 =
Catherine Daguesseau
*1663–†1729
☐ Seigneuries of Lux,
Tilchatel, and l. 50,000

Léon-Charles
*1685–†1705

HENRI-CHARLES
*1686–†1761
Lieutenant-General
Comte de Tavanes
= 1712 =
Marie-Anne Amelot
*?–†1741
☐ l. 250,000

Charles-Nicolas
*1690–†1759
Archbishop of Rouen
Cardinal
Grand Almoner of France

Charles-Henri
*1695–†1768
Marquis de Saulx

CHARLES-MARIE-GASPARD
*1713–†1784
Brigadier
Menin du Dauphin
Chevalier de la Reine
= 1734 =
Marie-Casimire
de Froulay-Tessé
*1715–†1753
Dame du Palais
☐ Aulnay (Normandy)
and ⅓ of Tessé fortune

Charles-Henri-Paulin
*1723–† before 1742

Nicolas-Charles
*1745–† ?
Abbe de la Creté
○ l. 64,135

Henriette
= 1731 =
L. de Vienne
○ l. 120,000

Françoise
= 1733 =
Marquis Desprez
○ l. 120,000

CHARLES-FRANÇOIS-CASIMIR
*1739–†1792
Marshall
Chevalier de la Reine
1st Duc de Saulx-Tavanes
= 1759 =
Marie-Eleonore-Eugénie
de Levis-Chateaumorand
☐ l. 400,000
(Separation, 1772)

Charles-Dominique-Sulpice
*1751–† after 1790
Colonel
= 1771 =
Feydeau de Brou
○ l. 100,000
(2 sons, died unmarried;
1 daughter = Benseval)

Marie-Anne
*1749–†1771
= 1767 =
Comte de Rieux
○ 80,000 l.
(1 son, died unmarried)

CHARLES-MARIE-CASIMIR
*1769–†1820
2nd Duc de Saulx-Tavanes
émigré
Peer, House of Peers
= 1786 =
Aglaé-Marie-Louise
de Choiseul-Gouffier
*1772–†1861
émigrée
☐ l. 600,000

Gaspard-Vincent-Joseph
*1766–†1768

Gabrielle-Charlotte-Eléanore
*1764–†1827
= 1784 =
Castellane
○ l. 200,000

Catherine-Charlotte-Eugénie
*1767–†1853
= 1787 =
Kercado
○ l. 200,000

ROGER-GASPARD-SIDOINE
*1806–†1845
3rd Duc de Saulx-Tavanes
Peer, House of Peers
(died unmarried; suicide)

Louise-Emiline
*1794–†1866
= 1817 =
Marquis de Rochefort

Charlotte-Clementine
*1795–†1855
= 1825 =
Vicomte Digeon
= 1830 =
General Lheureux

Gabrielle-Isaure
*1802–†1871
= 1822 =
Comte Greppe (Italian)

* born   † died   = married

Portions and dowries:
received by the family ☐
paid by the family ○

I

FROM RENAISSANCE "CAPTAINS"
TO COURT NOBILITY

A grand seigneur was once a man of illustrious birth who possessed large estates and the great offices of the Crown," wrote Cardinal de Bernis with a certain nostalgia. "Master of his own region, he was not ashamed to reside there. He had influence with the King, but he seldom went to Court."[1] In the sixteenth century, Gaspard de Saulx was such a *grand seigneur*. Ardent champion of the Counter-Reformation, soldier of both Henry II and Charles IX, Gaspard combined his Catholic royalism with a large measure of local influence: he was a royal "captain" in Burgundy when the power of Paris was not yet secured in the province, he was *Grand Bailli* at a time when royal governorships were much more than honorific sinecures. His château of Sully—sturdy stone pierced by small apertures and encircled by a wide moat—was the center of a chain of twenty-four domains and seigneuries, comprising over forty villages and extending from Autun northeastward through the Dijon plain almost to Langres in Champagne. Behind Gaspard was a semi-feudal retinue of some eighty families of lesser nobility, in addition to a host of *robins, procureurs, prévôts,* receivers, sergeants, and clerks, not to count tenants, sharecroppers, winegrowers, artisans, and *censitaires*—all dependent on the *Bailli*. Basking still in the glory of his recent victories at Renty and Cerizolles, Marshal Gaspard presided over the local Burgundian estates in the midst of a civil war. Here was no docile royal agent, but a great captain whose military successes against the Imperial troops in Italy or the Huguenots in the Saône Valley were more marks

[1] Cardinal de Bernis, *Mémoires et lettres,* ed. F. Mason (Paris, 1903), I, 101.

of personal fidelity than obedience to a sovereign.[2] Surely Gaspard had gilded the coat-of-arms of an old family—the Saulx-Tavanes.[3]

Yet, if the sixteenth century had witnessed a brilliant revival of a noble family that had once served the dukes of Burgundy, the luster of fortune and position was not to endure long into the following century. Less than fifty years after Gaspard's death in 1579, the house of Tavanes came upon hard times. The large revenues accumulated by Gaspard were diminished, domains were alienated, and debts were mounting. War and heroic combat, which had earned Gaspard fame and glory, seemed to work against the fortunes of the family as the new century advanced.

During most of the seventeenth century, northeastern Burgundy was the French frontier, open to frequent invasion by Imperial troops or marauders from Franche-Comté across the Saône River. The Tavanes seigneuries along the Saône and Vingeanne rivers were exposed to these incursions. In 1636, the seigneurie of Beaumont was sacked by the Imperials; by the end of the year, 800 villagers had perished either by the sword or in the aftermath of starvation and disease. The same thing happened on other properties of the family along the Vingeanne—at Dampierre, Champagne, Blagny, Renêve. The sieges of Mirebeau, Fontaine-Française, and Saint Jean-de-Losne would long be remembered in the Dijonnais; it was a story of extreme brutality, with the worst atroci-

---

[2] This "society of *fidélités*" and a "hierarchy of dignities" have been treated extensively by Roland .Mousnier, in his *Les hierarchies sociales de 1450 à nos jours* (Paris, 1969), pp. 81–82, and *Problèmes de stratification sociale*, Actes du Colloque international, 1966 (Paris, 1968). See also O. Ranum, *Richelieu and the Councillors of Louis XIII* (Oxford, 1963).

[3] For the genealogy of the family, see Père Anselme de Sainte Marie, *Histoire généalogique de la maison royale de France, des grands officiers de la couronne...*, 9 vols. (Paris, 1730), VII, "Saulx" and "Saulx-Tavanes". See also L. Pingaud, *Les Saulx-Tavanes* (Paris, 1876). Pingaud is principally interested in the sixteenth and seventeenth centuries. He has edited selections of the correspondence of Gaspard, Jean, and Guilleaume de Saulx in his *Correspondance des Saulx-Tavanes au XVIe siècle* (Paris, 1877). See the Bibliography for *Mémoires* of Gaspard and Jacques de Saulx. For an excellent portrait of Gaspard de Saulx in sixteenth-century dress, see Bibliothèque Nationale, *Manuscrits Français, Nouv. acqu.*, 1773. A similar portrait can be found at the château of Bussy-Rabutin in the Côte d'Or. Gaspard's most authentic ancestor was Jehan de Saulx, Chancellor of the Duke of Burgundy, 1405–20. See R. Vaughan, *John the Fearless* (London, 1966), pp. 134–36. For the history of Burgundy in Gaspard's time, see H. Drouot and J. Calmette, *Histoire de Bourgogne*, 4 vols. (Dijon, 1927–37), and H. Drouot, *Mayenne et la Bourgogne: Etude sur la Ligue*, 2 vols. (Paris, 1939). Both are conventional, essentially political histories.

ties following the first breach in the town walls. Only the extensive tracts of forest of Velours and Longchamps, bridged by the marshes of the Tille barely ten miles east of Dijon itself, prevented a direct attack on the capital. The physical devastation was nothing compared to the famine and pestilence which followed—and Swedish allies were not much better than the Croats of the army of Gallas. The Peace of Westphalia did not bring an end to this "time of troubles," for marauding groups of disbanded troops continued to pillage the region periodically until the final annexation of Franche-Comté in 1678. The inquest of the Intendant Bouchu presents a picture of utter desolation, of a rich agricultural area being turned to waste and fallow. It is therefore easy to understand why there is a gap in estate accounts of the Saulx-Tavanes in the middle years of this disastrous seventeenth century.[4]

The reign of Louis XIV brought little relief. If falling agricultural production marked the first two-thirds of the century, stagnant rents characterized the years after 1680. Fortunately, a partial record of the Tavanes leases in this period has survived.

TABLE I.1   RENTS OF THE TAVANES FAMILY IN THE SEVENTEENTH CENTURY

Seigneurie of Beaumont		Seigneurie of Lux		Seigneurie of Tilchatel	
Lease	Annual Rent Livres	Lease	Annual Rent Livres	Lease	Annual Rent Livres
1608–18	3,500	1652–61	4,000	1644–	6,000
1622–28	4,100	1669–75	4,500	——	——
——	——	1690–99	3,100	1673–79	10,200
1668–74	5,400	1699–1708	3,500	1679–89	10,000
1674–83	5,400	1708–17	3,600	1689–98	9,500
1689–95	5,200	1717–26	3,550	1698–1706	8,700
1696–1702	5,200			1706–14	9,000
1704–13	5,047			1714–23	9,500
1711–16	5,047				
1718–30	5,011				

SOURCES: A. D., Côte d'Or, E–1767, E–2022.

From the income side alone, then, the agricultural picture was not a very favorable one for a noble seigneur who had land in the Dijonnais during the reigns of Louis XIII and Louis XIV. But with careful attention to the expenditure side of the ledger and with assiduous manage-

[4] G. Roupnel, La ville et la campagne au XVIIe siècle : étude sur les populations du pays dijonnais (Paris, 1955), pp. 12, 26, 238n, and passim. Roupnel's work is a classic of its kind.

ment of the land, a noble family might do better than just survive. The noble magistrates of Dijon had proven that. Could the warrior clan Saulx-Tavanes make the adjustment? Family tradition and temperament did not appear auspicious. Gaspard's two sons had fought on opposite sides in the Wars of the League, and their grandsons in turn would oppose one another in the Wars of the Fronde. Such continuous soldiering was not conducive to husbanding the resources or to developing the skills and attitudes the economic situation required.

Preservation of a noble fortune meant more than surveying rent rolls and keeping current expenditures down. More important in the long run was the problem of managing the division of the family estate over the generations. Marshal Gaspard de Saulx had been aware of the necessity of family discipline in these matters. An active military life did not prevent him from spending his last years writing a manual on the education of nobles. He was very firm on the vocation of children.

> Wealthy *gentilshommes* with three children should place two in the army, and middling nobles only one. The rest should enter either the Church or the Law, and only the eldest should have children. Marry few daughters, for that is the ruin of a noble house.[5]

Under the Burgundian customary law, younger children of noble families could claim equal shares to one-third of the fortune of their parents.[6] Much depended on a father's ability to keep dowries, portions, and "gifts in life" from exceeding these limits. In other words, the eldest son should be assured his maximum legal claim to the inheritance. When families were large and sons-in-law prestigious and stubborn, a father would be under considerable pressure to make incursions on the eldest son's two-thirds. But even under the best conditions, the family fortune had to be constantly increased in order to compensate for the loss of one-third of the estate each generation. Here again the virtues of frugality and measured expenditure would not alone solve the problem, unless

[5] *Mémoires de très noble et très illustre Gaspard de Saulx, Seigneur de Tavanes, Maréchal de France, Amiral des Mers du Levant, Gouverneur de Province, Conseiller du Roy et Capitaine de Cent Hommes d'Armes* (Lyon, 1657), p. 11. The *Mémoires* were edited by Gaspard's son, Jean de Saulx. See Pingaud, *Correspondance*, Introduction. Gaspard's views on education are cited copiously in W. L. Wiley, *The Gentlemen of Renaissance France* (Cambridge, Mass., 1954).

[6] M. Bouhier, *Les coûtumiers du duché de Bourgogne avec les anciennes coûtumes et les observations de M. Bouhier, président à mortier*, 2 vols. (Dijon, 1742–46), I, 12ff, "Des successions".

very substantial savings could be made from current income and rein-vested in the land.

Much more promising was the effort to contract "good alliances" for eldest sons, attracting dowries large enough to provide a net increase in the income-producing capital of the family. In this quest the Saulx-Tavanes were better favored by tradition and temperament. The role of the military captain, in addition to providing a wide field for dramatic action or an "illustrious" stroke, was an admirable lure for a wealthy heiress. Properly employed, a great name founded on a reputable military past could restore a family fortune without tarnishing its coat-of-arms. On this point, Marshal Gaspard's manual on education was subtle. Men of noble virtue should not contract *mésalliances* from which only "demi-virtue" can be born. But the race of *gentilshommes* should not be con-fined to the military. "Stupid is the opinion of brutes that presidents and councillors [of the parlements] are not *gentilshommes*."[7] However, the Tavanes had to wait for the Marshal's grandson Claude to follow this wise counsel concerning the selection of wives.

A review of the family's wills and marriage contracts in the late six-teenth and early seventeenth centuries reveals that Gaspard's stern ad-monitions were not followed, not even by the Marshal himself. Emo-tional considerations and unforeseen contingencies had a way of inter-vening. The fact that Gaspard's two sons fought against each other in the Wars of the League did not facilitate a normal family settlement. Perhaps this is what led to the equal division of Gaspard's properties be-tween his two sons "without any *préciput* or right of the eldest."[8] And this incision in the estate had been preceded by two dowries of 100,000 and 80,000 livres to each of Gaspard's daughters. These were enormous sums for the late sixteenth century and contrasted sharply with the dowry Gaspard's wife had brought to the family in 1546—a modest 20,000 livres.[9]

The same pattern persisted in the second generation. Guilleaume, with a marriage portion from his wife of only 20,000 livres, dowered each of

[7] *Mémoires de Gaspard de Saulx*, p. 11.

[8] *Archives Départementales*, Côte d'Or, Series E, number 1662, *Partage*, 1581. Hereafter cited as *A. D.*, followed by the series and number *only*. See "Abbrevia-tions," at the beginning of the book.

[9] *A. D.*, E–1727, *Inventaire des titres*. Marriage contracts of January 9, 1566; Octo-ber 9, 1588; and December 16, 1546. This is an inventory of family contracts and titles, giving only a summary of each.

5

his three daughters an average of three times this sum.[10] Marshal Gaspard's warning was far away. Worse, his most distinguished son-in-law, a Rochechouart from outside the province, obtained a court order requiring Guilleaume to deliver land as security for an unpaid dowry.[11] Guilleaume, toward the end of his life, partially disinherited his eldest son, Claude, limiting his portion to the family properties in the Bailliage of Dijon.[12] No wonder that the family papers in the early seventeenth century began to bulge with law cases, sentences, and foreclosures over portions. Leaving aside the cost of Guilleaume's countless campaigns in the Wars of the Three Henrys, his family charges were assuming dangerous proportions. His choice domains were threatened with court action and seizure.[13]

Claude de Saulx, grandson of the Marshal, made a concerted effort to halt the disintegration of the family fortune. In 1613 he negotiated an excellent marriage with Françoise Brulart, daughter of the First President of the Parlement of Dijon. Her dowry of 120,000 livres was a welcome relief. Within two weeks after the marriage contract was signed, Claude had received 27,000 in silver and 57,000 more assigned to his creditors.[14] A few years later it was Brulart money that repurchased the land of Arc-sur-Tille, alienated previously to pay family debts.[15] Claude de Saulx had employed his name well, for the Brularts were also willing to use their legal capacities on his behalf both in Paris and Dijon.[16]

Claude even obtained an unexpected bonus in the administrative acumen of his new wife. Françoise de Brulart has left an account book of her estate management at Beaumont between 1632 and 1636. Every small purchase was itemized, and, more important, every bit of agricultural produce was mustered, even to the point of sending artichokes, butter, and eggs to her husband with his company at Auxonne on the Saône. When Madame was at Dijon, she had her food sent from the estate, 20

[10] *A. D.*, E-1663, Marriage contracts of October 18, 1570; December 31, 1596; October 9, 1608; September 27, 1604; and August 29, 1613.
[11] *A. D.*, E-1663, *Arrêt du Parlement*, December 20, 1613.
[12] *A. D.*, E-1727, Will of December 13, 1635; Codicil of May 4, 1637.
[13] Roupnel, *La ville et la campagne*, pp. 236-37, 237n.
[14] *A. D.*, E-1727, Marriage contract of August 14, 1613; receipts of September 1, 1613.
[15] *A. D.*, E-1741-42, *Remises et retrocession*, 1641-42.
[16] Françoise de Brulart had an uncle who was *maître des requêtes* at Paris. He very kindly resold Arc-sur-Tille to his niece for the same price he had paid for it. See Roupnel, *La ville et la campagne*, p. 187n.

miles away. She bought her clothes in the local villages, including "thread to mend the coat of Monseigneur," an item that future generations of Tavanes women would find incredible. She paid the three livres her son had borrowed from his seminary comrade at Dôle. And when the Imperial troops threatened, instead of fleeing westward, Comtesse de Beaumont stocked the château with grain and powder for a siege.[17]

Françoise de Brulart was the ideal wife at this stage in the financial history of the family. From this point of view she had only one "fault," for which her husband and the contemporary state of medical knowledge had to share the blame: Claude de Saulx and Françoise Brulart had eleven children who survived childhood and had to be portioned. Yet even this prodigious threat to the family fortune was dissipated in a manner that suggests conscious planning. Three of the four girls became nuns in local convents (Dijon, Châtillon, and Semur) and two of the seven sons became abbots in Champagne. Portions for children who entered the Church could almost always be reduced to a few hundred livres. Two more sons died bachelors. This left one married daughter and three married sons whose portions had to be paid in full. Jacques, the eldest, received his two-thirds under Burgundian custom on condition that he pay the others.[18] Luckily, Claude's married daughter died childless and her dowry plus some of her husband's property returned to the elder branch in 1657.[19] One married son established a cadet branch of Mirebel and the other, Louis, willed his portion to his only daughter.[20] Thus, with reasonable luck and through good planning, only two portions in eleven were fully paid and permanently lost to the family.

By a prudent marriage and a careful ordering of family obligations, the generation of Claude de Saulx had begun to restore the family fortune. By 1662, Claude's thrifty widow felt secure enough from family creditors to entail the domain of Arc-sur-Tille to her grandson, thus legally securing part of the estate from alienation in the next generation.[21] Had a new family discipline been established, one that put financial equilibrium before generosity to younger children, or even before family *éclat*?

[17] *A. D.*, E–1808, Register, 1632–36; Roupnel, *La ville et la campagne*, p. 321n.
[18] *A. D.*, E–1727, Wills of September 12, 1638 and August 3, 1662.
[19] *A. D.*, E–1727, Will of March 7, 1658; *A. D.*, E–1666, Transaction of August 1, 1657.
[20] *A. D.*, E–1727, Will of February 15, 1680.
[21] *A. D.*, E–1727, Will of August 3, 1662.

If new discipline implied any departure from military function, no change is discernible in the last half of the seventeenth century. All four of Jacques's sons fought in royal regiments and two of them paid with their lives—René killed by the Turks in Crete in 1668, and Gaspard by the Hanoverians at Kassel in 1677. Henri became *maître de camp* in the Orleans regiment and Charles-Marie, the eldest, lieutenant-governor in Burgundy.[22] Yet something else had changed. One can not peruse the transactions and accounts of the family in this generation without an awareness that the Tavanes were becoming "domesticated" in the armies of Louis XIV. The quest for promotions and the purchase and sale of commissions and regiments suggest a narrowing of options and almost a scramble for prestige posts in the professional army of Louvois. The sons of the house made their way from standard-bearers to ensigns, lieutenants to colonels, brigadiers to lieutenant-generals—all appropriately attached to elite regiments bearing the names of the royal household or the Princes of the Blood. No longer were the Tavanes winning fame and fortune as *condottieri* captains in a frontier province on behalf of an insecure monarchy. Institutions, especially military institutions, had changed.

Even in the single generation from 1650 to 1680 the differences were marked. Jacques de Saulx, *Frondeur*, had not hesitated to place his first loyalty at the service of the Prince de Condé. When Condé broke with the court of Mazarin and the Queen, Jacques made it a point of honor "to follow the fortunes of his master." He remained faithful to the house of Condé even after the Prince had been abandoned by the Parlement of Paris and had to rely on Spanish mercenaries. Neither courtier nor statesman, this Tavanes saw himself as a "valiant and vigilant warrior," for whom unwavering personal loyalty was the highest virtue.[23] When he finally withdrew from Condé's army in 1652, he denied that he had been "bought" by Mazarin.

> In order to remove from the thoughts of Your Highness [Condé] that any base interest has made me seek the friendship of this minister [Mazarin],

---

[22] Père Anselme, *Histoire généalogique*, VII; L. Pingaud, *Les Saulx-Tavanes*, Appendix.

[23] *Mémoires de Jacques de Saulx, comte de Tavanes*, ed., C. Moreau (Paris, 1858), Preface. The *Mémoires* were first published in 1691, eight years after the death of the author. They emphasize acts of valor and dramatic *escarmouches*, evoking strong emotions—hate, vengeance, and—above all—personal loyalty.

I am protesting to him and giving him my word that I do not intend to appear at Court nor assume any government post. I want only the joy of seeing Your Highness there with the rank that is his due.[24]

The words, at least, were in the very best tradition of Gaspard, Guilleaume, and Jean de Saulx, of a century earlier.[25]

The military career of Jacques's son, Charles-Marie, was different. The years from 1655 to 1675 were decisive in the establishment of the new French army. Le Tellier and the war ministers had done their work well. The crown at last gained control over the appointments of general officers, and by regulating billeting, medical aid, and the flow of supply in general, the Ministry of War undercut the military independence of the *condottieri* captains. The prestige of a military career had scarcely begun to suffer, but the very size, recruitment, and training of the new royal army left less place for individual combat and, most important, for personal loyalties.[26] A family loan contracted in 1684 reads: "to be employed for the equipment of seigneur comte de Tavanes so that he can serve His Majesty during the present campaign."[27] The Ludovican state made sure there was no other to serve.

In the society of the Sun King there was still a very large place for a *grand seigneur* with a military tradition to uphold—provided he did not remain in the provinces or, worse, cabal for local power. If it is too simple to posit a sudden mutation from provincial magnate to domesticated courtier among the French aristocracy, it is certain that a military career followed a more prescribed course by this time. Sooner or later *les grands* had to come to terms with the Secretary of War in the capital. How much more advantageous and fitting to approach the new bureaucracy with the recommendation of the Court! It may well be true that, in obtaining regiments under Louis XIV, the vintage of a family played a lesser role than royal favor.[28] Better to have both.

A move to Paris seemed increasingly mandatory. The Tavanes could

---

[24] *Mémoires de Jacques de Saulx*, p. 220.

[25] Pingaud, *Correspondance*, pp. 76, 292–305, 310, 330–31. These letters express in the finest sixteenth-century manner the sense of personal loyalty of Gaspard, Guilleaume, and Jean de Saulx.

[26] J. B. Wolff, *Louis XIV* (New York, 1968), 148–51; A. Corvisier, *L'armée française de la fin du XVIIe siècle au ministère de Choiseul* (Paris, 1964), I, 130–42.

[27] *A. D.*, E–1673, *Obligation*, April 24, 1648.

[28] A. Corvisier, "Les généraux de Louis XIV et leur origine sociale," *XVIIme Siècle*, XLII (1959), 42.

9

not have been entirely unaware of its dangers. One did not have to wait for the moralists and physiocrats of a later date to appreciate the costs of living in Paris and Versailles. However, there were also opportunities for a family with a name like that of the Tavanes. Their pedigree was irreproachable. The Tavanes were among the oldest houses of France, with proofs establishing their nobility in 1234.[29] This placed them securely among such illustrious names as Polignac-Polignac, Estaing, Montmorency, La Rochefoucauld, and La Tremouïlle. As Duclos, that cryptic commentator on social mores, put it, "a Tavanes has no need of any title other than his birth."[30] Such a name commanded respect of Parisian as well as Burgundian society.

Residence near the Court promised at least three practical advantages the Tavanes would lose little time in procuring. It brought them close to the national money-market, a mixed blessing, but indispensable in the search for large capital sums. Second, it promised pensions and gratuities from the Royal Treasury—pecuniary honors that could more than defray the higher cost of living. And finally, it was the center of the marriage market. Paris offered what no provincial capital could: a wide choice of heiresses from respectable, highly-placed robe families, with the world of "Finance" but one generation removed. A good marriage in the capital could do more at one stroke to restore a sagging fortune than a lifetime devoted to painstaking domain-building and economy in the provinces. Moreover, despite the example set by Françoise Brulart, how could a Saulx-Tavanes settle for the life style of a provincial magistrate? A permanent move to Paris, of course, meant to reject provincial independence and local leadership for good. However, after the reign of Louis XIV, the provinces no longer offered a family of military nobility the role it had enjoyed in the past. In the end, it was easier to change the family's residence than to change its vocation. To continue in the *métier* of military service in a style befitting the descendants of Marshal Gaspard de Saulx, the Tavanes had to accept the importance of Paris and the Court.

How conscious these motives and arguments were is impossible to say, but it is certain that the Tavanes benefited from each of the advantages outlined above.[31] The move to Paris provided the family with a standard of living they had never enjoyed before—aided, to be sure, by borrowed

[29] F. Bluche, *Les Honneurs de la Cour* (Paris, 1957), "Saulx-Tavanes."
[30] C. P. Duclos, *Oeuvres complètes* (Paris, 1806), X, 188–89.
[31] There are no extant letters or other appropriate sources for these years.

capital from the City's "bankers." They obtained highly prestigious, if not always highly functional, posts. They frequented the very best of "society." By the standards of material consumption and social status, the move proved a clear success. On the other hand, domestication exercised more subtle changes on the members of the family in the eighteenth century. Gradually, the military role became secondary to that of courtier. Prerogatives and pretentions grew apace, unrelated to any new "illustrious action." Duclos's observation about the sufficiency of the Tavanes name seemed confirmed. As the court replaced the battlefield as the arena of social competition, family name and family connection had to bear the full weight of family advancement. For, in the more fluid society of Paris, not even a *grand seigneur* could afford to stand still: he had to develop skills, techniques, and even masks to retain his preeminent position in society.

Charles-Pinot Duclos had a way of exposing some of these techniques in his *Considérations sur les moeurs* (1769). In an article on the *grands seigneurs*, he pointed to a certain evolution in the use and meaning of the term "noble."[32] Once an exterior sign of strength and courage, he wrote, it has since become mere usage. "Children, inheriting the rank of their fathers, have nothing to do but to enjoy the fruits of the accomplishment of their ancestors." Duclos pursued the physical aspects of the change. Ancestors with athletic physiques and imposing mien have been replaced by *beaux soldats* with delicate and weak faces, *sophisticates* of more polish than strength. One cannot help but contrast Marshal Gaspard's seventeenth-century portrait at Bussy-Rabutin to that of Henri-Charles at Lux painted in the eighteenth century. Duclos was not the only one to make this observation. Serious educational reformers emphasized that a cardinal weakness in the education of the court nobility was the lack of physical exercise.[33]

Duclos, however, was suggesting a more fundamental weakness, when he discussed how *les grands* maintain their place near the apex of the social pyramid. An "imaginary power" upholds them, Duclos said, built

[32] C. P. Duclos, *Considérations sur les moeurs de ce siècle* (London, 1769), pp. 85–92.

[33] *Ephémérides du citoyen, ou bibliothèque raisonnée des sciences morales et politiques*, V (1766), 163ff. This refers to an article in the physiocratic periodical condemning "excessive delicacy" in the physical upbringing of children of the upper nobility.

on ostentation and pomp which artificially widens the distance between "the Great" and their inferiors. It is an ostentation won by intrigue for high office and exhibited by conspicuous and exacting ceremony. The dignities and trappings of position are absolutely vital to the existence of the *grand seigneur*. Moreover, insisted Duclos, the court noble half-consciously senses the insecurity and futility of his position, and thus he needs an escape in the world of pomp and circumstance.[34] Half-consciously indeed, for it is doubtful that the Tavanes discerned anything unusual about ceremony and the distinctions of rank. Yet Duclos, with all of his "modern" assumptions about meritocracy, was perhaps not entirely wrong in detecting a certain insecurity, even futility, in the daily existence of "the great families." The lives and careers of several members of the Tavanes family in the eighteenth century would seem to substantiate Duclos's general assessment.

*

Henri-Charles, comte de Tavanes, became head of the family after the death of his elder brother, killed in the campaign of 1705. He was only nineteen, a soldier in Villeroy's army in Flanders, when he received all of his brother's appointments and titles from the King.[35] A young musqueteer recently off to war with six horses, four camp mattresses, seven months' supply of wine, and 800 livres for incidentals, Henri-Charles had suddenly become Lieutenant-General and Royal Bailly in Burgundy.[36] His subsequent military career had all the marks of a prepared ascent. He was standard-bearer at 19, lieutenant in the Dauphin's Light Horse at 22, First Ensign in the Queen's Light Horse at 25, captain in the English Gendarmes at 30, brigadier at 33, and *Maréchal de Camp* at 48. Wounded on the Scheldt in 1708, his remaining years in the army were not arduous. After Utrecht, his assignments were elsewhere.[37]

In 1721, Henri-Charles assumed direct command of the province of Burgundy and took up residence at Dijon. The new regent, Bourbon-

[34] Duclos, *Considérations sur les moeurs*, pp. 90–92.

[35] Marquis P. de Dangeau, *Journal de la cour de Louis XIV*, ed. A. de Montaiglon, 19 vols. (Paris, 1857–60), X, 307.

[36] *A. D.*, E–1675, Accounts of Pierre Jouvancourt, 1703–05.

[37] Duc de Saint-Simon, *Mémoires*, 42 vols. ed. A. de Boislisle (Paris, 1930), XVIII, 103n; Dangeau, *Journal*, XVI, 450; *A. D.*, E–1673, *Obligation*, January 31, 1708; *A. D.*, E–1678, Sale of September 13, 1716.

Condé, had not forgotten past services of the Tavanes dating back to the Fronde.[38] In the absence of the official military governor, Prince de Condé, Henri-Charles assumed the title of "commander-in-chief" with wider powers than are usually associated with this office. He presided at the provincial estates where he acted alongside of the intendant as the King's man. It was hardly a sinecure in the first half of the century.[39] In the 1750s, for example, Henri-Charles received royal instructions that he ask for a million livres in taxes, negotiate loans at five per cent, establish barracks and studs for the army, raise money for the coast guard, build highways, supervise forest conservation, and encourage trade and industry. All this was in addition to the usual verification of titles and accounts from other local government bodies such as the *Chambre des Comptes* and Bureau of Finances. His hardest task was negotiating with the local Parlement. Among his papers we find a memorandum including such phrases as "make a short speech on the wishes of the King regarding the edicts to be registered" or "insist that His Majesty intends no changes in the Edict and prevent the officers of the Parlement from leaving" or "the First President can have the floor if we have so agreed the night before." Tavanes was to act as d'Aiguillon did in Brittany, receiving *lettres de cachet* from Paris if voluntary registration of the edicts failed. His instructions from Paris specified that his speech to the magistrates be both "sentimental and energetic." Later, during the Seven Years' War, Henri-Charles was to order the Parlement to register the new twentieth taxes "as if We were there in Person."[40] In short, the count was acting in a capacity that required administrative and diplomatic talents. How well did he perform?

Henri-Charles's long tenure in Burgundy—he remained commander until 1761—would seem to speak well of him as a royal agent. But the Parlement of Dijon clearly thought otherwise. If his role was to soften the resistance of the local magistrates, he failed miserably. That matters were not proceeding well is indicated by the claim of the Parlement that

[38] Duclos, *Oeuvres*, X, 188–89.

[39] Drouot and Calmette, *Histoire de Bourgogne*, IV, 284–85; J. Richard, *Histoire de la Bourgogne* (Paris, 1957), pp. 96–97. Richard suggests that the lieutenant-general was the spokesman for the intendant who remained *officieux* in Burgundy. One might add *"officieux"* but not impotent.

[40] *A. D.*, E–1678, *Instructions que le Roy a ordonnées être remises au Sr. Comte de Saulx-Tavanes . . . principal commissaire aux Etats dud. Pays de Bourgogne; Etat des pièces renvoyées à M. le Comte de Saint Florentin*, September 22, 1760.

the office of lieutenant-general was extinguished with the death of the governor, the seventh duke of Bourbon-Condé, in 1740. Tensions between the two branches of government were endemic, but Henry-Charles did not help matters by insisting on every formal prerogative of his office. He demanded that, in the absence of the governor, he enjoy the same honors, including the registration of his credentials by the Parlement to be followed by a formal visit by a deputation of magistrates, *pour lui faire compliment*. The count insisted on the ceremony to the last detail according to documented precedents of 1611 and 1651. Even for a very ceremony-conscious society, this was too much. The magistrates protested, and an exchange of correspondence on the issue began with Paris, apparently to the annoyance of the ministry.

Yet Henri-Charles persisted. Long memoranda were dispatched to the capital on such vital issues as the composition of the visiting delegation and the form of reception at the ducal palace. A portion of one of these papers will impart some of the flavor of the controversy.

> ...There is an indecency and inconvenience in this part of the ceremony.... The iron gate is too far away from the stairway leading to the governor's apartment. This might easily result in the Governor and deputies having too long a distance to cross in case of rain.... Moreover, when the deputies enter the court by coach, the Governor or Commander-in-Chief must stand on the very last step of the staircase.[41]

Having cited precedents for this and the appropriate salutations to be exchanged, the count outlined the proper order of march, explaining why he thought the Treasurers of France must follow the Chamber of Accounts. He was concerned over whether, as royal commissioner, he should be addressed as "Monseigneur" or "Monsieur" by the *Tresoriers* at Dijon. He promised to consult the practice at Toulouse and Rennes, other *pays d'états*, on this vexing problem. He ended his dispatch with an unexpected concession.

> It seems convenient to restrict this kind of ceremonial, tiring for the companies [Parlement and Chamber of Accounts], to times when the governor and commander-in-chief return from court or after an absence of six months. For shorter periods of absence the companies can decide themselves whether to send a deputation or not.[42]

[41] *A. D.*, E-1680, *Mémoire*, ca. 1744.
[42] *Ibid.*

14

In 1744, in the middle of the War of the Austrian Succession, Henri-Charles's contest with the Parlement over the forms of respect due his office attained exaggerated proportions. During the *Te Deum* celebrating the French victory at Courtrai, Tavanes requested the same honors performed for his predecessor, Prince de Condé. The crux of the ceremonial turned on the count's right to sit in a special, raised arm-chair in the ducal palace. This opened the *Affaire du Fauteuil* which recalled in some ways Saint Simon's famous *Affaire du Bonnet*. The magistrates of Dijon categorically refused the count this "new honor."

A controversy over precedence was clearly developing, one that a less pretentious and hypersensitive lieutenant-general might have avoided. True, it was something more. One must recall that such elaborate customs of precedence were not considered patently ridiculous by contemporaries. The attachment of all officials and magistrates to the prerogatives and rights of their "corporations" or "administrations" was legendary. Indeed, sensitivity to protocol was heightened by the increasing institutional rivalry between the Parlement of Dijon and the royal administration represented by the intendant and the lieutenant-general. Assertions of ceremonial etiquette and respect were most likely to be contested in marginal cases where an indisputable precedent had not been established. Was Comte de Tavanes the authentic successor of Prince de Condé in all the attributes and prerogatives of the office? Tavanes obviously thought so and he asserted all the formal rights of his predecessor. And once the Parlement sought to contest even a few of these ceremonial forms, the crown was obliged to come to the support of its agent.[43]

---

[43] J. Ormancey, "L'affaire du fauteuil, 1744," *Annales de Bourgogne*, XXXVIII (Apr.–June, 1966), 81–99. De la Custine, the historian of the Parlement of Dijon, claimed that Tavanes's actions were prompted by the central government in order to "humiliate" the Parlement. Ormancey does not go this far. The government had not supported Tavanes in 1741, when he requested special marks of *condoléance* from the magistrates on the occasion of his wife's death. Nevertheless, in 1744, the royal government backed Tavanes with a series of *lettres de cachet*, enjoining the *Parlementaires* to execute the honors due the count in every detail. Ormancey asserts that Tavanes was skillful enough to mix the privileges of his office with the interests of the sovereign. It is not certain, however, that this was a skill, an *habileté*, the crown appreciated. A decade later, the intendant persuaded the count to forego insistence on all his prerogatives. It is difficult to believe that the intendant was acting on his own initiative. See *Archives Nationales*, H–122 (hereafter cited as *A. N.*, followed by series and number), Joly de Fleury to Controller-General, November 23, 1757.

The royal government ordered the magistrates to execute the formalities and honors due the count in every detail. Twenty-five magistrates refused the order. Six of them, including the famous President de Brosses, were exiled.[44] It is difficult not to sympathize with Brosses when he wrote from his exile in the hills of Auvergne:

> What I find most painful is suffering for such a ridiculous thing as if it were serious business affecting the public welfare. To speak frankly, this is a stupid vexation without example. To exile six people for the idiotic and miserable vanity of one individual, while an affair of State over *lettres patentes*, remonstrances, and *lettres de jussion* ends in the exile of one or two, I swear that, when I think about it, this affair is even more comical than absurd.[45]

Brosses and his colleagues fought back by making the name of Tavanes synonomous with fatuous pretension. Henceforth, Brosses referred to the commander as "the little count." Tavanes even crept into the characterizations of solemnity and pretense in the *Italian Letters*.[46] Exasperated by exile and the failure of a parlementary deputation sent to Paris, Brosses finally gave way. "When I think of that impudent impostor of a little pigmy count writing to Paris that we are 'Austrians' at heart ...!" The final humiliation came when Brosses was selected to present the respects of the Parlement to the commander on his return to Dijon in 1745. Understandably, Brosses referred to this speech as "laconic."[47]

Brosses and the magistrates could take some solace from the flood of epigrams that circulated during their exile. Brosses thought some of the verses worth recording, especially the one depicting the count as a windbag who fought over armchairs and as a soldier who served the nation by waging a puerile war on the Parlement. The meanest sally of all questioned even the count's pedigree.

Monsieur le petit commandant,
Ma foi, vous vous moquez des gens.
Respectez mieux les robes noires

[44] *Lettres du Président de Brosses*, 2 vols., ed. Y. de Bezard (Paris, 1929), I, 118, 119n (July 2, 1744).

[45] *Ibid.*, p. 121 (July 25, 1744).

[46] C. de Brosses, *Lettres familières sur l'Italie publiées d'après les manuscrits*, ed. Y. de Bezard, 2 vols. (Paris, 1931), I, 9, 49; *Lettres du Président de Brosses* I, 137, 150.

[47] *Lettres du Président de Brosses*, I, 129 (August 6, 1744); 164–65, 164n (March 28, 1746).

Vos pères étaient gens à rabat
Vous en pouvez lire l'histoire
Dans les fastes de l'Almanach.[48]

The whole affair had apparently soured the Secretary of War, and he complained to the Chancellor about this man whose thirst for honors had obstructed, or at least complicated, the execution of royal policy in Burgundy. Such open criticism of Tavanes could not have been easy for Saint-Florentin, since Chancellor Daguesseau was Henri-Charles's uncle by marriage. The count lost no time in responding.

> It has not been easy for me to stand quietly by and be misrepresented to you by M. le Comte de Saint-Florentin as a man tormented by a thirst for honors and who, in consequence, causes all kinds of difficulties.... I assure you, my dear uncle, that in this province where I have had the honor to command for many years, everyone knows me as an enemy of vain ostentation and justly regards me as a man always ready to conciliate, prevent disputes, and maintain peace.... For the rest, my dear uncle, I hope that this affair will not hurt me in the eyes of His Eminence, Monseigneur Cardinal Fleury.[49]

If the count's relations with the Parlement were far from harmonious, his relations with the Estates of Burgundy were much better. Thirteen years after the *Affaire du Fauteuil*, Tavanes appeared to exercise his role, together with the intendant, as royal representative at the local estates with tact and competence. His letters, and those of the intendant, concerning the assembly in 1757 and 1760, reveal that Tavanes could plead on behalf of the tax-payers of Burgundy as well as bargain with the estates over the budgetary requests of the crown. His principal task was to steer the royal requests through the assembly with the greatest possible dispatch and with a minimum of compromise. His relations with the intendant, Joly de Fleury, were apparently good. Both men wrote in flattering terms about the actions of the other on the king's behalf. In 1760, as the war began to turn for the worse, the crown requested an additional tax of the province to defray the cost of the militia and the coast guard. Both the count and the intendant anticipated trouble. Tavanes wrote to the minister:

---

[48] *Ibid.*, I, 124 (July 25, 1744). Brosses found two mayors of Dijon named Tavanes in the Almanach.

[49] *A. D.*, E–1680, *Mémoire écrit par Tavanes au Chancelier d'Aguesseau*, ca. 1744.

17

> But we hope that by the close concert that exists between him [the intendant] and myself, and by the zeal with which we are both animated we will engage the Estates to conform to the orders of the King.[50]

The intendant substantiated this close cooperation over parlementary tactics in a letter a week later.

> We have decided, M. le Comte de Tavanes and myself, to reserve this article [on the new tax] for the end, not only to get through the easy articles first, but also because a number of delegates have already left and there will be less confusion in the assembly later. We have already spoken to the presidents and principal members of each house. There have been a number of objections and we have answered them as well as possible.[51]

The cooperation between intendant and lieutenant-general was so close that their reports on the proceedings of the assembly were almost identical, even to the choice of words. At the end of the session of 1760, the intendant said that the resistance to the tax on the *milice* had been overcome in large part by the efforts of Comte de Tavanes, Comte de Vienne, the bishops of Autun and Dijon, and the mayor of Dijon.[52] The count reciprocated with a compliment perhaps slightly tinged with condescension.

> Monsieur Joly de Fleury has exercised his functions with the greatest zeal, and beyond what his fortune permits. He has terminated his intendance with marked proof of his zeal ... and he leaves Dijon with our regrets.[53]

Tavanes's functions were not limited to those connected with persuading individual notables to cooperate with the crown. The count reported a proposal by the Estates to authorize exchanges of property without legal fees and to permit enclosure on one-fourth of a proprietor's land in each parish, "without prejudice to the right of common pasture or of the *dîme*, ecclesiastic or infeudated." Tavanes stressed the last clause which does not appear in the intendant's complementary report.[54] No doubt the

[50] *A. N.*, H–126, Tavanes to M. Clautier, November 25, 1760. The count apparently had the same relation with the intendant in 1727. *A. N.*, H–109, Tavanes to Controller-General, May 13, 1727.

[51] *A. N.*, H–126, Joly de Fleury to Controller-General, December 2, 1760.

[52] *Ibid.*, Joly de Fleury to Controller-General, December 4, 1760.

[53] *Ibid.*, Tavanes to Controller-General, December 9, 1760.

[54] *Ibid.*, Compare the letters of Tavanes and Joly de Fleury, both sent to the Controller-General on December 6, 1760.

count had opportunities to "qualify" the legislative initiatives of the Estates.

As the count's tenure at the Estates drew to a close in 1760, there is less evidence of his insistence on protocol. In 1757, the count gave way to the intendant's request that he not demand a formal visit by the entire *corps* of the Estates. He also gave way on the question of whether the presidents of each chamber should come to his townhouse every day to receive instructions and make a report. It was agreed that they would only come for "special instructions" and for "several at the same time." Perhaps the count had profited from his experience with the Parlement. Perhaps the refusal of the Estates to vote Duc d'Aignan, the previous "commander," a pension of 20,000 livres was a warning. In any event, good relations with the Estates seemed confirmed when the assembled members solicited the King for a regiment for the count's grandson, "a public expression," wrote the intendant, "of their affection and recognition."[55]

Whatever his reputation with the Parlement, the Estates of Burgundy, or the ministries in Paris, Henri-Charles remained in his "functions" until his death in 1761. His "thirst for honors" was not limited to the formal variety. Thirty years of royal service had netted him a substantial number of pensions from the public treasuries at Paris and Dijon. From early in his career he had been generously treated. In 1727 he had received 130,000 livres to help defray the cost of two commands in Burgundy.[56] By 1754, his income from various pensions was as follows:

TABLE I.2 ROYAL PENSIONS OF HENRI-CHARLES, COMTE DE TAVANES (1754)

Commander in Burgundy	26,250 livres
Octrois on the City of Dijon	500
Bonus from the Estates of Burgundy	5,400
Bonus from the General Receipts of Burgundy	1,797
Pension from the Royal Treasury	3,328
Pension from the Order of Saint Esprit	3,000
Exceptional Appointment from the Department of War and Royal Treasury	2,625
Total Revenue	46,900 livres

SOURCE: *A. D.*, E–1687.

[55] *A. N.*, H–122, Joly de Fleury to Controller-General, November 23, 1757 and December 3, 1757.

[56] *A. D.*, E–1677, *Donation*, January 8, 1727; *A. D.*, E–1678, *Brevêt de retenue accordé*.

Henri-Charles had made his office pay, and pay well. He even managed to be selected as representative of the nobility on the tax committee of the provincial Estates, a position which paid 40,739 livres for the three-year term.[57] His father's appointments as lieutenant-general fifty years before had returned only 7,000 livres. When he was not writing letters to Paris about the local Estates or ceremonial etiquette, he was soliciting the Ministry of War for "provisions," "indemnities," and "gratuities." When Saint-Florentin did not answer, he wrote to his uncle. Despite the irritation he caused and a performance as royal commander that can not be rated higher than average, his requests were not denied.[58]

At a time when the office of lieutenant-general was becoming less functional and more honorific throughout the kingdom, Tavanes maintained an administrative position that still had value to the crown. But in retrospect at least, he seems to have been among the last of his kind. His insistence on the honors of his rank and function may have been due as much to a sense of threatened position as to a ceremonious, not to say carping, temperament. Magistrates like Brosses might have seemed his most acrimonious rivals, but at root it was an intendant like Joly de Fleury who threatened to replace him as the King's man in Burgundy. But for the moment, Tavanes seemed secure enough. He was well protected at Paris. Not every commander in the provinces could claim a chancellor of France for an uncle. And how many had a younger brother who would attain one of the highest preferments the French Church could bestow?

* *

The procession began about four o'clock in the afternoon in the following order. The mounted company of *Cinquantenaires*, a carriage belonging to His Eminence with his two almoners and his two *gentilshommes*, then the carriage bearing His Eminence with Monseigneur the Bishop of Rodez at his side ... and the cross-bearer with the archiepiscopal cross on the box. Each of the carriages was drawn by six horses. The mounted police escorted the carriage of His Eminence, followed by those of the town notables. A huge crowd filled the air with shouts of joy....[59]

[57] *A. N.*, H–143, Tavanes to Controller-General, June 8, 1754. These were the famous *Elus*, a committee of the Provincial Estates in charge of tax assessment, collection, and disbursement.

[58] *A. D.*, E–1675, *Etat*, 1703–5.

[59] J. de Beaurepaire, ed., *Entrée à Rouen du Cardinal de Saulx-Tavanes*, (Rouen, 1903).

In these dignified and festive circumstances, Monseigneur le Cardinal de Saulx-Tavanes returned to Rouen in 1756.

An eminent protector, the prescribed preparation, good birth, and a measure of good luck helped Abbé Nicolas de Saulx-Tavanes from his Parisian college of Plessis in 1703 to a cardinal's hat in 1756. The protector was none other than the famous Archbishop of Cambray, François de Fénelon. According to Luynes, Fénelon, before his death in 1715, conducted a thorough search for a successor "qualified as much by birth as by the regularity of his morals and doctrine." The Jesuits recommended M. l'abbé de Tavanes, "whose birth was well-known" and who was then at the seminary of Saint-Nicolas du Chardonnet. Fénelon then ordered a careful investigation of the candidate, directing his own people to attend the defense of the abbé's thesis at the Sorbonne, follow the progress of his studies, and record all of his daily activities including the company he kept. Apparently the report was exemplary, for although Fénelon died before the appointment was made, his successor at Cambray, Monseigneur d'Estrées, offered the young abbé the post of grand vicar of Pontoise with the clear understanding that this was only the beginning. This assignment led to contact with Cardinal de Bissy at Paris who reviewed the original report on Tavanes and concluded, with some exaggeration, that "Providence had apparently intervened with the eminent Archbishop of Cambray."

After this, Monsieur l'Abbé de Tavanes became representative of Sens at the General Assembly of the Clergy of France at the age of 25, Bishop of Châlons at 31, Archbishop of Rouen at 43, Grand Almoner of the Queen at 53, Cardinal at 66, and Grand Almoner of France at 67. Little wonder that Archbishop Tavanes felt a certain debt to the Fénelon family. When he became Grand Almoner, he used his first opportunity, writes Luynes, to find out if there was "some abbé de Fénelon properly recommended" whom he could appoint to a dignified post in the Church.

In 1737 the archbishop took up permanent residence at Versailles and in 1742 he occupied apartments directly above those of the Queen. His twenty-year tenure as almoner of Marie Leszcynska had begun. From the Luynes *Mémoires* we snatch glimpses of him—in the company of Cardinal de Rohan marking the cross of ashes on the royal brow at the beginning of Lent, on the dais at the Sorbonne examining the thesis of Fleury's grand nephew, at the opera entertaining the papal nuncio with Cardinal Auvergne and other high Church dignitaries, or in the cortège

21

at Notre Dame in full ceremonial vestment. More frequently he would be found in the more intimate circle of the Queen as her constant spiritual companion at Marly, Fontainebleau, and even at Metz during the illness of the King in 1744. So dependent did the pious Queen become on her chief almoner that she only reluctantly permitted him to leave Versailles even for short absences.[60]

The prelate's influence extended to policy matters. In 1750 when Machault proposed that the new *vingtième* tax be paid by the clergy, the Queen turned against the new controller-general, according to Luynes, because of her attachment to the Archbishop of Rouen.[61] Not that he limited his opposition to giving advice to the Queen. In 1751, while his older brother was urging the Parlement of Dijon to register Machault's tax edicts, Archbishop Nicolas was one of the presiding officers at the Assembly of Bishops in Paris which protested the entire fiscal program of the minister. A year later, he was one of four ecclesiastical commissioners, including Cardinals La Rochefoucauld and Rohan-Soubise, sent to represent the First Estate in a dispute with the Parlement of Paris involving Jansenism. Luynes commented that the commissioners were chosen "not only for their personal merit, gentleness, and intelligence, but also because they were titled," of the most honored nobility.[62] Of the archbishop's precise political views we know little, but a number of his personal characteristics come through strongly. Nicolas de Tavanes was a man of tact and self-control, a master of ceremonial etiquette equally effective when presiding at the Assembly of Bishops as when directing protocol for the royal chapel service.[63]

If the archbishop's visits to his diocese were infrequent, he was able to

---

[60] C. P. d'Albert, Duc de Luynes, *Mémoires*, 17 vols., ed. L. Dussieux and E. Soulié (Paris, 1860–65). Rather than cite more than a dozen references for these few paragraphs, the author refers the reader to the excellent index in the last volume of this edition.

[61] Luynes, *Mémoires*, X, 433. "The Queen, who got on well with the Controller-General before, has reacted quite differently since the Clergy Affair. The views of the Archbishop of Rouen, her Grand Almoner, whom she likes very much, are the cause of this change of attitude. It appears that the entire royal family has adopted the tone of the Queen regarding the Controller-General" (September 21, 1750). See also M. Marion, *Histoire financière de la France depuis 1715*, 6 vols. (Paris, 1914–26), I, 175 and *passim; Machault d'Arnouville* (Paris, 1891), 240.

[62] Luynes, *Mémoires*, II, 26; XI, 299.

[63] *Ibid.*, IV, 64; IX, 73–75; X, 283; XII, 26; Cardinal de Bernis, *Memoirs and Letters*, 2 vols., transl. K. P. Wormley (Boston, 1901), II, 59–60.

find more time for sojourns at his country house, Gaillon, some twenty-five miles from Rouen near Elbeuf. Georg Forster, the future Jacobin of Mainz, was struck by the beauty of it a few years before the Revolution.[64] The Duc de Luynes, who visted Gaillon in 1745, gives an excellent description of the château and the archbishop's interest in its upkeep. Luynes was particularly taken by the marble sculpture and medallions of the double court, along the circular stairway, and above the chapel altar extending to the vaulting. The archbishop's apartments were ample; the dining room was 42 by 27 feet. A "delightful terrace" adjoined the bed-room. The wing beyond the billiard room contained four or five other apartments with fine views on the gardens. Looking out toward the *orangerie*, Luynes commented on the stables, recently enlarged and re-paired by the archbishop to house some fifty horses. The *orangerie* itself boasted a comfortable music room some 52 feet by 27 with a 20 foot ceil-ing. The French windows faced a terrace freshly planted in lindens, a particular passion of the archbishop's. From there, gently sloping ramps led to the château park—five hundred acres of woods surrounded by a high wall. Beautification work was progressing on a small canal near the kitchen-garden and on a new terrace. The archbishop had obtained per-mission from the village of Gaillon to move the road around his new garden. The ensemble was most enticing. The château was set on a hill-side and provided an excellent view of the Norman countryside from almost any one of its twenty-six furnished apartments.[65]

The prelate had few material worries. In addition to his portion of 42,573 livres in the family estate, promptly paid by his elder brother, Nicolas had obtained a comfortable benefice near Cluny from the Abbot of Auvergne when he was only 27. With a touch of envy Dangeau de-scribes the priory as *très noble*, worth 10,000 livres rent not including substantial seigneurial rights. The benefice was apparently obtained with the help of Chancellor Daguesseau, Nicolas's uncle. By 1745, he had added a second benefice, and in 1757, after promotion to cardinal, the King donated a third one near Rheims, worth over 38,000 livres revenue and supplemented by a royal pension of 6,000 more.[66] Gaillon remained

[64] Georg Forster, *Briefe und Tagebücher*, ed. A. Leitzmann (Halle, 1893).

[65] Luynes, *Mémoires*, VII, 34–40 (August 23, 1745).

[66] *Almanach Royal* (1757), p. 49. The *Almanach* put the new cardinal's revenues at 80,000 livres. See also, *A. D.*, E–1673, *Partage*, August 5, 1729.

Archbishop Tavanes's country residence until the end of his life when it passed to his successor in the diocese of Rouen.

Archbishop Tavanes placed a certain confidence in what his contemporaries called *"usages du monde."* Unlike his colleagues, the Archbishop of Bourges and Abbé Harcourt, he was surprised and not a little shocked by the appointment of Monseigneur Beaumont, Archbishop of Vienne, as new Archbishop of Paris in 1746. Not that Tavanes coveted the post. His friend, the Duc de Luynes, was certain that he was "quite content with his station." What disturbed men like Tavanes and Luynes, so they affirmed, was the royal intervention in clerical appointments, "especially to archbishoprics." It had been the practice for all appointments of this kind to be made by a special clerical officer, Monseigneur Boyer, Bishop of Mirepoix, in consultation with his colleagues. Boyer had seen Beaumont "only three or four times" during a short one-month stay in Paris. This was the root of the problem. It was not a matter of Beaumont's moral and doctrinal integrity—he never gambled, it seems—but his "lack of social graces" which had already caused a number of blunders attributed by some people to a lack of *esprit*. As Luynes said, "No one imagined that he could be in the running." In such cases, it was wiser to choose from a Parisian family.

Conservative in matters of ecclesiastical appointments, Tavanes was equally conservative in matters of local disorder. In the spring of 1752, the Grand Vicar of Rouen, Tavanes's executive officer in residence reported a riot of workers in the cotton and wool industry of Rouen, leading to the pillaging of the city's grain supplies. The disturbances of April, 1752, extended beyond the city itself and were not completely over by the following fall. At one point, the situation seemed serious enough to warrant a trip to Rouen with Intendant La Bourdonnaye. It did not come to this, but Tavanes expressed his views on the causes of the "sedition."

According to the archbishop, the riot had not been provoked by the closing down of the shops. He went on to explain to his friend Duc de Luynes that regulations in the textile industry were essential to its prosperity. The rules required the women spinners not to sell their product to individual merchants, but only to specified *entrepreneurs des manufactures* on certain days of the week. Frequently, he continued, the women claimed that they could not wait for their pay until this specified day;

24

joined by other women, they quickly became excited, shouting that they were starving to death. At this point, the women were joined by an undetermined number of vagrants (*gens sans aveu*) and outside trouble-makers, and these were the people who raided the city's grain magazines. For the future, the archbishop suggested better police protection, including at least two permanent army regiments in the outskirts of the city, though not in the center where they would disturb commercial circulation. The new barracks could be paid for by the city itself.[67]

In retrospect, the archbishop's attitude may seem somewhat short-sighted. In fact, his reaction to the Rouen riots was quite typical of his contemporaries. The "riff-raff" theory, sometimes supplemented by allegations of "alcoholism" and "shiftlessness," was quite common. There was also considerable doubt that misery and shortage of food was the issue. Even Luynes stressed the participation of at least one rioter with 800 livres income. As for the archbishop's proposals for the future, these too were not exceptional. The intendant favored "examples." Five rioters were hanged and dozens more arrested.[68]

If the intendant and a number of local observers shared these views, how could one expect an archbishop whose duties kept him at court to be more sympathetic or understanding? Name, family, calling, the court—perhaps the Queen's circle in particular—all conspired to make Nicolas de Tavanes a man of order and accepted ways. He gave much thought to such issues as the distance of the royal *prie-dieu* from the chapel altar, or to the correct seating of prelates and court dignitaries at Notre Dame. The usages he followed in these ceremonial matters could not have been so different from the rules he thought preferable in tax policy, ecclesiastical appointments, and local administration. He could not be considered uncharitable, certainly not in the formal sense. Every Christmas, Cardinal Tavanes dispensed 100,000 livres from the royal treasury for various charities; half of this sum was spent at his own discretion.

Nicolas de Saulx-Tavanes was a prelate of the Old Regime, whose career belongs somewhere between the expansive indiscretions of a Rohan and the public works of a Brienne. Portly, dignified, conventional, Cardinal

[67] Luynes, *Mémoires*, XI, 499–501.
[68] G. Lemarchand, "Les troubles de subsistence dans la généralité de Rouen," *Annales historiques de la Révolution française*, (October–December, 1963), 401–27.

Tavanes had learned how to succeed in his calling, and if tact, *bon ton*, and family name were relevant, he possessed them in full measure.[69]

Fortunate indeed were members of the family who could claim blood ties with the illustrious Archbishop of Rouen. In 1742, when the honorific post of *Chevalier de la Reine* became available, Henri-Charles, Comte de Tavanes was considered. Nicolas insisted so vociferously that he had *not* solicited the office on his brother's behalf that one suspects he was helpful. It was natural to identify members of the family at Court by referring to them as relatives of "Monseigneur the Archbishop of Rouen."[70] The connection was especially useful to the eldest son of Henri-Charles, future head of the family.

Charles-Marie-Gaspard, known as the Comte de Saulx to distinguish him from his father, was only twenty-seven when he was promoted to *brigadier* in 1740. He had passed through all the lower grades even more rapidly than Henri-Charles. At the age of nineteen, he had been married to Marie-Catherine de Froulay-Tessé, an excellent choice joining a very promising inheritance with a distinguished name. Gaspard was raised in Paris and apparently visited his father in Dijon only occasionally. A good soldier, he fought in the War of the Austrian Succession, first under Prince de Conti in Italy, and later under Maréchal de Saxe in Flanders. His valor was proven when he was lightly wounded in the Alpine campaign of 1744 in the company of such noble officers as Stainville and Mirepoix.[71]

At the same time, Gaspard was learning proper court manners and frequenting the best of Parisian society. In the spring of 1742, Luynes mentions him at a royal supper at Fontainebleau. Later in the evening, the Queen asked four couples to dance the minuet, and Gaspard was given the opportunity of exhibiting his talents in the company of the dukes of Chartres and Rohan, and Marquis de Bissy. A few years later, we again find "Monsieur de Saulx, the nephew" at an intimate *souper du Roi*, in the company of the marshals of France—Luxembourg, Soubise,

---

[69] See the picture of Archbishop Tavanes in J. de Beaurepaire, ed., *Entrée à Rouen du Cardinal de Tavanes* (Rouen, 1903).

[70] Luynes, *Mémoires*, IV, 253; 30–31.

[71] *Ibid.*, VII, 185; V, 403.

Duras, Noailles, Villeroy. In 1743, he was formally presented at Court, an honor even his father had not obtained.[72]

Gaspard's entry into court circles at age thirty was facilitated by the favor the Tessé family enjoyed in the entourage of the Queen. The death of young Comte de Tessé near Prague in 1742 had moved the Queen to offer the post of *dame du palais* to Gaspard's young wife. Luynes described Madame de Saulx's qualifications for the position.

> She has a pretty face and a pleasant personality. She is the daughter of the Marquis de Tessé and, consequently, niece of the First Ecuyer of the Queen. Her husband is nephew of Monseigneur the Archbishop of Rouen, Grand Almoner of the Queen. For all these reasons, the Queen believes herself justified in soliciting this favor....[73]

This was probably the first occasion for Gaspard and his wife to learn how precarious court position could be. The King overruled Marie Leszcynska's choice and selected Madame de la Tournelle, his new mistress, for the post. It was characteristic of Louis XV to use the Queen's household as a berth for his favorites. Before obtaining the coveted post, Madame de Saulx had to wait until after the King's illness at Metz in 1744 and the subsequent fall of Madame de Châteauroux.[74]

By 1747, good fortune, no doubt assisted by the most assiduous court diplomacy, again favored Gaspard and his wife. Court dignities and military promotions came rapidly. In January, the couple moved into the new wing of the royal palace at Versailles; it was a large, comfortable apartment, complete with kitchen and wine cellar. In September, Gaspard was named "Companion" (*Menin*) to the Dauphin and he joined the entourage of the King's pious and lethargic son.[75] The pension was 6,000 livres for the life of the pensioner.[76] A year later, the countess was

[72] *Ibid.*, IV, 132; IX, 226.

[73] *Ibid.*, V, 401.

[74] Marquis d'Argenson, *Journal et mémoires du marquis d'Argenson*, 9 vols., ed. E. J. B. Rathery (Paris, 1859–67), IV, 232–33. For a general introduction to the Court at Versailles, see G. P. Gooch, *Louis XV: The Monarchy in Decline* (London, 1956); J. Levron, *La vie quotidienne à la cour de Versailles au XVIIe et XVIIIe siècles* (Paris, 1965). For the mid-century, the *Mémoires* of duc de Luynes and the *Journal inédit* of duc de Croÿ (see the bibliography) are among the most informative and most objective. For the late century, those of Madame Campan (see bibliography) are recommended, despite their obvious partiality.

[75] Luynes, *Mémoires*, VIII, 77, 299; XIII, 50.

[76] A. N., O¹–3744, *Maison du Dauphin, Etat des Menins*.

presented to the King and the count was made lieutenant-general. In 1752, he was made Governor of the Fort de Taureau, an honorific command of 10,000 livres revenue, and three years later, he was named *chevalier d'honneur* of the Queen, a place worth 12,000 more.[77]

At forty-two, Gaspard had already accumulated an array of pensions and honorific offices that matched his father's. But unlike Henri-Charles, he had no administrative duties, and his attendance at the Estates of Burgundy in 1752 was surely voluntary. This is not to say that he did nothing, for court life had its own demands—a constant nervous strain, a perennial alert against new turns of favor or disfavor. If Gaspard ever thought that any single courtier was indispensable, he must have been brought up short in 1753. At the age of only thirty-eight, Madame de Saulx was struck down by smallpox. Following the implacable process of court politics, the position was filled the very next day by the Marquise de Mirepoix.[78] If Pompadour lived her brief life constantly on the brink of a nervous breakdown, each courtier in a smaller way faced the same uncertainties. No wonder there were educational reformers who seriously advocated rigorous physical training for court nobility.[79]

It is generally assumed that life at Court was excessively expensive, consuming every bit and more of the pensions it dispensed. No doubt there were dangers, not the least of which was *gros jeu* at the King's table. Yet it was possible, at least in the middle years of the century, for courtiers like the Saulx-Tavanes to avoid such pitfalls. There were, in fact, four courts at Versailles in the 1750s. The King and Pompadour ruled the most prestigious, of course, and the one with the largest favors to bestow. But there were also the courts of the Queen, the Dauphin, and the sisters of the King. These last three had a decidedly different tone and hardly constituted the same menace.[80]

The court of Marie Leszcynska had a justifiable reputation for solemnity, piety, and dullness. Duc de Richelieu severely but accurately captured the atmosphere of the Queen's evenings "in her chambers."

There everyone was comfortably seated, but the conversation was far from brilliant. Hours passed in deadly silence in the English manner, and the

[77] Luynes, *Mémoires*, XII, 72; XIV, 295; Brosses, *Lettres*, 267n; *A. N.*, 0¹-3793, *Maison de la Reine*.
[78] Luynes, *Mémoires*, XIV, 33.
[79] See article in the *Ephémérides du Citoyen*, V (1766), 163ff.
[80] G. Maugras, *Le Duc et la Duchesse de Choiseul* (Paris, 1924), pp. 100ff.

drowsiness of the entire company characterized the calm of the Queen's "little committee."[81]

No nocturnal orgies here. The less delicate members of the King's circle referred to it as the Holy Week.[82] The Queen preferred a small group including the Duke and Duchess de Luynes, Cardinal de Luynes, Archbishop Nicolas de Saulx, and a half dozen ladies-in-waiting, including Gaspard's wife. The Queen's day followed an inflexible routine beginning with prayers, moral readings, mass, and some painting in the morning; the afternoon passed in playing the harpsicord in her apartments or reading in one of four languages (Marie Leszcynska was a linguist). At 6 P.M., the Queen arranged tables for *cavagnole*, a kind of lotto not to be confused with the gambling that went on at the King's tables. Dinner was at nine or ten after which the Queen retired with five or six of her ladies, while conversation turned more likely to moral aphorisms and a scandal or two than to politics or intrigue.[83] A dull existence to be sure, but there was no threat here to the Saulx fortune.

The court of the Dauphin to which Gaspard was attached was scarcely different. If possible, it was even less animated. Marquis d'Argenson depicted the Dauphin's existence as decidedly sedentary.

> He has the taste of Philip V (of Spain). He never leaves his wife; she will govern when he is King. From noon until six in the evening he remains alone with her talking and reading. She does some needle work. But he rarely goes out even on the terrace at Versailles, except for a few hours of riding. He shows no strong inclinations; he loves rest and food. He has given up his study of music, though he retains some taste for it. He attends a concert twice a week.

Duc de Croÿ was more terse. "The Dauphin, heavy and indolent, was not fond of hunting or, for that matter, of much else."[84]

Under such conditions, one wonders what his official companions were doing. There is some question whether the Dauphin even had a "court"

---

[81] Maréchal duc de Richelieu, *Mémoires*, 2 vols., ed. F. Barrière (Paris, 1868), II, 156. Richelieu's authorship of these *Mémoires* has been questioned. See Gooch, *Louis XV*, p. 279.

[82] Richelieu, *Mémoires*, I, 430.

[83] Luynes, *Mémoires*, I, Introduction by MM. Dussieux and Soulié, based on the Queen's correspondence.

[84] A. Brette, ed., *La France au milieu du XVIIIe siècle (1774–57) d'après le journal du marquis d'Argenson* (Paris, 1898), pp. 74–75; *Journal inédit du duc de Croÿ (1718–84)*, 4 vols., ed. Vicomte de Grouchy and P. Cottin (Paris, 1906), I, 81.

in the usual sense of the word. Clearly, Gaspard was not threatened here by gaming or by an example of extravagant living, but by boredom. This was not yet the court of Marie Antoinette.

There is evidence that Gaspard liked the ladies. Both Marquis d'Argenson and President de Brosses agreed that Madame d'Estrades was Comte de Saulx's mistress, though her dismissal from the court of the King's sisters during an economy wave in 1755 must have impeded the affair.[85] Less reliable was the rumor that the count also pursued Madame la Duchesse de Luxembourg. This might have had dire consequences. The duchess was a model of elegance with a reputation for prodigious spending, gambling, and all that goes under the rubric of *coquetterie générale*, before she settled down to conducting her salon in lessons of etiquette.[86] Either Gaspard was unusually discreet or his pursuit was unsuccessful. It seems that Gaspard had avoided any financial disaster from that quarter.

Having weathered the storms of the early 1750s, Gaspard hastened to assure the position of his eldest son, Charles-Casimir. In 1758, he placed him in the Dauphin's household and, a year later, married him to Mlle. de Lévis-Châteaumorand, *Dame du Palais* in the Queen's Household.[87] So secure was the family's position at court that neither the death of Gaspard's uncle, the cardinal, in 1759 nor the passing of the Queen and the Dauphin a decade later altered its circumstances. Gaspard remained *Menin* of the Dauphin and *chevalier d'honneur* of the Queen with all the prerogatives of these posts.[88] He spent forty years of his life at Court, retained his position despite all cabals, all family feuds, and all changes in the royal household.

How did Gaspard negotiate the transition to the reign of Louis XVI? Apparently, it presented no special problems. The count and his family avoided any obtrusive role among the politically-oriented factions of the Court. The Tavanes could be labeled neither *dévôts* nor followers of Maupeou; they were not among those noble families who followed Choiseul into seclusion at Chanteloup. By 1772, young Casimir and his

[85] Argenson, *Journal*, IX, 126 (November 8, 1755); Brosses, *Lettres*, I, 267 (August 16, 1755).

[86] *Horace Walpole Correspondence*, eds., W. S. Lewis and W. H. Smith, (New Haven, 1939–), VI, 84; G. P. Lévis, *Souvenirs et portraits* (Paris, 1813), p. 53; Luynes, *Mémoires*, XV, 126; H. Buffenoir, *La maréchale de Luxembourg, 1707-1787*, (Paris, 1924), p. 31.

[87] Luynes, *Mémoires*, XVIII, 57; A. D., E-1699, *Inventaire*, 1784, fol. 217.

[88] A. N., O¹-3744, 3793.

wife had obtained appointments in the household of the new dauphine, Marie-Antoinette. The entire household of the elder dauphine, mother of Louis XVI, had already been transferred *en bloc* to the new dauphine.[89] Two years later, the new Queen announced that she would retain all the old pensioners of Marie Leszcynska. The Queen's household was expanded to make room for all the older courtiers. It would seem that Gaspard's post had become hereditary. The notation in the accounts of the Queen's Household for 1774 refers to the office of *chevalier d'honneur* belonging to Michel-Gaspard de Saulx-Tavanes *and* Charles-Casimir de Saulx, "his son *en survivance*."[90]

Casimir even improved on his father in the matter of accommodations at Versailles. By the 1780s, he had six rooms (three *à cheminée*) in the aristocratic North Wing adjoining the apartments of Vintimille, Narbonne, and Talleyrand.[91] Moreover, in addition to the customary *gages, livrée*, and maintenance allowance of 12,000 livres as *chevalier de la reine*, he received such supplements as "two dozen candles a month" and transport for all his baggage during the Queen's trips into the country.[92] But the company was worth more than the emoluments. The *Almanac Royal* lists a distinguished group of aristocratic families in the household of the new queen. Among the ladies one notices Lamballe, Chimay, Ossun, Luynes, Choiseul, Duras, and Tavanes; among the men, Polignac, Tessé, and Tavanes.[93] In March 1778 the French consul at Madrid addressed a letter to Comte de Tavanes "*à la Cour*," requesting that he intercede with Comtesse de Polignac, the Queen's favorite, to obtain "a position" for a friend.[94] Is there a better proof that the Tavanes were well-established in the new reign?

* * *

All members of the Tavanes family were not equally useful in the quest for prestige, place, and affluence. All cadets were not as successful

[89] *A. N.*, O¹-3744; Madame Du Deffand, *Correspondance complète . . . avec la duchesse de Choiseul, l'abbé Barthélemy et M. Craufurt*, 3 vols., ed. Marquis de Saint-Aulaire (Paris, 1866), II, 162–63.

[90] *A. N.*, O¹-3793. Although court *charges* were not hereditary, it was considered a disgrace if the post were not kept in the family. See Croÿ, *Journal inédit*, I, 137–38.

[91] *A. N.*, KK–540, *Logements à Versailles*, 1787.

[92] *A. N.*, O¹-3793.

[93] *Almanach royal*, (1785), pp. 126–27.

[94] *A. D.*, E–1678, Paulo to Tavanes, March 30, 1778.

as Archbishop Nicolas. Consider the case of Charles-Henri-Gaspard de Saulx, known as Vicomte de Tavanes. He was a grandson in a cadet branch of Jacques de Saulx, the *Frondeur*, and first cousin of Henri-Charles, the commander at Dijon. His career, like his cousin's, had started well enough. Favored by his father's reputation in the wars of Louis XIV, he became a *brigadier* in 1719 and, a few years later, First Chamberlain of Duc de Bourbon, lieutenant-general in the Mâconnais, and honorary councillor in the Parlement of Dijon. In 1721, he had married Elizabeth Mailly du Breuïl, daughter of a receiver-general of finance in Touraine. Here was Duclos's alliance of Court and Finance in its most open form. The receiver-general offered a handsome dowry of 300,000 livres.[95]

Despite all these advantages, the vicomte demonstrated an amazing capacity for recklessness. A year after his marriage, he managed to lose 300,000 livres in one evening, playing *faro* with Comtesse de Livry. Marais put it succinctly: "There goes the dowry for the honor of *gros jeu*." Two years later, he created a scandal by publicly accusing his wife of infidelity and sending her back to Touraine when it was common knowledge that he was having an affair with his wife's sister.[96] Even a society somewhat jaded in these matters found this too much. Having squandered his dowry and destroyed all possibilities of an inheritance from his wife's family, the vicomte apparently embarked on a number of speculative ventures that lacked care or foresight. In the midst of the Law Boom, he sold family lands in Normandy to John Law himself for 200,000 livres in paper and lent part of it to his cousin at 2.5 per cent subsequently paid in coin.[97] Many nobles used the inflation in land values of the Law Boom to liquidate their debts, but here the vicomte was selling land to buy *rentes* at a fixed return.[98] Selling land was always a bad sign and, as a descendant of a cadet branch, he could not have had much to sell.

In 1736, we find the vicomte appealing to his cousin at Dijon to purchase his command in the Mâconnais. Though in tight circumstances, he

[95] Père Anselme, *Histoire généalogique*, VII, 239ff. Dangeau, *Journal*, III, 53; IV, 264. *Journal et mémoires de Mathieu Marais sur le règne de Louis XIV et le règne Louis XV, 1715–37*, 4 vols., ed. M. de Lescure (Paris, 1863), II, 337.

[96] Marais, *Journal*, II, 337; III, 134.

[97] *A. D.*, E–1678, *Constitution de rente*, February 21, 1720.

[98] F. V. Forbonnais, *Recherches et considérations sur les finances de France depuis 1595 jusqu'en 1721* (Liège, 1753) VI, 380.

revealed a certain unwillingness to live in the country. He mentioned an offer for his office of 160,000 livres, 60,000 in coin and a domain near Château-Thierry for the balance.

> ... it is worth 3,750 livres revenue, guaranteed. But I do not want land in that region where there is a large château which probably has not been lived in for a hundred years and which might possibly cost me immense sums to put in shape.[99]

The vicomte had another proposal that suited his personality better. If his cousin would pay him 150,000, half could be applied to liquidate his debts and the other half invested in a life-time annuity.[100] "At my age, I can get eight per cent, but I must have the 75,000 in coin." Such an arrangement left little for the vicomte's posterity. But Henri-Charles did not appear anxious to buy another command and neither did the Marquis de Tessé, a second prospect. By 1738, the vicomte was forced to lay his cards on the table.

> My property totals only 50,000 livres, 24,000 lent to you and 26,000 invested in government bonds (*hôtel de ville*).... My father gave me a donation of everything he had so that I could buy his office. He even consented to the sale of a farm in Normandy that was all I owned in order to pay for it.

Clearly the prestige of the office of lieutenant-general had been too highly valued. It returned only 2,814 livres revenue. Together with his *rentes* above, the vicomte could not have had an income much in excess of 5,000 livres, a miserable sum for a man of his pretensions.[101]

The vicomte died in 1753 in the provincial town of Aisey-le-Duc in Burgundy. His will revealed the full measure of the debacle. Aside from his wardrobe which he willed to his valet, the family was obliged to sell all of his effects, including his silverware, snuff-box, watch, and even his Cross of Saint Louis, to pay his debts and the back wages of his servants. His assets came to 73,680 livres, his obligations to 54,834 livres,

---

[99] *A. D.*, E–1732, Vicomte de Tavanes to Henri-Charles de Saulx-Tavanes, January 3, 1736.

[100] For the *rente viagère* see R. J. Pothier, *Traité du contrat de constitution de rente* (Paris, 1763), pp. 230–32; 249–53; 260–63. See also G. V. Taylor, "The Paris Bourse on the Eve of the Revolution, 1781–1789," *American Historical Review*, LVII (July, 1962), 951ff., for speculation in *rentes* of all kinds.

[101] *A. D.*, E–1732, Correspondence of Vicomte de Tavanes with Comte de Saulx, 1736–38.

leaving a net *fortune* of only 18,846 livres. Among unpaid obligations were his younger brother's portion and a 300-livre pension to his sister, abbess of Saint Andoche. How far this was from the episcopal splendor of Archbishop Nicolas!

The elder branch of the family was more immediately concerned with the last line of the will.

> I name my universal heir, Monsieur le Comte de Saulx, lieutenant-general and Companion of M. le Dauphin, and, in the event of his death, his eldest son and then the other children in order of their birth.... I am very sorry that my legacy is modest, but since I received nothing from my paternal side, I can not be more generous.[102]

A rapid perusal of the will and inventory quickly revealed that there was almost nothing to claim. After a futile effort to hold on to the meager *rentes*, the heirs renounced the inheritance as "more onerous than profitable," which was their right under the law, and none too soon, for the vicomte's creditors were besieging the heirs within a year. Henri-Charles's reply to one of these creditors is an interesting commentary on the risks of lending.

> ...I must confess, Madame, that you very much surprised me when you asked me if I were the heir of M. le Vicomte de Tavanes.... Having renounced the inheritance, I am in no way obliged to pay his debts. [Moreover,] it was only by good will toward your father...that M. le Vicomte delegated [the *rente*], without any formal guarantee, to your father and mother from a claim on MM. Trêmes and Blerancourt...I was heir only with "benefit of an inventory" a legal status which does not oblige me in any way toward the inheritance. *Voilà*, Madame, all that remains is to assure you of the attachment, etc.[103]

Repercussions of the vicomte's checkered career were not over. In December, 1754, only one year after his demise, the local police at Verdun reported an unfortunate series of events. An officer from the army of Holland had attempted to borrow 400 livres at the château gate of the Seigneur de Marcheville. He was refused. Shortly thereafter Marcheville received a number of threatening notes and called the local mounted police to investigate. Searching the neighboring countryside, the police discovered "a poor vagabond, dressed in a tattered brown *redingotte*, accompanied by a white hunting dog." The servant at the château identi-

[102] *A. D.*, E–1732, *Testament*, October 1, 1753; *Etat de mes fonds*, 1753.
[103] *A. D.*, E–1732, Comte de Tavanes to Madame de Coiseul, April 8, 1755.

fied the man as the one who had requested the 400 livres. Lacking any papers, he was arrested and put in jail at Verdun. Upon interrogation, the man claimed to be Léonard de Saulx of the Saulx-Tavanes family. Incredulous, the police nonetheless informed the intendant, who wrote to the Controller General and to the Archbishop of Rouen. There were no replies from higher circles until May, 1755, when an order arrived transferring the accused to the prison of Fort Evêque in Paris. The intendant found the accompanying letter from M. le Comte de Saulx, *Menin* of Monseigneur le Dauphin, most curious. The count denied any blood relation with the prisoner, but assumed all the costs of the transfer. The Verdun police report subsequently referred to the case as involving a *"gentilhomme vagabond."* Never had a Tavanes fallen so low. On the other hand, it was to the credit of the elder branch that they would not ignore their illegitimate cousin altogether.[104]

A generation later, the Tavanes at Paris received letters from one Monsieur de Petitville at Nancy, requesting the continuation of an allowance. Was this man Léonard de Saulx under a more discreet name, or was he another product of the vicomte's *amours*? His efforts to obtain a royal pension of 1,000 livres after thirty-six years of service in the army had been frustrated by the failure to procure a valid birth certificate for the War Department. The old soldier asked Comte de Saulx for help. In 1783, Petitville claimed a legacy of 650 livres per annum from his father, the vicomte, now dead thirty years. "There is no doubt," he wrote, "that one can leave a legacy to a bastard, even one born in adultery. All the law books are full of *arrêts* confirming this." Petitville went on to cite the customary law of Normandy and other precedents at law. In 1786, the first duke of Saulx-Tavanes was still paying a small pension to the *"enfant naturel"* of Vicomte de Tavanes—a cadet branch not easily forgotten.[105]

Petitville was not the only member of the family—the "extended family"—requesting aid from the elder branch. In 1769, for example, Charles-Marie-Gaspard received a letter from a Monsieur de Crécey, claiming he was a relative by a marriage with the Saulx-Tavanes in 1364. Crécey wanted proofs of his "alliance" to facilitate his advancement. He

[104] *A. N.,* H–1141, *Mémoire au sujet de la capture et de l'information faite en 1754 et 1755 contre Léonard de Saulx*, Verdun, July 19, 1757. I found this police report quite by chance, in connection with another research project unrelated to this book.
[105] *A. D.,* E–1732, Petitville to Comte de Tavanes, 1779–83, 1786.

said that he was not well educated in such genealogical research, having entered military service at fifteen. On another occasion, a Monsieur de Bourgogne, who needed a recommendation for his son trying to enter a royal military school, assured the count that he, too, was a relative by a marriage in the sixteenth century. "Although I have never had the honor of meeting you," he wrote, "your glorious name and beneficence toward everyone prompts me to write to you and ask you to honor me with your powerful protection."[106] A Tavanes would not have found this appeal anachronistic.

Most distressing were supplications from cousins in real financial trouble. In 1772, Gaspard de Saulx received this message from Palerma, Spain.

> Monsieur and Dear Cousin, Woe for me! I have had the misfortune of losing my husband eighteen months ago.... I have had a great deal of trouble working the land all year. Three years have passed without enough harvest to furnish seed. If you would have the goodness to provide my two sons ... with only half their pensions....[107]

With financial problems in his immediate family, Gaspard must have breathed a sigh of irritation when he scanned this letter.

During the same years that Vicomte de Tavanes was trying to sell his command, Henri-Charles was presented with a more flagrant family scandal. He received word that his cousin, Marquis de Mirebel, a young captain in the Condé dragoons, had "abducted" a Mademoiselle Le Brun from her château and taken her to Besançon in Franche-Comté. Before the count at Dijon could hush up the affair, the girl's father had written to Condé, the governor, demanding retribution and embroidering the complaint with the charge of rape. A long and ugly lawsuit followed, where all the fine points of the law were exposed to public eye. Could "abduction" take place with the consent of the girl? Was it "abduction" or "insubordination" whereby "rape was no longer rape"? As Marais put it, the father was a regular devil, claiming that Mirebel's action violated human rights and "those of hospitality," and that it was a clear case of premeditated attack.[108] Henri-Charles, as lieutenant-general in the prov-

---

[106] A. D., E-1727, Crécey to Tavanes, January 30, 1769; Bourgogne to Tavanes, February 4, 1769.

[107] Ibid., Marie-Gertrude de Tavanes to Comte de Saulx, September 27, 1772. This was probably Gaspard's niece.

[108] Marais, Journal, IV, 370, 381; A. D., E-1736.

ince and head of the family, felt obliged to counter these charges in a letter to Prince de Condé. Whatever his failings with the Parlement of Dijon, Henri-Charles was not devoid of diplomatic skill on this occasion in 1732.

> In all honesty, the action of M. de Mirebel can perhaps be regarded as extravagant, but in the extremity in which he found himself, it had something almost noble about it.... M. de Mirebel visited M. Le Brun at Dôle and, dressed in his riding clothes, entered M. Le Brun's bedroom. He threw himself at the foot of the bed.... Opening his coat and pointing his sword to his chest, he declared he would not fight against a father-in-law he esteemed. He begged him to forgive his daughter, who was very ill. As for himself, he demanded only death.

The rest of the letter described in more prosaic terms what took place. Altercations between the two men lasted for over an hour, M. Le Brun holding the rapier all the time, and ended with the young marquis riding back to Besançon, thirty miles away. A second encounter had taken place at a *cabaret* in Besançon, in which Mirebel refused a duel with Le Brun. The purpose of the count's appeal to Condé was to establish the inflexibility of Le Brun and the touching gallantry of his young cousin. "He deserves more pity than anger, and I throw myself on my knees before you to intercede for him!" He thought it relevant to add that Mirebel was in financial difficulties, and that he would not want him to lose his company which, in fact, Condé had obtained for him.[109]

The count was not successful, and Mirebel was condemned to death by the courts *in absentia*. But the damage was not permanent, at least not to the marquis. He emerged ten years later at Versailles at the beginning of the War of the Austrian Succession, having gained valuable military experience in the employ of the Elector of Bavaria. He presented a useful report on Prague and its defenses. This undoubtedly led to a formal pardon in 1746. Mademoiselle Le Brun did not fare so well. A letter from Dôle has survived, in which she pleads for a reconciliation with her family, "after a disgrace of fourteen years." The reply of her parents was uncompromising. "You have not followed religion, honor, or conscience."[110]

[109] *A. D.*, E–1736, Tavanes to Condé, July 8, 1732.
[110] Luynes, *Mémoires*, IV, 30–31; *A. D.*, E–1736, Letters of February 26, 1746, and September 15, 1746.

The *Affaire Mirebel* has many aspects of comic opera, but it was the reality. As far as the participants were concerned, there was nothing comic about it. The count's manner and technique of upholding the family name seem particularly pertinent. A Tavanes and a Condé might be expected to share a certain tolerance toward older, noble traditions of gallantry and impetuous actions.

Cadets like the vicomte and Mirebel taxed family solidarity to the limit. If one could not always demand "illustrious acts," one might at least expect discretion. Henri-Charles's youngest brother was of this middling sort, non-heroic but unobtrusive. No one could accuse Charles-Henri, Marquis de Saulx, of asceticism. The inventory taken at his death indicates that he lived well in Paris. His town house on the Rue du Bac, with its imposing carriage gate was kept in constant repair and housed eight servants and a coach. The marquis was a fastidious dresser: he owned no less than fifty suits and seemed to have a special weakness for velvet waistcoats.[111] On the other hand, he was hardly flamboyant in a dangerous way. A bachelor all his life, there is not the slightest evidence of an affair, much less a scandal.

As a field-grade officer, he was apparently active into his sixties. His last years were spent in the circle of Madame du Deffand, during the lean years between D'Alembert and Horace Walpole. It should be remembered that the salon of Madame du Deffand had never competed with the most intellectually demanding salons of Paris. This was especially true after Mademoiselle de Lespinasse lured the most stimulating guests elsewhere. Nevertheless, proud of measured *esprit* and moderate towards all enthusiasms—religious or secular—the entourage of this clever, blind old lady formed an aristocratic supper club after 1765.[112] Madame du Deffand mentioned the Marquis de Saulx in a letter to Walpole.

> Although I like to write to a man of *esprit* like yourself, there is no more sentiment in these letters than in those I write to M. de Saulx. Poor M. de Saulx! He passes for an intimate friend. Each time he returns from some campaign, people make me compliments on his return and talk of my

[111] *A. D.*, E–1676, *Vente après décès*, 1769. Duc de Croÿ refers to the cost of two dress suits in the 1740s—5,000 livres! Duc de Croÿ, *Journal inédit*, I, 75; II, 372. "Everyone is ruined *en broderies*", he wrote later. See Chapter III below.

[112] M. Glotz, *Salons au XVIIIme siècle* (Paris, 1949), 203ff.

missing him during his absence. That is the tone of our nation; you are not used to it....[113]

Madame du Deffand was notorious for her lack of sentimentality, and her few references to the Marquis seem harsh. In her eyes, he appears as a self-effacing individual, with little intellectual pretension, but a certain fortitude. She was most impressed by his last days.

My good friend, M. de Saulx, is in a terrible state, but he is resolved not to die at home. He can hardly walk, much less speak, and seems to be in agony. He dined Sunday with me, and yesterday with the President (Hénault). I have ... stayed with him to spare him the fatigue of a *souper*.

Two weeks later, however, she wrote to Walpole that he was "right about Marquis de Saulx; he is easy to forget and difficult to replace."[114] Her cruellest remark was made after a particularly tiring *souper* for sixteen guests.

As for M. de Saulx, if we removed the particle [de] from his name, changed the spelling, and left only the sound, he would be perfectly named.[115]

If the marquis added no luster to the family name in salon circles, at least he had done nothing to tarnish it. His mother's inheritance had left him well fixed with the domain at Beaumont and he willed it to his nephew, Gaspard, when he died.[116]

Granting that a half-dozen scattered and incomplete biographies do not constitute a definitive profile of the Tavanes family in the eighteenth century, a number of conclusions can still be drawn. Allowance made for a wide range of eccentricity, the Tavanes could not be labeled lazy, shiftless, or fundamentally foppish. True, they seemed to avoid, perhaps consciously, the appearance of earnest and persistent application, characteristic of the magistrates of parlement and the intendants of the King. Well-connected with the highest echelons of the robe, they still kept a

[113] *Walpole Correspondence*, III, 197, December 12, 1766. Lewis notes that the Du Deffand–Saulx correspondence has not yet been discovered. Perhaps it is just as well, given the marquis's limited talents as a man of *esprit*.

[114] *Walpole Correspondence*, V, 108, July 13, 1768; V, 121, July 27, 1768.

[115] *Ibid.*, III, May 26, 1766. *Saulx* becomes *sot* or silly fool.

[116] *A. D.*, E–1676, *Compte testamentaire*, 1769.

certain distance from the magistrates, preferring the company of the military noblesse—a Richelieu, a Duras, a Lévis—marshals all. Yet it can not be said that they failed to "adapt" to new roles in the army, administration, church, court, or Parisian society. Indeed, they were most successful in obtaining the best positions and prestige offered by contemporary society. But perhaps it had been almost too easy. The prerogatives of birth and family connection had permitted the Tavanes, and so many like them, to infiltrate the higher circles at almost every point. A combination of royal favor and carefully planned marriages could work wonders, at least for the elder branch of the family. However, success increasingly depended on the spell of name and title, without the complementary assets of rigorous training or exceptional capacity.

Although Henri-Charles was not incapable of serving royal interests in dealing with the Estates of Burgundy, his troublesome insistence on the honors of his office—both ceremonial and pecuniary—makes one wonder if, on balance, his services to the crown were very valuable. It could be argued that a more rigorously trained intendant, such as Joly de Fleury, could do as well without the "commander" in Dijon. As for the archbishop, he underwent the prescribed theological preparation and clearly mastered the etiquette of a court prelate,[117] but he had neither contact with nor deep understanding of the problems of his diocese, and his views on Church privileges and the criteria for the selection of bishops could hardly be called imaginative or even flexible. The eldest sons in the two following generations were apparently competent officers, willing to serve at the front in wartime, but their tours of duty in the army were very short compared to the long years they spent at court. In all four cases, it might well be asked whether their pecuniary and honorific rewards were justified by their services to state and society.

Younger sons and flamboyant, bankrupt cousins are perhaps stock-in-trade in the history of any great noble family. Cadets were to be sacrificed in the distribution of family inheritances, so that the elder branch might retain its luster. One cannot help but sympathize with the family head, constantly plagued by the entreaties of distant relatives, some of doubtful authenticity. Yet the dependence, not to say futility, of these cadets would seem to make it all the more important that the elder

---

[117] This thesis can be found in the Bibliothèque Nationale. See also Bibliothèque Nationale, *Manusc. fr.*, 2447, fol. 203–5, (1708). The odes accompanying the thesis evoke a glorious ancestry.

branch aspire to excellence and service. Where was the response to the "illustrious actions" of a famous ancestor? Duclos had expressed it well:

> The principles of ambition were no more just in the past than they are today. Motives were no more praiseworthy, nor demands more innocent. But their endeavors could be useful to the community and sometimes even inspire emulation.[118]

Did the Tavanes sense a decline in their value to the state? Was the near-obsession of Henri-Charles with the outward forms of respect a sign of insecurity? Did the restlessness of the vicomte or of Mirebel imply more than eccentric cadet behavior? Perhaps the utilitarian values of a Duclos were too foreign to the world of the Tavanes to cause the slightest psychological tremor.

But, whatever the reason—whether the need to compensate for a vague sense of futility or simply the necessity to maintain the "state of a gentleman" in a very demanding capital—the Tavanes were increasingly concerned about money. Efforts were directed toward mustering revenues and taking stock of the heavy financial price the family had paid for its ascent to the giddy heights of court society.

* * * *

One benefit of the move to Paris was the procurement of royal pensions. Both Henri-Charles and his son Gaspard had added about 40,000 livres to their annual income from royal gratuities alone. Proximity to court was of no small advantage here. The Tavanes were also profiting from the increasing demand for general officers in the latter half of the reign of Louis XIV.[119] Even more important was the availability of a large number of eligible heiresses in the Paris marriage market. Charles-Marie's marriage with Catherine Daguesseau in 1683 was the first of a series of alliances with Parisian nobility, of robe and sword, that accompanied and encouraged permanent residence. Clearly, the dowries and inheritances that these brides brought to the Tavanes estate were essential to the family's survival at the capital. A review of the principal marriages and maternal inheritances from 1680 to 1770 will show how fresh infusions of outside capital came to the rescue at every critical phase in the financial history of the Saulx-Tavanes.

---

[118] Duclos, *Considérations sur les moeurs de ce siècle*, 105.
[119] Corvisier, "Les généraux de Louis XIV . . . ," pp. 23–53.

However successful the heads of the family were in avoiding the worst perils of conspicuous consumption in Mirabeau's "bottomless pit," there were certain expenses that could not be avoided. One of these was the cost of army commissions. The market for commissions varied with the prestige of the unit as well as with the rank. Cavalry and elite units, so dear to families like the Tavanes, cost considerably more than regular infantry commissions.

TABLE I.3   THE PRICE OF MILITARY COMMISSIONS

Rank	Price		Rank	Price
	Infantry Livres	Cavalry Livres	Elite Corps	Livres
Lieutenant	20,000		Guidon	100,000 (1743)
Captain	40,000		Ensign	56,000 (1716)
Colonel	30– 75,000	120,000	Captain	120,000 (1716)
Maître de			Maître de	
Camp		42,000 (1693)	Camp	280,000 (1703)
Lieutenant-				
General	150–240,000 (1750)			

SOURCE: A. Corvisier, "Les généraux de Louis XIV et leur origine sociale," *XVIIe Siècle* XLII (1959), 39; A. Babeau, *La vie militaire sous l'Ancien Régime* (Paris, 1890), vol. II, pp. 143–44; Dangeau, *Journal* IX, 153; XVI, 450; III, 53; IV, 264; XVIII, 147; *A. D.*, E–1673, E–1678·

Although the exact price depended on conditions at the moment, there seems to have been a steady inflation in the commissions market, despite all efforts of the crown to stabilize prices.[120] In the early reign of Louis XIV Charles-Marie de Saulx-Tavanes seems to have been satisfied with cavalry posts—a colonelcy for 30,000 livres in 1690, *maître de camp* for 42,000 livres in 1693—relatively modest prices.[121] His sons, Henri-Charles and Marquis de Saulx, preferred grades in the Light-Horse Guards or the *Gendarmes* selling at 100,000 livres or more. It is true that the King was often generous, reducing the price in an individual case or making an outright gift of the initial commission. Both Henri-Charles and his cousin, the vicomte, received reductions of over 100,000 livres on the price of their lieutenant-generalcies. But it was not always so. As one moved up the scale of ranks, each promotion cost more. The burden of the army career of Marquis de Saulx is indicated in a passage from the accounts of his mother, dowager Comtesse Daguesseau-Tavanes.

[120] A. Babeau, *La vie militaire sous l'Ancien Régime*, 2 vols. (Paris, 1890), II, 144.
[121] Dangeau, *Journal*, III, 53; IV, 264.

Marquis de Saulx acquired the rank of ensign, giving his grade of flag-bearer in payment, and later bought a captaincy in the *gendarmes* by ceding his grade of ensign. All these operations cost Dame Daguesseau-Tavanes 82,000 livres of which 40,254 livres were borrowed.[122]

To be sure, officers were paid, their salaries representing a return on the original investment. In time of war, this might attain nine or ten per cent, but in peacetime it seldom represented more than five per cent for field-grade officers.[123] Even this assumed that salaries were paid regularly, which was far from the case. Worse than the *gages* of parlementarians, payments of army wages were delayed in war-time. In the Seven Years' War, payment on the German front apparently broke down altogether, and many officers had to pay their dragoons out of their own pockets.[124] At the same time, opportunities to make money by selling army stores seem to have become less numerous. Crucial were the extra expenses which threatened to exceed the stipend. A French officer was not only responsible for his own equipment but also for the replacement and equipment of deserters. And deserters, needless to say, were numerous.[125]

Most of the sums borrowed by the Tavanes in the first two-thirds of the century were employed to supplement the costs of campaigning or to sustain the rank of lieutenant-general at Dijon. The reports to the War Department of comfortable living in the officer corps are legion. An ordinance in 1707 attempted in vain to confine colonels and brigadiers to one wagon and twenty horses each. No cavalry officer could do with less than six horses and three valets, and many had more. Henri-Charles had six horses, worth 1,765 livres, in the campaign of 1705. The Treasury paid only 250 livres for each horse killed, the officer paid the balance. But the greatest drain was for food. There were few officers of field rank that could join the lieutenants in the *"cabaret."* It was customary for colonels and above to provide "open table," complete with silver plate and appropriate table linen. In the middle of the Seven Years' War, Saint Germain, Minister of War, attempted to limit the number of courses served at the officers' tables. The officers evaded the ordinance by putting the meat, fowl, and pastry on the same tray. Under

---

[122] *A. D.*, E–1673, *Partage*, August 5, 1729.
[123] Babeau, *La vie militaire*, II, 1–15, 144.
[124] Luynes, *Mémoires*, I, 6n.
[125] Corvisier, "Les généraux de Louis XIV...," 39n.

such conditions, a colonel was fortunate to keep his table expenses below 1,000 livres per month.[126]

The costs of a command in the provinces during peace time might be
expected to be less. But Henri-Charles at Dijon was hardly the sort to
skimp. One look at the Ducal Palace on the Place Royale tells a great
deal. As Brosses put it, "those immense apartments consume half the
revenues of the office in wood and candles."[127] The frugal parlemen-
tarian no doubt exaggerated, but even 40,000 livres income was not too
much to keep up appearances, especially when we recognize that Tavanes
presided at the Estates across the square. How many places were set at
the tables in the palace when Henri-Charles returned from Paris we do
not know, but they must have counted by scores. The bills in the hands
of the caterers of Dijon are there to prove it. By the 1750s Henri-Charles
needed between 1,800 and 3,500 livres per month for household expenses
alone, not including his trips to Paris.[128]

The increasing family obligations of the 1720s reflect the coming to
maturity of three sons. Their father died when they were still young,
and their mother, Catherine Daguesseau, assumed responsibility for the
careers of two royal officers and one potential prelate. Like Françoise
Brulart in the seventeenth century, Catherine Daguesseau had many of
the sober, earnest qualities of the robe *noblesse*. Even Saint-Simon, no
great admirer of the robe, lauded the exceptional *esprit*, application, and
incorruptibility of Catherine's brother, the new Chancellor of France.[129]
Her father, a *maître des comptes*, would have no truck with "false
luxury" and the women of the family feigned none of those "little weak-
nesses" so common among ladies of good birth.[130] In short, Catherine
Daguesseau brought the Tavanes not only an inheritance, but her own
personal intelligence and application which she exhibited in more than
twenty-five years of widowhood.

This is not to minimize the inheritance. In addition to 50,000 livres in
coin and 20,000 livres in precious stones, Catherine's fortune included two

[126] Babeau, *La vie militaire*, II, 151, 168, 170n., 173, 176; *A. D.*, E–1675, Jouvancourt Accounts, 1703–5. Duc de Croÿ spent 35,000 livres for the campaign of 1760
(*Journal*, I, 500–501).

[127] Brosses, *Lettres familières*, 289.

[128] *A. D.*, E–1687; *A. D.*, E–1688, Seguin Accounts, 1749–61.

[129] Saint-Simon, *Mémoires*, XXXI, 26–29.

[130] *Lettres inédites du Chancelier d'Aguesseau*, 2 vols., ed. D. B. Rives (Paris,
1823), I, 18, 41.

important domains in Burgundy, Lux and Tilchâtel, which doubled the value of the landed property of the Tavanes.[131] The countess lost no time in assuming active management of this estate. In 1703 she renounced the "community of property" with her recently deceased husband, thus securing her own land and income following the terms of her marriage contract. She then proceeded to liquidate her husband's debts. It was a long task. High noble creditors such as Estrées, Bethune-Charost, Choiseul, and Pontchartrain were paid, though often by negotiating fresh loans with members of the robe such as Godard at Paris and Le Grand at Dijon. The accounts of the countess furnish an insight into the involved procedures of "assigning" *rentes* and transferring obligations to third parties. Such "assignments" avoided any major transfers of liquid capital and facilitated an old custom of borrowing from Peter to pay Paul. Moreover, in addition to changing creditors, the transfers might procure other advantages for *une femme de tête* like the countess. In 1720, for example, she liquidated capital sums in Law paper, some of it borrowed from the famous vicomte at low rates of interest.[132] She also attempted to spread the loans more widely in lots of twelve to 20,000 livres and at four per cent instead of five per cent when possible. All these operations were long and complicated. The cost of new army commissions for her two sons added to the harassment. Payments for the new grades had to be spaced in such a way as to synchronize with the receipts from commissions sold. Few buyers ever paid the full sum outright. In 1716, when young Henri-Charles sold his company of Light Horse for 56,000 livres, he received only 4,500 livres in immediate payment and a promise of the rest over the next three years.[133] Even this type of contract was relatively advantageous, for many purchasers preferred to negotiate a constituted *rente*, paying five per cent of the capital in perpetuity.[134]

In 1714, the countess was forced to sell the barony of Sully. Sully, with its fine Renaissance château and *parc* some twenty miles from Autun,

---

[131] *A. D.*, E–1727, *Contrat de mariage*, February 3, 1683; *A. D.*, E–1673, *Extrait du testament de Madame Hausset*, September 3, 1703; Roupnel, *La ville et la campagne*, 234–35. In 1716, Lux and Tilchâtel were estimated at 400,000 livres; the Tavanes family domains at Beaumont and Arc-sur-Tille were valued at 450,000 livres. *A. D.*, E–1673, *Rente constituée*, September 7, 1716.

[132] *A. D.*, E–1673, *Renonciation*, September 11, 1703; Receipts, April 8, 1720; *A. D.*, E–1678, *Rente constituée*, February 21, 1720.

[133] *A. D.*, E–1678, *Vente*, November 13, 1716.

[134] See Pothier, *Traité du contrat de constitution de rente*.

had been the choicest domain of Gaspard de Saulx in the sixteenth century. Perhaps only a Daguesseau bent on keeping her own lands free of debt could have persuaded her young family to part with it. Perhaps it was the prestige still attached to Sully that made it saleable. It brought 198,000 livres, 1,000 in *louis d'or* and the balance "delegated to pay a similar sum to the oldest creditors of the estate of Charles-Marie de Saulx."[135] To the "oldest creditors": this implied that there were still others. Despite such efforts to reduce the overall indebtedness, the countess was forced to contract, by the mid-1720s, substantial loans from some of the richest "bankers" in Paris, including a loan for 38,000 livres from the famous Crozat, one for 24,000 livres from President of the *Grand Conseil* Fortia, and one for 30,000 livres from Abraham Peyrenc de Moras.[136] Here was the convenience and the danger of the Paris money market. By the time of her death in 1729, the countess had heavily mortgaged the estate.

It is curious that the last will of Comtesse Daguesseau-Tavanes is not among the family papers, otherwise so complete. Is it possible that the story of her strange disappearance from the château of Lux in 1729 is true?[137] What accounts for the equal division of her fortune among three sons, when the customary law of Burgundy would have permitted an advantage for the eldest? True, the damage was not permanent, for both younger sons died bachelors and all the Tavanes land was willed back to the main branch. Nevertheless, Henri-Charles, the eldest, now had substantially more to pay his brothers in portions at a time when other expenses were mounting. Henri-Charles lost the domain of Beaumont, worth 6,000 livres revenue in 1730, to his younger brother, Marquis de Saulx, and had to pay Nicolas, the Archbishop, 42,573 livres capital or 1,702 livres annual *rente*.[138]

Fortunately, another marriage with a member of a robe family in the next generation again came to the rescue. In 1712, Henri-Charles married

[135] *A. N.*, T–109[6], *Vente à Paris*, April 26, 1714.

[136] *A. D.*, E–1686, Register, 1754; For these bankers, see Luethy, *La banque protestante*, II, 788–89.

[137] Marquise de Créquy, *Souvenirs*, 10 vols. (Paris, 1840), I, 185ff. More than one "tale" about the old Château of Lux is related in these *Souvenirs*. We are also told that Comtesse de Tessé-Tavanes was buried alive in the crypt of the château. Since the work is reputed apocryphal, such stories fall into the domain of nineteenth-century folklore.

[138] *A. D.*, E–1673, *Partage*, August 5, 1729.

the daughter of Michel-Jean Amelot de Gournay, Councilor of State. Amelot, like Chancellor Daguesseau, was a talented administrator, having completely reorganized Spanish financial and commercial policy as advisor to the new Bourbon king at Madrid.[139] No doubt the marriage of his daughter to a Tavanes was part of an effort to consolidate his position at court after a long absence abroad. For the Tavanes it represented a new type of inheritance. Like other members of the Parisian robe, Amelot had most of his fortune in *rentes* and urban real estate.[140] In 1724 when Amelot died, the promises of his daughter's marriage contract were fulfilled, and she received half of his estate.

TABLE I.4   THE INHERITANCE OF MARIE-ANNE AMELOT, COMTESSE DE SAULX-TAVANES IN 1725

Nature of Capital	Amount Livres	Rente or Interest Livres	Rate of Return %
Rentes on:			
Four Houses in Paris	200,000	10,000	5.0
the Wine Brokers of Paris	30,150	1,370	4.5
Rentes on the *Tailles*	50,000	500	1.0
Rentes on *Aides et Gabelles*	367,938	8,198	2.5
Sub-Total:	*648,088*	*20,068*	*3.1*
One-Half "Movables" and Silverware	21,025		
Cash on Hand	43,050		
One-Half Sale-Price of a Townhouse in Paris	81,761		
Total Capital:	803,924		
Costs of Litigation	67,500		
Net Fortune:	736,424		

SOURCE: *A. D.*, E–1677, July 5, 1742.

Although the inheritance included no rural property, it had the advantage of liquidity. Henri-Charles had cause for satisfaction. He sold all the urban property immediately along with the silverware and the

[139] Marais, *Journal*, III, 112; Saint-Simon, *Mémoires*, XIII, 445; XVIII, 81ff.; Balteau, Barroux, Prévis, *et al.*, eds., *Dictionnaire de biographie française* (Paris, 1932–   ), "Amelot."

[140] On the fortunes of Parisian robe nobility see F. Bluche, *Les magistrats du Parlement de Paris au XVIIIe siècle, 1715–71* (Paris, 1960); D. Roche, "Recherches sur la noblesse parisienne au milieu du XVIIIe siècle: La noblesse du Marais," *Actes du 86me congrès national des Sociétés Savantes, Montpellier, 1961* (Paris, 1962), pp. 554, 558–59.

Councilor's fine collection of paintings and used the proceeds to pay for his rank of lieutenant-general and to buy some provincial *rentes* at four per cent. In 1731 and 1733, Henri-Charles's two daughters married with dowries of 100,000 livres each, assigned from their mother's fortune. In 1734, his eldest son, Gaspard, was given 222,000 livres in a special legacy, also from his mother's inheritance. As a result of these payments, by 1742 the Amelot fortune was reduced to 307,188 livres capital, returning 6,942 livres interest or only 2.3 per cent.[141]

When his wife died in 1740, Henri-Charles proposed a special arrangement with other members of the family, to avoid dividing the Amelot inheritance. He argued that it would be less expensive for his two daughters to renounce claims to their mother's estate and be satisfied with their dowries alone. The core of his argument was that debts on this estate had to be paid in hard coin and that the *rentes* could not be converted into cash "without excessive loss." Apparently it was not possible to convert government bonds at full face value in 1740. There is good reason to believe that Henri-Charles had purposely exaggerated his mother's debts, since the account presented to his daughters is unusually vague on this matter. His memorandum ended with an admonition to accept his more advantageous "arrangement." He sweetened the offer by promising to divide the inheritance of his deceased son, Abbé Nicolas-Charles (not to be confused with Archbishop Nicolas-Charles). When it was objected that the abbé's debts threatened to "bankrupt" the inheritance, Henri-Charles replied that "it is certain that these debts can be reduced to their true value" and that the abbé's accounts were unreliable. It appears that Henri-Charles was interpreting the family accounts to the advantage of his eldest son and, as he was the head of the family, his advice was not easily contested. Yet despite these efforts, it appears that most of the Amelot fortune was employed to pay family obligations and for the office of lieutenant-general. Although the *rentes* made it easier to service older debts, they were not used to reduce overall indebtedness. Henri-Charles even borrowed 5,456 livres to pay for part of his wife's funeral expenses "having in the inheritance no capital that can be converted into coin without too great a loss."[142]

But if the Amelot marriage had not fulfilled all its promise, the mar-

[141] *A. D.*, E–1677, *Effets*, 1742.
[142] *A. D.*, E–1677, Amelot Papers.

riage of Gaspard to a Tessé in the next generation most surely would. It was a brilliant match from every point of view. The Tessé family had proofs of nobility from 1065, predating even the Tavanes by 169 years. Marshal Tessé had won honor and fortune like Michel Amelot as advisor to the Bourbon king of Spain. The elder branch of his family had entered court and married into the families Noailles, Ayen, and Lafayette.[143] The younger son of the marshal, a naval officer, had married Françoise Castan, the only child of one of the richest merchant-bankers of the reign of Louis XIV.[144] They had two daughters, one of whom was disinherited; the other married Gaspard de Tavanes in 1734. Gaspard had married the heiress of an heiress.

Unfortunately, Gaspard's wife died suddenly and without a will in 1753, so that he did not receive the Tessé fortune until after the death of his father-in-law in 1766.[145] It was often a long wait from the promises of the marriage contract until the delivery of the inheritance. As a consequence of this delay and of expenses associated with Gaspard's new post at court and his son's campaign in Germany, the 1750s brought on a major financial crisis.

In 1754, the aging Henri-Charles decided to transfer the care of his affairs to his son, Gaspard, who agreed to seek a "solid arrangement for the liquidation of our debts." Henri-Charles claimed the royal pensions worth about 40,000 livres for himself and assigned all the other revenues totalling about 50,000 livres to his son. From this 50,000 livres Gaspard agreed to pay all the interest charges due and employ the remainder, "if there is any," to liquidate the capital owed. Gaspard had these obligations summarized in a large cow-hide register. The accumulated burden was heavy. Dating back to the 1720s, there were 45 loan contracts negotiated at Dijon and 80 more loans signed at Paris, adding to a capital of 752,363 livres and bearing an annual interest of 52,222 livres. It could not have taken Gaspard more than a moment's reflection to realize that the interest charges exceeded his assigned income by about 2,000 livres

[143] Luynes, *Mémoires*, VII, 423; L. Gottschalk, *Lafayette Comes to America*, (Chicago, 1959).

[144] H. Luethy, *La banque protestante*, I, 197–221; II, 249. Luethy claims that Castan needed Tessé's "protection" at Court. On this occasion, Samuel Bernard made some bitter comments about this marriage and about aristocrats in general.

[145] *A. D.*, E–1700. Gaspard also lost his wife's income which was in the form of a life-time annuity of 15,000 livres. Luynes referred to this *rente viagère* as if it were a gamble that failed. Luynes, *Mémoires*, XIII, 32.

yearly. Gaspard de Saulx was technically bankrupt. In 1734, Henri-Charles's debts had totalled 300,300 livres; in the following twenty years, they doubled.[146]

How had it happened? The accounts would suggest that the Tavanes paid for nothing in cash. Henri-Charles and his immediate family accumulated 45,000 livres in debts to local merchants and shopkeepers—tailors, jewelers, grocers, perfumers, wine merchants. Henri-Charles even recorded 5,000 livres owed to "a lady at Dijon," without any further explanation. Yet these obligations were less pressing, since the merchants charged no interest. More serious were the loans contracted to pay military expenses of various kinds. There is good reason to believe that the Seven Years' War had been especially costly for Gaspard's son, Casimir, since regular payment of the army ceased altogether.[147] But most important was the fact that, by 1760, the family fortune had to support three generations of Tavanes. This was the consequence of the longevity of both Henri-Charles and Gaspard, both of whom lived past 70, and the young marriages of the eldest sons—Henri-Charles at 26, Gaspard at 21, and Casimir at 20. This was to fall even below the low average age of bridegrooms among the French peers as a group (23.6 years).[148] The early search for an heiress meant young marriages, and young marriages led to the clustering of generations. Three generations of Tavanes could not, or would not, live as one establishment. The same problem would arise again in the next generation.

Somehow, Gaspard managed to keep up appearances through the 1750s. Deficits, however, mounted on the accounts of both father and son. In 1756, Gaspard borrowed 45,000 livres; in 1757, he borrowed another 15,500 livres. In 1759, he sold the silverware at Dijon for 22,347 livres—an ominous sign.[149] The death of Henri-Charles in 1761 brought some relief, permitting the liquidation of one expensive establishment at Dijon, but it was not enough. Gaspard now began to default on his

---

[146] A. D., E-1687, *Récapitulation générale*, September 14, 1754; A. D., E-1700, *Mémoire*, August 7, 1767.

[147] Luynes, *Mémoires*, I, 6n. According to Luynes, young Duc de Chevreuse spent over one million livres to pay his dragoons and maintain discipline during the Seven Years' War.

[148] C. Lévy and L. Henry, "Ducs et pairs sous l'Ancien Régime . . . ," *Population* (1960), 812–14.

[149] A. D., E-1688, Seguin Accounts.

interest payments, giving his creditors the legal right to demand their capital. Pressed on all sides, he decided to sell land.

The decision to sell was difficult enough. Which domain should it be? Part of the estate had been entailed either by will or marriage contract and was "not subject to division or dismemberment." In less troubled times, Henri-Charles had entailed to Gaspard's children the domains of Lux, Bourberain, and Tilchâtel, so that, under the law, Gaspard could not sell them. The other properties of Arc-sur-Tille and Pailly had been entailed to Gaspard, but he had already renewed them for another three generations.[150] However, entails were not impossible to break. Gaspard's legal advisors argued that the newest entail had not been "published" and that the count could petition the courts to "discharge" the entail and sell the land to pay off his debts.[151]

The seigneury of Pailly was chosen for several reasons. Gaspard was advised to keep his lands around Dijon free of debt and sell a domain of "mediocre value situated in a different province." Pailly was in Champagne, under a customary law of inheritance more generous to younger sons than that of Burgundy.[152] Gaspard sold Pailly in 1764 for 190,000 livres, or thirty-two times the revenue, an excellent price. The purchaser was *maître* Toussaint, *chevalier d'honneur* at the *Chambre des Comptes* of Dijon, a magistrate on his way to nobility.[153] Toussaint paid 10,000 livres in coin and received a list of creditors of the Tavanes estate to reimburse. Most of them would settle for a guarantee of regular payment of interest. Investment opportunities were not so numerous in the eighteenth century that men with capital "placed" at five per cent would want their capital reimbursed.[154]

The worst was over. The death of Gaspard's father-in-law in 1766 com-

---

[150] The Ordinance of 1747, sponsored by Chancellor d'Aguesseau, limited entails to three degrees. See J. Brissaud, *A History of French Private Law* (Boston, 1912), 732.

[151] *A. D.*, E–1947, Entails at Pailly; E–1700; Bouhier, *Coûtumiers*, I, 12ff.

[152] *A. D.*, E–1947; *A. D.*, E–1700, *Mémoire*, August 7, 1767.

[153] *A. D.*, E–1679, fol. 279–80. Members of the *Chambre des Comptes* at Dijon became ennobled after twenty years of service or death in office.

[154] *A. D.*, E–1686, Register, 1765. Until a general history of *rentes* in the eighteenth century is written, see B. Schnapper, *Histoire d'un instrument de credit : Les rentes au XVIme siècle* (Paris, 1958) and R. de Roover, *L'évolution de la lettre de change du XIVe au XVIIIe siècle* (Paris, 1953). See also G. Chaussinand-Nogaret, *Les Financiers de Languedoc au XVIIIe siècle* (Paris, 1970).

pleted the financial recovery. The will of Marquis de Tessé was worth thirty years of waiting. A model of sobriety, the will assigned 2,000 livres to cover all funeral expenses and charities and apparently applied the formula "without ostentation" conscientiously. Making Gaspard's son his heir, the marquis willed to him his lands in Normandy, worth 14,000 livres a year, that more than compensated for the loss of Pailly two years before. But the most satisfying provision was buried in the center of the will.

> The property in cash (*argent comptant*) is close to 500,000 livres, consisting of about 180,000 in gold in the desk of my study and about 100,000 in silver either in the desk or in the strong box above the clothes closet, and 120,000 with M. de Merland, Receiver of the *Généralité* of Paris, payable according to his drafts to be found in my secretary for which Madame de Tessé [my wife] has the key.[155]

Apparently, Marquis de Tessé preferred the strong-box to any other form of "saving" or investment. Nor was this all. Although Tessé obviously preferred hard coin, he had *rentes* worth 120,000 livres, a claim to an inheritance valued at 200,000 livres, and a promising lawsuit over a house on the Place Royale in Paris. All this was in addition to provisions made for servants, the jointure of widow Tessé, and a 3,000-livre diamond for the executor of the will. The marquis had mobilized his fortune tightly, leaving little to servants or charity. Indeed, so frugal was the will, that the Tavanes felt obliged to violate the specifications regarding the burial. "A wooden coffin did not please the family nor did it seem appropriate to the priest." But they lost no time in auctioning off the marquis's household effects in his townhouse on the Isle of Notre Dame.[156]

Gaspard was anxious to assign at least two-thirds of this fortune to his eldest son, following the provisions of his marriage contract. However, his wife had left no will and, since the Tessé fortune was governed by the Custom of Paris, the two cadets had an equal claim with their older brother. A compromise was arranged, whereby the landed property went to the eldest son, and the gold and silver was divided into three equal lots of 160,000 livres and invested in the Estates of Brittany at four per

[155] *A. D.*, E–1702, Will of June 30, 1766.
[156] *Ibid.*, "Observations on the burial expenses."

cent. When the accounts were closed, it appeared that Gaspard had accumulated about 500,000 livres in land and *rentes*.[157]

The Tessé inheritance contained another unexpected item. Marquis de Tessé had capital in shipping ventures at Cadiz, no doubt inherited from his father-in-law, the banker Castan. Gaspard now took possession of a packet of correspondence and memoranda treating *pacotiles*, *grosses aventures*, and *armements*. How exotic to find, alongside of constituted *rentes* and silver *écus*, accounts in *piastres*, *pistoles*, and other coin that evoked a world of affairs eons away from the seigneuries in Burgundy! Gaspard had claims to ten ships which, in the years before the Seven Years' War, were bound for Lima, Cartageña, Havana, and other ports of the Spanish Empire. The investment totalled 111,594 livres and earnings had exceeded 28,000 livres. The correspondent at Cadiz in those years promised profits of 41 to 45 per cent.[158]

But this had been ten years earlier. In fact, the last dividend on this exotic parcel was declared in 1753. On the eve of war, the agent at Cadiz was assuring Marquis de Tessé that the new convoy system and a few years of peace would surely revive the trade. The Seven Years' War proved a bitter lesson to more than one investor in the Spanish and French colonial trade. The permanent damage caused by the English blockade should not be underestimated. If ships and exports could still be had, capital was not equally forthcoming. Moreover, the colonials had a perfect excuse for not paying.[159] The phrase "in arrears" (*retard de paiements*) plagued the Tessé account after 1755, and the end of the war apparently brought no relief. A memorandum from Cadiz dated December, 1766, was not of a kind to encourage further investment.

> But to the extent that the debts are of long standing and the debtors are far away and either insolvable or of bad faith, one must be happy with what one can get.[160]

---

[157] A. D., E–1700, *Mémoire à consulter*, 1766; A. D., E–1702, *Etat sommaire des objets de la succession Tessé*.

[158] A. D., E–1700, Correspondence Giradon-Tessé, 1751–56.

[159] On this general problem of a relative decline in colonial trade after the Seven Years' War see the works of H. Robert on La Rochelle, Gaston-Martin on Nantes (see bibliography) and especially the chapters by F. Crouzet, in *Bordeaux au XVIIIe siècle*, ed. E. Pariset (Bordeaux, 1968), pp. 313–15 and *passim*. On the preference for land even among merchant-bankers see Luethy, *La banque protestante*, II, 42–44, 177–88.

[160] A. D., E–1700, *Mémoire*, December 17, 1766.

The Paris marriage market had no doubt put the Tavanes in contact with family fortunes that contained other elements than royal pensions and landed revenues. The Amelots had brought public *rentes* and urban real estate; the Tessés now contributed overseas investments. But as Gaspard and his son entered the last third of the century, the original components must still have seemed preferable. *Rentes*, coin, and even urban real estate were most easily divisible for the payment of family creditors. Regarding overseas ventures, the Court *milieu* was clearly more favorably disposed and better placed to obtain technical knowledge of the trade than the average provincial town. Nevertheless, for a family with the current-income needs of the Tavanes, the colonial trade must have seemed much too uncertain.

The end of the reign of Louis XV had seen the Tavanes through difficult times. The death of old patrons, the uncertainties of the Court, and the close race between expenditures and inheritances had provoked crises. Yet as Gaspard approached his sixtieth year, his family seemed secure on all sides. His son, Casimir, was winning a new place at Court after his return from the war; the number of scandalous cousins had apparently fallen, and the Tessé fortune had not only put the family creditors at a distance, but also provided the Tavanes with new pretensions as Norman seigneurs. As Gaspard leafed through the papers in his study in the townhouse on the Rue Saint-Dominique, his thoughts turned at some point to the estate accounts. Perhaps the land deserved closer attention. Was it not, upon reflection, the most reliable of investments, the solid basis of aristocratic prestige, and the hope of increased revenues. Gaspard's eldest son must not forget that the Tavanes had drawn income from Burgundy for more than three centuries.

II

THE BURGUNDIAN ESTATE AT THE
END OF THE OLD REGIME

*I*n 1780, Charles-François-Casimir de Saulx, Comte de Tavanes, *Maré-chal de Camp*, became the head of the house.[1] He was 41 years of age, retired from active military service, and already eight years separated from his wife. His mother had died of smallpox when he was only 14; his father, Comte de Saulx, had waited until his 67th year before he transfered the bulk of the family property to his eldest surviving son. Such a long minority would not seem to prepare the young count for an active role in estate management. Since the Seven Years' War, in which he performed commendably with Broglie's army on the Elbe, the Comte de Tavanes had been attached to the Royal Court at Versailles. Like his father, he accumulated a number of prestigious, honorific posts in the royal service, most notably the office of *Chevalier de la Reine*, attached to the Queen's Stables. Although Madame Campan, that keen court ob- server, insisted that the *écuries* formed a department of first importance by its "dignity and expense," it was hardly a proving ground for the serious application land administration required.[2]

Moreover, from the young count's point of view, the terms of the family pact whereby his father relinquished control of the estate were far from ideal. The aging Comte de Saulx, like his own father twenty years earlier, retained a substantial—and the most secure—share of the reve- nues. These were the royal pensions, appointments, and gratuities ac-

---

[1] *A. D.*, E–1878, *Transaction*, March 31, 1780.
[2] Madame J. L. H. Campan, *Memoirs of the Court of Marie-Antoinette* (Lon- don, 1850), I, 23, 288.

cumulated over two generations and totaling almost 40,000 livres, a third of the family income. Deducting this sum from the inheritance, the count's father gave him the landed property, but on condition that the younger count pay all the debts of the house.[3] Now new obligations were added to old ones. For the act of donation necessitated arrangement for the payment of portions to members of the family. The young count was obligated to pay the interest on his younger brother's portion of 100,000 livres and on his sister's dowry of 80,000 livres. Furthermore, even a noble family had to pay the property transfer tax, the *centième denier*. One per cent of the capital value of the Saulx-Tavanes estates was no small sum. The lands in Burgundy were taxed at almost 12,000 livres, and those in Normandy at about half this amount.[4] Perhaps it was the sudden realization of the full weight of these and other obligations that spurred the new head of the house to action.

Even a cursory glance at the meticulous annual statements of the family intendant, Jean Godard, must have been a revelation to François-Casimir. No doubt the prodigious daily consumption of his wife, before and after the separation of 1772, not to mention his own, had accustomed the count to the costs of Parisian living. But the annual service charges on the total family obligations were sobering indeed. They were approaching 50,000 livres, not including the interest on portions of 9,000 livres more. What resources were available to meet these fixed expenses?[5]

In 1780 the properties in Burgundy and Normandy were yielding a net revenue of 80,000 livres while rents and annuities added another 8,000 livres. At first glance, a margin of 30,000 livres income would seem sufficient to cover the fixed obligations and even leave something to amortize the debts. But such an estimate did not take into consideration two major threats to budgetary equilibrium. The count's three children were reaching twenty, the marriageable age of French court nobility.[6] No Tavanes could be dowered for less than 100,000 livres, not to speak of the expense of a wedding fitting for a great house. Moreover, could the count maintain a dignified establishment in the Saint Sulpice quarter of

---

[3] *A. D.*, E–1699, 262, *Transaction*, March 31, 1780.

[4] *A. D.*, E–1878, *Mémoire . . . pour payement du centième denier dû par Monseigneur Comte de Tavanes.*

[5] *A. D.*, E–1712–19, *Compte Godard*, 1786–90.

[6] C. Lévy et L. Henry, "Ducs et pairs sous l'Ancien Régime: Caractéristiques démographiques d'une caste," *Population* (1960), 807–30.

Paris and perform his services at Court on 30,000 livres per annum? Few noblemen would attempt to maintain the state of a gentleman in Paris on less than 50,000 livres, exclusive of fixed obligations.[7] The count was scarcely prepared by either habit or education to follow the frugal precepts of a provincial *gentilhomme campagnard*. After all, the count was on the verge of becoming a "hereditary duke of France," an honor he could hardly regard with indifference. This was not the moment to skimp on the inevitable legal and ceremonial expenses associated with creating a duchy of Tavanes. Obvious retrenchment on the count's part would be unbecoming in the extreme. Had the family attained new heights of dignity and honor, recapturing in a certain measure the glorious days of Marshal Gaspard de Saulx, famous captain of Henri II, only to discover that their resources were painfully inadequate to sustain the rank?

François-Casimir had good reason to review his accounts and search for new sources of income. He had not been totally oblivious of money matters in the past. Three years earlier, he had invested 20,000 livres in the Guiana Company, an overseas commercial venture that had a family precedent in the investments of the count's maternal grandfather a generation ago. But his tentative investment was not to produce the six-digit profits of his grandfather in the 1750s.[8] In 1781 it was already clear that the Guiana Company was in serious trouble. The count did not attend the stockholders' meeting in March of that year and, like other shareholders, he not only refused to subscribe further capital, but also denied that he was liable for more than the amount of his original investment. Appeals by the directors of the company were to no avail.[9] If François-Casimir had ever been tantalized by the letters from his grandfather's agent at Cadiz in the 1750s, he was apparently unwilling to risk any more money on the West Indies trade. Better to write off the original

---

[7] On the cost of Parisian living, see H. Carré, *La noblesse de France et l'opinion publique au XVIIIe siècle* (Paris, 1920), ch. I; F. Bluche, *Les magistrats du Parlement de Paris au XVIIIe siècle 1715–1771* (Paris, 1960), Part III, ch. IV.

[8] *A. D.*, E–1700, *Mémoire instructif concernant . . . differents interêts . . . tant à la grosse aventure qu'en armement et pacotilles de differents navires de Cadiz . . .* ; *Correspondance*, 1751–56.

[9] *A. D.*, E–1708, *Compagnie de la Guyane*, Report of 1781. A plaintive report of the company management reads: "It cannot be hidden that the general appeal [for more capital] has failed, a number of shareholders imagining that they are not responsible for the debts and loans of the company and are obligated only for the amount of their shares. . . ."

investment as a mistake not to be repeated. Given the consumption pattern of both the count and his father, one wonders where he found the 20,000 livres. The count had better luck with his connections at Court. In April, 1780, the King granted him a new pension of 15,000 livres per annum, presumably in recognition of military and courtly services in the previous reign.[10] But this would hardly be enough. A more promising alternative remained—the land.

*

The oldest and most important family properties were in northern Burgundy. Scattered over twenty parishes, these properties were grouped in three major clusters. The seigneury of Arc-sur-Tille, eight miles east of Dijon in the rich Saône plain, embraced 2,000 acres of domain, a third in grain, a third in meadow, and a third in forest. The second cluster extended along the Vingeanne River, twenty miles northeast of Dijon and consisted of almost 1,400 acres, half in grain, half in forest. Adjoining this *comté* was a third cluster, reaching westward to the main royal road from Dijon to Langres in Champagne. Centering on the parishes of Bourberain, Lux, and Tilchâtel, with dependencies in a half-dozen others were 5,000 acres of Tavanes domain, 80 per cent of it in solid tracts of forest, helping to fuel an important iron forge on the Tille River.[11]

Altogether, the Burgundian properties totaled 8,100 acres, 5,500 acres in large solid blocks of woodland and 2,600 acres in scattered plots of grain and meadowland. These scattered plots were rarely more than 15 acres each, and most of them were less than one acre each, often no wider than an adjoining road, and completely interspersed with peasant holdings. Maps of the estate reveal a patchwork of rectangular plots, the count's property colored in brilliant red.[12] This was domain land, but completely different in configuration from the compact *métairies* of the

---

[10] A. D., E–1727, *Inventaire des Titres, Série 2, Brevet, April 1, 1780.*
[11] See map, below.
[12] A. N., T–109[1–2]; A. D., E–1762, 1765, 1781, 1916. These bundles contain sectional maps of the property, drawn up by the agents in the 1780s. See Documents VII and VIII (map of Lux).

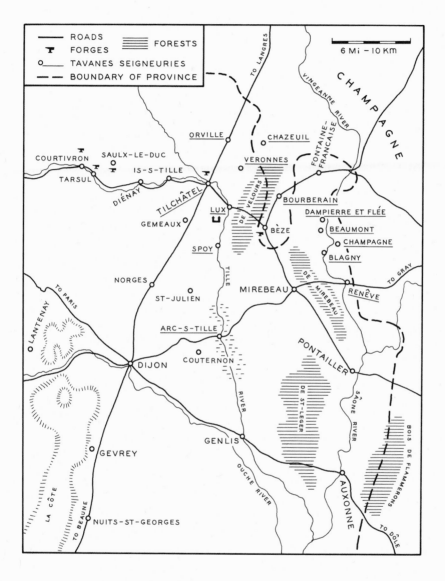

Figure 1. The Burgundian Properties of Duc de Saulx-Tavanes

Toulousain or even the smaller family farms of Upper Brittany, not to speak of the large commercialized farms of the Beauce or Flanders.[13]

In addition, the Tavanes had claims to seigneurial dues on some 20,000 acres. They included the usual array of quit-rents (*cens*) in coin, *banalités* of mill, oven, and press, mutation fees, fines, and a few *corvées*. But the most important seigneurial right was the *dîme inféodée*, a claim to the thirteenth sheaf of grain on at least 13,000 acres of grain land. In 1780, the gross receipts from the Burgundian estate reached 61,707 livres, a third from seigneurial rights.[14] The family property in Normandy was a more recent acquisition, and less extensive. An inheritance of the count's mother, it included the barony of Aunay near Caen, returning 18,000 livres, and the *dîmes* of three parishes near Calais, producing 10,000 livres more.[15]

The total income from land was therefore just under 90,000 livres in 1780. This was a large estate by French standards. The Saulx-Tavanes were among the 30 *émigré* peers who received the largest indemnities by the Restoration government in 1825.[16] There is reason to believe the estate was typical of the high aristocracy, not only in acreage and income, but also in the quality of the land (especially the predominance of woodland), the configuration of the domain, the proportion of income in seigneurial rights, the types of leasehold, and the kind of management employed.[17] Arthur Young claimed that wherever he encount-

[13] See R. Forster, *The Nobility of Toulouse in the Eighteenth Century* (Baltimore, 1960), ch. I; J. Meyer, *La noblesse bretonne au XVIIIe siècle* (Paris, 1966), Part II, ch. IV; G. Lefebvre, *Questions agraires au temps de la terreur* (La Roche-sur-Yon, 1954), pp. 58–90.

[14] *A. D.*, E–1721, *Comptes Billard*, 1780. See also Table of Rents, Document V.

[15] *A. D.*, *Calvados*, E–710, *Fermages*, 1778–80. The precise acreage of the Norman estate is unknown.

[16] A. Gain, *La restauration et les biens des émigrés* (Nancy, 1929), II, 475. The Saulx-Tavanes received an indemnity of 475,271 francs capital. Gain labels indemnities over 225,000 francs as "*gros*." It should also be stressed that the Tavanes were indemnified for less than half of their estate; about 60 per cent of the domain land was in forest and was returned to the family under Napoleon. Hence, the indemnity probably underestimates the value of the Tavanes' estate relative to other members of the peerage.

[17] "Reason to believe" does not mean statistical proof. Very few studies of individual estates exist. See D. Roche, "Aperçus sur la fortune et les revenus des princes de Condé à l'aube du XVIIIe siècle," *Revue d'histoire moderne et contemporaine*, XIV (July–Sept., 1967), 217–43; B. Hyslop, *L'apanage de Philippe-Egalité, Duc d'Orléans, 1785–91* (Paris, 1965); P. Lefranc, "Les propriétés privées de Charles X dans la Vienne,"

ered large tracts of forest he could be sure it belonged to some absentee nobleman. Yet absentee landlords need not be careless ones, as the Saulx-Tavanes example will make clear.

How was this land administered? One is immediately impressed by the simplicity of management, the small number of agents, and the low cost of administration. In 1780, the entire administration consisted of four men, not including the forest wardens and three domestics in the country château at Lux in Burgundy. The four were Jean Godard, the chief steward at Paris; Antoine Billard, the Receiver at Dijon; Jean Duboy, steward at Lux; and M. Rossignot, the steward at Aunay in Normandy. All four had some legal training. Godard was an advocate attached to the Parlement of Paris, hence a lawyer of some standing, having attended a faculty of law and still pleading cases in the kingdom's highest sovereign court.[18] Billard was an advocate attached to the Parlement of Dijon, less prestigious but clearly near the top of the professional hierarchy in the provinces. Duboy and Rossignot were local notaries whose legal competence and prestige scarcely transcended the local parishes where they lived. They worked exclusively for the Tavanes family. The wages for the entire staff, including the forest wardens, were not excessive, when one remembers that a day-laborer's annual wage was about 200 livres.

Jean Godard became chief steward or intendant of the Tavanes estate in 1780. The previous count had not centralized his accounts in the hands of a single steward at Paris. He had depended on his receiver at Dijon to keep the accounts for his lands in Burgundy, make disbursements for his obligations there, and send the balance of the revenues to Paris. He did the same with his Norman estate. The elder count had a separate account of his Paris expenses kept by a Monsieur Chennevière, to whom he assigned only the revenues from his royal pensions.[19] Pre-

---

Bulletin de la société des antiquaires de l'Ouest, VII (1964), 521–46; Louis Gottschalk and Janet MacDonald, eds., "Letters on the Management of an Estate during the Old Regime," *Journal of Modern History*, VIII (1936), 64–81; M. Vovelle, "Sade et Mirabeau," *Provence historique* (1967), 160–71. There are, of course, references to estates of the upper nobility in the more general works of Paul Bois, Jean Meyer, Louis Merle, Pierre de Saint Jacob, Marc Venard, and Georges Lefebvre, but little on estate management.

[18] See F. Delbeke, *L'action politique et sociale des avocats au XVIIIe siècle* (Louvain, 1927).

[19] *A. D.*, E–1710, Miscellaneous Accounts, 1777–83.

Table II.1   Salaries of the Administrative Staff of the Comte de Tavanes, 1780

Staff	Salary Livres
M. Godard, *Intendant* at Paris	800
M. Billard, *Procureur-Fiscal* at Dijon	400 (raised to 600 in 1780)
Sr. Duboy, *Régisseur* at Lux, Burgundy	400 (raised to 600 in 1782)
Sr. Rossignot, *Régisseur* at Aunay, Normandy	400
Sauloville, Chief Forest Warden and *Concièrge* at Lux, Burgundy	600 (and livery)
Seven forest wardens in Burgundy (5,300 acres of wood)	1,400 (and livery)
Two forest wardens in Normandy	400
Three domestics* (1 maid, 1 gardener, 1 messenger) at the Château of Lux in Burgundy	210
Total	4,610 livres

* There were fifteen more servants in the townhouse at Paris, but they cannot be considered part of the estate administration.
Source: *A. D.*, E–1712–19 (Godard); *A. D.*, E–1721 (Billard); *A. D.*, E–1728 (Duboy); *A. D. Calvados*, E–1710–12 (Rossignot).

sumably, the older Tavanes had a complete financial picture of his estate, but no reader of the voluminous yet scattered family records can reproduce it.[20]

François-Casimir, when he became the head of the family, instituted some important changes in estate bookkeeping. Billard at Dijon began to submit concise trimester accounts of receipts and expenses, a definite triumph of lucidity and precision over previous disarray. Similarly, Godard at Paris produced the first clear picture of the entire estate, including the properties in both Normandy and Burgundy, and, after the elder count's death in 1784, he itemized all of the income from the royal pensions. For the first time, the debts contracted in Paris are revealed in their impressive entirety, chapter headings identifying annuities, perpetual rents, *obligations*, and drafts (*billets*) of all kinds. The young count now had annual statements on printed forms in duplicate, which he reviewed with Godard in January of every year.[21]

Despite these indubitable improvements in accounting, however, the statements revealed two shortcomings. First, they were not double-entry, and the rubric "receipts" often included such items as "new loans," an awkward and misleading accounting technique at best. Second, although the separate Norman and Burgundian accounts make it certain that

[20] Perhaps the older count destroyed the evidence.
[21] *A. D.*, E–1712–19.

Godard in Paris received all the revenues, the intendant prefaced each annual report with the following statement:

> Monsieur Jean Godard, Advocate at Parlement, declares that, although he is the Intendant of Monseigneur le Duc de Saulx-Tavanes, he does not receive the revenues directly from the tenants, *rentiers*, and debtors, but from Monsieur le Duc himself to whom he gives receipts for each item.[22]

Apparently, the Comte de Tavanes reserved the right to withhold a portion of the revenues from the eyes of his chief steward.

Godard was a professional intendant, working for the well-known Luynes family as well.[23] Although he was no expert on agriculture, he was something more than a meticulous bookkeeper. In 1788, he drew up a complete summary of the family obligations and proposed a budget whereby rents would be increased by some 20,000 livres and the duke's household and personal expenses reduced by a similar amount. Godard planned to balance the Tavanes budget by 1790, and in 1788 everything pointed to success.[24]

Antoine Billard, Dijon advocate, had been in the family employ since 1761, when the Tavanes took up permanent residence in Paris. In 1780, the new count drew up a memorandum (*mémoire*) in the form of a questionnaire regarding Billard's functions. Among the questions appeared a basic query: "Is Monsieur Billard only a collector and disburser of revenue or does he administer the land?" The reply did not answer the question directly. "In correspondence with Comte de Saulx, M. Billard conducts all the count's affairs, including collecting rents, selling wood, renewing leases, pursuing delinquent tenants, and paying local creditors of the estate.... For this purpose he must have the appropriate papers and titles."[25] It is not surprising that Billard was most frequently referred to as *Chargé de la Recette* for some twenty *fermes* or leaseholds. Although

---

[22] *Ibid.*

[23] *A. D.*, E–1710, In these accounts Godard is referred to as *"intendant de M. le Duc de Luynes."* His residence was usually noted as Hotel de Luynes, rue St .Dominique, St. Germain quarter, an even more respectable "neighborhood" than St. Sulpice. Recall that the Luynes and Saulx-Tavanes families had both been part of the Queen's circle in the previous reign.

[24] *A. D.*, E–1715, *Detail net . . . de toutes les charges de l'Etat de Comptabilité de Paris, 1788.* In the light of subsequent events the optimism of Godard seems misplaced. *"En 1790 la Recette augmentera de 19,898 livres [et] la Recette ne manquera que de 6,222 livres."*

[25] *A. D.*, E–1878, *Questions à repondre par M. Billard.*

the same memorandum stated that "M. le comte has had no other advisor for his affairs since 1761," it is clear that Billard had neither incentive nor opportunity to act as an agricultural entrepreneur. In fact, the count's conception of estate management precluded any such function. From the count's correspondence, there is little doubt that Billard was performing his duties best when he placed a maximum number of sacks of gold and silver in the stagecoach that left Dijon every month for the count's residence on the Rue du Bacq in Paris.[26] In short, Billard was a collector of rents and not much more.

In 1780, the new head of the family surprised "his people" in Burgundy by announcing a provincial journey to inspect his properties on the Tille River. A certain flurry of preparations shook the quiet routine of the half-deserted château of Lux. Duboy, the resident steward, called his skeleton staff of three together and ordered Sauloville, the chief forest warden, to alert his seven men scattered over some 5,000 acres of forest. Duboy spent 500 livres making hasty repairs on the château—a sixteenth-century structure always in need of new plaster or tile—and stocked the cellar with 800 bottles of good wine from the Côte.[27] The forest wardens were outfitted in new green livery complete with silver buttons, blue-gray capes, and the Tavanes coat-of-arms.[28]

Billard at Dijon prepared a list of business to be discussed with the count during August. Included were such items as renewing leases, nominating a new *bailli* at Bourberain, a village of 87 households, repairing the church at Arc-sur-Tille, arbitrating a dispute between the subtenant at Beaumont and the parish priest, and preparing for the renewal of the *terrier* of the village. The prospect of dealing with these details was not made more attractive by Billard's new estimate of the *centième denier* (one-per-cent inheritance tax) which the count would have to pay upon official reception of his father's property. For his part, the count promised

---

[26] *A. D.*, E–1878. Insurance for the transport of gold and silver from Dijon to Paris was 10 sous per 100 livres, or only 0.5 per cent. Billard sent as much as 5,000 livres per trip, presumably in silver *écus* of 3 livres each. The threat presented by such notorious bandits as Cartouche seems exaggerated in the light of such a low rate.

[27] The "*Côte*," a ridge of vineyards stretching from Dijon south to Beaune, was fast becoming the most famous wine-growing area in Burgundy. The robe nobles of the Parlement of Dijon owned most of the best *crus*. A. Colombet, *Les parlementaires bourguignons à la fin du XVIIIe siècle* (Dijon, 1937), 133–34; G. Roupnel, *La ville et la campagne au XVIIe siècle* (Paris, 1955), 80 and *passim*.

[28] *A. D.*, E–1723 (Duboy).

to send a complete list of those to whom the revenues should be paid after Billard collected them. Many of the family creditors were local residents of Dijon.[29]

The tone of the new count's instructions to Billard was crisp, stern, and businesslike. They included the following information:

Pursue the affair against Collard for the *cens* of 6 sols. The count will intervene if necessary.

Show the tenant at Bourberain the map of the land, but in any case, press him to pay what he owes and make no deductions because he is not going to get any.

Since Claude Bourget, the forest warden, has been deaf for the last two and a half years, replace him.

Claude P. ... has built a tannery on the commons at Arc-sur-Tille [at the rent of] 2 livres 10 sous. We believe that Comte de Saulx can ask for the same *cens*.

Marginal comments, apparently in the count's own hand, were even more terse. "Demand the *cens* and, in case of refusal, go to the law," or simply, "Raise the lease from 260 to 300 livres." On points of law the count's instructions were equally decided, not to say unyielding.

Terminate the subject of water rights with M. de Longecourt one way or another. ... If M. de Longecourt does not want to make a reasonable arrangement, M. Billard will order Sr. Rochet [the count's tenant] to harass M. de Longecourt's tenant until he gives up all claim to these water rights.

Regarding his own tenants' rights, the count was not diposed to a generous interpretation of the law.

Tell Sr. Richard, tenant at Arc-sur-Tille, that M. le Comte de Saulx will sell 400 feet of oak trees on his own account. Sr. Richard is too reasonable to claim that the price of these trees belongs to him.[30]

Tavanes never made his projected trip to Burgundy. Instead, he decided to send two professional assessors from Paris to inspect his properties for him. The task set for Messieurs Fleury and Dubois makes clear what the count considered essential in estate management. They were to estimate the precise yield in kind and money from each domain, each

[29] *A. D.*, E–1878, *Mémoires* (for Billard).

[30] *A. D.*, E–1878, *Mémoire contenant instructions pour M. Billard relatives aux Affaires de M. de Saulx-Tavanes.* (The hand is shaky; is it the count himself?)

track of forest, each enclave, and, above all, from each of the varied seigneurial rights. On these detailed estimates, the count would base his rents—and he wanted them raised. In a letter to Billard in August, 1780, he wrote:

> The quantity of debts and charges imposed upon me by my father in the transaction [March 31, 1780] requires me to raise 15,000 livres more annually from the land. I have no other choice at this time but to raise the leases and rents. Those at Tilchâtel and Arc-sur-Tille are the largest. Therefore, it is of utmost importance to obtain most of these new revenues from these two leases.[31]

The special agents did their work well. The surviving statements leave no doubt about this. Each domain and its dependencies had its own estimate. Columns of rents and dues bore such headings as "actual return," "anticipated return," or "maximum possible income." In an effort to determine the profit margins of each principal tenant (*fermier principal*), Fleury and Dubois examined the lease terms of each subtenant (*sous fermier*).[32]

The rents of the subtenants were usually paid in kind at a fixed rate per acre. For example, rents were usually fixed by custom at seven or eight measures of grain per *journal* (0.8 acre), and even the smallest plots could be calculated as fractions of this amount. Seigneurial rights such as the *dîme inféodée* were more difficult to estimate since they were a proportion of the harvest and hence changeable from year to year. The major variable was of course the market price for grain. The price schedule employed by Fleury and Dubois was naturally open to debate, especially by the principal tenants. As a double check, the count sent his agents to Burgundy in alternate summers in order to compare estimates. The summaries of these estimates and the bids made by the prospective new tenants were then sent to the count in Paris. Table II.2 gives the summary for the *comté* of Beaumont.

The principal tenant at Beaumont, who received the income of all these subleases, had paid the count a rent of 13,000 livres in coin since 1776. With the expiration of her lease after nine years, Tavanes saw an

---

[31] *A. D.*, E–1991, Comte de Tavanes to M. Billard, August 20, 1780.

[32] *A. D.*, E–1878. See the various *Etats* of Fleury. For example, *Produit extrême possible de la terre de Lux, May, 1784.* On subleasing in this region see P. de Saint-Jacob, *Les paysans de la Bourgogne du Nord au dernier siècle de l'Ancien Régime* (Paris, 1960), pp. 387, 435–38, 484–85.

TABLE II.2   AMOUNT OFFERED FOR THE LAND OF M. LE COMTE DE TAVANES FOR RENEWAL OF
THE LEASES BEGINNING JANUARY 1, 1786 (BEAUMONT AND DEPENDENCIES)

Name of Land to be Leased	Name of Bidder	Amount of Bid *Livres*	Pot de Vin* *Livres*	Fleury *Livres*	Dubois *Livres*
				Estimates of	
Beaumont and Dampierre	Moniotte (present subtenant)	7,000	700	7,350	7,340
Farm of Bessey and *Dîmes*	Pilletrel and Widow Baignot (subtenants)	1,650	165	2,010	1,694
Champagne and Mills	Bigiver (*laboureur*)	2,550	255	2,968	2,386
Blagny	Sr. Gland (*laboureur*)	2,800	280	3,347	2,748
Renêve and *Dîmes*	Escuyer (miller)	1,412	147	1,629	1,671
The Ponds	No one	——	——	1,000	800
Total of Subleases		15,412	1,547	18,304	16,639

* *Pot de vin:* An entrance fee of ten per cent of the annual rent; literally, a "bribe."
SOURCE: A. D., E–1878, *Etat des prix offerts des terres de M. Le Comte de Tavannes . . .*, January 1, 1786.

opportunity to raise the rent. Not unnaturally attracted to Fleury's estimate, the count decided to raise the rent by 5,000 livres. Following the usual practice, he notified Billard at Dijon to auction the lease for Beaumont and to accept the first bid to reach 18,000 livres.[33] But it was not quite so simple. Billard had great difficulty finding a tenant who would pay this much. In the fall of 1783, he wrote to the count in Paris:

> On February 15, 1776, M. Billard leased this land for M. le Comte de Saulx for nine years for 13,000 livres per annum, an increase of 4,900 livres over the previous lease. This leasehold has, therefore, been increased by one-third, not in the last thirty years as on the land of other seigneurs in the Kingdom, but in nine years. Despite this increase of 4,900 livres, Monsieur Fleury, in various memoranda that he has presented to M. le Comte de Tavanes, claims that this lease can still be increased by 5,308 livres, 10 sous. This means doubling it in nine years.[34]

Billard went on to explain that Fleury's "forced estimates," based on verbal bids of the subtenants, had frightened off prospective takers of the Beaumont lease. He pointed out that the subtenants were in debt to the principal tenant, Madame Noirot, and that she had quite possibly kept them from appearing at the auction by threatening them with fore-

[33] It was customary to auction money leases. For important leases, the landlords "advertised" by posting bills (*affiches*). See Document II.
[34] A. D., E–1767. Billard to Comte de Tavanes, November 15, 1783.

closure. Billard was especially distressed that the count should blame him for the failure to obtain a new tenant at the rent specified.

> I am sure, Monsieur, that everything you have written in your letter is not directed at me but at the bidders who have intrigued and caballed as they always do before the auctions. I am innocent of any blame. I have been attached to Monsieur le Comte de Saulx [the elder] and to you, Monsieur, more by honor than by interest, for over 25 years. Madame la Duchesse de Luynes has confidence in me; I have been named guardian of M. le baron de St. Julien, and I have never been reproached. At the end of every lease, I have always increased rents.
>
> Monsieur le Comte de Saulx gave me his confidence in 1762, and I have [subsequently] increased all of his leaseholds by a third or a quarter as I have detailed to M. le Comte de Tavanes. I have done everything in my power to conduct the auction in a way to raise the rents to the estimations of M. Fleury. Despite all my efforts and all my prayers, it has not been possible to engage the bidders. M. Fénéon, the elder [a prominent local *feudiste*], M. Genret, clerk at Arc-sur-Tille, and M. Huet, your solicitor at Lux, who were all present at the auction, will testify to my efforts to raise the rents to the level specified in the estimate of M. Fleury. Surely, I do not merit the reproaches you have made.... You should come here yourself, Monsieur, and lease your land and you will see that it is impossible to lease them at the rents set by M. Fleury.[35]

Aside from its obvious plaintive quality, the agent's letter suggested a certain resentment toward M. Fleury. Billard could hardly welcome such special emissaries, dispatched by an absentee *grand seigneur* at Paris, whose task it was to extract a maximum rent from the land. That this technique was not limited to the Saulx-Tavanes is further indicated by Billard's observation that the "Dames of Saint Cir," who had just bought the Comté of Charny near Dijon, had sent such an individual from Paris to make a rent assessment. "He fixed the rent at 40,000 livres, but the proprietors have had to lease the *comté* for only 28,000."[36]

The problem was not so much that Fleury had overestimated the price of grain, though Billard accused him of this. It was rather that his calculations left such a narrow margin of profit for the principal tenant. One mistaken estimate of the *dîme*, one small dip in the grain or wood market, one delinquent subtenant, and the principal tenant was in trouble.

---

[35] *Ibid*. Like Godard, Billard also worked for the Luynes family. We are dealing here with a professional class of estate administrators.

[36] *Ibid*. See also *A. N.*, T-153[114] for this technique on the estate of Comtesse de Choiseul-Beaupré in Lorraine.

To make matters more difficult for the tenant, the new leases required the payment of supplementary fees, clauses that were not present before 1780. The new tenant was to pay one year's rent in advance in addition to a reception fee (*pot de vin*) of ten per cent of the first year's rent. For the *comté* of Beaumont, this meant an initial payment of over 20,000 livres. Pointing to the number of bankruptcies among tenants and iron-masters in 1783, Billard affirmed that there were not two people in the entire Saône Valley with 20,000 livres in ready capital.[37]

It was customary to announce lease auctions on large bills or posters and circulate them in Dijon and throughout the villages and *bourgs* of the countryside. Billard announced auctions for Beaumont on three separate days throughout the autumn of 1783, but to no avail. He reported in December that the third effort had produced only one subtenant, "even though M. Duboy [the steward at Lux] had visited the others in their homes in order to persuade them to come to the auction."[38] The old tenant, Madame Noirot, offered 14,000 livres without the *pot de vin*, an increase of 1,000 livres over the previous lease, but still unacceptable to the count.[39]

Faced with tenant resistance, the count decided upon a new course of action. In early 1784 he decided to lease Beaumont in smaller lots or *en détail*, to employ the contemporary French term. Tavanes's agent at Lux argued that, given the extreme fragmentation of the soil, it was relatively easy to lease directly to the subtenants, and that the profit of

---

[37] *A. D.*, E–1768, *Mémoire detaillé des Revenus du Comté de Beaumont*, December 11, 1783.

[38] *Ibid.*

[39] *Ibid.*; *A. D.*, E–1767, *Baux*, December 30, 1765; February 15, 1776. Madame Noirot not only signed but also negotiated leases for her husband who was a *marchand* at Pontailler, the river port on the Saône ten miles south of Beaumont. Such *marchands-fermiers* were apparently men of some means since they had to pay large money-rents. In addition to collecting money-rents from subtenants, they also marketed the produce rents and seigneurial dues in kind which were considerable in this region. No doubt they also acted as rural usurers. Saint-Jacob speaks of this "rural bourgeoisie" as avaricious and "engrossing," and they may well have seemed so to the small peasant owner. Saint-Jacob, *Les paysans de la Bourgogne du Nord*, pp. 484–85, 502n. But it can also be argued that they were the only section of the rural hierarchy that was market-oriented and had developed some skills of agricultural entrepreneurship. See R. Forster, "Obstacles to Agricultural Growth in Eighteenth-Century France" *American Historical Review*, LXXV, N°. 6 (Oct., 1970), pp. 1600–1615. See also Table of Tenants, Document IV.

the principal tenant could be eliminated entirely.[40] The chief advantage of the larger tenant was his greater solvency compared with the small subtenants, which assured a regular return, and his management of the many small details of everyday farming. In this case, however, it was easier to obtain the desired rents from subtenants than from a single tenant. No doubt the subtenants would have to manage their own marketing and collect seigneurial dues, but they were apparently willing to shoulder this burden. In fact, they may have welcomed the chance to market their produce directly. Therefore, when Noirot's lease expired in 1785, Beaumont was rented to eight tenants, most of them former subtenants. The total rent from these eight leases was 16,462 livres, in addition to a *pot de vin* of 1,381 livres. The count had thus circumvented the resistance of the tenants and was able to come within 1,600 livres of Fleury's "forced estimate" of the revenues of Beaumont.[41]

* *

Tilchâtel was the count's most important property in Burgundy. It consisted of 4,000 acres of forest in an almost solid mass east of the main royal road from Dijon to Langres. Tavanes owned about one-third of the forest in the *Bailliage* of Dijon and his holdings were matched only by those of the robe nobles of the local Parlement who held tracts of woodland southeast of Dijon.[42] At the center of this substantial tract of woodland was the count's iron foundry.

The royal inquest of 1772 concluded that the provinces of Burgundy and Champagne alone produced about half of the iron of the kingdom.[43]

---

[40] *A. D.*, E-1878, *Etats*, May, 1784.

[41] *A. D.*, E-1768, *Etat du Prix des Amodiations des Fermes de M. le Comte.*

[42] *A. D.*, E-1771, *Etat Général du bois en Bourgogne*, June 2, 1763; *A. D.*, Q-1117, *Declaration que fait Jacques Fénéon aux Citoyens administrateurs du District d'Is-sur-Tille....* May 18, 1793, Chapter 7, *Bois*; *A. D.*, Q-1118, *Liquidation des Créances*, 1793-An VIII. For the holdings of the robe nobility see *A. D.*, Q-546, *Biens des Emigrés: District de St-Jean de Losne* and Colombet, *Parlementaires bourguignons*, 137-40.

[43] B. Gille, *Les forges françaises en 1772* (Paris, 1960), 96-100. The national survey of 1772 estimated the annual production of the foundry of Tilchâtel at 600,000 livres of cast iron (*fonte*) and 400,000 livres of wrought iron (*fer forgé*), thus ranking the establishment among the twenty largest producers in the Subdelegation of Langres. There were few foundries in the entire kingdom that produced more than a million livres of cast iron. Contemporaries observed that the quality of iron produced in this region was high, and thanks to river transport, the market regular. The royal govern-

The region northeast of Dijon was especially favored for surface mining, and the rivers Ignon, Tille, Bèze, and Vingeanne served as a source of power for a dozen important iron forges. In addition to an adequate supply of mineral and water power, the count's foundry at Tilchâtel had an abundant supply of wood. Its iron shared a high reputation with the forge of neighboring Bèze. The geographer Courtépée made special mention of Tilchâtel in the late eighteenth century.

> They produce good marketable iron and iron-rods at the forge at Tilchâtel. ... They can make 400 *milliers* of iron yearly, without stopping, the same as at Marey, Moloy, Villecomte, Courtivron, Compasseur, and Buffon. All the rest produce about half this much....[44]

Tilchâtel had a furnace for smelting and a trip-hammer forge for converting the cast iron into wrought iron for blacksmithing. The iron works employed 34 workers, 20 for the mining and 14 for the foundry, in addition to a score of woodcutters. Here, in relative isolation on the edge of a forest, the ironmaster needed managerial as well as technical skill, dealing as he was with a labor force known for its grossness.[45]

No iron works could survive in the eighteenth century without accessible transportation to market, and for a heavy commodity this meant water. The Saône River was possibly the most important artery for iron transportation in the kingdom and was navigable as far north as Gray. The iron from the count's foundry was carried in carts to the Vingeanne River ten miles to the east, then sold and reloaded at Chalon-sur-Saône,

---

ment was solicitous of the production of such a vital raw material and in an effort to allocate and conserve both ore and wood fuel, it was hesitant to authorize the establishment of new foundries. For obvious reasons, this policy was favored by existing owners such as Tavanes.

[44] M. Courtépée, *Description générale et particulière du Duché de Bourgogne*, 4 vols., (Dijon, 1847), I, 317. In 1801, Tilchâtel produced 22,500 myriagrams or 247.5 English tons of wrought iron annually. This represented about eight per cent of the production of the District of Dijon. Vaillant, *Statistique du Département de la Côte d'Or* (Paris, An IX), 454–55. Claude Fohlen concludes that, at the end of the eighteenth century, the iron industry in neighboring Franche-Comté reached a point of technical perfection but that it operated on an artisan scale that would not survive the competition of the next century. C. Fohlen, "La décadence des forges comtoises," *Mélanges d'histoire économique et sociale en hommage au Professeur Antony Babel* (Geneva, 1963), II, 134, 146.

[45] A. D., L–1895, *Enquête—Bois et Forges—1790*; M. Vaillant, *Statistique du Département de la Côte d'Or*, (Paris, An IX), pp. 454–55; B. Gille, *Les origines de la grande industrie métallurgique en France* (Paris, 1950), p. 166. Gille quotes Bouchu in the Encyclopedia on the problems of the ironmaster.

a major river port serving all the forges of the Dijonnais. The iron was then shipped to the slitting mills of Forez where it was worked into hardware or nails and then sent to the fair at Beaucaire for sale.[46] The foundry of Comte de Tavanes was therefore an integral part of an important industry.

Although labor costs for such an enterprise were not excessive—perhaps 10 to 12 per cent of total costs—charcoal for fueling furnace and forge absorbed at least 25 per cent of the outlay.[47] Fortunately, the count was well provided. He assigned 2,250 acres of wood to the foundry (250 acres to be cut every year), leaving no less than 3,000 acres more for the open market. He had three major outlets: neighboring forges, such as Bèze, which lacked forests of their own; firewood consumers in Dijon, especially the townhouses of the *parlementaires*; and naval procurement officers who came from as far as the naval arsenal at Toulon.[48] However, this surplus did not deter the count from joining other proprietors in contesting the establishment of more iron forges in the region. By an *Arrêt du Conseil* in 1777, the count obtained a royal order prohibiting the construction of any forge that would threaten the wood supply of his furnaces.[49]

---

[46] B. Gille, *Les origines*, p. 107 and *passim*; also, his *Les forges françaises en 1772* (Paris, 1960), p. 96.

[47] Gille, *Les origines*, 140–41. These estimates, Gille insists, are most approximate. The iron prices charted by Labrousse are even less reliable; *ibid.*, 137–39. On the whole problem of the relative costs of labor and fuel and their consequences for technological change, see Michael W. Flinn, "Timber and the Advance of Technology: A Reconsideration," *Annals of Science*, vol. 15, no. 2 (June, 1959), 114–15. If charcoal made up such a large part of total costs, and wood prices were rising much faster than iron prices (as the tables suggest in C. E. Labrousse, *Esquisse du mouvement des prix et des revenus en France au XVIIIe siècle* (Paris, 1933), II, 345, 351), then was it not more profitable to sell wood on the open market than to use it to fuel forges? Also, why did not iron prices follow wood prices?

[48] *A. D.*, E–1770, *Vente des coupes de bois*; A. D., L–1895, *Enquête*, 1790; E. Picard, "Le commerce du bois de chauffage et du charbon de bois à Dijon au XVIIIe siècle," *Mémoires de l'Académie des Sciences, Arts, et Belles Lettres de Dijon*, V (1896), 165–264. Before the family moved to Paris, Tavanes's own townhouse at Dijon consumed more than 280 *moules* (411.6 cubic meters; see Table of Measures, preceding Ch. I) per annum. The *moule* cost about eight livres between 1730 and 1775, and then rose steadily to reach 13 livres by 1788. In 1783, a group of Dijon wood merchants claimed that "twenty years earlier, one fire per family was enough; now they need three or four." Picard, "Le commerce du bois," 199–202, 222–24. For naval procurement, see *A. D.*, C–270, 273, 275–76.

[49] *A. D.*, E–1991 (Tilchâtel).

Whether sold to professional merchants or included in the lease of a foundry, wood was an excellent commodity to own in the last forty years of the eighteenth century. This was especially true in this part of the Saône plain where transportation costs either to Dijon or to the river ports at Pontailler or Auxonne were not prohibitive. The sales of wood at Beaumont tell the story over a century.

TABLE II.3   SALES OF WOOD PER ARPENT AT BEAUMONT

1694—25 livres	1749—63 livres	1786—110 livres
1700—30	1758—67	1788—138
1729—48	1776—73	1789—160

SOURCE: *A. D.*, E–1770, *Bois de Beaumont*

This is an increase of 139 per cent between 1758 and 1789, greater by at least 50 per cent than the national average increase in the price of wood in this period.[50] By contrast, prices of winter wheat rose only 22 per cent in the *Généralité* of Burgundy between the five-year periods of 1756–60 and 1785–89. Moreover, wheat prices were vulnerable to much greater seasonal fluctuations than wood.[51] A temporary depression in grain prices in the early 1780s had much to do with Billard's difficulties at Beaumont. Wood was another matter, and Billard's tone in 1785 differed markedly from his supplications two years before. "Given the scarcity of wood and the high prices, we can easily get the 120 livres per *arpent* M. le Comte de Tavanes is asking."[52]

Woodland was comparatively simple to manage. The chief expense was for forest wardens or guards to keep out the poachers and foragers for brush wood and to enforce the royal conservation ordinances. The new count raised the number of wardens from five to eight and increased their annual wage from 75 to 200 livres in addition to new livery. The

[50] Labrousse, *Esquisse*, II, 343–48. This is a minimum differential since Labrousse uses the earlier base period, 1726–41.

[51] See below, Document X. The extreme variation in the price of grain makes comparisons with the steady increase in the price of wood difficult. Even averaging five-year periods does not tell the full story. For example, if the period 1761–65 is selected, the increase for 1785–89 is 56 per cent, since grain prices fell in the early 1760s. See Labrousse, *Esquisse* I, 107, giving annual prices for Burgundy. For grain prices on the Dijon market from 1774–91, see P. E. Girod, "Les subsistances en Bourgogne et particulièrement à Dijon à la fin du XVIIIe siècle," *Revue Bourguignonne* XVI, no. 4 (1906), Appendix III; and *A. D.*, Q–734, Arc-sur-Tille, *Prix des Grains*, 1777–90.

[52] *A. D.*, E–1770, *Bois de Beaumont*.

chief warden received 600 livres instead of 150, as much as the local steward at Lux. As for the wood sales, the count sold the wood "on the spot" and avoided all expense of felling the trees or hauling them to market. Duboy, the resident steward, simply marked the trees to be cut or assigned the sections of forest to be exploited. The wood merchants did the rest, and assumed all the risks once the contract of sale had been signed and delivered. It was in the count's interest to enforce the conservation ordinance regulating the number and kinds of trees to be cut and replanted. There is good reason to believe that he did so.[53]

Until the 1780s, the elder Tavanes had included the woodland in the nine-year leases. Negotiations with wood merchants were left to the principal tenants, who might profit from rising prices within the period of their lease. In 1783, however, Fleury argued against leasing the wood over nine years and urged the new count to auction his wood directly to the wood merchants in lots on an annual basis. He proposed a rotation system whereby the count could sell about 50 acres of properly aged trees every year. Thus the count would receive the full benefit of inflation. The proposal was a response to the regular increase in wood prices which avoided the short-run fluctuations of other commodities. The grain market was much less steady, and here a nine-year lease was necessary to assure regular returns.[54]

Since 1774, Tilchâtel had been leased to the Rochet brothers, ironmasters from the neighboring *bourg* of Bèze, for 24,000 livres per annum. In August, 1780, the new count wrote to Billard that he appreciated the prompt rent payments the Rochets had made in the past and knew them to be good tenants, but that his present financial position did not permit him to make any "sacrifices" in their favor. He instructed Billard to estimate the amount of wood available, the price per acre, the price of iron, the quality of the local ore, the amount and kind of land adjoining the forge, "in a word, [to make] an inventory that will adjust this leasehold to its true value and ... establish an acceptable profit for the tenant."[55] Adding every *dîme* and *cens*, Billard calculated the income

[53] *Ibid.*

[54] *A. D.*, E–1878, Fleury Visit, August, 1783, ". . . *il ne faut point du tout amodier des bois, mais en faire tous les ans une adjudication au plus offrant* . . ."; *A. D.*, E–1991 (Tilchâtel); *A. D.*, E–1818, *Etat* (Velours).

[55] *A. D.*, E–1991, Comte de Saulx-Tavanes to Billard, August 20, 1780. See Document III, for the lease of Tilchâtel in 1790.

of the property at 40,029 livres yearly, 67 per cent above the Rochet's rent.

The count responded with a proposal for renewal which he considered generous. He set the new lease at 36,000 livres, a fifty per cent increase over the old rent. Moreover, he continued, if the Rochets would pay 12,000 livres in advance and 18,000 livres *pot de vin* the day the new lease was signed, the count would reduce the annual rent to 34,000 livres. These advance payments, he said, would cover his royal taxes on the transfer of his new inheritance.

> If Monsieur Rochet accepts these propositions, M. le Comte de Tavanes will authorize M. Billard to serve the lease conforming to the model the count will send him. If not, post auction proceedings immediately for the leasing of the forge and notify M. le Comte de Tavanes who will post a similar announcement in Paris.[56]

The count also responded firmly to a number of propositions put to him by the Rochet brothers. The two ironmasters were anxious to contract a longer lease in the hope of benefiting from inflationary trends and gain flexibility. But the count would have none of it. An eighteen-year lease was entirely out of the question. "M. le comte de Tavanes is not familiar with that manner of leasing in advance. He will never extend a lease for more than nine years." Billard was instructed to tell the neighboring tenant at Bourberain the same thing. The count will "not even consider negotiating leases five years in advance." As for the Rochets' complaint that good wood and ore were only to be found at increasing distances from the forge, the count replied that all these "difficulties" were compensated by the reduction of 4,000 livres from Billard's assessment of the income of the Tilchâtel lease.[57]

Rochet responded a week later that he and his brother could not afford a rent of 34,000 livres together with the other fees and consented to an auction of the lease. Billard reacted quickly. He announced the auction of the lease throughout Burgundy and even in neighboring Champagne. He was especially careful to post bills and pass the word at Chalon-sur-Saône, the major river port for the southward transport of grain, iron, and wood. Here, on All Saints Day (November 1st), the

---

[56] *A. D.*, E–1991, Comte de Saulx-Tavanes to Billard, September 20, 1780.
[57] *Ibid.*

ironmasters and iron merchants of the two provinces, as well as those from the Lyonnais further south, would meet, presumably for the purpose of bargaining and arranging sales. As a further precaution, Tavanes announced the auction in Paris, not only by wall poster but by newspaper, in the eighteenth-century equivalent of the classified advertisement.[58] This was the count's largest single leasehold and he was leaving no stone unturned in his efforts to obtain a maximum income.

Whether the count had set his rent so high for bargaining purposes or was pressed for ready capital, he was willing to settle within a month for 30,000 livres rent and 18,000 livres *pot de vin* or reception fee. The Rochet brothers were not so badly off as first appeared. Like other ironmasters in the region, they did not limit themselves to one forge. The name of "Sieur Rochet" appeared either as manager or owner of seven forges from Bèze in Burgundy to Vezoul in Franche-Comté in 1772.[59] The Rochets were ironmasters of some importance, good examples of rural mining capitalism.[60]

By provincial standards, 18,000 livres was a large sum of money to pay in advance. How did the Rochets raise it? In 1783, they signed a partnership agreement with one Claude Courtois, Dijon *négotiant*, for eight and one-half years. Its purpose was to exploit forges in the region, including Tavanes's. Two-thirds of the profits would go to the Rochets, and one-third to Courtois. By the agreement, the Rochets were obliged to provide a specified quantity of wood fuel and to make all necessary repairs on the forges. Courtois in return promised to advance the Rochets up to 200,000 livres—not too much, given the high fixed costs and the uncertain market for iron. The interest was fixed "according to commercial custom" at six per cent, which, incidentally, was contrary to the usury

---

[58] *A. D.*, E-1991, *Mémoire*, September 29, 1780. The *"petites affiches"* or classified ads are a part of the provincial and Parisian press that deserves more attention from economic historians.

[59] Gille, *Forges françaises*, pp. 41, 42, 44, 50, 59, 97, 99. The count's former tenant, Quillard, also appears as manager of three forges in 1772. In fact, Rochet appeared to be among the most prominent ironmasters in Franche-Comté. See Fohlen, "La décadence des forges," p. 136.

[60] Gille, *Les origines*, pp. 160–67, and *passim*. The fact that a nobleman like Tavanes owned a foundry did not make him a "capitalist entrepreneur." Men like Rochet were the entrepreneurs. Even the operating capital did not come from the count.

laws. The interest payments were made a mortgage on the Rochet property.[61]

Trapped between interest obligations and high rents, it is not surprising that the Rochets had difficulties meeting rent payments, much less making any capital improvements on the forge. Moreover, like cereals, iron prices tended to level off after 1772, further narrowing the margin of profit. In early 1784, after the lease had run for only four years, the count evinced concern about delinquent payments from the Rochets. In a crisp letter he told Billard to keep careful account of the due dates and to prevent accumulation of back-rents.[62] Then, suddenly in 1785, the count ordered seizure of the Tilchâtel property and evicted the Rochets in the middle of their lease.

The Rochets were replaced by two new tenants, M. Lagnier, ironmaster of Loeuilley on the Vingeanne River, and M. Berger, *négotiant* of Lyon, who agreed to pay 28,000 livres annual rent. In addition to delinquency in paying their rent, the Rochets had been condemned in court for damaging the forest in violation of the royal conservation ordinance. With little room to maneuver, they had been overanxious to cut timber and sell at good prices.[63] The new ironmaster, Lagnier, barely escaped a similar fate. The count's forest wardens reported that he was cutting the wood badly and had failed to replant the requisite number of saplings. Lagnier replied that tree needles and rocky soil made the cutting very difficult and that he was "forced" by the local peasants to sell wood to fuel the bread ovens, placing an extra burden on his work

[61] *A. D.*, E-1991, *Société*, May 9, 1783. The lease of 1790 suggests a similar partnership. *Ibid.*, *Bail*, October 19, 1790. Fohlen argues that a lack of capital was the principal cause of the decline of ironmaking in this region in the nineteenth century. "For many proprietors, as under the Ancien Régime, forges were only an adjunct to a landed estate, a supplementary rent added to the soil." Fohlen, "La décadence des forges," p. 141. This was certainly the view of Tavanes.

[62] *A. D.*, E-1722. Comte de Tavanes to Billard, February 18, 1784.

[63] Apparently, the Rochets lost their forge at Bèze as well. A government survey in 1790 reads: "Forge belonging to the creditors of Guilleaume Rochet." *A. D.*, L-1895. Just before the Revolution he was imprisoned for "fraudulent bankruptcy." He sold his other forges during the Revolution to three Strasbourgeois. It appears that his eviction from Tilchâtel marked the beginning of a series of financial disasters for the Rochets. See Fohlen, "Le décadence des forges," p. 144; S. de Montenay, "L'établissement d'une manufacture à Bèze sous la Révolution," *Annales de Bourgogne* (1966), p. 190n. However, by 1802 the Rochet brothers had fully recovered. See Chapter V, below.

force. The new tenant denied that he would ever fell trees "unauthorized by the ordinance, in a forest belonging to a *grand seigneur.*" He pleaded with the count's agent not to go to court.

> Why fill volumes with writing for the profit of some solicitor? All we ask is the good will and equity of M. le Duc de Saulx and we defer to his judgment alone.[64]

In a lengthy legal battle the duke was at a distinct advantage and he knew it. Violation of the royal ordinance was a legal excuse to terminate the lease. It is not deference to a noble family that is implied in the plea, but a keen awareness of the old adage, "better a bad arrangement [among contesting parties] than a good lawsuit." The tenant's overhead expenses were high enough as it was. Worse, he might lose the lease altogether.

Despite their efforts, Lagnier and his partner Berger lasted only five years. In 1789, Tavanes found still another tenant willing to pay 30,000 livres for the lease.[65] Although the count and his agent had not come as close to the "forced estimate" as at Beaumont, they had increased the return on Tilchâtel by 33 per cent between 1780 and 1789. Furthermore, they encountered no difficulty finding new tenants to replace those who fell behind in their rent payments. No doubt, an iron forge set in 4,000 acres of forest was a more attractive lease than the scattered parcels of grain land at Beaumont. There were other ironmasters in Franche-Comté to replace those who had failed.[66] A few years later, the forges of the area were working full time for the war effort.

* * *

The domain of Arc-sur-Tille, eight miles east of Dijon, was in the center of the fertile Saône plain. Tavanes had good reason to be pleased with this property. There were 2,000 acres of domain land—some in large tracts—and most of it recently drained and planted in wheat and grasses. There was also a *dîme inféodée* of one-thirteenth the harvest of 1,600 acres more.[67] Despite at least three bankrupt tenants, the rents had risen

[64] *A. D.*, E-1770, Lagnier to Billard, September 13, 1786.

[65] *A.D.*, E-1991, Lease of October 19, 1790. See Document III.

[66] Like Rochet, Lagnier was manager of several other forges in Franche-Comté, owned by Comte d'Orsay. Gille, *Les origines*, p. 178; Gille, *Forges françaises*, pp. 45, 48.

[67] *A. D.*, E-1744 (Arc-sur-Tille); *A. N.*, T-109[1-2].

dramatically from 8,000 livres in 1750 to 19,000 livres in 1781. In 1788, two years before the current lease was to expire, Tavanes prepared for renewal and a further increase in rent. He had Fleury's "forced estimate" of 1783 before him in Paris. It stood at exactly 25,153 livres.[68]

The auction began promptly in March, 1788. Four prospective tenants competed for the lease, supplementing their cash offers with letters to the new duke at Paris. The letter of Calignon, grain merchant (*marchand-fermier*) of Dijon, combines apparent deference and respect with special pleading.

> I cannot hide the fact, M. le Duc, that only by working the land directly myself and maximizing the profits even on the smallest items can I pay the rent you are asking. I must say that it is impossible for anyone but a real farmer (*cultivateur*) to pay that much rent. Anyone who makes an offer based on an armchair calculation is certain to ruin all your vassals (*vassaux*) and all the peasant farmers to whom he sublets. Moreover, he will ruin himself and his very audacity [in taking the lease] will discredit your leasehold.
>
> M. le Duc, it is only a proof of my zeal that I risk this observation. You are the final judge of who should lease your domain.... You have informed M. Billard in your letters that you prefer me because I manage the land directly.
>
> Perhaps I am the one to increase the value of your land. It needs an agri-culturalist.... I hasten to repeat what I said in my first letter: my heart's wish is to become one of your vassals.[69]

Calignon touched another issue. How much margin of profit was left for the tenant after the rent was paid? Much depended on the accuracy of the assessment of the experts Fleury and Dubois. Sr. Conner, another potential tenant of Arc-sur-Tille, made a careful assessment of his own, checked Fleury's account at Dijon, and claimed that the special agent had overestimated the revenue from the *dîmes* by 2,000 livres, making the lease worth only 23,153 livres. Since the duke was asking a rent of 23,000 livres, this left a profit margin of only 153 livres. In a letter to the duke, Conner contrasted this sum with "the 2,155 livres that you counted on giving him [the tenant]."[70]

It is the last comment that concerns us here. Does it mean that the duke considered the 2,153 livres (or 8.6 per cent of the total income of the

[68] *A. D.*, E–1744. Sr. Conner to M. Duc de Saulx-Tavanes, March 24, 1788.

[69] *A. D.*, E–1744, Sr. Caligon to Duc de Saulx-Tavanes, March 22, 1788.

[70] *A. D.*, E–1744, Conner to M. le Duc, March 24, 1788.

property) an appropriate profit for the tenant? This would be a rent-income ratio of 91.4 per cent, an incredibly high rate.[71] Nonetheless, there is little doubt that such margins of tenant profit were considered normal, at least by absentee landlords in Paris. Among the Tavanes papers is a memorandum advising the count against direct management. Supervising a large number of tenants meant frequent trips to the provinces and running the risk of their insolvency. But the main argument was that the profit made by the principal tenant (*fermier général*) could not be eliminated by direct administration. "A salaried steward (*régisseur*) would absorb the approximate profit of a *fermier général*." Since a steward for a large noble estate was seldom paid over a thousand livres, it appears that the tenant was not supposed to make more than a well-paid steward. The role of entrepreneur, improver of land, or even creditor for insolvent subtenants was not considered in the determination of a fair return. As the memorandum put it: "The *fermier général* [on the Norman property] does not cultivate the land himself and earns at least 2,600 livres *without doing any work*."[72] What a contrast with Quesnay's article in the *Encyclopédie* where the role of *fermier* as one who invests in the land is so lauded!

It is doubtful that Tavanes even thought about "appropriate profits" for his tenant, much less in terms of rent-income ratios. He would take what the market would bear and set his rents as close to Fleury's estimates as possible. That he found tenants at these rents suggests that they had nowhere else to go, that is, that there were no alternative employment opportunities.[73] No doubt the larger *marchands-fermiers* hoped to make up for small-unit profits by contracting more than one lease and still benefit from inflation during the nine-year term. In any case, it is interesting to compare Fleury's estimate of the income of the property in 1783 with the actual rents paid in 1788 (see Table II.4).

---

[71] Clark and Haswell give the rent-income ratio for France as a whole as 39 per cent in 1788 and 45 per cent in 1815, rates comparable to parts of China in 1928 and Chile in 1960. When rent takes half of the gross product of the land, low-income agriculture is in evidence. C. Clark and M. Haswell, *The Economics of Subsistence Agriculture* (New York, 1966), pp. 99, 105–7. The Tavanes case is not really what is meant by rent-income ratio since we are dealing here with a tenant (*fermier*) who sublets. Nonetheless the point is clear; the profit-margin of the *fermier* was to be kept narrow.

[72] *A. D.*, E–1700, *Mémoire*, November 11, 1766 [italics mine].

[73] Clark and Haswell, *Subsistence Agriculture*, pp. 99–100.

TABLE II.4   PROFIT OF TENANTS ON THE TAVANES ESTATE

Name of Property	Fleury's Estimate of Income from Subtenants in 1783* Livres	Rents in 1788* Livres	Profit of Tenant Livres	Rent-Income Ratio Per Cent
Beaumont and Dampierre	7,350	7,000	350	95.2
Bessey and Dîmes	2,010	1,715	295	85.3
Champagne and Mills	2,968	2,550	418	86.6
Blagny	3,347	3,000	347	89.6
Renêve	1,629	1,462	167	89.7
Ponds of Beaumont	1,000	800	200	80.0
Lux	5,635	4,500	1,135	79.8
Spoy	1,991	1,800	191	90.4
Bourberain	5,735	5,600	135	97.5
Arc-sur-Tille	25,153	23,000	2,153	91.4
Tilchâtel	40,029	32,000	8,029	79.9

* Grain prices in 1783 and 1788 were almost identical (A. D., Q-734; Labrousse I, 107); wood prices had risen about 30 per cent.
SOURCE: A. D., E-1878 (Etats); A. D., E-1744 (Baux); A. D., E-1767 (Baux); A. D., E-1817 (Baux); A. D., E-1991 (Baux); A. D., Q-1118 (Revenues-1790); A. D., E-1721, 1724 (Billard accounts).

Assuming Fleury's estimates were accurate, the principal tenants were able to pocket from ten to twenty per cent of the total income from the subtenants. If Fleury had "forced" the estimates as Billard claimed, their profits would be even smaller. In practical terms this meant only a few hundred livres annually for most of the tenants. Only the Rochets at Tilchâtel or Calignon at Arc-sur-Tille could count on four-digit profits, sums that placed them clearly above the income levels of village artisans and other peasant proprietors.

Did the economic position of the tenants on the Tavanes estate in the 1780s mark any radical departure from their position thirty or forty years before? There is no question that rents in Burgundy had risen steeply after 1750, and especially after 1780. The combined Burgundian rents were 49,435 livres in 1754 and 86,269 livres in 1788, an increase of 75 per cent in thirty-four years.[74] The prices for farm produce which the tenants marketed had not risen so fast. In the period between 1756-60 and 1785-89, the price of wheat in the Dijonnais rose only 22 per cent, the lesser grains in proportion.[75] The exception was wood which, as we have seen above, rose 139 per cent between 1758 and 1789. Not only had

[74] See Table of Rents, Document V.
[75] See note 51 above.

grain prices risen more slowly than rents, the seasonal fluctuations made the profits of the tenants very uncertain. None, except the tenant at Til-châtel, could count on a regular rise in prices, and after 1783 even he was allotted only the strict minimum of wood needed to fuel his forge.

What happened to a tenant in a bad year? Take the case of Bour-berain, where revenues were largely in *dîmes* of one-twelfth the harvest. In 1756 the *dîmes* yielded 100 *emines* (1,455 bushels) of grain selling at 2,895 livres while in 1783 (a bad year) they yielded only 71 *emines*, selling at 2,850 livres. A drop of 30 per cent in production had almost been compensated by the seasonal rise in price.[76] However, the rent in 1783 was 700 livres more than in 1756. It is very doubtful that the tenant at Bour-berain made any profit in 1783. The assessments of Fleury and Dubois were presumably based on an "average year," but there were many complaints that they selected the highest prices of the season for their calculations. In any event, with such narrow margins of profit, a bad harvest hurt any tenant whose revenues came from *dîmes* or *champarts*, that is, from rents calculated as a proportion of the harvest. Where the subleases stipulated a fixed rent of grain per acre, the principal tenant was not directly affected by a drop in production. But he still had the unenviable task of collecting those rents in kind from hard-pressed subtenants.[77]

In any case, it appears that the tenants' profit margins were narrowing. Since prices failed to keep pace with rents, the alternative was to increase the rents of the subtenants. This is what Calignon, the principal tenant of Arc-sur-Tille, suggested, when he alluded to "armchair calculators" who would ruin their subtenants. Indeed, in other regions of France, this was the source of considerable antagonism between peasants and *fermiers*.[78] In the Dijonnais, however, it was scarcely possible to make any substantial changes in the lease terms of the subtenants. Rents in kind were fixed by tradition. At Arc-sur-Tille, Bourberain, Lux, Blagny, or Beaumont, rents on domain lands were fixed at six to eight measures

---

[76] *A. D.*, E–1818 (Bourberain). See also Document VI. This is evidence against the assertion of C. E. Labrousse that a drop in grain production is *never* compensated by the rise in price. See D. Landes, "The Statistical Study of French Crises," *Journal of Economic History* X (1950), 195–211. See also the Table of Measures, above.

[77] This was especially true in the early 1780s. Saint-Jacob, *Les paysans*, p. 475.

[78] G. Lefebvre, *Questions agraires au temps de la Terreur.*

of grain per *journal* (0.8 acres). They were the same in the 1780s as in the 1750s. The seigneurial dues were also fixed by tradition, though in proportion to the harvest, not to the area. Only the mills, ponds, and the more substantial pieces of meadowland were sublet at money rents and were susceptible to increase, but these accounted for only a small part of the revenues of each principal tenant.[79]

Fixed rents in kind were made necessary by the extreme fragmentation of the land and the stagnation of productivity per acre.[80] One might picture the 500 acres of arable domain at Arc-sur-Tille as made up of broad, contiguous fields of waving grain. It was nothing of the kind. The seigneur's land was made up of 56 pieces completely interspersed with the strips of small peasant proprietors. The fragmentation was even more pronounced at Bourberain, Beaumont, and Lux. Sometimes, as at Blagny, a single *laboureur* rented as much as 100 *journaux* from the principal tenant, but this was exceptional. Much more common were subleases in lots ranging from one-half to ten *journaux*.[81] Rather than attempt share-cropping on such small plots, the land was rented at a certain number of measures of grain per *journal* regardless of the harvest. In fact, the six or eight measures usually collected represented about one-third of the gross harvest. There is no evidence that these rates changed in the course of the century, and given the stagnation of production, it is difficult to see how they could be raised further. All the agricultural costs, including seed, *dîmes*, taxes, and dues, were taken from the subtenant's income, which easily absorbed another third of an average harvest. Unless a sub-

[79] *A. D.*, E–1768, 1818, 1878, *Etats.* Saint-Jacob insists that the *sous-fermiers* were ruined by the *principaux fermiers* who raised the subleases too high. Saint-Jacob, *Les paysans*, pp. 484–85. However, by his own production and rent figures (*ibid.*, 503–6), an increase in produce rents seems scarcely possible.

[80] Saint-Jacob, *Les paysans*, 491, 503.

[81] *A. D.*, E–1818 (Bourberain); *A. D.*, E–1916 (Lux); *A. D.*, E–1765 (Beaumont). The fragmentation of the land in this part of Burgundy was extraordinary. The scattered strips of the seigneur, colored in red and yellow on the duke's map, were identical in size and shape with the adjoining strips of the local peasants. Rows of rectangular plots measured in fractions of an acre were frequently no wider than the secondary roads passing through the parish. Occasionally, one detects a larger piece of land marked *"au seigneur—9,761 perches"* or about twenty acres, but pieces of 200 to 300 *perches* (less than an acre) were much more common. At Lux, one sectional plan embraces an area of 116 acres divided into 172 pieces. See Section Map of Lux, Document VIII.

tenant held a large number of such strips, he was already close to the subsistence level.[82]

The principal tenants, therefore, were squeezed between subleases largely fixed by tradition and the increasing rents demanded by the counts of Tavanes since 1750. Until 1775, cereal prices rose rather steadily, and partially compensated the tenants for their higher rents. But between 1776 and 1786, there were as many bad years as good years, while rents continued to rise at an accelerated rate. Even the Rochets at Tilchâtel experienced difficult times as the price of iron began to level off after 1772 and their rent rose from 21,000 to 30,000 livres in the early 1780s.[83] Most discouraging of all, for the tenants in the 1780s, was the increasing precision of the count's estimates of landed revenues. The assessments before Fleury's survey of 1783 had been more carelessly done, the yields and acreages certainly underestimated, thus favoring the tenant. After 1783, this escape valve was closed, and the rents absorbed more and more of the revenues of the land.[84]

It was the smaller tenant who was most likely to fail. If the new head of the Tavanes family seemed harsh, he was little different from his father before him. A glance at the table of tenants since the middle of the century indicates how few tenants lasted more than one term of nine years, and how frequently leases were prematurely terminated by the counts of Tavanes. Tenant debtors were relentlessly pursued.[85]

Cold accounts rarely depict the more human aspect of a foreclosure, but occasionally a clear picture emerges. Consider the case of Georges Villers, tenant at Bourberain, east of Tilchâtel. A letter to the elder count in 1764 warned of difficulties. Villers claimed that his subtenants were in debt, that the local peasants were paying the oven (*banalité*) fees of one-

[82] Saint-Jacob assumes that the produce rents represented a third of the gross harvest. Saint-Jacob, *Les paysans*, p. 504n. Tavanes's land produced between 16 and 21 measures of wheat per *journal*. His produce rents ranged from six to eight measures, i.e., between 38 and 50 per cent of the gross harvest. *A. D.*, E–1878 *Etat*; Q–734 (Arc-sur-Tille). This comes very close to the rent-income ratio estimated for the entire kingdom. See Clark and Haswell, *Subsistence Agriculture*, pp. 105–7.

[83] For grain prices see Girod, "*Les subsistences*"; Labrousse, *Esquisse*, I, 107; see also Document X. For iron prices, see Labrousse, *Esquisse*, II, 351, 354–55. Saint-Jacob alludes to an "agrarian crisis," characterized by low prices in the early 1780s. Saint-Jacob, *Les paysans*, pp. 470, 478–80.

[84] *A. D.*, E–1817, 1818. Compare the *Etats* of 1756, 1765, and 1770–73 with Fleury's survey of 1783.

[85] See Table of Tenants, Document IV.

twentieth instead of one-twelfth, and that they had refused to pay the mutation fees *(lods et ventes)* altogether. He pleaded with the count to give him the seigneurial titles to enforce the rights and a bit more time to pay his rent arrears. But to no avail. The count obtained a sentence from the Parlement of Paris authorizing his agent to appropriate Viller's effects and sell them to liquidate the debt.

In January, 1765, Villers' household furnishings, farm tools, grain, and livestock were sold at auction at Bourberain. The sale netted 30,212 livres, only 750 livres shy of his debt to Tavanes. Villers and his wife refused to attend the foreclosure proceedings or to sign any legal document whatsoever. But the inventory of sale revealed the futility of their resistance. Everything they owned—kitchen utensils, bed linen, plows, pigs, even firewood and straw were sold to local merchants, tenants, peasants, and artisans. Still not satisfied, Tavanes arranged a second foreclosure and obtained Villers' last cash reserves, which he had hoped to use for his taxes, salt, and house rent. It is not surprising that Villers' name did not reappear as a tenant of the count or his son. He was ruined.[86]

In 1786 the new duke served a similar sentence. Bachet, the tenant at Bourberain, died only a few months after signing the lease, and his widow owed the duke more than 3,000 livres in back rents by 1786. On this occasion, judicial proceedings were even more rapid than in 1764. Tavanes's new seigneurial bailiff at Bourberain handed down a judgment only two weeks after the rent was due. The sentence left no doubt of intent. "We authorize the seigneur-plaintiff to constrain the debtors, seize their possessions, furniture, and other effects found in the buildings of the seigneur's *ferme*." Somehow, the widow Bachet held on. But three years later, in the hard winter of 1789, Madame Bachet and her new husband were again behind by 2,800 livres. And again, the seigneurial judge issued a prompt warning that if payment was not forthcoming the tenants would have their possessions confiscated *"sur le champ."*[87]

Although the situation of the tenants in the two periods seems little different, it appears that the younger Tavanes had tightened his seigneurial justice at the local level. Rather than obtaining a sentence from the Parlement of Paris, the duke economized on time and expense by ordering his seigneurial judges on the spot to take prompt action. What-

[86] *A. D.*, E–1817, *Saisis et ventes . . . sur Georges de Villers, fermier de Bourberain et Flée*, 1764; *Vente*, February 20–21, 1765.
[87] *A. D.*, E–1817, *Procedure contre Sr. Bachet et Sr. Paris*, 1786–89.

ever its initial cost, the new *duché* involved an enlargement of a local staff of seigneurial bailiffs that was not purely ornamental. Delinquent tenants as well as "vassals" and *censitaires* could now be more efficiently dealt with.

* * * *

The distinction between large and small tenants remained. The Rochets at Tilchâtel, Calignon at Arc-sur-Tille, Jacotot at Lux might still net over a thousand livres per annum from the duke's properties even in 1788. Unlike the smaller tenants, these three at least had not yet been reduced to the role of rent collectors. Moreover, they could still stock their grain, wood, or iron, and wait for a better market. Men like Calignon and Rochet had commercial contacts in the river ports, and came close to monopolizing the market for farm produce. They were still *coqs de village* on whom lesser men depended to provide loans, leases, work, and a market outlet when there were a few sacks of wheat to sell.[88] Is it surprising that Calignon, disliked by the subsistence peasantry about him and no doubt contemptuous of these pigmies in turn, was accused of "monopolizing" wood on one occasion and of "terrorizing" a village assembly on another?[89] At times it seemed that only the local royal officials had some sympathy for the *fermier*. In 1786, the subdelegate of Dijon observed that the low price of grain in that year might provide even the poorest inhabitants with enough to live on, but that unless prices rose, the *fermiers* would be unable to pay their rents.[90] Yet it was not economic deprivation—and certainly not misery—that plagued these larger tenants; it was rather a sense of frustration regarding future expectations. Other obstacles placed severe limits on tenant initiative and minimized opportunities to enlarge profits by increasing productivity.

The extreme division of the land was the first obvious obstacle. An agent's report to Tavanes in 1784 on the revenues of the barony of Lux exposed once again the problem of enclosure in France. The agent, no

[88] Saint Jacob, *Les paysans*, 502, 502n. See Lefebvre, *Questions agraires*, for the role of the *fermier principal*.

[89] Picard, "Le Commerce du bois," p. 222–23; Saint-Jacob, *Les paysans*, p. 430n. The reciprocal attitudes between *fermier* and peasant were probably ambivalent—hostility mixed with begrudging admiration. See R. Redfield, *Peasant Society and Culture* (Chicago, 1956), ch. II.

[90] *A. D.*, C–100.

doubt the steward, Duboy, stated that while the "seigneur-proprietor" had the undeniable legal right to enclose his meadow, there were good reasons not to do so. Enclosure would deprive Tavanes of badly needed animal fertilizer provided by the grazing livestock of the community. Second, since the duke's meadowlands were interspersed in a large tract of grassland, the cost of building and maintaining walls would be excessive. It would be best for the tenant at Lux to sublet most of these plots of meadow and work a few directly with day labor.[91]

If the duke had any thought of increasing production, his agent's observations hardly encouraged him to apply them.

> It is not practical to introduce large-scale farming. The cultivator lacks the necessary capital, and hard money is very rare. The population is not large enough. Therefore, in good harvest years when the demand for farm produce is low, trade in such produce declines. The mentality of the small peasant is opposed to any form of innovation. There is not a single intelligent risk-taker, willing to alter the traditional crop courses.[92]

Observations such as this were made from one side of France to the other. Nothing could be done with routine-minded peasants. What puzzled foreign observers like Arthur Young was the apparent dependence of French agricultural progress on the initiative of the small peasant cultivator who was handicapped by lack of both capital and vision. Why, asked Young, could not the larger proprietors supply this deficiency?[93] Proprietors like Tavanes were absorbing close to 90 per cent of the tenants' income and probably close to 50 per cent of the marketable surplus of the soil in rents.[94] How much of these rents were reinvested in the land?

In the course of the century, the Tavanes had evinced little interest in farm improvements. Probably the most active estate manager was the dowager countess Daguesseau-Tavanes who brought the seigneuries of Lux and Tilchâtel into the family as her dowry at the beginning of the

[91] *A. D.*, E–1878, *Etats* (1784).

[92] *Ibid.* Whatever demographers may discover, some contemporaries thought the consumer market limited.

[93] Arthur Young, *Travels in France* (Dublin, 1793).

[94] The estimate of 50 per cent is based on the assumption that the subtenants retained 40 per cent and the *fermiers* the remaining 10 per cent of the "marketable surplus." This is little more than a guess, but it probably overestimates the share of the subtenant since all the expenses (seed, *dîmes*, seigneurial dues, royal taxes) had to come from his portion.

century. Sister of the learned and active Chancellor of France, the countess lived at least part of the year on her lands in Burgundy, made frequent inspections of the domains, negotiated the leases in person at the château, and kept her forge and mill-wheels in repair.[95] Her son, Henri-Charles, resided at Dijon, though he was decidedly more interested in the prerogatives and emoluments of his lieutenant-generalcy than in farm management. Nevertheless, the same man who worried about the correct form and deference that robe nobles should display toward a resident military governor also concerned himself with a substantial drainage project. In cooperation with sixty-six other local proprietors, Henri-Charles hired the engineers and crews to drain several hundred acres of marsh at Arc-sur-Tille for conversion into grainland. As a result, he not only made his own domain lands more productive, but also increased his returns from the *dîme* on neighboring plots under his seigneurial jurisdiction. Since the *dîmes* were collected on land in cereals and not on land in hay or forage, conversion to grain permitted the count to extend his seigneurial claims.[96] This is the only case of a major capital land improvement by the Tavanes family in the course of the century. After 1761, all of the Tavanes family lived at Paris, and management of the Burgundian estate depended exclusively on the activities of local agents.

At the end of the 1750s, the property of Arc-sur-Tille was leased to an unusually energetic tenant. Sieur Joachim Huvelin had come from Belfort where he had been a procurement officer of the crown, an ironmaster, and [*sic*] *a conseiller secretaire du roi.* He was a man of larger capital and wider vision than most of Tavanes's tenants who were usually *marchands-fermiers* or *marchands-négotiants* from Dijon or the small *bourgs* of the upper Saône valley. Huvelin had taken over the lease of the previous tenant who had gone bankrupt in the middle of his nine-year term. Between 1758 and 1761, Huvelin proposed at least three projects for capital improvements on the count's land. In a memorandum entitled "Objects for Amelioration," Huvelin urged investment in further drainage, the money to be spent on new canals and dikes. He suggested that an investment of 10,000 livres by Tavanes might spur contributions from the local inhabitants. Indeed, he even suggested that his lease terms include such an arrangement. On a second occasion Huvelin proposed to

[95] *A. D.*, E–1998.
[96] *A. D.*, E–1745, Arc-sur-Tille, 1753; *A. D.*, Q–734 (*Dîmes*).

increase the yield of hay by spreading potash (*cendre de lessive*) as a special preparation for the soil. He estimated that the project would require 4,000 cartloads of potash, good seed, and about six years before the results would appear.[97] It would cost Tavanes about 10,000 livres. On still a third occasion, the tenant boldly urged a venture in commercialized farming—cheese production. Among other expenses, the project would require the construction of stables for 80 cows at a total cost of 4,000 livres. "If you can advance me half, Monsieur, I can put this land to value," wrote Huvelin to the count in Paris.[98]

Huvelin's energy and enthusiasm did not receive a warm welcome in the Saint-Sulpice quarter of Paris. The count seemed more concerned about his tenant's interpretation of the lease. Far from conceding any loans, Tavanes commented that Huvelin had not read the lease carefully regarding *his* responsibilities to maintain the canals and ditches. As for the project to increase the yield of hay, the recommendation of the count's agent seems to have been conclusive. Huvelin's project promised an increase in revenue of 2,000 livres. "This 2,000 livres, and more, will come to us anyway at the next lease without planting any new crop."[99] Clearly, the elder Tavanes had little confidence in the long-run benefits of capital improvements urged upon him by his tenant at Arc-sur-Tille.

Understandably, Huvelin exhibited some signs of frustration. He had signed a nine-year lease in 1759, agreeing to pay 13,000 livres rent, an increase of 5,400 livres over the previous lease. A letter to the new Comte de Saulx revealed a certain anxiety.

> I must not count on any help from Monsieur le Comte de Tavanes. He has reached an age where nothing affects him, but I attribute this change to his advanced years. I wish with all my heart that your affairs [at Paris] will allow you to travel to Burgundy this summer. You can then manage your own affairs here, which would be much better. I hope, Monsieur, that you will have a word to reply.[100]

Huvelin had to give way on his interpretation of the lease. He succeeded only in enlisting the new count's support against the neighboring

---

[97] Young commented that it was this delay that made French landlords skeptical about such improvements. Young, *Travels*, I, 235–36.

[98] *A. D.*, E–1744, *Mémoire* of Huvelin, 1758; Huvelin to Comte de Saulx-Tavanes, March, 1761; Mémoire of February, 1760.

[99] *A. D.*, E–1744, *Mémoire*, 1761; Comment on *Mémoire* of 1758.

[100] *A. D.*, E–1744, Huvelin to Comte de Saulx-Tavanes, March 1761.

proprietor whose sand banks kept filling in Huvelin's drainage canals. It is doubtful whether the count's intervention in this instance had a salutary effect. He wrote a very sarcastic letter of protest to the neighboring proprietor, one Seigneur de Bressey, reminding the man of his modest rank as a member of the *petite noblesse*.[101] The reply of Bressey does not suggest an amicable or satisfactory settlement of the problem. Huvelin died in 1764, and it is not surprising that there were few successors with his interest in capital improvements among Tavanes's tenants.

The frustrations of Huvelin were due to the attitudes of the new duke's father and grandfather in the 1760s. But the attitude of the head of the family in the 1780s was no different. He would not spend one sou beyond the essential maintenance costs of the estate. The accounts for estate repairs during this decade make this quite apparent.

The following table makes it abundantly clear that farm improvements or even annual repairs were not the count's primary concern. Taxes on the land he did pay, though the three *vingtièmes* after 1784 claimed much less than their fifteen per cent. Renovation of the *terriers*, the employment of a *feudiste*, and the elevation of the land into a *duché*, as we shall see, were far more important to the count. Duboy, the steward, was assigned the revenues of the property at Lux—about 8,000 livres—with which to pay the expenses of the entire Burgundian estate, excluding the *vingtièmes*. One heading on his accounts reads "*Réparations faites par Économie*," apparently meaning that they were not to exceed the income from Lux. These expenses included the wages of the forest guards and his own 600 livres, which hardly qualify as investments in the land. In short, gross agricultural investment amounted to about four per cent of the total receipts from the estate. This might be compared with an English reinvestment rate of 12 to 25 per cent in the nineteenth century.[102] Moreover, modern agricultural economists focus

---

[101] *A. D.*, E–1745, Correspondence Bressey-Saulx, 1758–64. The tenor of the correspondence is indicated by the following remark of Sr. de Bressey to the count: "*Permettez-moi, Monsieur, de vous écrire pour la dernière fois et de me plaindre amèrement du ton aigre et imperieux que vous prenez avec moi dans une affaire que j'ai cru aussi juste et simple. . . .*"

[102] Nathaniel Kent recommended 11 per cent on small farms, seven on large, "once in good repair." N. Kent, *Hints to Gentlemen of Landed Property* (London, 1775), p. 207. Individual examples tend to be higher. Habakkuk notes 7.5 per cent for the Bedford estates in the early eighteenth century, while Grigg places it at 25 per cent for three estates, throughout the nineteenth century. David Spring, again for

TABLE II.5   ESTATE EXPENSES, 1781–89

Date	Annual Repairs Livres	Wages Livres	Taxes Livres	Terriers Livres	Other Expenses* Livres	Total Expenses Livres	Total Receipts Livres	Expenses as % of Receipts
1781	5,040	2,130	2,381	4,700	979	15,230	47,609	31.9
1782	3,950	2,376	4,907	2,000	—	13,233	78,080	16.9
1783	2,343	2,626	5,856	4,500	2,000	17,325	81,466	21.3
1784	3,683	2,514	6,786	4,900	773	18,656	81,589	22.9
1785	3,065	2,746	6,788	5,109	627	18,335	88,378	20.7
1786	3,148	2,722	6,788	5,701	—	18,359	78,967	23.2
1787	3,637	2,634	5,886	13,351	800	26,308	95,952	27.4
1788	3,400	2,125	4,978	4,141	300	14,944	95,928	15.6
1789	3,160	1,980	4,977	3,948	1,000	15,065	95,713	15.7
Annual Average	3,603	2,428	5,483	5,372	720	17,495	82,654	
% of Receipts	4.3	2.9	6.6	6.5	0.9	21.2	100.0	

* "Other Expenses" includes the sum of 772 livres for rural charity in 1789.
SOURCE: A. D., E–1723 (Duboy Accounts); A. D., E–1721 (Billard Accounts).

attention on "net investment," that is, gross investment minus annual repairs and replacements. Since the expenses here include repairs on mills and forge, new retaining walls, masonry and carpentry work on old granaries, and a new roof for the château, "net investment" cn the Burgundian estate evaporates altogether. In the course of the century, net investment in the land had surely never exceeded five per cent, but in the last decade before 1789, it shrunk to nothing. The new steward was to complain about such excessive economy in 1790. If his intention was to

the nineteenth century, indicates an 18 per cent average expenditure on Sir James Graham's estate between 1819 and 1845 and over 30 per cent on the Duke of Bedford's estate between 1842 and 1861. H. J. Habakkuk, "Economic Functions of English Landowners in the Seventeenth and Eighteenth Centuries" in W. E. Minchinton, ed., Essays in Agricultural History (Plymouth, 1968), I, 194; D. B. Grigg, "A Note on Agricultural Rent and Expenditure in Nineteenth-Century England," Agricultural History XXXIX (1965), 150–51; D. Spring, "A Great Agricultural Estate; Netherby under Sir James Graham, 1820–45," Agricultural History XXIX (April, 1955), 80–81; D. Spring, The English Landed Estate in the Nineteenth Century: Its Administration (Baltimore, 1963), p. 192. See also W. M. Postan, "Investment in Medieval Agriculture," Journal of Economic History XXVII (December, 1967), 579. Postan estimates gross reinvestment on a number of thirteenth-century English estates at two to five per cent. Admittedly these English examples are late for an exact comparison with French estates in the eighteenth century.

plough back a strict minimum of his revenues into the land, the new duke had been thoroughly successful.

Lease terms did not encourage farm improvements either. The larger part of each lease was directed to prohibitions, not permissions. No major repairs could be undertaken without written permission of the seigneur-proprietor. Most of the wood—the basic building and repair material—was reserved for the seigneur. Subletting had to be authorized by the owner. All rents had to be paid in gold or silver, and tenants were encouraged to find *"cautions,"* third parties who would guarantee prompt payment in full. After 1757, the leases at Beaumont and Bourberain explicitly prohibited the tenants from claiming any reduction in their rent because of war, hail, flood, or "for any other cause, predictable or unpredictable, whatsoever."[103] Emphasis was clearly placed on close control of the tenant, to the detriment of agricultural improvement.

* * * * *

In 1765 and again in 1785, the Tavanes drew up inventories of the titles and papers concerning the estate in Burgundy. These two dates mark two offensives by the family, in a process that Marc Bloch labeled "seigneurial reaction." The two inventories list family leases, transactions, sentences, judgments, sales, exchanges, acquistions, and a large category of seigneurial procedures and titles—*terriers, bail à cens, reprise de fiefs, visites*—dating back to the late fifteenth century. The inventories reveal a cluster of such seigneurial titles in the sixteenth century, relatively few in the seventeenth, and another cluster in the mid-eighteenth century, becoming especially voluminous in the 1780s. Although Saint-Jacob in his work on the Burgundian peasantry has made us aware of successive waves of "seigneurial reactions" since 1670, the Tavanes case points to a distinct offensive after 1750.[104]

A concern for more vigorous collection of seigneurial dues can be detected in the Tavanes leases, corresponding roughly to the period in which regular rents began to rise. The lease of 1730 at Beaumont, for example, devoted considerably more space than previous leases to fixing payment of seigneurial judges, furnishing "manuals" of the rights,

[103] *A. D.*, E–1767, Lease of October 28, 1757; *A. D.*, E–1817, Lease of February 8, 1784. These should be compared with earlier leases in the same bundles.

[104] *A. D.*, E–2022 (1765); *A. D.*, E–2023 (1785).

dividing the revenues of the fines and the *lods et ventes* (mutation fees), projecting a new land survey, and obtaining declarations from the *censitaires*. The lease even specified that a certain part of the *seigneurie*, previously exempt, "will pay the thirteenth sheaf like the rest of Bessey."[105] In 1751, the count made a "pact" with his *fermier* at Lux, dividing the expenses and future revenues of a project to "revive (*faire revivre*) the rights neglected on the lands of Lux and Spoy.[106] At Tilchâtel, between 1755 and 1757, there were nine law suits brought before the Paris courts by Comte de Tavanes against a number of proprietors in his jurisdiction, condemning them to come before his clerk at Tilchâtel and pay from twenty to thirty years' *cens* arrears of about one bushel per acre.[107]

The duke's father, Charles-Marie-Gaspard de Saulx-Tavanes, would brook no threat to his property rights in the forests. Far from conceding that the inhabitants of Lux had communal rights in *his* wood, Tavanes had obtained a formal act by the village assembly, authorizing the cutting of trees in the *communal* wood for château repairs.[108] The contiguity of his own forest with that of the village community, however, provoked continuous disputes over the right of usage. In 1761, Tavanes wrote his agent that he would make no concession to a claim by the inhabitants to use fifteen acres of his wood. "I ask only for justice in all affairs. I do not have that stupid vanity which requires that I make an arrangement with the inhabitants.... I leave such foolish vanity to the lawyers." The count insisted that Duboy "go to court." The results were rapidly forthcoming. Two weeks later, Duboy reported that the *usagers* did not have enough money to go to Dijon to conduct a lawsuit and had come to Tilchâtel to beg the count to halt proceedings against them. They agreed to pay for their past use of *his* wood.[109]

There is no doubt, then, that a more vigorous enforcement of seigneurial rights as well as whittling away village claims to wood occurred before Charles-François-Casimir became seigneur in 1780. But the new count's changes in administration included a thorough renewal of all seigneurial claims and a maximum effort at strict collection. The first duke placed his own stamp on the "seigneurial reaction." In addition to

---

[105] *A. D.*, E–1767, Lease of June 12, 1730.
[106] *A. D.*, E–1878, Agreement of August 28, 1751.
[107] *A. D.*, E–2023, Nine lawsuits before the *Requêtes de l'Hôtel à Paris*.
[108] *A. D.*, E–2022, Act of the Assembly of Lux, May 1, 1743.
[109] *A. D.*, E–1843, Tavanes-Duboy Correspondence, March, April, 1761.

the second major inventory of titles, the new seigneur drew up a complete set of new *terriers* (records of seigneurial dues) with supporting maps, sectional plans, and special manuals for the tenants and seigneurial officials. For this purpose, the count employed a professional expert, a *feudiste*. He was Jacques Fénéon from Saulieu in the northwestern part of Burgundy, a man of some reputation in the region. Fénéon was more than a surveyor and cartographer, even more than a specialist in "feudal law." He was an estate manager as well. In 1789, Billard, the chief agent of the Tavanes in Burgundy, died after 28 years of service. Fénéon took his place and, significantly, moved not to Dijon but to the family château at Lux.

The count attached great importance to the renovation of his *terriers*. He was willing to spend considerable sums on this project which extended over several years. By contract in early 1781, he agreed to pay Fénéon and his assistants between three and four thousand livres a year in addition to the costs of travel, materials, and legal proceedings. In the 1780s, the annual cost of "reviving" the seigneurial rights averaged over 5,000 livres, almost one-third of all estate expenses including taxes.[110]

What did Fénéon do to justify this added cost at a time when the count was keeping all other estate expenses at a strict minimum? First, he conducted in *arpentage*, surveying every scrap of land in Tavanes's four major seigneuries. Then he had to record all of the count's claims on each strip, including the precise area, boundaries, name of peasant proprietor, and authentic title to each *reconnaissance*. The count's domain lands extended over 8,000 acres; his claims to seigneurial rights extended over at least 20,000 more.[111] There were a lot of stone markers to plant and proprietors to identify. Every *dîme*, every *champart*, every mutation fee, every *banalité*, every *taille seigneuriale*, every *cens*, and every *corvée* was recorded for each *"censitaire"* and *"justiciable."* The attached colored maps indicated each plot in an intricate patchwork measured in *perches* (9.5 square meters) rather than *journaux* (0.8 acres). No wonder a number of *terriers* were in two volumes because of their size and weight.

---

[110] *A. D.*, E–1723 (Duboy); *A. D.*, E–1721 (Billard). See Table of Estate Expenses, above, p. 91.

[111] This estimate is based on claims for compensation for the *dîmes* abolished in 1789. *A. D.*, Q–733, 734. The *dîme* was also collected on the duke's domain land. It is not always possible to keep the two jurisdictions distinct. See also Document VII.

Fénéon compiled no less than seven *terriers* and six atlases in the 1780s.[112] They replaced *terriers* drawn up between 1548 and 1610.

But however slow and exacting this was, the hardest task was not measuring and recording. The local inhabitants had to be persuaded to confirm these claims. Fénéon's treatment of this problem was not above criticism. When the *terrier* of Beaumont was completed in 1784, he notified the inhabitants of the seigneurial jurisdiction that the old and the new *terriers* would be available to them for inspection and comparison at the clerk's house. Fénéon chose the summer recess of Parlement, when no legal council was available, to publish his *terriers*. But the inhabitants complained that he did not give them enough time to look at them. They wanted three months instead of a few days to read the new *terriers*. Fénéon replied that this was unnecessary and summoned the inhabitants before the parish church to confirm the new rolls. He observed that there were fifteen men present, representing "the most important part of the community," and that they had accepted the new *terrier*. Apparently, Fénéon's dispatch of the task was not altogether successful, for the inhabitants were able to make a mild protest via Duboy, the steward. "The inhabitants say that they have no intention of contesting the rights of Seigneur Comte de Saulx-Tavanes that are legitimately substantiated by his titles..., but that certain rights, such as the *péage*, which had been abolished, should be explicitly excluded." Moreover, they wanted Fénéon to specify the weights and measures, since terms such as *mesure* or *boisseau* varied from village to village.[113]

Subsequent protests were less mild and accommodating. Fénéon encountered increasing opposition from the local villagers. They failed to answer his summons to assemble and recognize the new *terriers*; they contested the new land markers; they began to question the smallest articles in the rolls.[114] In 1786, the people of Renêve, a village of 150 households, claimed that Fénéon should have based the new *terrier* on the previous one of 1611, not on the *terrier* of 1545. In a letter to the count himself, they claimed that Fénéon had assumed that no one knew about the *terrier* of 1611, but that they had found it at the notary's house in Beaumont, a few miles away. Armed with this new documentation, the villagers denied the *feudiste's* claim to one chicken per inhabitant.

[112] *A. D.*, E–2023, List of *Terriers*.
[113] *A. D.*, E–1780, *Terrier de Beaumont*.
[114] *A. D.*, E–1795, 1869.

For them this was no insignificant matter. "There is a surcharge that Monsieur Fénéon wanted to introduce," they wrote.[115]

The new agent was surprised at this opposition. He was especially struck by the legal resourcefulness of rather ordinary artisans and peasants. At first he was inclined to attribute the resistance to the example of non-resident property owners, the *forains*.[116] Then he shifted the blame to local "trouble-makers" such as one Morizot, a lawyer from Tilchâtel. He advised the count in Paris about this man. Responding promptly, Tavanes addressed the intendant at Dijon.

> Comte de Tavanes finds it absolutely necessary to renew his *terriers* which are all very old and poorly written. His purpose in this expensive operation has been to establish the respective rights of the seigneur and the communities in a clear, precise, and equitable manner, thereby ending all legal disputes. He has chosen reputable commissioners of *terriers* and the communities have cooperated in the project. Beaumont would have concurred. Lux would have been no less reasonable, had not this Maître Morizot from Tilchâtel fanned the flame of discord. This man, who is known for his dishonesty, lives at the expense of the communities, for he encourages them to undertake unwarranted lawsuits.

The count went on to explain that Lux had agreed on all but three of the thirty-one articles in the *terrier* when this Morizot "incited the inhabitants to appeal to the Parlement."

> Comte de Tavanes has reliable information indicating that this dangerous individual, a real troublemaker (*vrai boutefeu de chicane*) is about to play a similar role in several other of the count's communities where he is trying to have himself named "special solicitor."

Tavanes then expressed a timeless view of seigneur toward villager that seemed to smack of wishful thinking.

> Abusing the blind confidence and lack of experience of people naturally good and simple, he will not cease encouraging them to oppose the commissioner of *terriers* on every point and without any foundation, contrary to their own interest and at considerable expense.

The count then put the weight of his name behind public order, an interest he shared with the local intendant. Certainly, Intendant Amelot

[115] *A. D.*, Q–734, Renêve.
[116] *A. D.*, E–1795, Fénéon to Duke, August 29, 1788.

could not have been unaware that the count's grandfather had married a member of his family earlier in the century. And had not the Tavanes always been close to the high robe, beginning with the Daguesseau, Amelot, Feydeau de Brou—chancellors, ministers, intendants all?

> Independently of his own interest in the affair, Comte de Tavanes must concur with the views of Monsieur Amelot regarding the welfare of the local communities and make such a conspirator (*intrigant*) known to him. He hopes that Monsieur l'Intendant will intercede and prevent the communities from employing this man as their agent and, if possible, exile him from the region. This will be the only way to restore peace and common sense between the seigneur and the inhabitants of Lux and prevent trouble in many other communities. . . .

The count ended his appeal by assuring Amelot of his "good intentions" and "love of public order," promising to instruct his agents in Burgundy to cooperate with the intendant and the "committee named to examine the requests of the communities concerning all matters in contention."[117]

But despite the count's efforts, protests continued in a proper legal form that betrayed the hand of special *procureurs* like Morizot whom the communities had hired. In 1786 the village of Champagne, represented by solicitors, made a direct appeal to the recently created duke. Prefacing their remarks with respect and devotion as "vassals" of the duke, they directed their criticism to his "agents."

> . . . the more they respect their illustrious seigneur, the more they are convinced that he wishes only justice to prevail. . . . They would not have thought it necessary to trouble Monseigneur le Duc de Saulx-Tavanes about the activities of his agents. They assumed that everything would be satisfactorily arranged with them. They were wrong. The following facts will prove it.[118]

Fénéon made his own comment in the margin of this village *mémoire*. If it had been the intention of the community to separate agent from seigneur, Fénéon would close the gap. He said that no village community had shown less respect for the duke than this one. Concentrating more on their attitude than on specific grievances, Fénéon again turned to the special *procureurs*.

[117] *A. D.*, E–1869, Comte de Tavanes to Intendant Amelot, ca. 1786.
[118] *A. D.*, E–1795, *Mémoire des Procureurs de Champagne*.

The countless tricks, the tone of superiority and air of smugness in the conduct of the *procureurs spéciaux* toward the agents of the seigneur is only too evident and in keeping with the style of this *mémoire*. It reveals how they can change their colors when their interests and passions dictate.[119]

Fénéon then separated the solicitors from the majority of the local populace. The villagers were not guilty of this aggressive tone; it was the solicitors from outside the parish. Again he insisted that their principal crime was the failure to conduct the negotiations in a polite and fitting (*douce et honnête*) manner "appropriate to people of this *état*." In fact, their "tone" was incompatible with their functions as representatives of the village. Fénéon ended by warning the duke that the only purpose of the village *mémoire* was to undermine his confidence in his agents.[120]

Were the special solicitors really "outsiders" with interests and attitudes distinct from the villagers? We cannot be certain about Morizot of Tilchâtel, but the four *procureurs spéciaux* of Champagne are identifiable. They were not city lawyers, but the parish priest, a *laboureur*, a *marchand*, and a *receveur des traites*—all members of the local community.[121] They were not the poorer members, to be sure, but they were neither lawyers nor "outsiders." True, there were occasions when Dijon lawyers were consulted, but the initiative came from the villages. No wonder Fénéon was shocked by such insubordinate behavior.

Tavanes, too, was astonished by the local opposition to the new *terriers*. He qualified the demands for a three-month period to inspect them as "frivolous;" four or five hours to compare the old and the new *terriers* would be quite sufficient. "Do they imagine that they can impose fresh delays? Have they not attempted such harassment (*tracasseries*) in the past?" Yet Tavanes said that he was "too noble" and "too generous" to seek any revenge. He agreed to give them two more weeks to inspect the *terriers* at Arc-sur-Tille.[122]

Tavanes had not been satisfied simply to renew the *terriers*, enforce

---

[119] *A. D.*, E–1795, Reply of Fénéon in right columns of *Mémoire*.

[120] *Ibid.* ". . . cet homme poussé par un zèle outré n'a pas craint, malgré son état passif dans les affaires du monde. . . ."

[121] *A. D.*, E–1795, *Mémoire*, May 14, 1785.

[122] *A. D.*, E–1743, quoted in N. Garnier, *Arc-sur-Tille: Les familles seigneuriales et quelques familles bourgeoises* (Arc-sur-Tille, 1913), 234. See also *A. N.*, T–109[1-2], *Mémoire pour . . . le Duc de Saulx-Tavanes contre les habitants d'Arc-sur-Tille, le 16 novembre 1786.*

neglected seigneurial dues, and integrate previously allodial property. Court favor was now to turn against him in a curious way; at least it would cost him more than it returned in livres and sous. In 1784, the count was made *Chevalier des Ordres de Saint Michel et du Saint Esprit,* and in 1786 his lands in Burgundy were "erected into a duchy" by the King. The new duke made every effort to give these new honors importance, and to make them locally prestigious as well as financially rewarding. There is little doubt that Tavanes' prestige was very much in play. He hardly needed the reminder about his "illustrious name"—so clearly engraved in the Letters Patent of 1784—but it no doubt hastened his efforts to give his properties a special judicial status.

> ...for these various reasons joined to those of an illustrious family, one of the oldest in Our Province of Burgundy, distinguished throughout time by its great offices, important appointments, and its alliances with the greatest houses of Our Realm. We have decided...to name him Chevalier in Our Order of Saint Michel and of Saint Esprit, in which he will be the sixth of his name admitted since the origin of these orders.[123]

In a letter to Billard, the count said that he intended to follow the example of the King, the Princes of the Blood, and the other great houses of the kingdom by establishing a ducal *bailliage*, complete with its own judiciary responsible directly to the Parlement of Dijon.[124] To Billard, well aware of the current heavy drain on the landed income, such an enterprise was fraught with danger. Tavanes was overly optimistic in thinking that the volume of lawsuits would produce a supplementary income. The *bailliage ducal*, Billard pointed out, consisted of only seven villages and 700 households and most of the wealthy proprietors were non-residents. Far from returning any revenue, judicial fines might not even cover the wages of local judges. Worse, since the ducal *bailliage* would take a certain amount of litigation away from the regular *bailliage* court, the new duke would have to compensate the royal judges. Nevertheless, the duke was determined to press on with the project and ended

---

[123] *A. D.*, E–1869, Letters Patent, June 8, 1784. The royal commendation stressed the count's distinguished military service at Astembeck, Creveley, Minden and during the "retreat from Hesse" and the "retreat on Cassel" during the Seven Years' War. Rossbach may have shaken other members of the officer corps; Tavanes had little reason to complain. For the Letters Patent creating the duchy, see Document I.

[124] *A. D.*, E–1687, *Mémoire.*

by arranging for itinerant seigneurial judges to pass on horseback from one village to another four times a year at the tenants' expense. In retrospect, the phrase *"grands jours"* seems somewhat pretentious for the number of cases that came before these judges. On the other hand, they did increase the duke's legal hold over the villagers.

The legal costs at Paris for the honor of a "duchy" were far more burdensome. Godard's accounts show an expense of 12,856 livres for 1786 and Billard's another 8,766 for 1787. How much of the extra legal expense incurred in these years is attributable to the "duchy" is impossible to ascertain. No doubt the duke took a particular satisfaction in adding a few seigneurial bailiffs and *greffiers* to his provincial staff. He probably hoped that this new judicial competence would serve to stifle the protest of the communities over the new *terriers*. The amount of detail concerning the size and decor of the seigneurial prison and *bailliage* court (actually a small house adjoining the château) suggests that not money but prestige and local pre-eminence were the duke's principal motives.[125]

If the duke would have his ducal jurisdiction at all costs, he also knew how to combine the assertion of seigneurial authority with a new source of revenue. An annex to the grant of *Chevalier des Ordres du Roi* authorized him to collect an old right known as the *droit d'indire*.[126] In origin this was a feudal aid, paid at the time of knighting, marriage of a nobleman's daughter, ransom, or crusade—the so-called "four cases." According to the customary law of Burgundy, the *droit d'indire* gave the lord a claim to double the seigneurial rights in that particular year. This right had not been applied in Burgundy for centuries, and there was no record of it even in the sixteenth-century *terriers*. Bouhier, in his new edition of the Customs of Burgundy, cited the most recent precedent as oc-

---

[125] *Ibid.* The duke insisted that his "officers" be advocates or "at least *licenciés*," qualified to judge criminal cases. Another memorandum devotes considerable space to court rooms and prisons. Although it had once been prohibited, "Today court rooms as well as prisons are tolerated in the châteaux. Thus, M. le Duc de Saulx can establish a court room (*l'audience*) and prison in his château at Lux. However, if he has a little house or other building outside of his château, he would be better advised to use it for the *Palais du Bailliage de Saulx* and the attached prison. This way he will avoid having sessions every day in his château, attended by all kinds of people. . . ." The memorandum proceeded to outline all the specifications for the ducal court including the number of keys for the *armoire* of the clerk and the color of the walls—*bleu celeste* with yellow *fleur-de-Lys*.

[126] *A. D.*, E–1869, Annex to Letters Patent of 1784.

curring in 1333, and this was not on Tavanes's properties.[127] The fragility of the precedent did not faze the duke in the slightest. Since he had claims to the *dîme* over several thousand acres, his agents calculated the revenue from the *droit d'indire* at 12,676 livres and proceeded to enforce collection.[128] Moreover, Tavanes not only claimed it in the year he became duke, but also on the occasion of the marriage of his eldest daughter, three years later. Surprisingly, all but one of Tavanes's parishes paid. On both occasions, Arc-sur-Tille, the one seigneurie outside of the new ducal *bailliage*, appealed from the royal *bailliage* court to the Parlement of Dijon, and even reached the *Conseil du Roi*—but to no avail. The courts sustained the House of Tavanes.[129]

The collection of this archaic right only added to the problems for Tavanes's agents. The inhabitants at Champagne, initially honored when their seigneur became a duke, were decidedly less enthusiastic when his agents asked for 445 livres, about four livres per household. On this occasion, the community consulted two advocates from the Parlement of Dijon, who discovered a title fixing the *droit d'indire* of Champagne at only 45 livres. The agents had to acquiesce, and Fénéon reported an increasing skepticism on the part of the villagers after this "error" was discovered. Both Billard and Fénéon were accused of "bad faith."[130]

The cost to the duke of renovating the *terriers* and enforcing even the most remote of seigneurial rights had been heavy and cannot be measured only in money. Before Tavanes's efforts in the 1780s to claim all his seigneurial rights, the subtenants and small peasants had not been directly affected by the seigneur's policies toward the land. True, the principal tenants, increasingly pressed by higher rents, bore down where they could, renegotiating mill leases, rigorously collecting grain fees and *dîmes*, raising what few money rents existed. But changes on the subleases were not easily made, since they were customarily based on so many measures of grain per acre. At Blagny, for example, the rent of 8 measures per *journal* was unchanged from 1741 to 1783, and probably

[127] C. L. Bouhier, *Les coutûmiers du duché de Bourgogne avec les anciens coûtumes et observations de M. Bouhier, président à mortier*, 2 vols. (Dijon, 1742, 1746), II, 287–88, 319–20.

[128] *A. D.*, E–1869, *Etat de ce que produira le droit d'indire en 1784.*

[129] Garnier, *Arc-sur-Tille: les familles seigneuriales*, pp. 231–33; *A. N.*, T–109[1–2], *Mémoire . . . 16 novembre 1786.*

[130] *A. D.*, E–1795, *Mémoire* and Reply.

after.[131] But now the seigneurial apparatus reached the average villager. By supplying the tenant with new *terriers* and seigneurial titles and employing special agents to enforce these claims, the duke made the smaller subtenant and *laboureur* more aware that he was their seigneur. The experience was especially irritating since it coincided with a decline in grain prices between 1783 and 1786, favorable to the average villager.[132] Previously a distant absentee lord known largely through his *fermiers*, Saulx-Tavanes was now known by his agents, above all by the vigorous Fénéon and a conspicuous corps of seigneurial bailiffs and forest wardens. By 1786, the absentee landlord was only too much in evidence on his Burgundian estate.

The question remains whether Tavanes's efforts represented a real economic loss to the peasant or simply a series of pinpricks, at worst, a threat for the future. Even without a thorough investigation of the burden of each seigneurial right, a few conclusions seem certain. Despite all efforts, certain rights were either contested or difficult to enforce. They were the *corvée* (only three days a year), the mutation fees, and seigneurial fines. The *taille seigneuriale*, representing a chicken or a few *deniers* per inhabitant, was also a light burden. The weight of the *cens* is more difficult to appraise. At Beaumont, it was only a half chicken and a few sous per *journal*.[133] At Bourberain, a 30-acre family farm paid 40 livres, unalterable to be sure.[134] At Tilchâtel, Tavanes collected the *cens* in kind at one *boisseau* per *journal*, perhaps five per cent of the gross harvest.[135] Taken alone, the *cens* was not a heavy burden and did not make up a large portion of Tavanes's seigneurial income. Efforts to increase the revenue from this source did not overly impress the agents. As Duboy said in 1784, "The new *terrier* at Lux gives hope of reviving a certain quantity of *cens* ... but we should not count on it."[136]

By contrast, the *dîme* and the *champart* had always been a substantial levy on the peasant and represented without question the most profitable of Tavanes's seigneurial rights. These were claims to a portion of the

[131] *A. D.*, E–1768, Blagny Sub-leases, 1741, 1774, 1783.
[132] See Document X (1755–90). Peasants were probably only aware of price changes over short periods (three to five years).
[133] *A. D.*, E–1780, *Terrier de Beaumont.*
[134] *A. D.*, E–1818, *Etat*, 1756.
[135] *A. D.*, E–2023, *Procès*, 1756–57.
[136] *A. D.*, E–1878, *Etat*, May 1784.

harvest, usually one-thirteenth of the four major grains (wheat, rye, barley, oats), maize and vegetables sometimes included.[137] Tavanes had these rights over about 13,000 acres, extending over a dozen parishes. Applied to such a large area, Fénéon's new survey could hope to bring additional revenue. Before 1783, the areas owing the *dîme* were rarely mentioned in either the leases or the periodic estimates of agents. Calculations were made on the basis of quantities of grain collected in the past. Hence, at Bourberain, for example, the *dîme* returned 70 *emines* of grain in 1765 and 71 in 1783; it had returned 83 *emines* in 1586.[138] But after Fénéon's survey, Tavanes had exact areas at his disposal on which to estimate the *dîmes*.

The result varied from parish to parish. But whereas before 1783 the *dîme* produced only about one livre per *journal* for the seigneur, after the land survey it produced between two and three livres per *journal*.[139] Price rise accounts for only a small part of this difference. What this indicates is that before the survey the small peasants were not paying their one-thirteenth, but considerably less. Perhaps this is what Duboy meant when he said that the peasants were very negligent in working the lands paying the *dîme* and *champart*. But by 1789, they were paying the full amount. And one-thirteenth of the gross harvest meant close to one-fourth of the net harvest.[140] From the peasant's point of view, this was increasing the *dîme*. When the canton of Bèze presided over the liquidation of the *dîme* in 1791, the local representatives could argue sincerely that "each *terrier* was a formal disavowal of the preceding one, because at each renewal the former seigneur of Spoy had always increased and extended the so-called right of *champart*."[141] Tavanes was within the letter of his titles, but he had clearly violated previous practice. His seigneurial revenues rose, and peasant revenues declined.

The "seigneurial reaction" practiced by Duc de Saulx-Tavanes represented real economic burdens to a substantial number of *dîme*-payers who otherwise had little to do with the duke or his agents. Not less im-

[137] *A. D.*, Q–734 (*Dîmes*); See Saint-Jacob, *Les paysans*, pp. 394–96, 454.

[138] *A. D.*, E–1818, 2022 (Bourberain). If there were 2,700 *journaux* subject to the *dîme* as Fénéon contended, Bourberain should have returned 170 *emines*, not 70.

[139] *A. D.*, E–1817–18 (Bourberain); *A. D.*, E–1768 (Blagny); *A. D.*, Q–733–34 (*Dîmes*); *A. D.*, Q–1117 (Reduction of rents due to abolition of seigneurial dues).

[140] Saint-Jacob, *Les paysans*, p. 133.

[141] *A. D.*, Q–733, Observations on the Rate of the *Dîmes*, Canton of Bèze.

portant, the whole process of renovation of the *terriers* caused a great deal of local friction and increased the distrust of the village inhabitants. Complaints tended to focus on Fénéon's methods of adding a fishing right here and a few sous there to the *terriers*. But most curious and novel was the lack of docility on the part of the local villagers, an aggressiveness and legal competence that startled both the duke and his agents. The day had passed when the threat of a lawsuit by the count was sufficient to bring the peasants to reason.

*   *   *   *   *   *

What conclusions are suggested by the experience of the Saulx-Tavanes as estate administrators in the decade before the Revolution? An estate of 8,000 acres with seigneurial rights over 20,000 acres more ranked among the largest in France, excepting, of course, the properties of the Princes-of-the-Blood. In 1788 it produced a gross income of 95,000 livres (one quarter from seigneurial rights), roughly equivalent to 4,700 English pounds. It was a sum about ten times the revenue of a provincial seigneur from Toulouse, Bordeaux, or Rennes, and a considerably larger proportion of the revenues of most French landlords. Put another way, it was a sum equal to the tax revenues of more than thirty Burgundian villages. It was a sum that surpassed all but the resources of the most opulent *negotiants*, bankers, and tax-farmers of the kingdom. Added to *rentes* and pensions, it permitted a nobleman to live the life of a *grand seigneur* at the capital, provided he placed some limit on consumption, display, dowries, and family *éclat*. For Tavanes was on the fringe of that rarefied stratum of French aristocracy called *"les Grands."* By English standards it was a modest landed estate indeed, but in France it placed a seigneur easily among the four hundred richest landlords.

Absentee owners like the duke, who visited their estates once or twice in a lifetime, were quite able to give their holdings close attention when need demanded. It has been said that it requires neither great skill nor constant application to raise rents. Tavanes's administration somewhat exceeded these limits, but there was still time for his duties and distractions at court. Moreover, the duke managed his land with a modest staff, even more modestly paid. Yet he could expect a great deal of effort from men like Billard and Duboy, relying, it seems, more heavily on personal loyalty than on economic incentive. At the same time, he employed special itinerant agents to estimate the revenues of the land at first hand and act as a check both on the tenants' margin of profit and on the performance of his permanent agents. In this manner the duke was able to maximize his rents, extracting close to ninety per cent of the income of the principal tenants. He kept estate expenses to a minimum, holding estate repairs and wages of personnel to seven per cent of the gross income. Because his leases had to be notarized (an absentee cannot negotiate verbal contracts), he paid higher taxes than most provincial resident nobles since he could not hide his rents. But even so, the *vingtièmes* (three in 1784) did not represent more than another seven per cent of revenue. The revival of seigneurial dues also cost about seven per cent. In brief, the duke was able to keep almost 80 per cent of his gross landed income for expenses in Paris.

Such estate management was not without repercussions on the principal tenants, often men of some means, grain merchants, and ironmasters with financial backing in the *bourgs* and river ports. The nine-year lease renewed at auction was not a novelty to the tenants, though they attempted to lengthen it. Nor was the rapid turnover of tenants, the dogged pursuit of delinquent rent-payers, sometimes leading to seizure and sale of the tenants' personal property. Yet there was something markedly determined and systematic about the new duke's efforts to make the land pay. It was not simply that rents rose faster than grain prices. More important was the technique of calculating the tenants' profits to the last livre. Given the inelasticity of the subleases, only the larger tenants had room to maneuver after 1780. Even for them, Tavanes made it difficult. They were consistently discouraged from speculation or experimentation with new farm methods or even modest improvements. Recall also that the duke limited the supply of wood to the amount required to fuel the forge and sold the rest annually on his own account. He refused all requests for longer leases. Like his father, he granted no loans or rebates on rents for capital improvements. Annual repairs, for the most part, were the tenants' obligation. Given the demand for the land, why risk capital? As Billard had said, the rents would rise anyway. The duke was not interested in farm production; he wanted immediate returns.

That the duke's need for money in Paris was the reason for his desire to maximize rents seems clear enough from his correspondence with Billard at Dijon. His motives for the renovation of the *terriers* and the enforcement of seigneurial rights seem less certain. Prestige played its part, as evidenced by the ducal *bailliage* and the holding of *Grands Jours*. But the desire for more income should not be completely discounted even here. More claims to seigneurial dues permitted the duke to raise rents higher, since they were included in the leases. The *dîme* and the *champart* were produce-rents worth collecting. The initial cost of the *duché* was high, but the duke, no doubt, assumed that this was temporary. A few more years—certainly by the mid-1790s—and the estate would pass 100,000 livres per annum.

The enforcement of these rights created fresh and unexpected irritation. Was it the added material burden as much as a new awareness of being "vassals" that spurred the villagers to action? In any case, they hired lawyers and began to question the legal propriety of the ducal agent and *feudiste*. They exhibited unexpected energy and competence. Unafraid to seek legal counsel, they fought back with appropriate weapons. It is also noteworthy that such legal counsel was available to the villages. It could not have been high legal fees that encouraged local solicitors to incur certain risks in contesting the rights of a great lord. The reaction of the village community reveals an emerging hostility, first aimed at the agent, Fénéon, but shifting by 1789 to the duke himself.

Unlike resident seigneurs, Tavanes was not well placed to whittle away peasant holdings by a process of loans and foreclosures or by using *cens* arrears and the right of option to absorb scraps of land into the domain. Such techniques required a close attention to small affairs that made residence mandatory. The principal tenants were in a better position to play the role of rural creditor and no doubt earned the dislike of many subtenants and small holders. But the overriding fact was that both tenant and peasant *censitaire* shared an increasing hostility—only partly economic—toward a common object. Label it the "feudal complex," the rigid landlord, or the meticulous agent, all pointed to the seigneur, Duc de Saulx-Tavanes. On this, tenant-grain merchant, ironmaster, *laboureur*, village artisan, and even day-laborer searching for fire-wood or forage could all agree.

Finally, where did the seigneurial agent stand in this increasingly frustrating situation? Permanent resident agents like Billard and Duboy were clearly irritated by the special agents the duke sent from Paris. They spoke plaintively, if not bitterly, about the difficulties of pushing rents so hard and so fast. The arrival of the *feudiste*, Fénéon, at the château of Lux could not have pleased Duboy, the master of Lux for many years, and Billard must have sensed that a professional manager

TABLE II.5   THE ESTATE OF THE SAULX–TAVANES FAMILY IN BURGUNDY

Property	Domain Area		Gross Revenues*			Seigneurial Dues
	1788	1800	1754	1788	1800	1788
	Acres	*Acres*	*Livres*	*Livres*	*Livres*	*Livres*
Arc-sur-Tille	1,955	631	9,600	23,000	6,214	6,895
Tilchâtel	4,035	3,981	21,725	30,000	18,169	6,684
Bourberain	198	——	3,300	5,800	——	4,826
Velours	——	——	1,000	1,827	——	1,827
Lux	289	2	4,000	4,500	——	1,850
1 mill			700	800		
Spoy	126	39	300	1,800	312	1,290
Orville	6	——	300	380	——	164
Veronnes	150	——	——	1,000	——	——
Beaumont and Dampierre	971	647	7,600	7,000	4,943	500
Champagne	101	20	†	1,250	——	100
1 mill			650	1,300	——	——
Blagny	143	——	†	3,000	——	185
Renêve	30	18	†	1,250	180	978
Bessey	116	——	†	1,100	——	500
Flée	——	——	260	360	——	360
Dîmes de Champagne	——	——	——	212	——	212
Dîmes de Bessey	——	——	——	615	——	615
Five Ponds of Beaumont	——	——	——	975	——	——
Total	8,120	5,338	49,435	86,269	29,818	26,986

* After deductions for annual repairs and wages of estate personnel.

† In lease of Beaumont.

SOURCE: For domain areas see *A. D.*, Q–1117 (1793) and *A. D.*, Q–1118 (Liquidation of Debts, 1793–1800; Indemnity of 1825–29). The last bundle also includes a list of rents from the leases of 1790. For the leases in 1754 and 1788, see *A. D.*, E–1867, *Mémoire* on the land of the *Duché* (1788) and the individual leases in the appropriate bundle for each property (Arc-sur-Tille, Tilchâtel, Beaumont, etc.). For the seigneurial dues see *A. D.*, Q–733–734; *A. D.*, Q–1117; *A. D.*, E–1867; and Documents VI and VII.

This table of rents poses three problems. First, it does not include all the wood which by 1788 was largely sold annually at auction and not included in the leases. Billard's accounts suggest that the wood sales could increase the annual income in the 1780s by as much as 10,000 livres. Second, the domain at Lux was not all leased. A part of the revenues (about 8,000 livres in the 1780s) were assigned to Duboy, the steward, who used them to pay the expenses on the entire Burgundian estate. For these reasons then the revenues here represent a minimum. According to Billard's and Duboy's accounts, the gross receipts in 1788 were 95,952 and not 86,269 livres, which is simply the total of all the leases. Finally, there were some rent arrears which would also tend to distort annual revenues, though this was not a major item until 1789.

was about to replace him. Billard had worked for the Tavanes family for a generation; he was paid 600 livres per annum in 1788. Fénéon arrived in 1781 as *procureur général* at a salary of 3,000 livres and expenses. Billard had many reasons to be dissatisfied with his employer. No doubt the prestige of serving a famous noble house helped sustain him. Yet had he lived to see the Revolution in Burgundy, what course would he have chosen? Would he have continued to serve through the 1790s as the agent of a *ci-devant* seigneur as Fénéon did? Or would he have put his legal and managerial skill at the disposal of the villages like that Monsieur Morizot, the man the duke called a "dangerous conspirator"? Babeuf, after all, was once a *feudiste*.

The duke's dogged persistence and singleness of purpose brought him the revenues to sustain his rank at Paris. His aversion to "waste" on the income side of the ledger was matched only by his aversion to economy on the expenditure side. For a *grand seigneur* had to spend freely on those objects that enhanced his prestige and fulfilled his conception of himself in that very special world on the Seine. But that "world" had little meaning for the villages of the Dijonnais. The very financial success of the operation had alienated or at least weakened the loyalty of the duke's tenants, *censitaires*, and even agents. Neither the prestige of royal favor, the trappings of a ducal *bailliage*, nor the coaches laden with silver from Dijon would compensate him for this loss. After 1789, the Burgundian estate of the Saulx-Tavanes had few defenders.

III

THE BURDEN OF STATUS

*T*he opportunities for adornment for people of means in the late eighteenth century should not be underestimated. The Goncourt brothers describe the inventive imagination that characterized female taste in these matters in the 1770s and 1780s.

There were gowns which ... called for the spoil of four thousand jays; there were gowns over which Davaux ran the most resplendent embroideries; there were gowns on which Pagelle, the tailor of the *Traits Galants*, threw *blonds* of silver lace, *barrières of chicoré* caught and held up with jasmine, little bouquets tied with little knots in hollows of embroidered festoons, bracelets, pompons—all the prodigious embellishments that brought a dress to the price of 10,500 livres and made Madame de Matignon to pay her tailor a life-time annuity of 600 pounds for one.[1]

Appropriately, the men were only slightly less fashionable. In 1751, Marquis d'Argenson complained that the expense of new coats ordered by the King for *fête* days had ruined two courtiers. Although men's apparel became somewhat less complicated at the end of the century, pages' coats could still command 1,500 livres in 1786. Words can only begin to describe what gentlemen's waistcoats were like—cream satin, chain stitch embroidery in pastel-colored silks, pounced and painted Indian cotton, or black satin with blue glass ornaments. Moreau's fashion plate,

[1] E. and J. Goncourt, *The Woman of the Eighteenth Century*, Le Clercq and Roeder trans. (New York, 1927), p. 220. See also, H. J. Baudrillart, *Histoire du luxe privé et public depuis l'antiquité jusqu'à nos jours* (Paris, 1878–80). Given the state of dry cleaning at the time, how many of these dresses were necessary in the wardrobe of a lady *à la mode*?

"La Grande Toilette" (1777), gives some idea of the nobleman in full dress complete with ribbon diagonally across the waistcoat, two fobs dangling from the breeches, sword and hat ready to stroll with his lady companion, also in superb walking attire.[2] To those clients who were tactless enough to mention price, an artist-tailor might justly reply, "Is Vernet paid simply for his canvas and paints?"[3]

The conversion of Marie Antoinette from simple muslin to *haute couture* after 1774 surely forced the competitive pace at court. The rise of the specialist, represented by the Queen's dressmaker Rose Bertin and the royal hairdresser Léonard, made the reign of Louis XVI the heyday of elaborate apparel. Nor was such sumptuous finery limited to the immediate circle of the Queen. It was a Parisian phenomenon, even a national distinction. Manuals were written about fashion. The "Treatise on the Principles of Women's Hairdressing," comprising 39 volumes and 3,744 identifiable hair fashions, was a classic of its kind. The *Monument du Costume* by Jean-Michel Moreau the younger is still a standard work of reference; its plates, a vision of beauty. The periodical of fashion, *Galérie des Modes*, was to follow. Even as intelligent and serious a woman as Madame de Genlis could expend considerable conversation on the latest in hoop petticoats and the proper adjustment of the bustle.[4]

The extreme elaboration of female attire did not end with dress, underwear, and coiffure, however intricate they might be. It extended to a host of accessories for both men and women that were the pride of the luxury trade. Jewelry in profusion to be sure, but also watches, watch fobs, fans, buttons "in gilding and silvering," snuff boxes, bonbon boxes, dancing-program boxes. Containers of all kinds, engraved exquisitely with heraldry, filligree, or weeping willows on classic columns were the rage. Recall that the gentleman's snuff box and lady's *étui* were as indispensable to polite society in the eighteenth century as the cigarette lighter is in the twentieth. From intimate supper to fancy dress ball, from *thé à*

---

[2] M. Davenport, *The Book of Costume* (New York, 1956), pp. 695–99.

[3] Goncourt, *The Woman of the 18th Century*, p. 226.

[4] Davenport, *Costume*, pp. 657, 688, 693–95. The reproductions of Moreau's plates recapture late eighteenth-century elegance in all its artifice and complexity. See also N. Waugh, *Corsets and Crinolines: A History of Women's Underwear* (London, 1954), 67–68; and André Blum, *Les modes au XVIIe et XVIIIe siècles* (Paris, 1928). Diderot's *Encyclopédie* defines technical terms and clarifies some of the complexities of women's dress. See, for example, *"Tailleur de Corps"* and the self-inflicted torture of the "half-boned stay."

l'Anglaise to *Jeu de Roi*, the *grande dame* and her escort required the proper ensemble for each social occasion.

In Paris, shopping was much more than a means to elegance. It was itself a diversion, a promenade, a setting for display.

> The "Merchant's Dream" is no more; we shop at the Palais-Royal. It is not at the "Ottoman's Loss," his very name has perished, but at the "Descent of the Pont Neuf," at the "Petit Dunkerque," at the "Petit" as it is known for short, that the fashionable flâneurs alight to linger a couple of hours agreeably over some petty futility.[5]

Elaboration in dress went hand in hand with an enlarged field of amusements. Theatre, suppers, promenades, balls, and firework displays were not new, nor was the elaborate game of love. The latter was no intermittent, shameful activity judging by the first fifty pages of Lauzun's *Mémoires*. But if the duke's conquests be ascribed to what a contemporary called his "chivalric imagination," he was not unique. One of the suitors of Madame de Genlis disguised himself as a beggar on the streets of Paris so that he could follow her everywhere.[6] More novel was the fashion for "true friendship" between women. Hours might now be spent in intimate conversation; Madame de Genlis would chat with her lady friends from eight in the evening until one in the morning.[7] For other spare hours, an array of newer diversions appeared—the passion for pets, the craze for puppets, the addiction to raveling and unraveling (the "mode of knots"), play-acting at home, and dabbling in philosophy, literature, and science. And "science" was an elastic word in the late century.

Mesmerism, pseudo-science, fortune-telling, outright sorcery were a welcome relief to the bored, the hysterical, the credulous.[8] The Prince de Ligne described his efforts to conform to this social prescription.

> In vain I passed whole nights at the house of the old Countess de Silly in the Faubourg Saint-Marceau where she saw spirits, or said she did, in my presence; in vain a certain Chavigny worked over me; and a man named Beauregard, on the night between Holy Thursday and Good Friday, per-

[5] Goncourt, *The Woman of the 18th Century*, p. 76.

[6] Comtesse de Genlis, *Mémoires*, ed. F. Barrière (Paris, 1857), pp. 95n, 126. Unless otherwise indicated, this edition is used throughout.

[7] *Ibid.*, p. 85.

[8] R. Darnton, *Mesmerism and the End of the Enlightenment in France* (Cambridge, Mass., 1968), ch. I.

formed the most horrible conjurations and tricks around me and the Ducs d'Orléans and Fitz-James. The latter in signing his name upset the inkstand over our compact with the Devil, who, apparently furious at this lack of attention, refused to appear.[9]

The Prince went on to describe the appeal of Cagliostro, Mesmer, the "great Etteilla," and other visionaries who were the rage of the moment. Efforts to communicate with the dead did not end, of course, with the departure of fortune teller or healer. Princess de Guemenée, governess of the royal children, was reported in constant trances which none of her contemporaries considered peculiar.[10]

And what of gambling? Comte Dufort de Cheverny, who liked the company of marshals and lieutenant-generals like Mirepoix, Duras, Richelieu, and Tavanes, had this to say about it.

Already at *collège* I knew all the games of chance as well as I do now. This science was part of our education and all our recreation time was spent at *piquet, trictrac, quadrille,* or at *quinze.* We were so well prepared that, when we entered society, Comte de Chabot, Monseigneur Brienne, the four Flamarens, and Monseigneur de Toris with whom we gathered every day at Monsieur de Saint Sauveur's were all dispensed from this apprenticeship. It is rather curious that no one of us was a real gambler, while Marquis de Genlis, though he was at my *collège* but not in our set, and Monsieur de Sillery, his brother, have become the biggest gamblers in Paris even though they were unacquainted with it at *collège.*[11]

That Cheverny had not entirely abandoned the habit is suggested by his subsequent remark that he had lost about a hundred *louis* (2,300 livres) "on this trip." The more prosaic account book of Marquis de Castries, also Marshal of France, tells a similar story. Castries calculated not in livres but in solid gold *louis,* the mark of a Parisian aristocrat. Interspersed with expenditures for travel literature, the *comédie,* cases of champagne, and trips to Marly and Fontainebleau such items as "won at gaming—45 *louis*" or "lost at gaming—15 *louis*" appear regularly.[12] It is this routine, habitual gambling that tells us more about the pervasiveness of the "vice" (or social asset) than the famous gaming tables of the

[9] C.-J., Prince de Ligne, *Memoirs, Letters, Miscellaneous Papers,* trans. K. P. Wormley (London, 1899), I, 212–13.

[10] G. Maugras, *The Duc de Lauzun and the Court of Marie-Antoinette* (London, 1896), p. 43.

[11] Comte Dufort de Cheverny, *Mémoires* (Paris, 1909), I, 44–45.

[12] Bibliothèque Nationale, *Manuscrits français,* 11438.

King.[13] Of course, someone had to win. Baron de Vioménil was reputed a winner for over twenty years and there were others with unbeatable luck.[14] But the losses were sometimes extraordinary. At age twenty, Marquis de Genlis lost 500,000 livres in a single evening to the same Baron de Vioménil. After this escapade, the Marquis' uncle locked him in Saumur castle for five years—one year for each 100,000 livres, he said.[15]

Gambling was not restricted to the backgammon tables of select residences. By 1775, horse racing had made its mark with the royal family; Duc de Lauzun brought English horses across the channel and Duc d'Artois enticed the young queen with enormous wagers on the "Plaine de Sablons," the Longchamps of the late century. The medieval tournament had succumbed to cupidity, commented one contemporary. Comte de Genlis bet Duc de Chartres that he could make the trip from Paris to Fontainebleau and back in less time than it would take the Prince to prick 500,000 pinholes into paper.[16] No wonder Duc de Villeroi lost at least one coachman in his regular carriage race from Paris to Versailles in one hour and five minutes. As Comte Dufort put it, "*C'était un bon enfant, voilà tout.*"[17] Aside from certain puerile aspects, there was more insidious danger in the habit of small gestures and petty vanities. "It is not the grand passions which ruin us," wrote Madame de Genlis, "for their danger is obvious, and the well-born can triumph over them by a concentration of will; but one is less aware of the petty, puerile sentiments which have nothing vicious about them, and yet, little by little, come to dominate us and lead us astray."[18]

Lauzun, a good representative of the "Young Court," scoffed at the older court traditions, the vexations of etiquette, and clamored for a more open, free and pleasurable life, ranging from new modes of dress *à la Henri IV* to a commitment to Anglomania or revolution in North America. But new tastes and enthusiasms ceded nothing to that other form of pettiness usually called "bourgeois" or "provincial." One simply should not count by livres and sous. Lauzun complained that his wife

---

[13] Duc de Luynes, *Mémoires sur la cour de Louis XV (1735–58)* (Paris, 1860), XII, 26; VII, 31; Duc de Richelieu, *Mémoires*, ed. F. Barrière (Paris, 1868), III, 154.

[14] Dufort, *Mémoires*, I, 44–45.

[15] Genlis, *Mémoires*, 47–48.

[16] Maugras, *Lauzun and Marie-Antoinette*, 82–84.

[17] Dufort, *Mémoires*, I, 75.

[18] Genlis, *Mémoires*, 117.

had brought him only 150,000 in *rentes* and he wanted her to be "magnificent."[19] Madame de Genlis defined this term as a desire among *grands seigneurs* to possess luxurious horses and carriages, numerous servants, and perhaps most important of all, to provide theater loges, *hôtel* apartments, and open table to all their friends, with sufficient leavings for the poor at the main gate.[20]

Duc de Choiseul maintained such a magnificent style of life, especially after his exile to Chanteloup. He managed to spend through a Crozat dowry, a generous government pension, and sumptuous royal gifts within a few years. Nothing was spared on his guests; Chanteloup became a veritable Houghton Hall, with a wine cellar to match. A staff of 54 liveried servants in the main house, and a table constantly prepared for 35 to 50 place-settings, served Choiseul's company 4,000 chickens per year, 30 sheep per month, and 300 pounds of bread per day! Between dinners and suppers, there was daily deer-hunting in the duke's 6,000-acre forest along the Loire; there was billiards, *trictrac*, chess, a superb library, and a collection of engravings inside the château; and an extensive formal garden was dominated by a Chinese pagoda of prodigious height.[21] A substantial number of Parisian aristocrats understandably followed the duke into exile and were infected by his notions of noble hospitality. His style of life, he said, was not simply a matter of personal taste, but an accessory to his birth and dignity, an obligation for a man of his station. It prompted Voltaire to quip: "My God, give him the post of controller-general and he will pick the Treasury bare in two years!"[22]

The higher one went in the social scale, the more demanding the obligation of magnificence became. It seemed worth almost any price; indebtedness, even open bankruptcy were risked and socially accepted. Lauzun, with his customary casualness best expressed in the untranslatable "*désinvolture*," alluded to his considerable debts in 1780, which was "not very extraordinary." He had an obligation of 1,500,000 livres and a fortune of more than 4,000,000 livres. All would have gone well, he re-

[19] Duc de Lauzun (Biron-Gontaut), *Mémoires*, ed. F. Barrière (Paris, 1862), p. 150.
[20] Genlis, Comtesse de, *Memoirs*, 10 vols. (London, 1825), X, 340.
[21] G. Maugras, *La disgrâce du duc et de la duchesse de Choiseul* (Paris, 1903), pp. 108–24.
[22] G. Maugras, *Le duc et la duchesse de Choiseul* (Paris, 1924), pp. 126, 122; Dufort, *Mémoires*, I, 390–91; 417–18.

marked, had not some avaricious speculators bought out all the old creditors and threatened to send him to prison. Refusing all financial aid from his many well-placed friends, Lauzun sold his land to Prince de Guémenée and converted his entire fortune into a life-time annuity of 80,000 which would keep him in proper estate for the rest of his days.[23] But without direct descendants, Lauzun was somewhat peculiar. Bankruptcies could be weathered without depriving posterity of its patrimony. The Rohan-Guémenée survived perhaps the most famous family bankruptcy of the reign—33 millions deficit. It is not clear whether the *spectacles* of the Prince or the "representations" of the Princess precipitated the "crash." The Polignacs, who followed the Guémenée as official tutors of the royal children, were reputed as "ruined" two or three times. But this did not prevent them from purchasing the magnificent domain of Chambord, in order to raise horses. Both the Guémenée and the Polignac were sustained by powerful court connections.[24] For who could be more understanding in these matters than the Queen and her flamboyant brother-in-law, Duc d'Artois? Marie-Antoinette had a reputation for being "very attached to her friends."

Indeed, the Princes of the Blood set the worst example of all. Clermont, in debt for over a million, saved by the royal treasury; Conty, whose wife loved to spend even more than he, sustained in large part by the fortune of his mistress, Madame d'Artic; the house of Condé rescued by the death of the duke and the efforts of the trustee, Comte de Charolais.[25] The death of the older Duc d'Orléans exposed the young Duc de Chartres to imminent bankruptcy. An enterprising member of the Genlis family saved him by proposing that the duke build shops and galleries in the inner court of his Parisian townhouse, the *Palais-Royal*.[26] Comte de Toulouse, bastard son of Louis XIV, left nine millions in debt when he died in 1737. Thanks to the efforts of the financial manager of the estate, Abbé Salabery, the debt was substantially reduced and the revenues increased to almost a million livres per annum. But in 1743, the

[23] Lauzun, *Mémoires*, pp. 150–54.
[24] Dufort, *Mémoires*, I, 430. Baron de Besenval, *Mémoires* (Paris, 1821), II, 44–45. On the intervention of the government on behalf of the Rohan-Guéménée, see J. Flammermont, "Lettres inédites de Marie-Antoinette: La banqueroute Rohan-Guéménée," *La Revolution française*, XXXIV (1898), 140–47.
[25] Richelieu, *Mémoires*, II, 144–48. See note 28 below.
[26] Genlis, *Mémoires*, pp. 236–37.

young Duc de Penthièvre assumed direct control of his fortune; two years later the estate was again unable to meet obligations of 800,000 livres.[27] Looking back, Abbé Soulavie, author of the memoirs of Duc de Richelieu, had this to say about the Princes of the Blood:

> All the Princes were wont to scandalize the public by their libertine habits, and almost all of them have been the most brazen corrupters of the Nation. In order to reestablish the old morals, the legislators and administrators of the Empire had to choose from that class of citizens called the *petite bourgoisie* where decent morals can still be found.[28]

All of aristocratic society cannot be judged by the "follies" of the Princes or the "magnificence" of a Choiseul. Expenditure of money was one aspect, to be sure, but expenditure of time and energy on the "whirlpool" of Paris was perhaps even more pervasive. In those sobering years after the Revolution, many noblemen of the older generation looked back on the "false vanities" and "fragile grandeur" of Paris at the end of the Old Regime. But Talleyrand's famous *douceur de vivre* is probably more historical. There was no perception of Ségur's "abyss under the carpet of flowers" in 1788. Madame de Genlis, one of that old society's finer products, remembered well what we have since labeled "the eve of the Revolution."

> A few individuals in our society foresaw storm and trouble, but in general, a sense of security prevailed in abundance. Duc d'Orléans and M. de Lauzun were with me one evening during the sessions of the Assembly of Notables. I said that I hoped the Assembly would reform a number of abuses. M. le Duc d'Orléans said that it would not even end the *lettres de cachet*.

Lauzun disagreed. Typically, they bet fifty *louis* on the question, Madame de Genlis keeping the written wager in her possession.

> I showed this wager to more than fifty people, and the ideas of M. le Duc were those of almost everyone. They regarded the idea of revolution as

---

[27] Luynes, *Mémoires*, VI, 253–55. On noble debts at Paris, see H. Carré, *La noblesse de France* (Paris, 1920), pp. 56–92.

[28] Richelieu, *Mémoires*, II, 146. Since the duke died in 1788, this is undoubtedly the comment of Abbé Soulavie, who was vicar-general of the diocese of Châlons when the Revolution broke out. Although it has been established that Richelieu transferred his personal papers to Soulavie, the memoirs were written by the abbé, later priest in the constitutional church. This authorship explains the moral tone of the memoirs as well as the controversy over their authenticity. See G. P. Gooch, *Louis XV: the Monarchy in Decline* (London, 1956), p. 279.

impossible. This sense of security had a disastrous effect; it kept us from taking measures that would have prevented it.[29]

Let there be no mistake about it. The cream of the old society—from the *Gens de la Cour* to more modest army officers—loved the world on the Seine. With all their affectation of blasé disdain, there was no other. For them, it was permanent and authentic. When Mademoiselle de Lespinasse described her day—dinner with Madame de Boufflers, social calls in the Faubourg Saint-Honoré, "Henry IV" at the Comédie-Française, the loge "on the Queen's side"—she seemed supremely happy, in her own words, a day "marvellously arranged."[30] It was the same for Genlis.[31] Or perhaps the outcry of the "exiled" army officer captures best the lure of Paris:

> I would rather kill myself than live in the provinces. I cannot find a single soul, a single wit to my liking. You, and all that is around you, have spoiled me for life.[32]

It would be wrong to characterize this high society simply as whirl of pleasure and frivolity. The puerilities, the inflexible etiquette, the apparently compulsive comings-and-goings—*visites, soupers, promenades*—imperceptibly merged into a more serious salon life, ranging, to be sure, from the lighter tone of Madame de Luxembourg or Madame du Deffand to the intellectual stimulus of Madame Geoffrin or Mademoiselle de Lespinasse. For the great attraction of Paris was not only the setting for magnificence, the opportunities to indulge one's tastes for the "finer things" that luxury industry could provide, but also the sense of being near the center of a civilization. Many of this privileged society merely went through the outward forms of urbane living, but there were others who pierced the surface to develop *esprit, goût, bon ton*, and even to think critically and imaginatively. It was the combination of *visites* and the Comédie-Française, of *soupers* and the latest novel, of château garden promenades and talks with English guests that made the capital all

---

[29] Genlis, *Mémoires*, p. 220.

[30] *Correspondance entre Mademoiselle de Lespinasse et le Comte de Guibert*, ed. Comte de Villeneuve-Guibert (Paris, 1906), pp. 245–46 (Lespinasse to Guibert, November, 1774).

[31] Genlis, *Mémoires*, p. 84. "I spent the winter in rather extensive dissipation." To be sure, the word carried less unfavorable connotations then.

[32] Lespinasse, *Correspondance*, p. 146 (Guibert to Lespinasse, September 9, 1774).

the more captivating. As Mademoiselle de Lespinasse wrote to Comte de Guibert, who was lamenting his exile in Quercy:

> We can say about the habit of living with people of *esprit* and merit what La Rochefoucauld said about the Court: it does not make us happy, and it prevents us from finding happiness elsewhere.[33]

But whether predominantly frivolous or serious, there was little place for the petty bourgois virtues to which Abbé Soulavie alluded. How unfortunate it was that Comte de Crillon was constantly occupied with business matters! It was, said Mademoiselle de Lespinasse, "a kind of occupation which results in more profit than glory."[34]

*

Aglaé-Marie-Louise de Choiseul-Gouffier was only fourteen when she married the son of Duc de Saulx-Tavanes in 1786. At this young age, she could be excused for a somewhat superficial view of her new father-in-law. She remembered him in her memoirs as a man of noble and generous sentiments, sincerely loyal to the Queen, though not a member of her intimate circle. Although he had been part of the royal court since youth, she said, the duke did not share the ideas of most courtiers. "I remember his saying that the office of *chevalier d'honneur* pleased him especially because it entailed no pecuniary advantage, and when the National Assembly ordered the publication of the Red Book recording all the secret pensions of the court, he laughed with complete indifference, confident, he said, that his name would not appear in it."[35] In fact, as his accounts show, the office returned the duke exactly 10,380 livres in 1786, after taxes.[36] Needless to add, the duke's correspondence with his estate agents exposes another side to the man. But to anyone who knew the duke in Paris, his "indifference to pecuniary advantage" seemed amply demonstrated.

That the duke, like his forebears, was quite capable of crying for strict economy from his agents in Burgundy while spending lavishly in Paris needs no comment. "Economy" was no religious fetish to Tavanes,

[33] *Ibid.*, p. 166 (Lespinasse to Guibert, September 23, 1774).

[34] *Ibid.*, pp. 203–4 (Lespinasse to Guibert, October 14, 1774).

[35] Duchesse de Saulx-Tavanes, *Mémoires 1791–1806*, ed. Marquis de Valous (Paris, 1934), p. 30.

[36] *A. D.*, E–1712.

but a necessary means to maintain his status in the capital. A lavish spender he was. Gaston Roupnel was right to characterize the Tavanes papers at Dijon as one mass of bills and debts.[37] And if these bundles of bills are any indication, spending for conspicuous display had increased after 1770.

The amount of time and money the duke and duchess spent frequenting those delightful shops along the Rue Saint-Honoré, Saint-Denis, or Richelieu was appreciable. The printed headings on the duke's bills give some of the flavor and attraction of such *traiteurs, fournisseurs,* and *marchands de modes*:

> *Magazin de toutes sortes de Marchandises de Fantasies les plus Nouvelles et le plus à la Mode. Rue de Richelieu, No. 13.*[38]

Judging by the frequency of the bills, the duchess was particularly fond of Bourjot's, though she hardly limited herself to a single shop.

> At the Silver Lion. Rue St. Denis near l'Apport Paris.
> Bourjot, merchant, selling all kinds of cloth, rich in gold and silver; embroidered, sown, and stitched in silk or velvet; taffetas of all styles; all kinds of cloth for furnishing or for the ladies and gentlemen.[39]

In 1771, the year before her separation from Charles-François-Casimir, Madame de Tavanes spent 3,804 livres for fabrics of this quality. The bill from Bourjot's was 4,063 livres the year before. The count was little more restrained in his personal dress. Between April and June of 1770, he spent 2,369 livres at Alexander's. The purchases included a dress suit, a coat, and a small wig (*en bouffant en blonde fine*) for 300 livres, plus ribbons, lace, cuffs and other sundries.[40]

Tavanes and his wife also had a great love of silverware, jewelry, crystal, porcelain, and other precious products of French craftsmanship, sold under signboards marked *Orfèvrerie* and *Bijouterie.* Gold spoons, silver

---

[37] G. Roupnel, *La ville et la campagne au XVIIe siècle: étude sur les populations du pays Dijonnais* (Paris, 1955), p. 314. Roupnel's cursory treatment of the Tavanes' accounts is misleading, however; Roupnel is too quick to separate the nobles of the Court from those of the robe in matters of estate administration. *Ibid.*, pp. 236–37, 322–23, and *passim*.

[38] *A. D.*, E–1728. Bundles E–1713, 1714, 1717, and 1720 bulge with receipts and bills for the 1780s. They are not classified.

[39] *A. D.*, E–1698. This is still another bundle of bills for the 1760s and 1770s.

[40] *Ibid.*

coffee services, an exquisite pair of earrings inlaid with precious stones (6,500 livres), and a mechanical watch and chain studded with jewels (5,900 livres) give some idea of the duke's taste. These last two purchases alone were worth more than his mother's entire jewelry collection, and the Tessés were notoriously rich.[41] In fact, the duke revealed increased interest in expensive gifts in the 1780s. The more traditional male accoutrements—walking canes with ball tops, decorated steel rapiers, ivory pen knives, or engraved snuff boxes—like those owned by his father, would not do.[42] He developed a weakness for mechanical dolls and cosmetic cases, gifts he showered on his new daughter-in-law, the fourteen-year old Aglaé-Marie-Louise de Choiseul-Gouffier. His wedding gift to her was a masterpiece of compact value; a rouge-box, pencil, scissors, knife, sewing set of silver and gold, all placed in a small chest of acajou wood. It cost 14,889 livres.[43]

Between 1784 and 1787, all three of the duke's children married. On these three occasions the duke spared no expense. For his son, in addition to a 20,000-livre pension and a cavalry company worth 5,000 livres more, the duke spent over 4,000 livres on new clothes and 700 livres on the ceremony itself, including 96 livres for the parish poor. In addition to his daughters' dowries, set at 200,000 livres each, Tavanes borrowed 30,000 livres for their trousseaus.[44] The new Comtesse de Kercado must have been splendid indeed. Bland receipts cannot begin to describe the richness of color and finery, from the *gaze d'Italie* to *velours frisés* and *satin rayé*.[45] For the tailors and shopkeepers who served the Tavanes family in these years, there were profits to be made. And let it not be said that clothes, jewelry, and other accessories were an inconsequential expense for a Parisian nobleman.

In the 1780s the Tavanes lived in a solid townhouse on the Rue du Bac, having left the Rue St. Dominique in the St. Sulpice quarter for something more suitable. They rented the house for 6,000 livres per annum, an outlandish rent by provincial standards, but not exaggerated for a good Paris address. The accounts of 1786 allude to recent additions and embellishments. In 1783, the duke laid new parquet flooring, and a

[41] *A. D.*, E–1720; E–1699, Inventory, 1784.
[42] *A. D.*, E–1699.
[43] *A. D.*, E–1720.
[44] *A. D.*, E–1717, *Detail*, 1788.
[45] *A. D.*, E–1714.

year later he built a library. Curiously, he sold his father's library of some 400 books the same year, including the works of his learned ancestor, Chancellor Daguesseau. A few years later, he paid to have a number of his books rebound, including some volumes on natural history and travel, and a one-volume seigneurial rent register—*terrier perpetuel.* One suspects that the decorative function of the library was worth more to the duke than its intellectual content. He paid equal attention to the redecoration of his bedroom and dressing room, especially the painting of the two shepherdesses, presumably of marble. But these do not seem to have been heavy expenses. Carpenters were cheap, and it cost the duke more to repair and polish his watches and snuff boxes in 1788 than it did to redecorate his townhouse. Heating such a house was something else. The August wood supply—no doubt for the winter of 1787–88—cost 2,835 livres. The duke could well appreciate the high cost of this commodity, since a substantial part of his revenues depended on it.[46]

What about other household expenses? The duke of course ate very well. The basic annual food budget was in the neighborhood of 5,000 livres. To this must be added the produce of specialty shops along the Rue St. Honoré. Here is a sample of purchases in January 1784:[47]

Turkey with truffles	21 livres
Chicken Patties of Rouen	6
Sauerkraut of Strasbourg	10
Olives of Marseilles	6
Rocquefort Cheese (in pot)	32
Anchovies in Oil	30
Spiced Bread of Rheims	20
Prunes of Tour	20
Levant Rice	12
Rhum from Jamaica	6
Brandy from Dantzig	9
Cognac	30
Muscat Wine from Toulon	3
Malaga Wine	3
Rhine Wine	5
Bordeaux Wine	3
Mocha Coffee	3
Cayenne Coffee	30

[46] *A. D.*, E–1699; E–1714; E–1713.
[47] *A. D.*, E–1712.

121

Although the household consumed less wine than Walpole's Houghton Hall, Tavanes kept a respectable *cave*. His main stock was Beaune and Médoc in 240-bottle lots supplemented by several hundred bottles of assorted wines ranging from white Champagne and Malaga to a few more exotic labels—Smirna, Cyprus, Montliban, Tokai, Noyau brandy and a Crème de Barbade. Yet the cost was not excessive. A cask of Médoc ordered from Bordeaux in December 1787 cost only 376 livres plus 2 per cent commission. The entire cellar was estimated at less than 1,000 livres in 1784. When the duke reduced the annual pension of his daughter because she lived with him, the 4,000 livres allotted for her maintenance was certainly more than ample.

What of the stables? The fact that the duke was officially attached to the royal stables does not mean that he had any particular interest in horses. His own stables were modest. Seven horses were sufficient for the carriages and cost about 1,400 livres a year to feed. Forage was expensive by the 1780s. The duke had seven carriages of various ages and sizes, including a large green English coach with silk draperies and a large "S-T" on the trains, another berline for the country, two diligences, two smaller phaetons, and a cabriolet. A new diligence cost 3,200 livres; a good horse, 1,000 livres; and new harness, 450 livres. Apparently, only two or three of these conveyances were used. The others were simply left in the stables, having almost no resale value. The coaches were kept in working order, polished and cleaned, under yearly contract for 540 livres. Altogether, expenditure for equipage was not excessive.[48]

If wages for carpenters and stable masters were modest, the salaries for domestics would surely be less. In the provinces, servants' wages rarely exceeded 200 livres and were almost always in arrears. It was considered sufficient for a servant to be housed, fed, and kept in livery. Moreover, except for the richest provincial families, four or five servants in the townhouse were usually adequate. But Paris standards were different, though still short of those set by English lords. The Paris household of the duke's father included fifteen servants at the following wages:

The Paris Household of the Saulx-Tavanes, 1786

Colmach (*Maître d'Hotel*)	600 livres
Poisson, Cook	945
Fauveau, Coachman	720

[48] *A. D.*, E–1713 to E–1719; E–1728; E–1699.

Frotté, *Suisse*	660
Henriot, Footman	432
Le Sans, Footman	432
Georges, Coachman	300
Duru, Cook's Assistant	612
Joly	360
Laveu	300
Duset	800
Fountaine, Valet	?
Desforges	?
Robert	?
Silvy	?
Total:	6,161 livres (minimum)

SOURCE: *A. D.*, E–1712, Legacies.

In contrast to provincial custom, these wages were paid promptly. Qualified domestics were probably harder to come by in the capital. Moreover, a break with family practice by the duke's father made the burden greater. Small legacies, usually a year's wages, were not unheard of in the provinces, but never legacies ranging from 1,200 to 6,000 livres. No doubt, the seventy-year-old count thought this fitting. His son, the duke, seemed less enthusiastic, for he converted most of the legacies into life-annuities at eight to ten per cent. Still, this represented an annual charge of about 4,000 livres, and many of the recipients had twenty years to live. The duke kept the younger ones on, but the obligations were there too.

What other expenses did the duke have? He reserved loges at the Comédie-Française and the Royal Academy of Music for the season for 1,625 livres. If other social obligations cost as much, the duke's amusements would have been a heavy burden. But judging from the bills, entertainment, excluding household provisions, does not appear high. Of course, it is quite possible that the duke did not record his gambling losses (or gains) like Marquis de Castries. What about his obligations at Versailles? Whatever else can be said about the court, it did not have to cost the courtier very much, apart from his attire. Apartments at Versailles were paid for out of the budget of the royal household and provisions of wood, oil, candles, and food could be had for less than 1,000 livres per month. Aside from the prescribed tips for each lackey or stable-boy, the opportunities for large spending were limited, strange as

123

this may seem at the pinnacle of high society. To be sure, one must make place for *trictrac* and *fara*; the Queen's gaming tables may account for the failure of the duke to live within Godard's 60,000-livre budget for personal expenses.

Education costs were almost negligible. Before her marriage, the future Comtesse de Kercado lived in a convent school for less than 500 livres per annum. Her piano lessons cost only 36 livres monthly. Medical care, such as it was, was equally cheap. The quaint medicines consumed by the duke's father before he died in 1784 cost 661 livres for an eleven months' supply.[49] But if teachers and doctors could be had for small sums, it was not the same for lawyers.

Tavanes had more than the usual family litigation in the 1780s. First, there was the considerable expense entailed by the elevation of the Burgundian property into a duchy—at least 25,000 livres in 1786 and 1787. Then there were the law cases over the *droit d'indire* and the new *terriers*. Equally important, though more difficult to estimate precisely, were legal expenses relating to inheritances. A great noble family like the Tavanes expended considerable energy on the arrangement of advantageous marriage alliances and the recuperation of legacies and inheritances. Not in vain had the Tavanes males married into wealthy robe families since the seventeenth century. But inheritances falling under the competences of various customary law codes required legal advice. Inventories had to be drawn up, settlement claims carefully established, mortgages and creditors classified. In the decade of the 1780s the first duke had more than his share of this kind of litigation. His wife's pension since their separation in 1772 never seemed to be enough; his father remarried at 70 and died at 71, leaving two legal tangles to unravel; his three children married. Moreover, his brother and nephew insisted that their paternal and maternal portions be paid. "Arrangements" with all of the ominous legal implications of the French expression had to be made.

In addition to the legal counsel of his agents—Godard and Billard were advocates—the duke employed at least two other lawyers in Paris. Monsieur Bro, family lawyer, negotiated with the creditors, occasionally liquidated debts, and more often arranged for new loans. Monsieur de Laune gave more technical legal advice to the duke, especially between

---

[49] *A. D.*, E–1717; E–1713; E–1710.

1782 and 1786. Here is a partial account, suggesting a considerable expenditure of time as well as money in the office of the advocate:

Consultation with M. de Laune	24 livres
Counsel regarding transactions on the second marriage	24
Drawing up 64 rolls	192
Counsel of the *terriers* of Lux	24
Examination of the extracts of all family acts	72
Consultation (five hours)	60

De Laune charged 12 livres an hour for his legal advice and presented a bill for 2,094 livres in April, 1786. Two months earlier, M. de Joigny presented his note for handling the inheritance of the duke's father; it was an additional 2,400 livres. The total legal costs for 1786 were 4,756 livres, not including the expense of the "duchy."[50] No wonder Tavanes was concerned about the threat of lawsuits from the villages of his Burgundian estate. He had enough legal expense in Paris.

Despite the fragmentary nature of the above expenditures, it is still possible to draw up an approximate annual budget for Duc de Saulx-Tavanes for the year 1788:

Personal Expenses of Duc de Saulx-Tavanes in 1788

Clothing, jewelry, gifts	20,000 livres
Townhouse (rent, repair, upkeep)	7,000
Heating	3,000
Food	6,000
Servants (including legacies)	10,000
Equipage (stables)	1,000
Versailles (three months?)	3,000
Legal fees	5,000
Education	1,000
Medicines	1,000
Theater	2,000
Charities (in Paris)	200
Taxes (in Paris)	2,800
	62,000 livres

SOURCE: This list is based on bundles of receipts and bills. There is no summary account available. *A. D.*, E–1713–20.

[50] *A. D.*, E–1712; E–1713; E–1721 (Billard accounts).

This list of expenditures suggests a great deal about what a Parisian nobleman considered important. A family budget, not unlike a national budget, establishes an order of priorities, a measure of consumer preference. Note the large proportion of total expenditure for outward display— 20,000 livres for clothing and accessories—almost one-third of the total spending for the year.[51] The maintenance of the household accounts for about one-half, including 10,000 livres for the servants.[52] By contrast, consider the small sums expended on education, medicine, or even theater, not to mention the negligible amounts set aside for regular charities. Possibly Tavanes distributed pocket-money to the ubiquitous Parisian beggars, sums not recorded on receipted bills.[53] As for other amusements, probably the most prevalent form of entertainment was the *souper* and the salon tea, so well documented by Horace Walpole and Madame du Deffand. These items would appear under household and food expenses. And food absorbed only about ten per cent of total expenses, a modest proportion by twentieth-century middle-class French standards. There is no evidence that Tavanes traveled, even though watering spas were already popular with the upper nobility. Taxes in Paris were light, about two per cent of revenue. If the two twentieth taxes paid in Burgundy and Normandy are included, the total tax burden was about six per cent of gross income.[54]

It has been argued that such conspicuous consumption has its economic advantages.[55] Heavy expenditures on luxury goods were certainly a boon to merchants and suppliers along the Rue de St. Honoré. Many a Pari-

[51] Jewelry might be considered more than an accessory to adornment; it is an investment or "hoard" of precious stones. Unfortunately, the bills are too scattered to present a meaningful breakdown. The jewelry of the duke's mother was valued at 5,000 livres in 1784.

[52] Legacies inflate this item by about 4,000 livres.

[53] Madame de Genlis remarked about the number of "poor" she had seen in one day's outing. She distributed her *"petite monnaie,"* about two *sous* to each beggar. Genlis, *Mémoires*, p. 126.

[54] Professor Behrens maintains that the French nobility was as heavily taxed as the English. Although the burden of the English land tax is far from established, it was certainly more than six per cent of gross income. See B. Behrens, "Nobles, Privileges, and Taxes in France at the End of the Ancien Régime," *Economic History Review*, Second Series, XV, No. 3 (1963), 451–75. The duke did not assume any of the taxes of the tenants by accepting lower rents.

[55] A. Lerner, *Everybody's Business* (East Lansing, 1961), p. 102 and *passim*, on "functional inequalities." See also W. Sombart, *Luxury and Capitalism* (Ann Arbor, 1967).

sian middleman might well regret the first emigration and look back on the Ancien Regime with some nostalgia. How much of this revenue "filtered" down to the producers of fine cloth (spinners, weavers, finishers) or to the handlers of luxury products (apprentices, *voituriers*, and barrel boys), not to omit coiffeurs, innkeepers, cooks, carriage makers, and stable boys? What we know about wages in these occupations does not suggest opulence, but without a luxury market, many of these individuals might have been unemployed or, at best, have inflated the ranks of agricultural labor. It is a fact that court aristocracy, with its outward disdain for the future and almost psychopathic need for display, did increase the savings-consumption ratio of which economists speak.[56]

The Tavanes "saved" nothing. They placed no fresh capital in land, *rentes*, or even in strong boxes. The family functioned like a sort of sponge, syphoning off public funds by sinecures, absorbing the capital of other families by marriage, and maximizing the revenues of the land at each new lease. This money was spent either on direct consumption or on portions and dowries that were in turn lavished on conspicuous expenditure. True, dowries were sometimes invested in land, when they were not used to pay old debts, but the land was promptly mortgaged to raise still more money for consumption. The Tavanes had absorbed more than one landed estate of the robe nobility, which served primarily to assure family creditors. And behind most robe fortunes was a maternal ancestor from the world of "finance" and perhaps even "commerce." In this manner, capital was drained from more than one social group, from more than one economic sector, to feed the appetite for luxury goods and services in the capital.

In a century that has some grasp of aggregate economic growth, one might well ponder the effects of this kind of demand on the allocation of resources and on the productive energies of the nation. Could the French economy in 1788, "afford" sewing sets at 14,000 livres or women's dresses at 10,000 livres? The Tavanes were draining their estates in Burgundy of every possible sou in order to spend profusely on luxury items in the capital. If a substantial portion had been reserved for reinvestment in the land, leading to an increase in food production, such conspicuous "waste" might have been tolerable. But a reinvestment rate of only four

[56] D. Landes, in M. M. Postan and H. J. Habakkuk, eds., *The Cambridge Economic History* (2nd ed., 1966), VI, Part i, 282.

per cent, including current repairs, was hardly enough. Had not Tavanes and his agents refused, because of the initial capital outlay, every proposal by the tenants that might lead to increased productivity? One does not have to make a moral case against luxury to establish the nefarious economic consequences of such an allocation of capital. Food production was deprived of the capital it urgently needed so that luxury trades could flourish.[57] Worse, members of the high aristocracy like Saulx-Tavanes imposed on the economy their own consumer tastes to the detriment of an industrial production more suitable to the consumption needs of the great mass of people.[58]

Maintaining an aristocratic style of life in Paris in the eighteenth century placed a greater strain on agriculture and manufacturing than is usually recognized. These economic consequences were much more important than the fact that this pattern of consumption left little for private charity. Furthermore, such "needs" encouraged a flagrant inequality of incomes that even the most tolerant society might call into question. Tavanes, far from the richest nobleman in Paris, had an income in 1788 between five and six hundred times the annual subsistence wage. He spent close to 80,000 livres a year on current expenses.

* *

Unfortunately, the duke's fixed obligations did not permit him this much current expenditure. In 1788, the interest obligations reached 120,689 livres, three-quarters of the income in that year. Indebtedness of this magnitude was not unknown to the Tavanes. A generation before, after the death of the duke's grandfather in 1761, the family underwent a severe financial crisis. They weathered the storm by the sale of a *seigneurie* and the timely division of the inheritance of the duke's mother,

---

[57] Even the food consumption of an aristocratic family tended to favor exotic delicacies and fine wines rather than vegetables and cereals. The physiological effects of such a diet on the working efficiency of the consumer are also worth investigation.

[58] See H. Luethy, *La banque protestante*, II, 21–25, for a discussion of aristocratic consumer habits. In a different context, C. E. Black writes: "A large investment in consumer goods will benefit the population but will reduce the productive capacity of the economy." Here the large investment in consumer goods by an elite of spenders would appear to do little for either sector of the economy. C. E. Black, *The Dynamics of Modernization* (New York, 1966), p. 19.

TABLE III.1   THE CHARGES ON THE HOUSE OF TAVANES

1763			1788		
Charges	Livres		Charges	Livres	
Perpetual *Rentes*	44,115		Perpetual *Rentes*	92,883	
Life Annuities	7,149		Life Annuities	11,864	
Interest on Capital	958		Notarized Bills	10,248	
			Private Signatures	5,694	
Total:	52,222		Total:	120,689	
Gross Revenue: (1754)	93,975		Gross Revenue:	165,504	
Paid at Dijon	8,984		Paid at Dijon	12,691	
Paid at Paris	43,238		Paid at Paris	107,998	
Family Charges	25,350		Family Charges	73,732	
Capital Repayable with Interest	19,278		Capital Repayable with Interest	319,840	
Capital Repayable without Interest	138,923				
(Approximately 33,000 to Dijon merchants and 12,000 to Paris merchants)			(Approximately 91,400 to Paris merchants)		

SOURCE: *A. D.*, E–1786 *Etat Général des dettes*, 1763; *A. D.*, E–1715 *Détail*, 1788.

heiress to the Tessé fortune. But in 1788, conditions were less favorable for reducing indebtedness. Let us compare family indebtedness in 1788 with the financial situation twenty-five years earlier (see Table III.1).

Notice that the margin between gross income and fixed obligations was about the same in both instances, between 40,000 and 45,000 livres. It was not a case of narrowing margin between income and interest charges. It was rather the greater difficulty of meeting current expenses with the same sum as in 1763. This was partly because the price of all consumer goods—and luxury goods—had risen over the time span of one genera-tion, but also because the duke found it necessary to spend more pro-fusely than his father or grandfather. This is indicated not only by the existing receipts, but also by intendant Godard's special review of family obligations in 1788. In this summary all the debts to Paris merchants date from 1770, contracted by either the duke or his wife. Over 50,000 livres of this capital was borrowed in 1786 and 1787 at the time of the marriage of the duke's children.

Even more important than the spurt of spending and wedding gifts, trousseaus, and the like were the terms under which the new loans were contracted. In 1788, a substantial amount of money was borrowed on notarized drafts (*obligations devant notaires*), with a stipulated time limit for repayment. Despite efforts to convert these drafts into perpetual *rentes*, eliminating the legal obligation to refund the capital, the duke was obliged to find ever larger sums of liquid capital to repay older drafts, many of which specified a one-year time limit. Equally striking was the difference regarding interest payments on such drafts. In 1763, almost all of these obligations were non-interest bearing, while in 1788 all the drafts explicitly stipulated an interest of five per cent, and in a few cases, six and seven per cent. The crisis of 1763 was apparently brought about by defaulting on interest payments on *rentes*; the crisis of 1788 was caused by increasing needs for cash to repay capital sums borrowed on short term.[59]

For example, before 1763 merchants and shopkeepers, whether at Paris or Dijon, did not charge any interest on Tavanes's mounting obligations.[60] But by the 1770s, explicit interest charges for this kind of obligation begin to appear and, by the 1780s, they are the rule. It is not likely that the duke frequented a more financially sophisticated type of shop or caterer than his father or grandfather had twenty-five years before. It is more likely that even small merchants were less and less inclined to extend credit to aristocrats like Tavanes interest-free. In 1787, Monsieur Normand, cloth merchant of the family for a number of years, submitted a statement for 10,641 livres "payable January 1, 1791 at six per cent."[61] In the same year, a master tailor made his bill for 10,777 livres "payable January 1, 1791," and specified on a separate note an interest of 777 livres, almost eight per cent.[62] The lawyers did the same. In 1789, Monsieur Roard, *procureur* at the Châtelet, lent Tavanes 20,000 livres, but withheld 1,000 livres interest in advance.[63] Clearly, the usury laws which prohibited any stipulated time limit for the repayment of capital as well as interest rates above five per cent were more or less openly flaunted. No doubt the money market was becoming tighter for everyone in these years of growing national financial crisis, but surely the Tavanes were

[59] For an excellent introduction to the problems of private finance in eighteenth-century France, see G. V. Taylor, "Types of Capitalism in Eighteenth-Century France," *English Historical Review* (July 1964), 468–97. See also A. R. Turgot, "*Mémoire sur les prêts d'argent*," *Oeuvres* (Paris, 1844), I, 119–20. The usury laws remained on the books, but business mores were changing, and in a manner less favorable to the debtor.

[60] *A. D.*, E–1687, Register of Debts, 1763.

[61] *A. D.*, E–1715, *Detail*, 1788.

[62] *Ibid.*

[63] *A. D.*, E–1717, Accounts, 1789.

an especially poor risk. More mature business practice was perhaps joined by less confidence either in the promises of the "Great" or, at least, in their unbounded capacity to pay.

As the table indicates, indebtedness to merchants or suppliers had doubled in twenty-five years. Yet these debts were not the most pressing obligations. They were dispersed among many creditors, and although individual debts often exceeded 10,000 livres, they were more easily converted into perpetual *rentes*. In the 1770s, the countess would buy "on credit" from Buffault, cloth merchants on the Rue Saint-Honoré, and eventually the count would "pass" a contract of "constituted rent" for the sum owed and pay five per cent annually.[64] More troublesome were obligations to financiers like the *fermier-général* Augerard. This loan combined all the worst features from the duke's point of view. It was for 21,000 livres, "interest included"; it was a draft by private signature (*billet sous seing privé*), renewable annually; it was subsequently converted into a notarized draft (*obligation devant notaire*). Much to be preferred were the two loans of Chalert, another *fermier-général*, for 65,000 livres in the form of "constituted perpetual *rentes*" at five per cent. Here the capital could not be demanded unless Tavanes defaulted on his five per cent for two consecutive years.[65] Apparently, the duke preferred to borrow from friends and private individuals rather than from "bankers." The register of debts for 1765 included a larger number of professional financiers such as Crozat (38,000 livres), Moras (30,000 livres), Fargès (30,000 livres), and Fortia (48,000 livres), in addition to at least three Dijon parlementarians—Bouhier (18,000 livres), Macheo de Premeaux (20,000 livres), and Charpy (38,000 livres).[66] In 1788 and 1789, there were fewer "bankers" among the seventy-two creditors of the Tavanes family. It may well be that professional bankers preferred safer investments. The history of the famous Rohan-Guémenée bankruptcy

[64] *A. D.*, E–1709, Bills of Comtesse de Tavanes.

[65] *A. D.*, E–1715, *Detail*, 1788. See R. J. Pothier, *Traité du contrat de constitution de rente* (Paris, 1763).

[66] *A. D.*, E–1686, Register of 1765; E–1698, Sequin and Billard Accounts; See H. Luethy, *La banque protestante en France* (Paris, 1960–61), II, 788–89. Abraham Peyrenc de Moras (1682–1732), was a *nouveau catholique*, and the brother of Fargès was *Trésorier, receveur, et payeur* of the Parlement of Dijon. See A. Colombet, *Les parlementaires bourguignons à la fin du XVIIIe siècle* (Dijon, 1937), pp. 75–77.

would suggest that the desperate borrower was forced to seek capital more frequently among the small creditors—*les petites gens*.[67]

In 1757, the family estate manager Seguin had suggested in the name of orderly accounting that the interest on all family obligations be paid on February first of each year. But the count's other financial advisors quickly cautioned that such a schedule would require too large a sum at one time. They advised paying at three- or six-month intervals from the date of the original contract and periodically renegotiating the schedule with individual creditors when money was short. This pragmatic, haphazard approach made it difficult for Seguin to estimate annual expenditure in advance, but it did give the Tavanes maneuverability.[68] A generation later, however, the intendant Godard seemed less able to echelon interest payments in this fashion. Creditors preferred January first and apparently had their way. Of course, the duke frequently renewed his drafts, extending them over several years, but he eventually had to pay, and often only by fresh borrowing.[69] Even the duke's own brother, who had lent him 45,000 livres by draft in 1780, would not be put off forever. Persistent, he was repaid in 1789, entirely in silver.[70]

Yet these adverse changes in the creditor-debtor relationship could have been circumvented, had it not been for the weight of the family charges (see Table III.2). Contrast the family obligations twenty-five years earlier: a son's annual pension of 24,000 livres, and only 1,350 livres interest due on the dowries of two daughters! This was quite a different situation, and since an eldest son's pension was the most easily deferred charge, the burden was certainly manageable, if not light.

What had altered the situation so radically by 1788? First, the generations had clustered, a direct result of encouraging young marriages.[71] The duke's children began to marry before the portions of his brother and sister had been liquidated. Indeed, it appears from the Rieux account that two generations of unpaid portions had accumulated. Second, the portions and dowries for the younger brothers and sisters were set con-

---

[67] *A. D.*, E-1715; E-1717. See Flammermont, ". . . La banqueroute Rohan-Guémenée," p. 144. The Prince carried a mass of small creditors down with him.

[68] *A. D.*, E-1688, Observations on the Account of M. Seguin, 1757.

[69] *A. D.*, E-1715.

[70] *A. D.*, E-1717. Vicomte de Tavanes promptly placed 21,000 livres in the Estates of Burgundy, a very poor investment in 1789 to say the least.

[71] L. Henry, and C. Lévy, "Ducs et pairs sous l'Ancien Régime," *Population* (1960), 807–830.

TABLE III.2   ANNUAL FAMILY CHARGES OF DUC DE SAULX–TAVANES IN 1788

Charges	Livres	Livres
Mme. la Duchesse, wife, interest on her dowry reimbursed after the separation of 1772		10,589
M. le Comte de Tavanes, son, assured income by his marriage contract		20,000
Mme. la Vicomtesse de Castellane, daughter, interest on her dowry		10,000
Mme. la Comtesse de Kercado, daughter, interest on her dowry		10,000
M. le Vicomte de Tavanes, brother:		
Interest on portion from mother's inheritance	3,080	
Interest on portion from father's inheritance	5,000	
		8,080
M. le Comte de Rieux, nephew:		
Interest on dowry of his mother, sister of duke	6,375	
Interest on loan to the duke, July 14, 1772	840	
Interest on loan to the duke, Feb. 22, 1788	925	
Incremental value on maternal inheritance	300	
Interest on his mother's portion of the inheritance of his maternal grandfather, father of the duke	3,082	
Interest on his mother's portion of the inheritance of his maternal grandmother, mother of the duke	3,541	
		15,063
Total Annual Family Charges		73,732

SOURCE: *A. D.*, E–1715, Godard Accounts, 1788.

siderably higher than they had been in the first half of the century, much higher than could be justified by an increase in income.[72] Some of this increase was made mandatory by the Norman customary law of inheritance which obliged the family to divide the Tessé fortune of the duke's mother almost equally.[73] But it is also clear that the duke wanted portions fixed at a very respectable round number, related more closely to those of other court families than to his own fortune. A duke could hardly dower a daughter for much less than 200,000 livres or fix a younger son's portion below 100,000 livres. Moreover, a *bonne alliance* could work both ways. To marry a daughter well placed one in the right company to marry an elder son. Had not the Tavanes followed a successful practice of attracting wealthy heiresses as daughters-in-law since 1600?

It was unfortunate that the duke himself had failed in this regard,

[72] See Genealogy, above.

[73] *A. D.*, E–1700. See briefs on the Tessé inheritance, especially the *Mémoire à consulter*, July 1766.

despite auspicious beginnings. At the age of twenty, he had been wedded to a Lévis-Chateaumorand, one of four daughters with a dowry of 400,000 livres and prospects of a substantial paternal inheritance.[74] A letter of the inimitable Madame du Deffand suggests an ominous combination of infidelity and hard-bargaining on the part of Comtesse de Tavanes twelve years after the marriage.

> One hears only about the adventure of Madame de Tavanes; no doubt you have heard about it. The separation is completed. She has 22,000 a year and will not have the care of the children. She will remain with Madame la Dauphine which displeases her husband a great deal. All of this has very much surprised me. I thought of her as a respectable woman (*une dame honeste*) and she is nothing of the sort.[75]

If the scandal was ephemeral, the financial blow to the duke was not. A valuable asset had been converted into a heavy mortgage made even worse by the spending habits of the duchess. The duke must have looked to the marriage of his own seventeen-year-old son to a Choiseul with hope that his own experience would not be repeated. The lavish gifts he showered on his daughter-in-law would surely be repaid in full.

There was one more aspect to this lottery of dowries, so critical to the financial history of aristocratic families. Although the Tavanes had not waited until their permanent establishment at Paris to contract marriages in the capital, their "alliances" in the latter part of the century seemed more ambitious. Consider the marriages of the younger children. In the 1730s the daughters had married into the Vienne and Desprez families, respectable families of the robe no doubt, but hardly heading the heraldic list of d'Hosier. It would not be seemly for such families to press a Saulx-Tavanes for the prompt payment of dowries. In the last third of the century, however, marriage alliances were contracted with the Feydeau de Brou, Castellane, Kercado, and Rieux, high robe and military nobility.[76] Such families were less reticent about money matters. The insistence of Comte de Rieux that every livre of his mother's portion be paid does not suggest a docile brother-in-law. The following letter captures some of the dryness of a financial agreement.

[74] *A. D.*, E–1707, Lévis Papers.

[75] Madame du Deffand, *Correspondance complète* (Paris, 1866), pp. 162–63 (Du Deffand to Duchesse de Choiseul, April 5, 1772). Madame du Deffand's shock was not to last; she was dining with Madame de Tavanes before long.

[76] Consult Genealogy, above.

I have just learned, my dear brother, that M. Le Boeuf, the notary, has absconded with the money which is supposed to come to us. It has considerably upset my affairs at this point and obliges me to ask you to send ... 2,500 livres of the 5,000 in reserve.... The money is necessary for the "establishment" of my son....[77]

The advice of the count's father on the form of payment is equally revealing. "As for the form of the contract ... it should not be a notarized bill (*un acte par devant notaire*)."[78] The Tavanes well knew that a notarized draft had to be paid promptly.

It was in January, 1789, that Godard presented his annual report of the previous year. It included the rather somber picture of indebtedness described above. But it also indicated a substantial rise in income over the year before. Regular revenues, after deductions for taxes and other estate expenses, including interest charges in Burgundy, appeared as follows (see Table III.3).

Despite the expenses of the *terriers* and the new duchy, Billard had sent more money from Dijon than ever: 15,000 more than the previous

TABLE III.3   GODARD RECEIPTS FOR 1788

Receipts from	Livres	Livres
Land in Burgundy (from Billard)	62,456	
Land in Normandy (from Poinant)	15,227	
Dîmes from the Calaisis	7,900	
Landed Income:		85,583
Pension from the Royal Treasury	15,000	
Commander of the Orders of the King	3,000	
Chevalier d'Honneur of the Queen	10,380	
Commander of the Château Taureau	9,900	
Lieutenant-General in Burgundy	900	
Appointments and Pensions:		39,180
Rentes on the Hôtel de Ville	6,276	
Rentes on the Marquis de Mirepoix	1,195	
Rentes on the Clergy of France	543	
Total Rentes:		8,021
Sale of Effects of M. de Saulx:		20,029
Total Revenue:		152,813

SOURCE: *A. D.*, E–1715.

[77] *A. D.*, E–1727, Rieux to Tavanes, August 14, 1780.
[78] *A. D.*, E–1727, Comte de Saulx to Comte de Tavanes, August 22, 1780.

year. The coming fiscal year would be even better. Godard predicted that the receipts for 1789 would increase by another 19,898 livres as new leases went into effect. If the duke could limit himself to 60,000 livres for personal "maintenance," the "administration" would be only 6,222 livres shy of meeting all annual obligations.[79]

In the meanwhile, however, substantial capital sums had to be raised in order to liquidate the drafts coming due. In the three years since January 1786, the duke borrowed 193,700 livres from ten new creditors, all by drafts with due dates occurring between 1789 and 1798.[80] Just as the rents and interest payments began to come into line, a torrent of new short-term loans increased the need for ready capital. The duke could not borrow fast enough to repay old debts. He had to sell land.

The decision to sell could not have been taken cavalierly. The prestige and security that only the land could bring were not easily parted with— even if it were but a small fraction of the total estate. A Lauzun who converted his land into life-annuities was an anomaly indeed. The duke's father had faced the same decision twenty-five years before. He ended by selling the *seigneurie* of Pailly in 1764. Pailly had been in Champagne, separated from the principal family domains in Burgundy, and governed by a customary law of inheritance less favorable to elder sons.[81] The same considerations applied to the Tavanes property in Lower Normandy. Furthermore, the Norman lands were a recent acquistion, part of a maternal inheritance in 1767.[82] It was easier to part with them than to sacrifice the patrimony in Burgundy with all of its memories of Gaspard de Saulx and Renaissance glory. The château-fort at Pailly had followed the fortress of Sully into the hands of some parvenue, bearing the elaborate and obvious titles of "new nobility." The Tavanes would not let Lux go the same way. The Norman lands it must be.

No effort was spared to sell at the best possible price. The land was sold in small lots of two to five acres at prices ranging from 400 to 1,000 livres per acre.[83] About half the price was paid immediately in coin and the balance over three to four years in fixed payments at five per cent. In

[79] *A. D.*, E–1715, *Detail*, 1788.
[80] *A. D.*, E–1712; E–1715; and E–1717.
[81] *A. D.*, E–1947 (Entail at Pailly); *A. D.*, E–1700, *Mémoire on Entails*, 1767; *A. D.*, E–2023 (sale of Pailly for 190,000 livres, thirty-two times the revenue).
[82] *A. D.*, E–1700, Tessé Inheritance.
[83] *A. D.*, *Calvados*, E–703 to E–708.

addition, the buyer had to pay a mutation fee (*lods et ventes*) of one-thirteenth the price of sale and a reception fee (*pot de vin*) at the time of transfer. Here is the Norman agent's report on these sales which began in July, 1789, and continued through December, 1791. Looking at this report, it would almost seem that no revolution had taken place. The duke simply put his land on the market slightly ahead of the National Assembly and apparently competed with the state on favorable terms.

TABLE III.4   PROCEEDS OF THE SALES IN NORMANDY

Date	Sale Price Livres	The 13th Livres	Pot de Vin Livres	Paid in Cash Livres	Sums Due Livres
1789	100,521	7,466	2,172	54,271	54,114
1790	69,986	5,722	1,729	35,067	34,515
1791	99,699	170	251	50,493	49,052
Total	270,206	13,358	4,152	139,831	137,681

SOURCE: *A. D., Calvados*, E–703.

Despite the famous decrees of August 4th, abolishing mutation fees, the "thirteenth" was paid into early 1791. Tavanes also retained a *cens*, to preserve his right of eminent domain and to remain seigneur. Domain land became *mouvances* in legal terminology. The duke also inserted the following clause in the contracts of sale:

> The *cens*, including *lods et ventes*, seizure, fines, and other rights ... will be redeemable if it is so decreed by the National Assembly and sanctioned by the King. But if these rights are destroyed and then reestablished, they will continue to be collected as in the past, notwithstanding any reimbursement that may have been made [to the seigneur] and without any restitution [by the seigneur]. This contract [of sale] will not be honored without this clause.[84]

The contract proceeded to specify that the buyer was to pay the *banalités*, *lods et ventes*, and other seigneurial obligations "like the other vassals." This is the kind of legal advice the duke received for his twelve livres an

---

[84] *Ibid.*, E–704, Contract of November 7, 1789. This was for the sale of about one acre (two *vergés*, Norman measure) to a "Sr. Renève." The sale price was 400 livres, plus 10 livres *pot de vin*, 34 livres, 3 sols for the "13th," and a *cens* of 2 deniers in perpetuity. Renève paid 210 livres *en espèce* and the 13th immediately, and agreed to pay the remaining 200 "without interest" on *Saint Michel* (September 28), 1790. It was more common to find an interest charge of five per cent in the abstracts of the contracts. See *ibid.*, E–708.

hour. The new buyers were reminded of the uncertainties of the times and advised not to redeem their seigneurial dues. The duke was apparently successful with this warning until early 1791. In March of that year the Châtelet court in Paris handed down a special ruling requiring Citizen Tavanes to declare "that he does not intend and has never intended to make use of any clauses in his contracts that might be contrary to the decrees of the National Assembly."[85] It was a curious situation indeed that required such a ruling. By this time, of course, the duke had collected over 13,000 livres in seigneurial rights, suppressed in principle twenty months before.

The financial results of this transaction were obvious and gratifying to the duke. The "Extraordinary Receipts" on Godard's account began to assume a new interest—54,000 livres from the Norman sales in 1789 and 58,000 in 1790. Tavanes was a step ahead of the sales of national property which no doubt added to his success. In 1789, a new category appeared on his books entitled "Reimbursements" of capital. Tavanes began to liquidate his drafts—45,000 livres in 1789, 46,512 livres in 1790.[86] Barring any new calamities, the duke had every reason to believe that bankruptcy had been avoided.

[85] *Ibid.*, E–707, Interpretive Act of March 16, 1791.
[86] *A. D.*, E–1717 (1789) and E–1719 (1790).

I V

REVOLUTION IN THE DUCHY OF
SAULX-TAVANES

*B*y January, 1789, reports of a severe winter in Burgundy reached the duke. He instructed his agents to distribute 600 livres among eleven parish priests to help "those on his lands hurt by the rigor of winter and the high cost of grain."[1] In the same month he donated another 300 livres to the poor of St. Sulpice in Paris.[2] These were the largest sums the duke had ever contributed to charity. Besides occasional gifts to the parish poor—at the time of his son's marriage, for example—the family accounts allude to only two regular charities. One was a foundation paying 36 livres annually for the poor at Beaumont and another paying 30 livres per year to help support a student at the Royal School of Design at Paris.[3] Given this background, local agents and priests had apparently impressed the duke with the seriousness of rural distress in early 1789.

There is no mention of the Great Fear in the duke's papers. It appears that peasant violence in the summer of 1789 passed the Tavanes properties, though the reverberations were very close indeed. Dijon stood at the outer reaches of the peasant risings in Champagne to the north and in Franche-Comté to the east. Arthur Young's encounter with two seigneurs in the provincial capital in July was not reassuring. They reported that three out of five châteaux along the road from Langres to Gray had been pillaged. Gray, the iron port on the Saône River, was only ten miles east

---

[1] *A. D.*, E–1723, Duboy Accounts, January, 1789.

[2] *A. D.*, E–1716, Curé of Saint-Sulpice to M. le Duc, January 10, 1789.

[3] *A. D.*, E–1719, Godard Accounts, 1790; *A. D.*, Q–8762, *Oeuvres de Bienfaisance*, 1792–An II, Beaumont.

of the duke's estate along the Vingeanne. Panic actually reached Chazeuil where the duke possessed seigneurial rights and *dîmes*, but his properties were spared. The *milice* at Gray and a detachment from Dijon helped keep order in the local countryside, despite riots at Auxonne and Saint Jean-de-Losne less than fifteen miles down the Saône from the new "Duchy of Saulx-Tavanes." If the peasant uprising that summer had frightened Tavanes, there was no change in the administration of his estate to indicate it.[4]

In brief, there was nothing cataclysmic about the year 1789 for the duke in Paris. In 1790, his correspondence with his new general manager, Jacques Fénéon, suggests little change from two years before. The lease for the forge and wood at Tilchâtel was signed with a new tenant on schedule for 30,000 livres per annum, 12,000 livres in advance. Fénéon began submitting monthly accounts on a new form which he insisted was considerably better than his predecessor's. Billard had collected some 58,000 livres before the summer of 1789, and Fénéon collected the rest by the end of the year. In fact, the duke received as much rent from his lands in Burgundy in 1789 as he had the preceding year—61,510 livres— and his rents for Normandy even rose by 5,000.[5] If there had been diffi- culty collecting seigneurial dues from the peasants and small holders, the principal tenants shouldered that task. In any case, prices had been good; the duke's *dîmes* were approaching an all-time high.[6] True, the financial plight of the government was reflected in delayed payment of royal pen- sions. In 1789, revenues from the duke's pensions fell from 40,000 to 20,000 livres. But in 1790, the treasury was not only able to remit the regular pensions but even pay the arrears for 1788. Even the *rentes* on the Clergy of France were paid for 1790. In March, 1791, the duke closed his annual account with Godard with a revenue (uninflated by new loans) of 231,038 livres, the highest sum ever attained.[7]

It was not until 1791 that the duke began to encounter serious difficul- ties, not all at once, but in gradual, irritating stages. First of all, taxes had risen. In 1788, he had paid only six per cent of his total revenue for

---

[4] G. Lefebvre, *La grande peur* (Paris, 1932), pp. 125–26, 155, 221–22, 206.

[5] *A. D.*, E–1721; *A. D.*, E–1724; *A. D.*, E–1717; *A. D.*, E–1725, Fénéon Correspond- ence, 1791.

[6] The *dîmes* from the region of Calais rose from 7,900 livres in 1788 to 8,800 livres in 1789, and to 12,700 livres in 1790. *A. D.*, E–1715, E–1717, and E–1719.

[7] *A. D.*, E–1717 and E–1719.

taxes. Although the twentieth taxes (*vingtièmes*) in 1788 were supposed to claim eleven per cent of the revenues established by the leases, the duke pared his assessment down to half this rate. In 1789, however, the new government made a fresh assessment of the land, based on acreages and subleases. The dreaded new *cadastre* had come at last. Revenue estimates jumped about 25 per cent. The government then established the tax rate at ten per cent of the income, no higher than the two *vingtièmes*, but with the full intent to grant no privileges. And in this instance the central government moved quickly. Tavanes was paying increased taxes for the last half of 1789. In 1790, the new *contribution foncière* was operating efficiently, and the duke paid over 12,000 livres in direct taxes.[8] The year 1791 was much worse. The government raised the rate on the "former privileged" to 7 sous 9 deniers per livre-revenue and collected over 10,000 livres on Tavanes's Burgundian properties alone.[9]

TABLE IV.1   ROYAL TAXES IN 1788

	Tax Livres	Revenues Livres
Vingtièmes:		
Burgundy	4,978	89,269
Normandy	1,231	27,173
Capitation:		
Paris	2,751	36,371
Servants	52	
Total	9,012	152,813

SOURCE: *A. D.*, E–1715; *A. D.*, E–1721; *A. D. Calvados*, E–711.

Fénéon did his best to keep the duke's taxes down. He protested that the duke had been overcharged at Bourberain in 1790 and supported his case with figures on acreage and revenues based in part on his own survey of 1782 and 1783 for the *terriers*. As usual, he was thorough and precise. He calculated the total revenues of the community at 48,980 livres, and the duke's share at 17,852 livres, including his *champarts*. Based on this ratio, the duke should have paid 2,032 and not 3,498 livres. More-

---

[8] The tax returns for this period are unfortunately incomplete. The land tax at Arc-sur-Tille was 2,543 livres; the lease was 23,000 livres. This is over ten per cent. *A. D.*, E–1744, *Impositions*, 1790. See also *A. D.*, E–1725, *Impositions*, 1789; *A. D.*, E–1719, *Contribution Patriotique* of 3,333 livres, 1790; and *A. D. Calvados*, E–710.

[9] *A. D.*, E–1878, *Impositions*, 1791; *A. D.*, E–1726, Fénéon Accounts.

over, argued the agent, even this smaller amount should be apportioned as follows:

1) for M. le Duc for all his taxes .... 1,001 livres
2) for Sr. Bureau, his wood merchant 655
3) for Sr. Paris, his tenant 376

Total   2,032 livres

Taxes at Bourberain, observed Fénéon, had risen by 2,434 livres, almost double the amount levied in 1789. Yet the duke alone had absorbed the entire amount. "Not one village *habitant* has suffered from this increase. On the contrary, his taxes have diminished, proving the injustice of the new apportionment."[10] Neither the local villagers nor the new tax officials drew the same conclusions. The full impact of the disappearance of the *Commission Intermédiaire* of the Provincial Estates, which had apportioned village taxes before 1789, was now becoming clear to the duke and his agent.

Still, the duke and his chief agent hoped that all this was a temporary dislocation. Fénéon wrote from Dijon in February, 1791, that the price of wood had fallen, but that if the duke could wait until the following year, he was sure that the trade would have revived by then. Wood consumption at Dijon had dropped because "all the rich families had evacuated the city." The seigneurial toll at Tilchâtel had been suppressed, and payment had stopped on the pension from the duke's lieutenant-generalcy. Yet Fénéon dismissed these items almost casually, promising to send a summary of the "deductions" necessitated "by the new order of things."

There was one serious problem. Rent payments from the *fermiers* had been delayed by the suppression of certain seigneurial dues which required an adjustment of the leases. By March, 1791, the duke was pressing Fénéon for more money. "I will do everything possible to send you a lot of money when I receive the first payments on the leases, assuming that the new taxes are no obstacle." He asked if the duke wanted to continue to pay the five doctors treating the sick on his lands. Together with the medicines, this cost 672 livres in 1790. "If this expense seems too great to you, I shall stop payments immediately and terminate the agreement which was only for one year anyway."[11]

[10] *A. N.*, T–109[5], Fénéon Observations, March 8, 1790.
[11] *A. D.*, E–1725, Fénéon Correspondence, Letters of February 9, 1791, March 20, 1791, March 6, 1791, February 21, 1791.

More disturbing was the activity in the local villages. The inhabitants of Renêve were submitting a constant stream of complaints to the new "Bureau of Peace and Conciliation" at Dijon about the duke's *dîmes*. This was the month when the mayor of Dampierre wrote directly to the duke on behalf of the commune, contesting the duke's rights to the village oven and a parcel of wood. The duke's response revealed an unshaken confidence in previous connections. "Was this mayor, Monsieur Maulbon, the son of Maulbon d'Arbaumont, former Secretary of the King? If so, please write to him and explain that his claims are unfounded."[12] He also suggested that Fénéon contact Monsieur Arnoult, advocate at Dijon, who had established the duke's claims at Dampierre a few years before. Arnoult had been recently elected deputy of the Third Estate from the Bailliage of Dijon and would surely prove helpful, thought the duke.[13] Fénéon replied in April that he doubted whether any letter from Arnoult (even if he could get one) would be enough. The situation was much more serious. "Without any authorization from the administration that is supposed to govern them," wrote Fénéon, "the municipalities are drawing up demands. The country people are convinced that all dues have been ended and the municipalities are committing the same error." The village of Chazeuil demanded the duke's titles in 15 days and threatened to cease payment of the *dîmes* of 1,800 livres. "I will try to change their minds, but their attitude will make it difficult." The agent then reported his difficulties collecting rents. He managed an agreement with Moniotte, the tenant at Beaumont, whereby the rent was reduced by 1,065 livres, to cover the seigneurial rights that were suppressed. But the peasants were less reasonable. After spending five days along the Vingeanne arguing with the municipalities, Fénéon was greeted at the château of Lux by a *'huissier'* (beadle) from Bourberain, claiming the inhabitants would not pay the twelfth-sheaf. "Suspicion is rampant in all of the municipalities, and any proposals in the name of a seigneur make little impression."[14]

Still, the duke had not grasped the "new order of things." He blamed Fénéon for poor administration, for not sending enough money to Paris,

---

[12] *A. D.*, E-1725, Letter of March 26, 1791.

[13] F. Claudon, "Journal de la réunion des trois ordres du bailliage de Dijon, tenue à Dijon (mars–avril, 1789)," *Enquêtes sur la Révolution en Côte d'Or* (Dijon, 1913).

[14] *A. D.*, E-1725, Letters of April 8, 1791, April 20, 1791.

and especially for failing to be sufficiently economical. Fénéon could be pardoned for feelings of frustration.

> I have received your letter of April 7th in which you express your discontent with my administration. Almost as unhappy as you, I have taken the 3,500 livres collected this month, rushed to Arc-sur-Tille to collect more ..., repaired the bridge ... and sent all the money and paper I have to Godard by the Saturday and Sunday stagecoach.

> Let me observe a few things. You think that my administration is expensive and you recommend the strictest economy in the future. I admit that you would be right to regret the demise of Monsieur Billard if his loss was the cause of the enormous diminution in your revenues. First of all, it is the result of unforeseen events beyond my control. Secondly, it would have been better for both of us if there had been a little less economy so that I would have found everything in better condition when I took over the management of your affairs.[15]

Fénéon went on to explain that, although his salary was higher than Billard's, he had performed the services of a *feudiste* as well as those of a land agent. Moreover, he had fired Saulaville, the chief forest guard, saved his salary, and more efficiently arranged surveillance of the duke's forests. The principal expenses, he insisted, were for taxes and interests to local creditors. As for repair of the château, forge, or mills, he would abandon these projects if so ordered. Despite his efforts to defend himself, Fénéon said nothing that would trespass the bounds of deference. The duke was still *maître*, and the agent would do his best. His subsequent letters to Paris invariably began with a report of the money sent to the Rue du Bac. But the registered letter was replacing the sacks of silver as hard money disappeared in the countryside. In May, Fénéon observed that not a single *écu* could be found in the Saône Valley. The tenants were paying their rents in assignats.[16]

The duke was only slowly coming to grips with the situation and his actions seemed unsystematic, not to say frantic. When the Committee of Finance at Paris refused to compensate him for his office of lieutenant-general the duke appealed to Monsieur Charlot, commissioner of the former Estates of Burgundy, to refund his money. There had been talk of a meeting of departmental commissioners in Dijon to liquidate all

---

[15] *A. D.*, E–1725, Letter of April 20, 1791.
[16] *A. D.*, E–1725, Letters of May 4, 1791, May 27, 1791.

arrears. The duke also claimed that he had paid too much capitation tax for 1790 and should receive a refund for this too. At the same time he sent Fénéon a collection of decrees of the National Assembly and a map of the new department. He also thought it best to send a portrait of the King to his château of Lux for safekeeping.[17] The duke was trying to come to terms with a new set of laws and institutions, but he was certainly unprepared for the changes taking place in the Burgundian countryside.

In the summer of 1791, the municipal revolution in the Saône Valley came into its own. It was not a unique event. Throughout France, the municipalities, down to the tiniest village, took full advantage of their new powers and the collapse of the old royal administration to contest the whole seigneurial system. They did not hesitate to bypass the new district government and to petition Paris directly. At last the peasantry had an institutional base of power—the village commune—and, more important, the will to use it.[18]

Even before the meeting of the Estates General in Paris, the local communes had begun to organize. On February 1, 1789, representatives of thirty-one rural communities assembled at Arc-sur-Tille. The deliberations were printed, an indication of the importance of the meeting and perhaps of support from the Third Estate at Dijon, eight miles away. The local communities, most of them located in the Saône Valley east of the provincial capital, sent from two to a dozen delegates. The *bourg* of 170 households must have bustled with some 200 country-lawyers, *marchands-fermiers*, and small landed proprietors. Arc-sur-Tille itself was represented by six men, the most important of whom were Pierre Jacquemard, an independent resident farmer with almost 100 acres of land, and his son. After a few words from the *échevin* Curot, who reminded the assembled delegates that their purpose was to suggest reforms of the

---

[17] *A. D.*, E-1725, Letters of June 6, 1791, June 20, 1791, May 19, 1791. These June letters were apparently written by the duke himself. They are awkward in their expression with numerous crossouts, inserts, and occasional misspellings. At fifty-two, the duke seems prematurely old or under tension, perhaps both.

[18] P. Sagnac, *La législation civile de la Révolution française 1789–1804* (Paris, 1898), pp. 123–30, 164–73; S. Herbert, *The Fall of Feudalism in France* (London, 1921); H. Martin, *La dîme ecclésiastique en France au XVIIIe siècle et sa suppression* (Bordeaux, 1912), pp. 332–39; M. L'Héritier, "La Révolution municipale: point de départ de la Révolution française," *Révolution française*, XVIII (1939), 135–36.

provincial administration, one of these six—almost certainly Jacquemard the younger—set a radical tone in an obviously prepared speech.

"This is the most important moment in our lives," he began, "a chance to remedy abuses," especially those affecting the distribution of taxes.

For too long the entire burden of taxes has fallen on us; for too long the Clergy, the Nobility, and the Privileged, paying only the lightest taxes, have enjoyed in perfect tranquillity the revenues from property that we unfortunate ones have acquired for them, while their fellow-citizens and brothers have sustained with tired arms this enormous burden [of taxes]. It is clearly destroying their will to work and their attachment for their privileged fellow-citizens.

Knowing that Jacquemard employed a number of day-laborers on his own fields, his suggestion that the revenues of the "privileged" were unearned may seem hypocritical, but it no doubt strengthened his argument against tax privileges. He added that the needs of the ordinary citizen had been hidden from the king by "perfidious hands," but at last the king had responded. "Let us profit from this precious moment ... so that he will permit us to vote in numbers equal to the first two orders combined in the Estates of Burgundy. I present this petition, Citizens, and solicit your support" (in writing).

Insisting on the importance of this moment when all the townships (*corps de villes*) are forming assemblies, the speaker proceeded to other grievances. "Agriculture, Sire, occupies at least five-eighths of your subjects. Yet it is discouraged ... for many reasons." Among these were the *corvées*, "the *droit d'indire* which is levied only too often by illustrious families," fines, *cens*, and other seigneurial rights. He ascribed the "almost total deprivation" of wood to the growing number of forges and to luxury heating (*feux de luxe*) in the towns. Less expected perhaps was his protest against the cost of local charities, "often forced on the poor and the vagabonds." On balance, the speech was a defense of the independent owner. He was the real "unfortunate." Burdened with fiscal and seigneurial payments, misunderstood and even misused by the townspeople, "the well-to-do farmers (*cultivateurs*) have sought other occupations (*états*) for their children, and the unhappy ones who remain grow only what is absolutely necessary to live on." Yet the solution would seem to lie in political changes. "Vote by head" and admission of curés to the Estates of Burgundy would presumably open the way for non-political reforms as well. Equalize and lower the fiscal burden, and hard

146

work would seem to do the rest. Arc-sur-Tille was not alone in condemning the idlers (*oisifs*) at both ends of the social scale. A final few words assured the crown that "the people continue their respect and hommage for the Clergy and the Nobility and will cooperate with them in maintaining equality and justice in the distribution of taxes." A touch of irony or sound political tactics?[19]

The speech had not been given in a void. Arc-sur-Tille had had considerable experience with seigneurial claims, communal rights, and tax privileges. Arc-sur-Tille had been the only one of the duke's nine villages to resist the *droit d'indire* for two years. This contest along with the renewal of the *terriers* and the enforcement of the *dîme* had not been forgotten. Nor had the duke's arrangement over the division of the *dîmes* and the responsibility of church repairs been forgotten by the curé. In 1777, Terguet, the curé of Arc-sur-Tille, had been summoned to the duke's townhouse on the Rue de Varenne in Paris where an "arrangement" on the *dîmes* had been concluded. In the light of subsequent increases in the *dîme*, one wonders how Terguet felt about his share or about the duke's refusal to contribute to church repairs. In any case, by 1789, the curé was clearly on the side of the community and against the duke's agent and tenant.[20]

In 1789, a new issue had developed over the communal right to 44 acres of wood that the duke's tenant Calignon had begun to clear. Fénéon had approved Calignon's project and the tenant, who had just accepted the new terms of the duke's lease, was hard pressed to maximize his profits. But he irritated the community further by employing woodcutters from outside the village and refusing to await the results of the legal action begun by the community. Conflicts over communal rights were hardly new in this region, but the year 1789 witnessed a broader conflict, a more active and better developed village organization, and a seigneurial agent and tenant clearly on the defensive.

The fact that the affair became known in Dijon and that several printed précis of the case were in circulation attests to its wider significance. Calignon was not without friends in Dijon, and he had the local support of Fénéon, the duke's agent, and Joannet, a local notary who had worked for Tavanes in the past. But the village community had its own

[19] *A. N.*, H–200⁴.
[20] *A. N.*, T–109¹⁻².

leaders in the Jacquemards, father and son. By the end of the year, the community had gained the upper hand against an isolated triumvirate.

One reason for this victory was a new local organization, partly inspired by events outside the village. In the fall of 1789, after a visit by fifty dragoons dispatched by the new Municipal Government at Dijon, Arc-sur-Tille turned its "provisional committee" into a permanent one, duly registered at Dijon. A few weeks later it formed a national militia and proceeded to elect officers. Now the village began to send delegations to the committee of Dijon defending its positions on communal rights. This was in marked contrast to previous representation by a mayor chosen by the Estates.

Calignon was not idle. He also made his case in Dijon, accusing the *habitants* of Arc-sur-Tille (or at least their present leadership) of having "committed excesses" on July 14 and of provoking "sedition" in general. The committee of Arc answered these charges. If they had "murmured" against the treason of the *grands* along with all other decent citizens (*honnêtes gens*), they were proud of it. If there were doubts about their attachment to order in the countryside, the committee reminded the authorities at Dijon that, during the past summer, the municipality had arrested a band of thieves, consigning one to the galleys for life and whipping and branding another. Brigands would be tolerated even less than vagabonds.

Jacquemard was apparently a popular figure at Arc in the fall of 1789. His election to major in the *milice bourgeoise* gave him legal authority to act. He arrested Calignon's woodcutters, hauled them before the local committee, expelled them from the village, and threatened to beat them up if they came back. Calignon's "indoctrination," which apparently consisted of generous servings of wine, was not enough to attract new workmen. To make sure, the municipality denounced Calignon to all the surrounding villages.

Calignon and Fénéon continued to fight what they called "Jacquemard and his band" with pamphlets at Dijon. They employed such terms as "criminal enterprise," excitement of the "fury of the people," and other phrases intended to capture the support of the sober lawyers at Dijon. The village delegated Jacquemard and the curé Terguet to plead their case before the November meeting of the municipality of Dijon. They also knew their auditors. They accused Calignon of contributing to the general shortage of wood in the region. Suspected of being a "hoarder" in the winter of 1789–90, Calignon was summoned before the municipal-ity of Dijon, and apparently escaped conviction only by exposing his lease terms and placing blame on the duke. Little wonder Calignon eventually dissociated himself from Fénéon and joined the new powers that be.

As for Jacquemard, he pursued a more consistent radical course. His rivals accused him of speaking publicly about château-burning. On one occasion, in a Dijon *cabaret*, in the winter of 1789–90, he allegedly boasted that he was seriously tempted "to lead the inhabitants of Arc-sur-Tille to Lux and to put the château to the torch, sparing no one but Fénéon's wife." Whatever the facts were, pamphlet wars could excite participants far beyond the original issues.[21]

Was it from ignorance that the "country people," as Fénéon called them, confused *dîmes* and *champarts* a year later? Indeed, the legislation of the National Assembly regarding the *dîmes* was sufficiently ambiguous and dilatory to provide the peasants an excuse.[22] By a decree in March, 1790, the *dîmes inféodées* were arbitrarily classed with those seigneurial rights which were "repurchasable." Then, a month later, it was decided to indemnify the owners directly out of the Public Treasury. But the National Assembly also decreed that the *dîmes* must be paid through 1790 and thereafter until the indemnities had been paid. The estimation of the indemnity caused further irritation, since the hired "experts" and even the district administrations were notorious for their overestimation of the capital value of the *dîmes*, perhaps encouraged by a consideration from the owners. But probably more decisive than these legal ambiguities, delays, and disappointments was the fact that the *dîme* had become a symbol for seigneurial dues of all kinds. "The *dîme*," writes Marcel Garaud, "was so unpopular that it symbolized in the minds of the peasants, more than any other seigneurial due, the most unfair, unjust, and arbitrary obligation of the Old Regime. And since it had profited so many seigneurs and was considered a *droit féodal*, the hatred of the country people focused on it."[23] Moreover, had not the famous decrees of August 4th proclaimed that "the National Assembly entirely destroys the feudal system"? Many a deputy at Paris may have regretted the wording

---

[21] *A. N.*, T–109¹.

[22] H. Martin, *La dîme*, pp. 323–32; M. Garaud, *Histoire générale du droit privé français: La Révolution et la propriété foncière* (Paris, 1958), pp. 247–55.

[23] Garaud, *La Révolution et la propriété foncière*, p. 255.

of that opening sentence, but it seemed clear enough to the peasants of the Dijonnais. In any event, at least four villages were refusing to pay Fénéon any dues at all. The agent said that he would attempt to refute their arguments, but "if the bad advice they are getting results in a refusal to pay, then we must go to court."[24]

Fénéon was soon before the justice of the peace of the Canton at Bèze, explaining, as he put it, "the real meaning" of the decrees of the National Assembly regarding seigneurial rights. The burden of his argument was that the *champart* was not a *dîme* and was still payable unless the owner was indemnified at 25 times the value of the annual rent. He got nowhere. He then proposed an "arbitration" of the case, only to be refused by the new president of the commune of Bourberain. Then the communes took the offensive. The municipal council at Bourberain forbade any proprietor or cultivator to pay any *champarts* to the tenants of the duke. This action was repeated in six other local communes. Some of the municipal councils asked for the duke's titles; some prohibited payment under any circumstances; and some kept silent when individuals openly refused to let the agents or tenants of the duke collect the thirteenth-sheaf in their fields. "The same epidemic has spread to Lux and Spoy," wrote Fénéon.

> People tell me that they are exempt from all types of *dîmes* and will not pay them in the future. Others at Tilchâtel say that the decrees of the National Assembly were passed *expressly for them*. You see, Monsieur, how far things have gone. This will cause further trouble with the leases. The tenants will now refuse to pay their full rents.[25]

Among the observations of the village communes regarding the *dîmes* was the bold protest of the community of Spoy, a village of 90 households. Not limiting their resistance to the *dîme*, they contested all seigneurial titles. The wording of the document is worth examining in some detail.[26]

The *terriers* were very suspect:

1. because all the acts of this *terrier* have been approved by notaries who were agents of the seigneur and had no right to do so;

[24] A. D., E–1725, Letter of June 6, 1791.
[25] A. D., E–1725, Letter of July 12, 1791. Italics mine. The French is *"fait tout exprès pour eux."*
[26] A. D., Q–733, *Tableau par district du taux de la dîme, Canton de Bèze, Observations* (Spoy).

2. because these *terriers* have been inaccessible to the former vassals and have not been examined or discussed by the interested parties;

3. because each *terrier* is a formal disavowal of the one which preceded it, since at each renewal the former seigneurs of Spoy have always increased and extended the so-called right of *champart*;

4. because under the Ancien Regime the former vassals, always fearful (*toujours tremblans*), preferred signing the articles that the hirelings of the former seigneur put before them to breaking their poor, frail earthen vessel against the iron kettle that was opposing them.

5. finally because the last *terrier* of the former seigneur of Spoy, begun in 1788, is not yet completed and therefore must be counted among those that the National Assembly has very wisely proscribed.

> 28 January, 1791
> and the Third Year of Liberty
> of the French Empire
>
> Guelaud,   Ballant,
> *Secretary*   *Commissioner*

It can be argued that this document reveals the hand of the articulate local notary—Fénéon's "trouble-maker"—rather than the authentic voice of the inhabitants of Spoy. But the village council authorized this protest and most surely read it. At the very least, it demonstrates a willingness on the part of the villagers to follow the lead of Guelaud and Ballant. The protest loses no opportunity to relegate "seigneurs" and "vassals" to an "ancien régime." It asserts that the obscure village of Spoy is entering a new era—"the third year of liberty" as part of a "French empire." By inference, a new peasant is emerging, no longer *toujours tremblant* before the *ci-devant*. Beneath the rhetoric, there is expectancy and the conviction that past injustices will now be made good.

Other villages of the "former duchy," if less strident in tone and vocabulary, left no doubt about their basic agreement with Spoy. The cahier of Beaumont had qualified the *droit d'indire* as "ridiculous and unjust" and demanded that the *terriers*, both old and new, be deposited in the village "so that every interested party could see them and make extracts of relevant articles." Then followed a host of other grievances regarding taxes and dues. But more indicative of a new awareness was the description of the assembly of the village inhabitants in February, 1789.

151

> Moved by the same Patriotism and filled with respect for the worthy citizens who have attempted to raise their voice and open the eyes of Our Beneficent Monarch to abuse of all kinds. . . .

Perhaps the hand of Bartet, local notary who convoked the assembly, was helpful here, although he was not alone. He had the confidence of the commune. A year later, the village council demanded in crisp terms that the titles of M. de Saulx-Tavanes be deposited in Bartet's house at Beaumont.[27] At Orville, Fénéon was summoned before the new "Bureau of Conciliation" by Citizen Perriquet, one of the duke's own tenants, chosen special solicitor for a group of proprietors who had refused to pay the *champart*.[28]

The commune of Renêve, outwardly respectful of the name of Saulx-Tavanes, accused Fénéon of willful fraud. The agent had conceded that critics of the new *terrier* might travel the five miles to Beaumont and compare the new one with those of 1547 and 1611. Reading these heavy tomes required something more than bare literacy, but in 1791 the villagers made the effort. They found the *terrier* of 1611 at Bartet's house and made a systematic comparison of articles, uncovering a number of "errors" in the new one. The essential part of their protest read:

> All the tenants are supposed to follow the articles of the *terrier* exactly. Nevertheless, Srs. Blandier and Guignon, the present tenants, have always demanded and still demand one chicken per inhabitant or 12 to 15 sous fine, although there is no mention of either in the old *terrier*.[29]

Was there a touch of irony in the sentence that read, "It could not be said that M. de Saulx ever intended that his tenants demand either one or the other"?

Even after the duke had given up all hope of collecting *dîmes* or *champarts*, Fénéon persisted. Perhaps it was his legal bent of mind as much as a desire to please the duke. Perhaps he had not fully appreciated what had happened to the local administrative machinery. The word *égarement* that Fénéon employed to fit the situation is revealing. It suggests that the whole affair was an aberration, a bewildering error that must soon pass. He would continue to test the courts and appealed

[27] *A. D.*, E–Supplement, *Cahier de Beaumont*, March 12, 1789; *A. D.*, Q–734, Beaumont, September 13, 1790.

[28] *A. D.*, Q–1117, Declaration of Fénéon to the Citizens Directors of the District (Orville).

[29] *A. D.*, Q–734, Renêve, January 31, 1791.

to the district tribunal at Is-sur-Tille. He soon discovered that the new district tribunal was a far cry from the *bailliage* court of the Old Regime, much less the ducal one. Fénéon was appalled when the court confirmed the non-payment of dues of any kind. Technically, the tribunal "suspended" payment, but the effect was permanent. He attributed this "illegal" judgment "either to the weakness of the judges working under pressure from the large number of interested parties in the audience or to a particular hatred toward the owners of such rights."[30] The observation indicated that the duke's agent was beginning to understand the meaning of recent events. The local courts as well as the communes were both in the hands of a new group of "interested parties" with a new "attitude," to use Fénéon's own words.

The district and departmental authorities had to bow before such local action. The directors of the district were suspiciously long in replying to Fénéon's protests and ended by denying his case.[31] The more conservative department, caught in the cross-fire between enforcing the decrees of the Assembly to the letter and yielding to local pressure, combined delay with a pro-forma defense of the law. The department "invited" the communes to pay their dues provisionally. As Fénéon put it, "the commune did not appear disposed to accept."[32] At the end of the year, he confided to the duke that further efforts to collect seigneurial dues would be fruitless.

What portion of the duke's landed income did the seigneurial dues represent? According to an estimate in 1793, they yielded 26,986 livres in 1789, 30 per cent of the income from the Burgundian estate in that year. The *dîmes inféodées* represented almost 20,000 of this sum.[33] The duke had not clung to these revenues only as a matter of principle or a mark of rank. Their loss was a heavy financial blow and may well have hastened the death of the first duke and provoked his son's emigration.

For more than a year, the duke waited for the compensation promised by the National Assembly for his *dîmes*. In December, 1791, he wrote to M. Arnoult, the advocate who had helped the duke establish his *droit d'indire* before the Revolution. Arnoult, deputy to the Estates General in

---

[30] *A. D.*, E–1725, Letter of September 6, 1791.
[31] *A. D.*, E–1725, Letters of July 12, August 10, September 6, 1791.
[32] *A. D.*, E–1725, Letter of December 14, 1791.
[33] *A. D.*, Q–1117, Declaration of Fénéon, May 18, 1793; *A. D.*, Q–733–734 (*Dîmes*); *A. D.*, E–1744, Letter of May 8, 1813.

1789, was now solicitor general of the department and in a position of influence. The duke's letter to Arnoult made no allowance for the possibility that the political rise of this Dijon lawyer since 1789 might have altered his relations with the *ci-devant noblesse*.

> I have not received my indemnity for the *dîmes inféodées*. We are waiting for the decision of the Department. It is very important for my affairs that this decision be made promptly. Accustomed, Monsieur, to your friendship and your assistance in the past, I dare hope that you will render me a new service and expedite the liquidation [of the *dîmes*].[34]

Again, former connections were insufficient. The Tavanes family was never indemnified for their *dîmes*.[35]

When Fénéon attempted to collect the September rents for 1791, the principal tenants had a good excuse to delay payment, for it took some time to adjudicate the portion of their rent represented by seigneurial dues. Collecting *dîme* arrears was, of course, hopeless, though Fénéon kept the accounts for future reference. The Revolution would not last forever and what had been done could be undone. But there was little doubt that Tavanes's finances had taken a bad turn, and Fénéon informed the duke that there would be little left for 1791 after the *dîmes* and taxes had been deducted. No longer could the duke count on those monthly packets and sacks of 5,000 livres, arriving regularly by coach from Dijon. In December, Fénéon began borrowing to pay off *local* creditors, something he had never had to do before. He was fortunate to obtain half in coin and half in assignats and at only five per cent.[36]

*

Since it has been suggested by some historians that the seigneurial dues were insignificant, it might be well to estimate what their removal meant in this instance. For the small holder on the Tavanes' seigneuries, a *dîme* of one-twelfth of the gross harvest was no insignificant burden. It should be measured as a percentage of the *net* harvest after deductions for rent, taxes and seed in order to understand what the tiller of a *journal* (0.8 acres) of grainland had gained. The *dîme* was paid on all grains, vegetables, and even flax in that region.

[34] *A. D.*, E–1725, Tavanes to Arnoult, December 27, 1791.
[35] *A. D.*, Q–1118, Idemnification of 1825–29.
[36] *A. D.*, E–1725, Letters of September 6, December 14, 1791.

TABLE IV.2   THE BURDEN OF THE *Dîme* ON RENTED LAND IN THE DIJONNAIS

A Maximum Estimate	A Minimum Estimate
Gross Yield: 16 measures	Gross Yield: 18 measures
Rent 8.0 (at ½) Taxes 1.0 (at 6%) Seed 4.0 (at 4 to 1 yields)	Rent 6.0 (at ⅓) Taxes 1.0 (at 5%) Seed 3.6 (at 5 to 1 yields)
Total Deductions: 13.0 measures	Total Deductions: 10.6 measures
Net Harvest: 3.0 measures	Net Harvest: 7.4 measures
Dîme (¹⁄₁₂): 1.33 measures	*Dîme* (¹⁄₁₂): 1.50 measures
% of Net Harvest: 44.4	% of Net Harvest: 20.3

SOURCE: *A. D.*, Q–734; *A. D.*, E–1878 (May 1784). P. de Saint-Jacob, *Les paysans de la Bourgogne du Nord au dernier siècle de l'Ancien Régime* (Paris, 1960), pp. 504–5; *A. D.*, E–1818 (Bourberain Revenues, 1783); G. Lefebvre, *Questions agraires au temps de la terreur* (La Roche-sur-Yon, 1954), p. 150. Although rents of one-third of the gross harvest were more common, there are examples of one-half. *A. D.*, E–1768 (Beaumont Revenues, 1783). In 1794, a petition from a village near Châlon-sur-Saône proposed that a tenant who demanded more than half of the harvest of a cultivator be regarded as a "suspect" and punished. Lefebvre, *Questions agraires*, pp. 208–9.

The burden on non-rented property was, of course, less, ranging from 11 to 12 per cent, using the estimates in Table IV.2 above. In fact, most cultivators at Lux, Arc-sur-Tille, or Beaumont were both owners and renters, but they rented more than they owned. The conclusions of Dupont de Nemours on this point appear to hold for the Dijon plain:

There are areas where the *dîme* at 1/25th costs only one-tenth of the net harvest, but there are *a greater number* where it takes one-sixth and others where it takes a third or even a half of what remains for the proprietor.[37]

For the small cultivator, therefore, the removal of the *dîme* and the *champart* represented a substantial gain. Not enough to provide any capital accumulation—the margins were too small—but enough to increase the level of family food consumption and, more important, to stimulate hope of better things to come. That is why the abolition of the *dîme* and the proscription of all seigneurial justice did not end peasant agitation. The village councils proceeded to reassert old communal claims that had not fared well in the courts of the Old Regime. In Northern Burgundy, woodland served as a focus for century-old friction between seigneur and village. Dispute over rights to the wood or outright pro-

[37] Martin, *La Dîme*, p. 122 (italics mine). Before the abolition of the *dîme* was finally legislated, some deputies proposed as a compromise that it be levied on the "net," not the "gross" harvest.

prietorship was made likely by the proximity of communal and seigneurial holdings. When village and seigneur owned portions of the same
forest tract, it was almost inevitable that boundary differences would
arise. It appears that the seigneurs of Saulx-Tavanes had won most of
these disputes in the course of the century, making good their rights of
triage at the expense of the villages.[38]

The tension had been greatly increased by the critical shortage of the
1780s. No other commodity rose so dramatically in price in the last third
of the century. Some communities had enough wood to enter the market
and provide a regular village income.[39] More important, the communal
wood provided brushwood for heating in winter and pasture for the
peasants' livestock, sheep, and goats. A large majority of the villagers
owned some livestock. Threats to the communal holdings were fiercely
resented. As prices rose and scarcity increased, the duke's forge at Tilchâtel must have been regarded as a veritable monster, consuming the
precious combustible at a prodigious rate. Little wonder that the peasants
often foraged for wood in the duke's preserve.

In 1790 and 1791, this foraging assumed major proportions. It is possible that the forest wardens were more inclined to overlook many of
these incursions; they had never been popular with the local peasantry
and the breakdown of the seigneurial system did not increase their
security from local agitation. In any case, ten guards were simply not
enough for over 5,000 acres of forest. Fénéon urged the duke to make an
inquest in preparation for formal court procedure, but Tavanes replied
that he preferred to let the other proprietors initiate such action.[40] In
June, 1791, the duke seemed more concerned with economy than prestige.
Moreover, he may have also recognized that the threat of going to the
law was no longer a sure weapon.

Encouraged perhaps by the duke's lack of action, the village communes
now seized the offensive. The commune of Chazeuil revived a transaction of 1761, to claim and cut fifteen acres of the forest of Velours. The

[38] Saint-Jacob, *Les paysans de la Bourgogne*, pp. 377–86, 488–89; see also M.
Bloch, "La lutte pour l'individualisme agraire dans la France du XVIIIe siècle,"
Annales d'histoire économique et sociale, II (1930), 329–83, 511–54; and G. Bourgin,
Le partage des biens communaux (Paris, 1908). The right of *triage* was a seigneurial
claim to one-third of communal property if it were divided.

[39] Saint-Jacob, *Les paysans de la Bourgogne*, p. 490.

[40] *A. D.*, E–1725, Letters of June 6, June 20, 1791.

commune of Veronnes unilaterally revoked the *triage* of 1730 and regained 150 acres of communal wood, lost sixty years earlier. Three other communes—Lux, Bourberain, and Arc-sur-Tille—basing their claims on similar acts of *triage* dating back to 1683 and 1747, seized and distributed parcels of woodland. Thus the communities were not only able to benefit from the abolition of the right of *triage*, but also to apply the new law retroactively and reverse earlier court decisions. Fénéon later explained that the duke had failed to take counter-action, not from lack of legal means, but "out of fear of exciting further violence."[41]

The threat of violence on the part of the communes was not lost on the duke's agent either. By 1793, Fénéon was cast in the curious role of defending the right of the local inhabitants to pasture their horses in the duke's wood "by a very old custom."[42] But even in the fall of 1791, after a summer attempting to collect *dîmes* and *champarts*, Fénéon had learned to temporize. The region was plagued by extreme dryness and the municipality of Lux threatened to force M. Bureau, the ironmaster at Tilchâtel, to open his sluice gates that were blocking the waters of the Tille. Fénéon claimed that there was so little water in the river it would be absorbed in the sand before it ever reached Lux, five miles away. "Nevertheless, I thought we had better do it, to calm the inhabitants of Lux. The privation of water, a real calamity in this region, might have otherwise led to damage to your forge."[43]

The "country people" were obviously restive, and the abolition of the *dîme* had not ended their agitation. On the contrary, it had apparently encouraged them to further action. The new commune was an ideal instrument for the assertion of older communal rights, especially to the forest. But would success even in this direction satisfy the villagers? How would they respond to the emigration, the new decrees from Paris, the flight of the King, and the events of 1792—war, inflation, counter-revolu-

---

[41] *A. D.*, E–1725, Letter of August 10, 1791; *A. D.*, E–1744, Letter of February 11, 1818; *A. D.*, Q–1117, Declaration of Fénéon, May 1793, chs. 7, 9.

[42] *A. D.*, Q–1117, Observation on the Wood. "The *laboureurs* will be reduced to poverty if this *usage* is abolished before the economic system of crops is changed at Lux and Bourberain by the establishment of artificial meadows. . . . In the meantime, the horses need the wood [for pasture]." Apparently, artificial meadows, sign of an advanced agriculture, were to be established in 1793, while the estate was under the administration of the government.

[43] *A. D.*, E–1725, Letter of September 6, 1791.

tion, the Republic? Much would depend on the action of the *fermiers* who still controlled the market for farm produce, provided leases, work, and credit to the countryside, and had political contacts in the market towns and provincial capital. Which way would the *fermiers* go?

The tenants welcomed the reduction in rents and were relieved of the nasty task of enforcing the array of seigneurial dues. Calignon, the tenant at Arc-sur-Tille, was able to overestimate the amount of *dîmes* included in his lease and to reduce his rent by over a third.[44] All tenants had a more secure margin of profit after the abolition of the dues, if only because seigneurial rights were difficult to assess and collect even before 1789.[45] At the same time, the local courts were more kind to tenants. Leases could still be broken, but the abuse was no longer the unique prerogative of the proprietor. For example, Bureau, the new tenant at Tilchâtel, refused to perform the cartage services stipulated in his lease. With little concern for historical accuracy, Fénéon complained that "the obscure clauses of a lease are always interpreted against the leasor, but in this case I find nothing obscure."[46] Bureau, like the *dîme*-payers of Bourberain, could now count on the courts, and Fénéon heeded the advice of the duke to avoid any legal expense. Henceforth, Fénéon paid the cartage costs at Tilchâtel.[47]

This is not to say that Fénéon was no longer able to drive a hard bargain. It was not only with the intent of impressing his employer that he wrote in late 1791:

> I want 800 livres for 12 years and the tenant to pay the taxes. I consider 21 years too long, given the lost opportunities to raise rents. If I don't get all of this, I will come close.[48]

As for wood sales, Rochet, the ironmaster at Bèze, offered 150 livres per arpent but Fénéon held out for 200 livres.[49] The precious combustible was selling better than ever. A new legal framework and a bureaucracy

[44] *A. D.*, E-1744, Letter of May 8, 1813. The lease was reduced by 8,140 livres; Fénéon claimed it should have been reduced only by 4,984 livres, Calignon having overestimated the area on which the *dîme* was collected.

[45] A. Colombet, *Les parlementaires Bourguignons à la fin du XVIIIe siècle* (Dijon, 1937), pp. 160–61.

[46] *A. D.*, E-1725, Letter of August 10, 1791.

[47] *A. D.*, E-1725, Letter of September 6, 1791.

[48] *A. D.*, E-1725, Letter of December 14, 1791.

[49] *Ibid.*

more responsive to tenant interests could not mitigate the shortage of wood and the pressures of the market.

But in 1791, the tenants were still hopeful. New legislation could go far beyond the abolition of seigneurial rights. And the tenant knew his grievances. Did not the petitions of 1793 and 1794 from all over France indicate increasing demand by *fermiers* for further agrarian reforms? Their departure from the grievances of other social groups in the countryside was not immediately apparent. Foremost among tenant demands was the longer lease-hold. Fénéon referred to a tenant who asked for 21 years; petitions throughout France proposed from 18 to 27, a major improvement over nine. Nine years hardly gave much incentive to improvements by the tenant, especially since proprietors used the opportunity to raise rents at each lease renewal.[50] Compensation by the proprietor for specific farm improvements by the tenant was a related demand. The *fermiers* also demanded legal preference for the incumbent tenant at the time of renewal in order to escape the practice of auctioning. Also related was the proposal that the landlord not be permitted to terminate the lease unilaterally before its expiration without compensation. Other demands included making the entrance fee (*pot de vin*) an annual payment or eliminating it altogether, diminution of rent in case of a weather disaster—a kind of calamity insurance against lightning, hail, or frost—and some guarantee regarding the sharing of the tax burden. These last demands touched on the tenants' margin of profit, though there is no evidence of an effort to establish a "fair" rent-income ratio.[51] Although these demands were never incorporated into a single national program, they clearly represent the principal economic grievances of tenants such as those on the duke's Burgundian estate. Were any of them implemented?

The high hopes of tenants for national legislation regarding farm leases were first dashed in September of 1793, when a proposal for tenant

[50] Contemporary critics of French agriculture such as Arthur Young and Antoine Lavoisier stressed the nine-year lease as a major obstacle to agricultural progress. Yet it appears from the English experience that brevity of the lease was not the only problem. Annual, even verbal leases were quite common in England. Yet it was not the "custom" to raise rents on a "sitting tenant." See J. D. Chambers and G. E. Mingay, *The Agricultural Revolution, 1750–1880* (New York, 1966), pp. 46–48, 165–66. But given the outlook and attitudes of landlords like Tavanes, a longer lease was necessary in France.

[51] G. Lefebvre, *Questions agraires*, pp. 80–88 and *passim*.

compensation for farm improvements was voted down in the National Convention. The Civil Code of Napoleon was to reaffirm the inviolability of contract. Given the continued, indeed increased, shortage of grain and the pressure of population on the land, freedom of contract gave the proprietor-leasor the full advantage of bargaining power.[52] The history of the tenant interest in the national legislature—National Assembly, Convention, or Council of Five Hundred—is still to be written, but there is no doubt that it will be a record of failure.

The Napoleonic Code did not go very far to recognize tenant grievances. True, the very fact that mutual obligations of proprietor-leasor and tenant-leasee were made explicit was of some advantage. The code, for example, specified what "ordinary repairs" included, what the consequences of default in payment were, or what standing a verbal lease had at law. It made some provision for "fortuitous events"—damage by hail, lightning, frost—providing compensation to the tenant if half or more of the harvest were lost. The code also provided for indemnification of the tenant in case the land was sold during the course of the lease. The new rural code actually did more for the subtenant by making him liable only for his rent to the chief tenant. Other tenant demands were not considered. And even in the case of calamities of weather, the appraisal of damage was in the hands of third parties (judges or experts) who in 1807 were no longer those of 1791.[53]

The nineteenth century brought few changes beneficial to the *fermier* of the Dijon plain. A table of leases for 31 properties in the department of *Côte d'Or* from 1817 to 1907 demonstrates the uniform use of the nine-year lease. As late as 1907, local societies of agriculture were still discussing the question of indemnifying tenants for an increase in the value of the land. Although the terminology of rents (*pot de vin, prélèvement*) may have changed, the rent-income ratio remained high, probably reaching a peak about 1877. A rough calculation based on the sample referred to above would put rents at 80 per cent of the net income of the land. Only with the agricultural recession after 1880 did rents fall and lease terms improve, but even then it is not certain that the rent-income ratio was more favorable to the tenant. In the Dijon plain at least the

---

[52] *Ibid.*, pp. 82–83.

[53] *Code Napoléon* (Paris, Collin Edition, 1807), Articles 1734–39, 1741, 1743–49, 1753–54, 1769–73.

fermier was unable to exploit the first breakthrough against the old order and obtain legislation providing him with security of tenure and encouragement to make improvements on the land.[54]

There is a certain irony in the failure of the *fermiers* to gain more from the Revolution. Part of the explanation lies in their inability to organize sufficient political support in legislative circles at Paris or in the country at large. After all, *fermage* was not a form of leasehold the majority of the peasants had an interest in reforming along lines advocated by the *fermiers*. For many small holders, especially in the Beauce and Flanders, *fermage* connoted exploitation and they thought it should be abolished altogether. What is more, the *fermier* was himself caught up in the *mystique* of proprietorship. How could it be otherwise in a country where the land was so widely distributed and where the landowner, especially the owner-occupier, was held in such high esteem? In the social world of the village and *bourg*, the *propriétaire*, even a small one, commanded a respect and confidence that a *fermier*, despite his economic hold on the rural community, might envy. But respect of the village community was only part of it. Tenants from Calignon to Bartet, who rented Tavanes's land, must have wondered whether outright ownership might not be preferable to leasing. Had the counts of Tavanes encouraged them to develop the land and increase their profits, they might have seen their interests differently. Proprietorship would offer less illusory profits and, above all, independence from landlords like the duke. For the *fermier*'s grievances were aimed at both "seigneurialism" and "landlordism." Could either one really be "reformed"?

Even before the *fermiers* were to see their desires for reform of tenure largely ignored, they might take advantage of the unsettled times to buy some land of their own. Here was a goal the *fermier* could share with the rest of the village community. When the national government embarked upon a plan of confiscation and sale of church and, later, *émigré* land, the *fermiers* demonstrated no hesitancy to buy. Perhaps the *fermiers* did not need this incentive to join the villagers in 1791. Given the way

[54] G. Martin and P. Martenet, *La Côte d'Or: étude d'économie rurale* (Dijon, 1909), pp. 98–100, 100n, 105–7. This work suffers from a failure to calculate the rent-income ratio systematically. A sample calculation for a domain of 268 hectares (204 in arable, 64 in meadow) in the mid-nineteenth century indicates a rent-income ratio of 82.4 per cent. This seems incredible. *Ibid.*, pp. 113–14.

events were developing in Paris, was there any reason (or sentiment) to defend the duchy of Tavanes—or even remain judiciously neutral?[55]

*   *

Mild and gradual though it may seem by twentieth-century standards, this was nonetheless a rural revolution. Although the local social groups involved were by no means identical in economic condition and social status, they revealed a remarkable unity of purpose in 1790 and 1791. Can a rural leadership be identified? Historians have frequently alluded to "rural bourgeois" who profited from the Revolution, but did they also lead it? The revolution on the properties of Saulx-Tavanes points to two categories of rural leadership—village notaries and tenants.

Fénéon alluded to the trouble-making lawyers like Morizot who set the villages against the seigneur even before 1789. It was Bartet, the notary of Beaumont, who made the *terriers* available to the protesting peasants in 1786. Later, he convoked the inhabitants to submit their grievances to be recorded in the village *cahier*. It was Joannet, notary of Arc-sur-Tille, who drew up the *cahiers* of twenty villages in the Dijon plain, and later rivaled Calignon for leadership in the new commune. It was Jacquemard, his rival and the radical leader of Arc in 1789 who became "commissioner expert" for the sale of the Tavanes' estate, and surely the same Jacquemard that fired at the windows of Verchère d'Arcelot, President of the Parlement, to encourage his emigration. The tax rolls make it quite clear that there was a large number of these rural notaries. They were of a more radical inclination than advocates such as Arnoult, the deputy of the *bailliage* at Paris and later departmental administrator. A certain idealism, or at least sympathy for the villagers, should not be ruled out among these notaries, despite Fénéon's charge of cupidity and "trouble-making."[56]

Less obvious as revolutionary leaders were the *fermiers*. Yet, like the

---

[55] Admittedly, much of this is speculation; correspondence or memoirs of *fermiers* are hard to come by. Were many of the new owner-occupiers of the nineteenth century former *fermiers*?

[56] *A. N.*, T–109$^{1-2}$, *Mémoires, précis*, regarding Arc-sur-Tille. N. Garnier, *Arc-sur-Tille: La Révolution, 1789–1802* (Dijon, 1913), pp. 39, 91, 159–60, and *passim*; H. Drouot and J. Calmette, *Histoire de Bourgogne* (Paris, 1928), p. 368; *A. D.*, Q–193; *A. D.*, Q–734 (the tax rolls for the Old Regime are in series C, the new *contribution foncière* rolls can be found in series L). See Chapter II above.

notaries, they had many of the attributes necessary to lead the communes. They were literate; they had contact with the market towns and river ports; they often leased property in different parts of the region. Their very insecurity of tenure made them search for other leases and, consequently, escape the isolation of one village community. Jean Calignon, for example, was *fermier* at Norges, then at Cessay-sur-Tille, finally at Arc-sur-Tille. He was also referred to as a *marchand* of Dijon, suggesting his dual economic function as well as his mobility. No doubt less active than the notaries before 1789, the tenants were often quick to adapt to changing times. Calignon is an excellent example. Known before the Revolution as "hard driving," he was still able to gain peasant confidence. Elected mayor of Arc in December 1791, he joined the Club of Friends of the Constitution, made speeches on the virtues of the new regime, and exercised his talents in the municipal council.[57] Perriquet, tenant at Orville, not only refused to pay his rents to Fénéon, but accused the landlord of illegal behavior. He represented what the duke's agent called "a large number of owners in a coalition" who refused to pay seigneurial dues and summoned Fénéon before the local tribunal.[58] Guelaud, who signed the truculent petition of Spoy as secretary of the commune, was Tavanes's tenant at Blagny. Was Bartet, the notary at Beaumont, the same Bartet who was tenant at Champagne?[59] The functions of notary and rent collector were not so different. The municipal council minutes at Arc expose the rivals for political leadership in the village—two *fermiers*, two notaries, and the village priest. It was the same at Saint-Julien and probably other villages of the Dijonnais.[60]

It would be wrong to depict the *fermiers* as forming a unanimous *bloc* of revolutionary leadership in the countryside. The inactive ones were not so conspicuous. Moreover, there is more than one way of "taking hold" of a revolutionary situation. Consider the case of Bureau, the *fermier* at Tilchâtel, probably the most affluent of the duke's tenants.

[57] Garnier, *Arc: La Révolution*; Saint-Jacob, *Les paysans*, pp. 430–31, 430n; *A. D.*, Q–1117, Arc, An v.

[58] *A. D.*, Q–1117 (Orville).

[59] *A. D.*, E–1768 (Beaumont leases).

[60] Garnier, *Arc: La Révolution*; M. Balotte, *La baronie de Saint-Julien à travers les âges* (Dijon, 1961). There is a great need for village studies during the Revolution. They will no doubt expose the petty political rivalries more related to personal feuds before 1789 than to ideological or economic conflicts, once the *ci-devant* seigneur had been disposed of.

Instead of entering local politics actively like Calignon at Arc-sur-Tille or Guelaud at Spoy, Bureau took advantage of the confiscation of the Benedictine monastery at Bèze to attempt to launch a cotton textile mill. His relations with the deputy Arnoult at Paris led to negotiations for the establishment of a Rouen spinning "machine," offered gratis by the new national government. Bureau's correspondence in the winter of 1789–90 does not suggest a man leading a village revolution, but an entrepreneur anxious to keep the countryside calm. No Rouen machine-smashers for him at Bèze.[61] Recall, too, that as ironmaster at Tilchâtel, Bureau was not dealing directly with peasant cultivators, but with a small industrial work force and a score of woodcutters. He was therefore not exposed to the same pressures as the tenants elsewhere on the Tavanes properties.

The tax rolls list a number of social categories for the village communities of the Dijon plain. Neither the *taille* rolls of 1780 nor the land tax of 1790 employed the term "peasant."[62] The first distinction from a fiscal point of view was that between the *habitant* and the *forain*, the resident and the absentee owner. Although the *forain* was suspected of tax evasion by the residents, he was not, in most cases, a *privilegié* from Dijon. He was more likely a *habitant* of a neighboring village, a cultivator or artisan like the other residents. All residents were divided into various categories, the largest being *laboureurs*, *vignerons*, *artisans*, *manouvriers*, and widows. These categories would seem to imply differences in function and wealth, but a closer look reveals that these were not the distinctive features. Many artisans tilled the soil, many winegrowers considered themselves artisans, and many *manouvriers* or day laborers were property owners. Functional distinctions were approximate at best. The tax rolls sometimes indicate a radical change in these categories, suggesting a shift from grain-growing to winegrowing, for example. Again, nothing of the sort was occurring. The tax officials had changed their

[61] S. de Montenay, "L'établissement d'une manufacture à Bèze sous la Révolution," *Annales de Bourgogne* (1966), 188–97. Letters of December 22, December 29, 1789, and January 3, 1790. Bureau formed a *société* (partnership) with 400,000 livres capital in early 1790; in 1794, we find him importing specialized workers from Neufchâtel in Switzerland. But there was no trace of the enterprise after 1797. The cotton spinning machine was probably Richard Arkwright's invention, employed in Rouen before the Revolution.

[62] The *taille* rolls for the villages of the Dijon plain are very complete and the reformation of the rolls between 1772 and 1781 makes them especially informative. The *contribution foncière* for 1790 and especially 1791 are equally complete. See Document IX.

terminology quite possibly in response to the desire of the residents for more perstigious labels. Better to be called a winegrower than a day laborer. The amount of prestige attached to one's place on the tax roll should not be underestimated. The search for status was not limited to the upper classes. The blurring of functions went hand-in-hand with an overlap in sources of wealth. In the case of the villages of the Dijon plain, the distribution of property was wide. In 1781, 61 per cent of the householders at Beaumont owned some land, and 68 per cent owned some livestock.[63] The *cahier* of Beaumont tells quite a different story. Article 16 reads:

> The *taille*, established in 1782 by the commissioner, was to be only about 1,000 livres which is still too much since the community has only 80 households among whom there are 15 tenant farmers (*laboureurs pour autrui*) and the rest winegrowers and day laborers and *not a single proprietor*.[64]

The tax rolls make it quite clear that the *cahier* had grossly distorted the actual case.

Jean Loutchitsky, almost 75 years ago, was the first to stress the wide distribution of ownership among the rural population of the Old Regime. Using the Dijonnais as one of his three regional samples, he denied the persistent view that the countryside was made up of a small number of property holders and a mass of property-less.[65] The distribution of *income* does not indicate great disparities of wealth either. Again at Beaumont, there were only six residents with incomes over 1,000 livres and 23 with revenues under 200 livres. The remaining 54 (65.1 per cent) had revenues between 200 and 1,000 livres. At Lux, the proportion of this middle groups was 61.8 per cent (84 of 136), and at Arc-sur-Tille it was 50.0 per cent (86 of 172).[66] This is not to say that there was no poverty. In all three villages more than one in four families had incomes below 200 livres. But it is to say that one finds a substantial *bloc* of middling cultivators, winegrowers, artisans, and even day laborers before the Revolution who were not desperately miserable. This is further substantiated by the large number of "active citizens" in these villages after 1789.[67]

[63] *A. D.*, C–5927 (1781).

[64] *A. D., E–Supplément, Cahier de Beaumont*, March 12, 1789. Italics mine.

[65] J. Loutchisky, "De la petite propriété en France avant la Révolution et de la vente des biens nationaux," *Revue historique*, LIX (1895), 85–92.

[66] *A. D.*, C–5927; *A. D.*, C–6018; *A. D.*, C–5916. See Document IX.

[67] *A. D.*, L–838 (Beaumont).

Since the tax assessments ignore wage payments in kind, even the lowest quarter of the population was not so deprived as their revenues suggest.

To conclude that material interests played a part in the revolt of the villages is one thing; to say that it was an uprising of the miserable, quite another. The majority of villagers who refused to pay their *dîmes*, contested the *terriers* and the right of *triage*, filled the tribunal at Is-sur-Tille to encourage the judges, demanded that the sluice gates be opened at Tilchâtel, and eventually bought the duke's land and château furniture— knew what was to their advantage. They also knew how to organize. Although the political experience of the villagers of the Dijon plain had been less extensive than among those of Provence, the new communal governments with elected mayors and general councils functioned effectively and forcefully. There is an impression of political awareness and a cohesiveness difficult to imagine among the desperate day laborers of Brittany or the property-less harvest hands of the Beauce. But one can imagine these small owners and artisans conversing across their narrow strips in the fields or across a work bench in the village shop. Marc Bloch reminds us that this was the region of open fields without hedges or other enclosures where communal rights were still strong. The land of the entire village was divided into three "cultures" (winter wheat, spring wheat, fallow) and each culture or *sole* was plowed, seeded, and harvested by all the cultivators at the same time. One walked over the neighbors' parcels to reach one's own plot. The sense of community in the daily farm operations was of long standing.[68]

In the early 1790s the countryside was alive with rumor and expectancy. Bartet and Jacquemard, Calignon and Perriquet seemed to know what to do, while Fénéon cut a more sinister figure as he rode from village to village after his rents and rights. Note that Fénéon was not physically harmed nor hounded out of the region, but rather worn down by litigation, obstructionism, and the threat of direct action. The villagers in the former *duché* of Saulx-Tavanes seemed remarkably respectful of human life and of "legitimate" forms of property. This comparative restraint may have been related to the stake they already had in society, modest as it was. Furthermore, to be above the subsistence level was to have time and energy for self-esteem.

[68] March Bloch, *Les caractères originaux de l'histoire rurale française* (Paris, 1952), pp. 34–49.

166

Material grievances alone do not account for the hostility the villagers felt for the seigneur. For "seigneur" implied its counterpart, *vassaux*. Anachronistic as this term may sound for the eighteenth century, it was common coin in all the seigneurial documents and the duke, his agents, and the peasants themselves employed it often. More important, it was employed with increasing frequency in the years immediately before 1789. The seigneurial reaction in this case had been marked as much by seigneurial pre-eminences as by seigneurial obligations. The ducal *bailliage*, the *droit d'indire*, the complete renewal of the *terriers* in a dozen villages at once, and the replacement of Billard by the *feudiste* Fénéon as chief manager of the estate are all examples of a new emphasis on the form and apparatus of seigneurialism as distinct from landlordism. The peasant was freshly reminded that he was a "vassal" of Duc de Saulx-Tavanes.[69]

In itself, this might not have been the cause of intense bitterness. But the peasant had reason to regard himself otherwise in the course of the century. The royal government had treated him differently. For whatever fiscal burdens they implied, the tax rolls employed another vocabulary. In the village *taille* rolls, the peasant was neither *vassal* nor *paysan*, but *habitant*, a word that in this context implied "taxpayer" or "citizen." By a curious coincidence in 1781, the year in which the duke began his seigneurial reorganization, the royal administration began to reapportion the burden of the *taille* in the communities of the Dijon plain. The reassessment was a response to local petitions and involved the convocation of the "general assembly of *habitants*" and the election of assessors. At Beaumont, the four nominated included a winegrower and a day laborer. Throughout the region, ordinary peasants were not only treated as taxpayers in public forms of address, but employed in the important task of tax apportionment.[70]

The contrast in treatment should not be ignored here. Almost simultaneously, the villagers were reminded that they were "vassals" of the Duke de Saulx-Tavanes and owed him deference and dues, while the royal government treated them as citizens who could apportion their own taxes. The public powers, as Tocqueville said, were "teaching" not only

---

[69] See Chapter II, above.

[70] See Loutchisky, "De la petite propriété," and *taille* rolls in *A. D.*, C–5911 to C–6113.

equality of treatment, but also a certain measure of citizen participation.[71] Together, the activities of the duke and the royal government in the 1780s must have disturbed and irritated the average winegrower or artisan of the region. Is it too much to speak of an ambivalent self-image? Could one be both "vassal" and "citizen"? Did the vocabulary of the modern state—"citizen," "nation," "rights"—that the remote village of Spoy could employ spring up over night? Self-respect played a role here as substantial as material grievance.

It has become almost commonplace to emphasize the rise of bread prices and of royal taxes in the years before 1789 as the twin blades squeezing the peasantry of France.[72] In the Dijon plain, however, neither grain prices nor taxes seem to have played an important role. Grain prices fell through most of the 1780s—so much so that in 1786 the royal subdelegate claimed that "grain and wine are at such a price that even the poorest inhabitants can live with a certain affluence."[73] It is true that prices began to climb dramatically in 1788 and 1789, but to ascribe rural tensions to the long-run effects of inflation in grain seems misleading. Wheat prices, as we have seen, rose only 22 per cent between 1750–55 and 1785–89.

As for the dreaded *taille*, complaints about inequities of assessment were often justified, though in the 1770s and 1780s a large number of communities in the Dijonnais thoroughly reformed their tax assessments and at rates that were not exorbitant.[74] But the most interesting fact is that the global tax figure for each village did not change much between 1760 and 1789. Royal taxes were always disliked, but there is little evidence that they were rising, at least in the villages where Tavanes was seigneur.[75] The standard economic explanation, therefore, does not carry us very far here.

[71] See the forthcoming work of Sasha Weitman on the relationship of centralization to demands for equality in the *cahiers*.

[72] This is the classic thesis of C. E. Labrousse, almost religiously reiterated in every French regional monograph. No doubt it holds for many parts of France, but not for the Dijonnais.

[73] *A. D.*, C–100; See Price Table in Document X.

[74] *A. D.*, C–5916, C–5927, C–6018, *Nouveau pied des tailles*, for the new tax rates which varied from five to ten per cent of gross revenues. On the value of this source, see Loutchisky, "De la petite propriété," pp. 85–86, 87n.

[75] See Table IV. 3 on royal taxes. The *cahier* of Beaumont claimed that its *taille* was set "at about 1,000 livres" in 1782; this is substantially true (the precise figure is 1,275 livres), but the villagers selected the lowest tax in 20 years.

TABLE IV.3   ROYAL TAXES IN THREE VILLAGES IN THE JURISDICTION OF THE SEIGNEURS OF TAVANES

Name of Village	Tax	1760	1765	1770	1775	1780	1785	1789
Arc-sur-Tille	*Taille* and *Vingtième*	3,096	3,165	3,251	2,959	3,542	3,251	3,825
	Capitation	684	717	621	712	859	600	612
Total		3,780	3,882	3,872	3,671	4,401	3,851	4,437
No. of Taxpayers		157	169	172	172	182	171	181
Beaumont	*Taille* and *Vingtième*	1,980	1,894	1,764	1,660	1,886	1,661	1,944
	Capitation	438	430	337	349	458	303	310
Total		2,418	2,324	2,101	2,009	2,344	1,974	2,254
No. of Taxpayers		82	85	82	82	82	94	94
Lux	*Taille* and *Vingtième*	2,012	2,264	2,108	2,323	2,482	2,481	3,172
	Capitation	447	426	412	557	615	497	506
Total		2,459	2,690	2,520	2,880	3,097	2,978	3,678
No. of Taxpayers		130	127	127	137	129	124	135

SOURCE: *A. D.*, C–5916 (Arc); *A. D.*, C–5926, 5927 (Beaumont); *A. D.*, C–6017, 6018 (Lux).

*   *   *

Slowly, between 1789 and 1791, the village communes became aware that they could take action on their own, that the local courts could hand down favorable decisions, and that the local administration from canton to district and from district to department would not obstruct communal action, even if it would not openly encourage it. Before 1789, the village communities had some corporate unity, but they had long been on the defensive against the Saulx-Tavanes who were almost always favored in the local royal courts. By 1791, the villages began to realize that there was a national legislature. For the first time there were men in high places doing something "expressly for them." To grievances both material and psychological was added the possibility of effective action by means of the new municipality and a distant but powerful benefactor, the National Assembly.

The new awareness that change and reform were possible did not come from the August 4th Decrees alone. Other issues were crowding the scene by the beginning of 1791. There was the discussion in the department about the new Constitution of the Clergy. It must have encouraged the rural municipalities to learn that 71 per cent of the local priests took the oath. Indeed, the *curés* must have reflected the views of the villages. the Côte d'Or was no Vendée. In February, the commune of Arnay-le-Duc, southwest of Dijon, arrested the aunts of the King who were bound for Italy, and dispatched them to Dijon where they were imprisoned for ten days despite the instructions of District and Department. In May, the new political club, *Amis de la Constitution*, with affiliates throughout the department, had a major reunion in the old Palace of the Dukes at Dijon. Did Calignon and Bartet mount the same steps which had caused such a battle of prestige for the duke's grandfather, thirty-five years earlier?

The countryside was also "politicized" by the national elections in September. Fénéon alluded to them as "occupying all the public officials" and interrupting his own legal proceedings.[76] This election, reinforced by new municipal elections, marked the real beginning of a second revolution in the countryside. An older generation of *gens de robe*, including moderates such as Arnoult, were being replaced by more active "patriots" recruited or supported by the *"comité des avocats"* at Dijon.[77] By 1792, the villages and *bourgs* were pushing the more conservative departmental administrations and openly supporting the *journées* at Paris. Dijon itself (population 20,000) was fast becoming Republican. A year later, the department would elect three future members of the Committee of Public Safety—Carnot, Prieur, and Guyton-Morveau—and one member of the Committee of General Security—Basire, known as "the implacable leveller" (*le farouche niveleur*) to his enemies. Again, unlike the Vendée, the rural communes were as "patriotic" as the departmental capital.[78]

---

[76] *A. D.*, E–1725, Letter of September 6, 1791.
[77] Montenay, "L'établissement d'une manufacture," pp. 189, 189n.
[78] Drouot and Calmette, *Histoire de Bourgogne,* pp. 359–62.

V

EMIGRATION AND RETURN

*A*ccording to his daughter-in-law, the duke had never been in good
health. The Revolution in Paris and the blows to his fortune both
there and in Burgundy had not improved it. In January, 1792, at the
age of fifty-three, he died. His son, Charles-Marie-Casimir, was only
twenty-three and knew almost nothing about estate administration. Outwardly at least, he and his young wife seemed scarcely aware of the
Revolution. The new duchess described him on his arrival in Brussels at
the end of 1791:

> Monsieur de Tavanes, having taken his mother to Switzerland and made
> an excursion to Italy, came to join me [at Brussels]. I welcomed him with
> pleasure. He pleased everyone in our group, imparting affability and gaiety
> allied with a natural charm and wit.[1]

A certain naïveté was to be expected in a couple so young and so
sheltered from the world outside the high society of Paris. In her memoirs, the duchess herself admitted the frivolity of these early years. She
recalled the moment of her marriage in 1786, when "birth, fortune, and
youth" were joined with "all the pleasures the court could offer."[2] The
description of her presentation at Versailles was even more vivid:

> I recognize the same leaves in the parquet floor I had counted so carefully
> to make the three prescribed bows. They were of great importance then
> and the subject of many lessons. ... Should I retrace the frivolous pleasures,

[1] Duchesse de Saulx-Tavanes, *Mémoires (1791–1806)*, ed. Marquis de Valous
(Paris, 1934), p. 24.
[2] *Ibid.*, p. 146.

recalling that the diamonds mixed with roses on my dress also adorned the head of the Queen.... I can still see the room where the King, the Queen, Madame Elisabeth, the Duc de Brissac, and Madame d'Ossun were seated at the same table....[3]

Since their marriage, the couple had their own townhouse on the Rue de Choiseul. A dowry of 400,000 livres and the count's pension of 20,000 livres was apparently enough to maintain them in those years before the Revolution.[4] Like his father, the young Tavanes knew the shops along the Rue de Richelieu. His recently purchased captaincy in the dragoons gave him an excuse to buy a number of fine rapiers and sabers, in addition to uniforms for himself and a splendid new outfit for his coachman. His purchases at Paris continued until the spring of 1792, when his acquisition of a brace of pistols, a horse, and a chest suggest preparations for emigration.[5]

After paying his respects to the princes at Coblentz and visiting his wife in Brussels, Charles-Marie-Casimir returned to Paris for his father's funeral. Travel of this sort was apparently no problem before the declaration of war in April, 1792. If the second duke knew little about estate management, he learned something about inheritances. An investigation of his father's fortune had something to do with his new interest in the Comte de la Baume de Montrevel, last of his line and relative of the first duchess. In fact, Montrevel had already made a donation of 300,000 livres to Charles-Marie's sisters.[6] As the duchess said quite blandly: "M. de Saulx was interested in cultivating the friendship of M. le comte de Montrevel whose fortune was destined for him."[7] And it was not in vain that the young duke and duchess pursued this inheritance through the Revolution. A short time before Montrevel went to the guillotine in 1793, he summoned a notary to his prison cell and entrusted his fortune to the Tavanes.[8] The duchess saw in this act a proof of "noble and generous sentiments."

Events moved very rapidly in the spring of 1792. Fénéon managed to

---

[3] *Ibid.*, p. 159.

[4] *A. D.*, E–1727, Contract of Marriage, April 9, 1786.

[5] *A. D.*, E–1728, *Mémoire*, June 7 and June 23, 1792.

[6] *A. D.*, E–1727, Gift of July 28, 1783. Each sister was to receive a *rente* of 7,500 livres after the death of Montrevel.

[7] Duchesse de Saulx-Tavanes, *Mémoires*, p. 32.

[8] *Ibid.*, p. 172.

send the second duke 14,788 livres during the first six months of 1792 before his final departure from Paris in July. This was a far cry from the receipts of 1790, but not so bad given the circumstances. With the outbreak of war, the new law on emigration, and the establishment of the Republic in August, it is not surprising that Fénéon remained as inconspicuous as possible. He held back his remittances to Paris, inflated the expenses, and paid off a few local creditors. In 1792, taxes totalled 11,489 livres, perhaps a quarter of the revenue of that year. There were 38 receipts, suggesting continuous government levies made necessary by the war.[9] Until July, Charles-Marie had sent his certificates of residence as required by law to the local mayors, and it was not until the end of 1792 that his name appeared on the government list of *émigrés*.[10] The second duke kept Fénéon informed of his whereabouts abroad and, in late 1792, the agent wrote to Tavanes at Maastricht, urging him to return before his absence was noticed. By a law passed in April, anyone who was absent from France after May, 1792 was liable to lose his property to the state.[11] The sequestration of *émigré* lands had been deferred for the moment in Burgundy, but there was no time to lose.

Brussels in the winter of 1791–92 had none of the features of a modern refugee camp. It apparently served as a gathering place for noble families, while husbands consulted with the King's brothers and cousins in the Rhineland. The young duchess found Brussels a convenient place for the regular winter season, the *plaisirs d'hiver*, as she put it. Nearby Spa had been frequented by the wealthy French nobility even before the Revolution. Chateaubriand described Brussels at this time as a small Versailles:

> The most elegant women and most stylish men of Paris, all dressed as *aides de camp*, waited amidst their amusements for the moment of victory.... Considerable sums that would have permitted them to live a number of years were spent in a few days; it was not worth while to economize since they thought they would be back in Paris any day.[12]

[9] *A. D.*, E–1726, Fénéon Accounts, October, 1791, to June, 1793.

[10] *A. D.*, E–1744, Fénéon to Tavanes, February 11, 1818.

[11] J. B. Duvergier, *Collection complète des lois, décrets, ordonnances, règlements, avis du conseil d'état* (Paris, 1834), IV, 93–95.

[12] Chateaubriand, *Mémoires* I, 391–92, quoted in J. Vidalenc, *Les émigrés français, 1789–1825* (Caen, 1963), p. 229. The history of the emigration of court nobles is still best studied from memoirs. Those of Echerolles, La Tour du Pin, Chateaubriand, Montlosier, and La Rochefoucauld are among the best known. The excellent work of J. Vidalenc brings together a wealth of this material; it does not pretend

The high aristocracy was represented this winter by the Rohan-Chabot, Montmorency, Arenberg de la Marck, and various branches of the Choiseul family. Most of the noble families were accompanied by their complete households, chambermaids, lackeys, cooks, preceptors. There was nothing to suggest undignified flight or financial distress. The young duchess even enjoyed the exictement, a welcome change from the oppressive boredom of Versailles.

The outbreak of the war in April, 1792, and the new law regarding *émigrés* produced a wave of serious activity in this otherwise unaltered court society. A number of noble wives who enjoyed personal fortunes decided to return to France to protect them. They were confident that elderly women would be safe.[13] The grandmother of the young duchess, Madame de Choiseul-Beaupré, answered the plea of her *chargé d'affaires*, returned to her estate, sold the silver, and sent the proceeds to her son abroad. There was complete confidence that the allied armies would soon restore "order" in France.[14] In July, Charles-Marie went directly from Paris to join Condé's *émigré* army in the Rhineland. But the events of the summer and fall of 1792 came as a rude shock.

The first disillusion came with the disaster at Valmy in September. Among other aristocratic officers, the young duke rejoined his family at Maastricht. However, threatened by Dumouriez's advance into the Austrian Netherlands, they could not stay long. It was at this point in late 1792 that Fénéon's letter arrived, informing the young duke that he might still return to Burgundy and save the estate from sequestration.

One can only speculate on why Charles-Marie declined the chance to return to France and decided to follow Artois to England. From his earliest youth, the second duke had been closely associated with the court noblesse, who considered loyalty to the princes a point of honor. Madame des Echerolles described it as a duty: "One must leave or lose status."

I remember it perfectly—the agitation of our families, their secret meetings, the haste to pass on the news from beyond the Rhine. When are you

---

to be a statistical study. See also J. Godechot, *La Contre-révolution: doctrine et action* (Paris, 1961), and Duc de Castries, *Le testament de la monarchie, III, Les émigrés, 1789–1814* (Paris, 1963).

[13] Duvergier, *Collection des lois*, IV, 444. The Law of September 9, 1792, attempted to deal with this problem.

[14] Duchesse de Saulx-Tavanes, *Mémoires*, p. 49; see note 15 below.

leaving?, people asked. You will be too late. Hurry! They will come back without you. It is for such a short time.[15]

Moreover, the duke was a captain in the dragoons and he was very young. His father had not given him any opportunity to administer the estate and he had never visited Dijon or the château at Lux. He seemed to have no interest in these matters. It is significant that, after the Revolution, the duke legally transferred all authority over the administration of the estate to his wife.[16] Furthermore, he was stubborn. He never admitted that the royalist cause had been defeated. His emigration was not simply a matter of waiting out a long storm; he revealed a constant desire to "disembark," after Valmy, after Jemmapes, after Fleurus, even after the disaster at Quiberon in 1795. Finally, there was a wooden, shallow side to the second duke. It is curious that the duchess, in memoirs that are not devoid of intimacies and emotional expression, speaks only twice of her huband's personality. She alluded to his "gaiety and wit" in Brussels and, later, to his interest in music and art stimulated by his stay in Germany.[17] But that is all. There is no evidence that he made a single speech as a member of the House of Peers from 1815 to 1820, when he was still in his forties. The one reference to him relates to his "indisposition" on November 23, 1815, during the trial of Ney.[18] If we can credit anecdotal testimony, the young duke's outstanding trait was his good looks and his success with the ladies.[19] In short, Charles-Marie-Casimir de Saulx-Tavanes was not very farsighted or flexible, not to say worse of him. He did what his court milieu expected, and in this he was doggedly stubborn.

After Charles-Marie's decision to go to England, the travels of the duke and duchess became less of an emigration in lace—*en dentelles.* But, compensating for poor inns and crowded channel boats, the English reception was a warm one. Together with Londoners, the Tavanes were shocked at the news of the execution of Louis XVI. The modest pension granted to them by the English crown did not permit them to remain in

[15] Alexandrine des Echerolles, *Mémoires* (Paris, 1879), 13.
[16] *A. D.*, Q–1118, Procuration of June 2, 1810.
[17] Duchesse de Saulx-Tavanes, *Mémoires,* pp. 24, 159.
[18] *Archives Parlementaires*, Second Series (Paris, 1888–1908) XV, 289.
[19] S. de Montenay, "Comment la maison de Saulx-Tavanes fut ruinée en dernier lieu par son homme d'affaires," *Pays de Bourgogne*, No. 45 (1964).

London.[20] At the end of 1793, for reasons of economy, they moved to Swansea in Wales, where their first child was born. Here they stayed until the spring of 1795, when the failure of the *émigré* landing at Quiberon in Brittany dashed any immediate hope of a return to France. Among the *émigré* losses on the Breton beaches was Comte de Rieux, cousin of the second duke. Rieux's incentive had not only been political. The duchess said he had debarked in Brittany in the hope of procuring money for his aged and needy father. Shot by Hoche's troops at Vannes, he was the last of the house of Rieux.[21] Dissension over family portions seemed far away then.

In the fall of 1795, the duke and duchess decided on a new voyage. The father of the duchess, former ambassador to Constantinople, had made his way to Saint Petersburg, where he had been pensioned by Empress Catharine.[22] Financial considerations now took precedence over honor. With difficulty the duchess persuaded her husband to leave their English friends who, she observed, for all the differences in mores, habits, and language, were tied to them "by interest and rank." After a long crossing of the Baltic, the duchess happily joined her father and his entire household at Cronstadt. The Tavanes reentered a familiar environment. So francophone was the Romanov court that the duchess found it odd that French was not the exclusive language of Moscow society. Here the emigration "in lace" could be resumed.

Yet court life no longer satisfied either the duke or the duchess. Once financially secured by his father-in-law and the Russian government, the duke was again off to England in the hope of participating in another

[20] On the payments by the English government and by private charities see H. Weiner, *The French Exiles, 1789–1815* (London, 1960), pp. 141, 103, 169, 223–34. The subscriptions to Wilmont's Committee totalled over three million pounds. The Duchess of York conducted a special subscription for noble ladies in distress, including the "Quiberon widows." The English government paid an allowance to the Duc d'Artois of 500 pounds per month (120,000 livres per annum) and to the Princes-of-the-Blood in proportion. The lesser nobility, La Ferronays, for example, had to get along on about 3,600 livres, while servants of noble families received only a guinea a month. Of course many nobles lived with English friends.

[21] Duchesse de Saulx-Tavanes, *Mémoires*, p. 57.

[22] J. Balteau, M. Barroux, M. Prévis, *Dictionnaire de biographie française* (Paris, 1936), "Choiseul-Gouffier." See also *Archives Nationales*, T–153. As a diplomat abroad, Comte de Choiseul-Gouffier was not considered an "*émigré*." His wife, the countess, effectively argued his case and that of her two sons before the Committee of General Security in May, 1793. She even regained possession of her property near Dieppe. See *A.N.*, T–153[147].

amphibious effort off the Breton coast. "He wanted to be at his post," wrote the duchess. But she was happy to learn later that the expedition had been abandoned. At twenty-four, the duchess evinced considerably more perception concerning effective *émigré* military action than many others of her class. She observed that the presence of Artois as leader was not enough to assure success. Quiberon had proved that. Why should the royalists expect the Breton peasants to leave their homes and harvests for long? The miserable failure of the Vendée uprising had demonstrated to the peasants that even Republican conscription was preferable to joining the Princes in the future. As for the nobility, the duchess was especially acute:

> The Breton and Poitevin noblemen, trained from youth in rough hunting, were the only ones capable of pursuing the kind of warfare which demands a robust body, a knowledge of the country, and a resistance to fatigue.... Besides, the royalists did not form a party. Having escaped the bloody regime of the Terror, each individual was afraid of the least disturbance. They did not think of the future. Their desires and needs were limited. They thought only of obtaining restitutions to guarantee their security.[23]

Indeed, it is hard to imagine the young duke de Tavanes as a partisan chief of the type described in Balzac's *Chouans*.

The daughter of an amateur Hellenist of some repute, the duchess had been educated in the classics and was apparently well-read in other literature as well. Somehow, the emigration had not hindered her education. On the contrary, it seemed to broaden it. With the financial support of her father, she was able to travel to Poland and later to Germany, Switzerland, and Austria. It was not common for a Parisian noblewoman to conclude that there was more to literature than the elegance and refinement of the eighteenth-century masters.

> There is a *je ne sais quoi* that awakened the genius of Chateaubriand and which has formed a talent here for his melancholy gravity. Imagination is stimulated by the stress of the times and has colored the stage with horizons much more vast than those of Versailles.[24]

There is little doubt that the duchess had imbibed something we call Romanticism. In Poland, she described the "vast deserted plains and

[23] Duchesse de Saulx-Tavanes, *Mémoires*, pp. 72–73; Castries, *Emigrés*, pp. 192–93.
[24] Duchesse de Saulx-Tavanes, *"Mémoires inédites"*, quoted in L. Pingaud, *Les Saulx-Tavanes* (Paris, 1876), p. 324.

somber forest" offset by her encounters with the descendants of another breed of French *émigrés*—those of 1685. Curiously, she referred to their "common disgrace," a consequence of the "ways of Providence and the unexpected in history."[25] In retrospect at least, her travels offered her excitement, old friends rediscovered by chance, new liaisons easily contracted, and an independence that "brought movement and activity into my existence."[26] The memoirs of the duchess leave the unmistakable impression that these years of exile marked the most stimulating time of her life. This response to a new experience demonstrates once again how difficult it is to predict human actions from social origins alone. New experiences and a changed environment count for something.

In the spring of 1797, with a new tzar in Saint Petersburg and with word of quieter times at home, the duchess decided to return to France. Her own mother had returned during the Terror and had regained her property in Normandy. In times less tense the duchess should do as well. For some reason, her name was not on the list of *émigrés*, and her passage from Switzerland to the Department of the Jura was not obstructed. The duchess reported that the country people were most cooperative. She had no difficulty obtaining a certificate of residence with the nine requisite witnesses.[27] She was even able to get one for the duke stating his continuous residence in a local commune in the Jura since April, 1792. Apparently the departmental authorities were satisfied, though they found it curious that the name "Saulx-Tavanes" appeared on neither the national guard muster nor the tax roll of the commune.[28] Near Dôle, thirty miles southeast of Dijon, the duchess found that "most of the administrators had been employed under the old regime and greeted us without any allusion to the emigration."[29]

The duchess then proceeded directly to Paris in the hopes of removing her husband's name from the list of *émigrés* and securing the return of his unsold land. But the chance of quick success was shattered by the *coup d'état* of Fructidor in September, 1797, which annulled the royalist election victory. The Directory became suspicious of all *émigrés*, and the knowledge that the father of the duchess, a Choiseul-Gouffier, was still

[25] *Ibid.*, p. 325.
[26] *Ibid.*
[27] Duchesse de Saulx-Tavanes, *Mémoires*, p. 121.
[28] *A. D.*, Q–1118, List of Certificates of Residence.
[29] Duchesse de Saulx-Tavanes, *Mémoires*, p. 122.

in Russia, did not strengthen her case. She was forced to go into hiding. She spent a few months in Normandy with her sister and husband "whom the Revolution had forced to become a *commerçant*." Later she found a more comfortable seclusion in her childhood convent at Belle-chasse in the countryside outside of Paris. It was two years before Napoleon's seizure of power "reopened the gates of France to the nobility." In early 1800, both her husband and father returned from abroad.[30]

Almost immediately, the Saulx-Tavanes were joined by other returning noble *émigrés*, notably the families Choiseul, Narbonne, Luynes, and Montesson, who seemed to form an inner circle within a larger group of aristocrats. The duchess described this reentry into the old society years later with a certain reserve. Perhaps she felt it then.

> Through Madame de Choiseul I met the old society which lived in the Faubourg St. Germain. It has since become a power even in the eyes of Bonaparte. Its members had kept the same language, the same formulas of civility, and a sort of exaggerated affability. They talked a great deal about the details of economy and the condition of their fortunes.... In their marriage projects they calculated the value of a title or a *grandesse* without realizing that their value had changed.[31]

Her views about the Marquis de Narbonne also suggested that the duchess could not return to the court mores of her youth.

> The importance of M. de Narbonne in society resided primarily in the empire that French frivolity accords to elegance, good taste, and a certain success founded on the reciprocal pleasures of vanity.... Something about him recalled the mores attributed to the former courtiers at a time when one was proud of his debts, mocked his creditors, and paid them with pretty words....[32]

But if the duchess of Saulx had some doubts about the authenticity of the new "court," she was not above taking advantage of old friends. If Madame de Montesson exhibited an excessive vanity and love of luxury, she nonetheless entertained influential members of the new government.[33] If the duke and duchess of Luynes had unfortunate political views, their kindness to returning *émigrés* helped one forget them. Moreover, some

---

[30] *Ibid.*, pp. 122–46. See also Pingaud, *Saulx-Tavanes*, p. 328.

[31] Duchesse de Saulx-Tavanes, *Mémoires*, p. 143. The duke pursued the *"Grandesse d'Espagne"* until 1819 when it was finally refused. *A. D.*, E–1678 (1724–1819).

[32] *Ibid.*, pp. 168–69.

[33] *Ibid.*, p. 156.

allowance must be made for release after almost a decade of absence from Paris. At twenty-seven, the duchess may be forgiven her momentary enthusiasm for balls, concerts, theatre, and the outdoor *fêtes* at the Tivoli and Elysée palaces.[34]

The Comte de Choiseul-Gouffier, ex-ambassador to the Porte, was well received by Talleyrand, and his daughter apparently impressed the vivacious Madame Bonaparte. Both connections were extremely helpful to the family.

> My father was pleased to meet the members of the diplomatic corps again and the foreigners he had known in Russia at M. de Talleyrand's.... He had lent considerable sums of money to the Austrian prisoners taken by the Turks when he was ambassador at Constantinople.[35]

The new regime, anxious to end the war with Austria, might find experienced diplomats such as Choiseul-Gouffier useful. Despite certain faults in the eyes of the duchess, Talleyrand was not without virtue. He had respect for his relatives, affection for his brothers, devotion to the interests of his family. "He valued domestic virtues regarding those with whom he shared an ancestor."[36] Clearly he was not the most disagreeable of the new men in high places.

The duchess could stoop to conquer. Her contacts with Madame Bonaparte during the "visits of winter" had been profitable. Despite Napoleon's express order that his wife stay out of *émigré* affairs, Josephine was very susceptible to entreaties by old noble families. It had not been easy for the duchess. The best she could say for the wife of the new First Consul was that, despite her frivolity and neglected education, she had a certain dignity and tact. Of course, one must avoid her "motley company"—*société bigarrée*. Most disagreeable had been the duchess's encounter with Fouché, new Minister of Interior. "It was not without a certain repugnance that I sat beside this minister at dinner at Malmaison."[37]

Patience, persistence, and diplomacy were finally rewarded. With the help of these "friends" and the intercession of the Russian and Austrian ambassadors, the father and husband of the duchess were removed from

[34] *Ibid.*, pp. 157, 138–39.
[35] *Ibid.*, p. 165.
[36] *Ibid.*
[37] *Ibid.*, p. 155.

the dreaded "list of *émigrés*." One can not but wonder what the ambassadors said to recommend the two men to Bonaparte—or was Talleyrand's approval sufficient? In any case, Charles-Marie-Casimir, Citizen Saulx-Tavanes was "definitively erased" in November, 1802. "The judgment of the Consuls declares that he will regain possession of his lands that have not been sold ... without any claim to an indemnity for property alienated."[38] How many *émigrés* read these words in 1802? How oddly neutral the word "alienated" must have seemed to them!

*

It had been ten years since Fénéon, the estate agent, had received word that the second duke would not return to France. What had happened to the estate in Burgundy during that time? Loyal to the family through four difficult years, Fénéon was alone to face the Year I of "Liberty" as an agent of the "former Duke de Saulx-Tavanes, *émigré*." This was not a popular professional title in 1793. To be remembered in the local community as a *ci-devant feudiste* could not have made his task easier. Yet he was determined to demonstrate his administrative competence to his new master, the French Republic. His tone toward the local administration had changed since 1791. His report to the district in January, 1793, suggested a busy and cooperative civil servant.

> ...I must go to Châlon-sur-Saône to submit my accounts to the municipal administration for the property of M. de Tessé, so that I can not make the declaration necessitated by the absence of the son of M. de Saulx until my return.... I am responsible for the receipts and expenses of the revenues of the inheritance of the late Citizen Saulx-Tavanes, the elder, and I assure you that no circumstance can make me deviate from the openness and exactitude that have always characterized my conduct.[39]

Citizen Fénéon now submitted monthly reports to the district. He took pride, as always, in arranging leases favorable to the proprietor, noble seigneur or French government. In September, 1792, he had negotiated a new lease for Beaumont, stipulating that the rent be paid in kind, no doubt to mitigate the effects of inflation. The grain rent claimed a good third of the gross harvest which assured the district a re-

[38] *A. D.*, Q–1118, *Radiation de la liste des émigrés. 12 Brumaire, An X.*
[39] *A. D.*, Q–876², Fénéon to Citizens Administrators of the District of Is-sur-Tille, January 10, 1793.

turn at least equal to the money rents paid in the 1780s. The mills were leased separately with the proviso that the tenant make all the repairs and even construct a second mill by 1794.[40] He continued to contest the claims of the local communes to the wood and even resumed his effort to claim arrears in seigneurial dues dating from before 1789. Among these was a claim to the *droit d'indire* at Blagny for 1787. After all, for a conscientious estate manager, an obligation was an obligation, regardless of the fact that it was no longer legally operative.[41]

On the debit side of the ledger, Fénéon recorded taxes of 11,489 livres paid from October, 1791, to December, 1792—close to one-fourth of the gross revenue.[42] He also deducted larger sums for repairs than had ever appeared on his accounts to the duke. True, there was some damage to the forge at Tilchâtel and to the mill at Arc-sur-Tille, possibly due to local disorders in 1789 and 1791.[43] But this does not account for over 12,000 livres spent for construction of two large barns for cattle and forage at Arc-sur-Tille, which proved an excellent selling point later.[44] Was Fénéon taking advantage of a more indulgent public proprietor, or was Calignon, the tenant at Arc, now able to have his way?[45] Mayor of Arc, Calignon had already taken advantage of the Revolution to reduce his rent by overestimating the *dîme* and to sell the duke's wood without authorization.[46] All indications are that Calignon was a strong and shrewd personality who knew how to organize local public opinion and intimidate his rivals. In 1793, men like Calignon had a command over the local community that Fénéon could no longer contest. After the Revolution, Fénéon attempted to collect from Calignon, but without written evidence, the agent was at a distinct disadvantage.[47]

Of Fénéon's "exactitude" there could be little doubt; his "openness" and charitable inclinations were another matter. He informed the public authorities that the establishment of five doctors in 10 parishes was *his*

---

[40] *A. D.*, Q–1117, Report on Beaumont.

[41] *A. D.*, Q–1117, Report of May 18, 1793.

[42] *A. D.*, E–1726, Accounts, 1791–93.

[43] *A. D.*, Q–1117, *Inventaire des titres et papiers de Régie* (Tilchâtel and Arc-sur-Tille).

[44] *A. D.*, Q–193, *Ventes* (Arc-sur-Tille).

[45] *A. D.*, Q–1117, *Etat des dettes passives* (Arc-sur-Tille).

[46] *A. D.*, E–1744, Letters of May 8, 1813 and February 11, 1818.

[47] *A. D.*, E–1744, Letter of February 11, 1818.

idea in 1789. He was quite willing to continue to pay them at 150 livres per year, but when Citizen Dr. Normand refused to work at such a low salary, Fénéon made no effort to raise it. He disagreed with the district about using an annuity of 36 livres established by a Tavanes three generations ago for a public granary (*grenier d'abondance*). He also argued against the administration of this charity by the municipalities.[48] From this correspondence in early 1793 it appears that Fénéon was not anxious to use the estate revenues to increase rural charity, especially under the auspices of the local communes. Was he protecting the duke's revenues or simply expressing his own views on such matters? That the government made inquiries into an annuity of only 36 livres gives some idea of its limited resources in that desperate year. It also suggests that the Republic's failure to help the rural poor in this instance was not a result of callousness.[49]

In April, 1793, the "movables" of the château of Lux were sequestered and sold at auction. Fénéon's inventory preserves the record. Some 931 articles were sold, bringing in 24,483 livres, a substantial sum by provincial standards. The best prices were bid for the beds and mirrors; chairs, buffets, *armoires*, linen, and kitchen ware sold very poorly, while the books brought rather better prices than might be expected in a rural community. The library varied in quality from Raynal's *History of the Indies* to *Theatre of the Boulevards*, but the books sold almost invariably at one livre each, suggesting that the discrimination of the buyers was not much different from the duke's. The inventory notes that the billiard table was "completely worn," implying that the steward at Lux, the chief warden, or perhaps even Fénéon did not spend all their time arranging accounts or inspecting the property. Fénéon managed to salvage the duke's cabriolet for himself. Two paintings, one of the Dauphin, father of Louis XVI, and the other of Jacques de Saulx, family ancestor, found their way to the Dijon public museum. The duchess attempted in vain to get them back in 1816.[50]

[48] *A. D.*, Q–1117, Report of May 18, 1793 (Chapter 10); *A. D.*, Q–876[2], *Oeuvres de bienfaisance: Beaumont-sur-Vingeanne, 1792–An II*.

[49] See A. Cobban, *A Social Interpretation of the French Revolution* (Cambridge, 1965), "Whoever won the revolution, the poor lost." The suggestion of callousness is implicit in the work of 0. Hufton, *Bayeux in the Late Eighteenth Century: A Social Study* (Oxford, 1967).

[50] *A. D.*, Q–1117, *Sequestre mobilier et archives, 1793–An III*; *A. D.*, Q–1118, Petition to Prefect, August 9, 1816.

The following month, Fénéon submitted a long report, summarizing
the financial condition of the estate, payments made to creditors, and
litigation in progress with tenants, communes, and other parties. He also
listed the wages he had paid from the receipts to the steward, the forest
guards, and the doctors serving the poor. Administrative expenses included his own salary of 2,400 livres and special outlays for the inventories at Lux of 4,729 livres more.[51] Anticipating the sale of the Tavanes
estate as National Property, Fénéon ended his report with appropriate
deference:

> Such is the report of my administration. The details are long. Perhaps the
> reader will find them fastidious, but I cannot make them more lively. My
> purpose has been to bring the Citizens Administrators up to date on all
> aspects of this administration. If I have not included everything, they are
> indulgent enough to know that I have tried my best. If during the short
> time that I will remain in the district, you need further clarification, I beg
> you to address yourselves to me with confidence.[52]

Three days later, Fénéon deposited all the titles and estate papers with
the District authorities.

A look at sectional maps of the Tavanes holdings makes it easy to see
how the pattern of ownership facilitated sale in small lots. Aside from
the wood, the duke's property was already divided into tiny scraps, rarely
over an acre and interspersed with the strips of peasant holdings. This
checker-board pattern was especially marked at Lux and Beaumont, but
only slightly less so at Arc-sur-Tille. An obvious impediment to rational-
ized grain production, this pattern was ideal for redistribution among
many small holders.[53]

The sales began in the spring of 1794 and continued through the
summer and fall. Thermidor apparently made no difference. Altogether
2,780 acres of grain and meadow land were sold in 864 lots. The domain
at Arc-sur-Tille fell from 1,955 to 631 acres, the one at Beaumont from
971 to 647, while the smaller domains at Bourberain, Spoy, Champagne,
Blagny, Bessey disappeared almost entirely. At Lux, for example, only
the château and two acres remained unsold. In the following winter

---

[51] *A. D.*, E–1726, Fénéon Accounts, 1791–93.

[52] *A. D.*, Q–1117, Report of May 15, 1793.

[53] See Documents VII and VIII; also, see maps of Lux (*A. D.*, E–1916), Beaumont (*A. D.*, E–1781), and Arc-sur-Tille (*A. D.*, E–1762); G. Roupnel, *La ville et la
campagne au XVIIe siècle* ... (Paris, 1955).

(1795–96) the forge at Tilchâtel (now Mont-sur-Tille) was sold, so that by mid-1796 the forests were the only substantial properties left. It was patently impractical to divide forest into small lots, so the woodland of the duke was held as a national domain. Judging from the number of lots sold, the Saulx-Tavanes were among the heaviest losers in the department, equalled only by such rich noble families as Bouhier and Legoux, both former presidents at the Parlement of Dijon.[54]

Who were the buyers of the Tavanes land? The question of who bought national property, despite a prodigious historical literature, has not yet been answered with statistical precision.[55] The answer requires a study, not only of transfers of land at the moment of sale of *émigré* properties, but also of subsequent transfers. No doubt, men of larger means bought out smaller buyers, and *émigré* agents, acting as "straw men," repurchased their masters' land, sometimes keeping it for themselves.[56] Even when these obstacles are overcome, it will still be difficult to identify precisely who "profited" from the sales. Loutchisky and his many disciples have reduced the issue to a choice between "peasants" and "bourgeois." The actualities of rural existence make such a simplification unhelpful. If the sales at Beaumont cannot resolve all the issues, they can at least emphasize the complexity of the problem and suggest that all elements of the local society "profited" in some degree from the land sales.[57]

[54] *A. D.*, Q–28, *Tableau des Ventes*; Q–403, *Liste alphabétique des différents propriétaires dépossedés* (246 names). See also *A. D.*, Q–1118, *Indemnisation*, 1825–29. The departmental summary of sales indicates only the number of *ventes*, not the areas. The district summaries, unfortunately incomplete, indicate that the sales were in lots of two to three acres in the vast majority of cases. The author is well aware of the imprecision of this remark. Hopefully the research project of Marc Bouloiseau on the transfer of *émigré* land will produce exact figures.

[55] For a brief review of this literature, see R. Forster, "The Survival of the Nobility during the French Revolution," *Past and Present* (July, 1967), 71–86. Lefebvre's work on the department of the Nord was a model of precision on this point but it was not followed rigorously by his successors.

[56] See F. Vermale, "Le retour de l'émigré," *Annales révolutionnaires* VII (1914), 149–64.

[57] J. Loutchisky, "De la petite propriété en France avant le Révolution," *Revue historique* LIX (1895), 71. Among his disciples one might include Lefebvre, Marion, Bouloiseau, and Soboul. Lefebvre, of course, was well aware of the nuances in the rural community; they were more important to him than the bourgeois-peasant dichotomy. Loutchisky himself asked if *both* peasant and bourgeois may have benefitted from the land transfers of the Revolution.

TABLE V.1   BUYERS OF THE LAND OF SAULX-TAVANES AT BEAUMONT

	Profession or metier	Area Purchased (in Journaux—0.8 Acres) Arable	Meadow	Revenue of Acquisition (Government Estimate) Livres and Sous
1.	*Cultivateur*	69.0	11.0	866.–
2.	Id.	15.6	——	181.–15
3.	Id.	12.5	——	102.–2
4.	Id.	10.0	——	89.–13
5.	Id.	7.5	——	70.–5
6.	Id.	6.3	——	65.–10
7.	Id.	5.0	——	46.–2
8.	Id.	5.0	0.3	44.–8
9.	Id.	4.0	——	40.–
10.	Id.	2.5	0.8	41.–
11.	*Artisan* (blacksmith)	6.3	0.5	87.–13
12.	Id. (blacksmith)	7.8	——	67.–
13.	Id. (wheelwright)	2.5	——	65.–
14.	Id. (stonecutter)	5.0	——	61.–5
15.	Id. (wheelwright)	4.3	——	42.–11
16.	Id. (mason)	4.3	——	41.–16
17.	Id. (mason)	4.3	——	41.–9
18.	Id. (mason)	1.8	——	21.–15
19.	Id. (mason)	1.8	——	17.–
20.	Id. (miller)	0.2	——	16.–1
21.	Id. (stonecutter)	1.3	——	13.–5
22.	Id. (weaver)	0.2	——	0.–15
23.	Winegrower	2.0	——	16.–
24.	Id.	3.0	——	25.–
25.	Teacher	0.5	0.1	21.–17
26.	Id.	0.1 (and one house)		26.–10
27.	*Manouvrier*	2.5	——	24.–10
28.	Id.	0.1 (and one house)		10.–5
29.	Id.	0.5 (and 0.2 vineyard)		6.–7
30.	Gardener	6.0	——	65.–
31.	Widow	9.5	——	93.–13
32.	Bourgeois of Dijon	23.5	0.8	207.–
33.	*Avoué* of Dijon	23.0	——	188.–13
34.	Unidentified	——	0.8	16.–6
35.	The Commune of Beaumont	——	22.1	708.–
	Total:	224.2	36.8	2,731.–4

SOURCE: *A. D.*, Q–1117, List of 34 new proprietors for the *Contribution foncière* of 1793; *A. D.*, L–838, *Contribution foncière* of 1791 with amendments. Taxes in 1793 were raised to 6 sous, 7 deniers to the livre or one-third of revenue.

The three largest buyers acquired about half of the arable land (115.5 *journaux*) and a third of the meadow (11.8 *journaux*) put on sale. Moniotte, the former tenant of the duke at Beaumont, added 64 acres (80 *journaux*) to his holdings, plus the mill worth an additional 600 livres revenue.[58] He increased his landed income from 441 to 1,913 livres. Perhaps more important than the added income was the fact that he was now the third largest *propriétaire* in the commune.[59] He was no longer primarily a *fermier* or *sous-fermier*. The two other largest buyers were *Sieurs* Petitjean and Bonnard, both *Bourgeois* residing in Dijon. Petitjean had been resident steward in Beaumont in 1792.[60] These two men bought 36 acres (45 *journaux*) of the duke's land *par moitié*, that is, as a single acquirer. The tax roll indicates that both Moniotte and Petitjean subsequently made other purchases and exchanges in the commune, apparently at the expense of a number of winegrowers. There is no evidence that any of these men played any political role during the Revolution in the commune or at Dijon, but they clearly "profited" from it. Perhaps they can be labelled "rural bourgeois," but more precisely, Moniotte was an agriculturalist (a farmer in the American sense), Bonnard a lawyer, and Petitjean an ex-administrator and non-resident landowner. Guelaud, former tenant at Blagny and active in communal government, made more modest gains, buying four acres to become a *propriétaire* for the first time.[61] The plot was too small to live on and Guelaud still needed land to rent. But his relation to the land was changing, just as Moniotte's was.

The other half of the land placed on sale at Beaumont was bought by thirty-one local residents, all living within a five mile radius of the commune. There were at least twenty buyers from Beaumont itself, a village of 94 households in 1789.[62] There were an equal number of new owners, men who had never owned any land before. The table indicates the distribution among social groups. The number of small buyers, some purchasing only a tenth of an acre, was facilitated by national legislation

[58] *A. D.*, L–838, Article 20. Moniotte must have owned at least 200 acres.

[59] *A. D.*, L–838, Article 4 (Juillet—4,584 livres); Article 11 (Petitjean—2,518 livres).

[60] The duke had no steward at Beaumont before the Revolution. Petitjean was probably employed by the government in 1792. *A. D.*, Q–876² Administration of Is-sur-Tille to J-B. Petitjean, *régisseur* at Beaumont. Petitjean was a resident of Beaumont by the tax roll of 1791, but a resident of Dijon later.

[61] *A. D.*, L–838. See Sections K and J indicating land transfers subsequent to the sale of the Tavanes property. See Article 182 for Gueland. Article 47 indicates "Bartet, notary" with a revenue of 98 livres. Apparently he was not a buyer.

[62] *A. D.*, C–5927 (1789). See *Source* of Table of Buyers, above.

which had become increasingly favorable to the small proprietor. By the law of July 25, 1793, local administrations were encouraged to divide the farms (*les corps de ferme*) and arrange payment in ten annual installments at five per cent. It was not until March, 1795, that the Convention began to demand down-payments of a quarter of the price and six-year payment schedules.[63] In addition to this favorable legal climate, the depreciation of the assignats, especially after Thermidor (July, 1794), must have aided anyone who could sell foodstuffs or even the wares of his shop or bench. It is still surprising to find twelve artisans, two wine-growers, and even three daylaborers with sufficient capital to buy land. One acre of grainland at 300 livres would cost 30 livres per annum, assuming no down-payment was required.[64] This sum represented about thirty days' wages. True, some of the buyers pooled their resources. Five of the artisans bore the same family name of Anselme. They may well have bid as a single buyer for the land and then divided it afterward.[65]

What of the other villages? At Arc-sur-Tille, 388 "lots" were sold under the supervision of Pierre Jacquemard, "*commissaire expert*" and local notary. Jean Calignon, the duke's former tenant and the new mayor of the commune, bought 39 of these "lots" or about 150 acres of land out of a total of 1,300 acres eventually sold. The purchase included the central *corps* of the farm, a fifty-acre piece containing the farm buildings—tenants' lodging, two granges, stables for 36 cows and oxen, large storage sheds, kennels, and barns which the government report characterized as "*beaux*" and "*considérables*," some built in "the last four years."[66]

Calignon had not permitted revolutionary politics to prevent him from making improvements. Could he possibly have anticipated in 1790 that the buildings would be his in September, 1794? Again like Moniotte at Beaumont, Calignon had become a *propiétaire* and *cultivateur*. Now at last he could fully exercise his talents as an agriculturalist. In 1801, Vaillant's new statistical survey of the department contained this interesting passage:

[63] M. Garaud, *Histoire générale du droit privé français: la Revolution et la propriété foncière* (Paris, 1958), 317–19.
[64] *A. D.*, Q–28. At Lux, prices varied from 200 to 300 livres per *journal*; *A. D.*, Q–193. At Arc-sur-Tille, they ranged from 400 to 500 livres on good grainland.
[65] *A. D.*, Q–1117, List of 34 new proprietors.
[66] *A. D.*, Q–193, *Ventes* (Arc-sur-Tille).

In the last years M. Calignon, *propriétaire* at Arc-sur-Tille has cultivated *arujutus* (white oats). Sixty kilograms of this seed has been planted on 70 *ares* (two acres) bearing wheat the previous year. It produced 1,350 kilograms or about 23 to one. This yield is incomparably higher than the yield of ordinary oats which never exceeds seven to one. Moreover, the white oats weigh a quarter more than the other.[67]

Calignon had gained regional notoriety as an agricultural improver. Independent ownership of 150 acres had been a greater stimulus, perhaps, than leasing 1,500 acres from Duc de Saulx-Tavanes.

The rest of the duke's arable and meadow land at Arc was sold to 80 buyers, 66 of whom became proprietors for the first time. As at Beaumont, they bought in lots of one to three acres; only Calignon's pieces were large.[68] At Lux, the largest buyer was one Claude Dugier of nearby Veronnes, who bought 112 acres of arable land and 21 acres of meadow, about forty per cent of the land sold in the commune. Here neither the tenant Jacotot nor the tenant at neighboring Tilchâtel bought any land. But Perriquet, the tenant at Orville, bought a few acres along with a half-dozen *laboureurs* and about sixty local artisans, winegrowers, and "little people" who purchased an average of one acre each.[69] At Tilchâtel, one Jean Meurtot bought a large lot of 104 acres of the duke's land, while the rest was sold in 52 "lots" of less than one acre each.[70]

There is no doubt that here were some large purchases, either by non-residents such as Petitjean or by former tenants such as Calignon. But it would be wrong to see these men as swallowing up all, or even most of the land placed on the market. There was also a swarm of very small buyers, many of whom now owned land for the first time. To be sure, Michelet's utopia of small independent owners was not suddenly created out of the débris of noble estates like Tavanes's. Independent ownership in the Dijon plain was already a fact before 1789. But the sales of national land did reinforce a sense of proprietorship at all levels of rural society, converting even the *fermiers* to the mystique of ownership.

[67] Vaillant, *Statistique du département de la Côte d'Or* (Paris, An IX), p. 420.
[68] N. Garnier, *Arc-sur-Tille: La Révolution, 1789–1802* (Dijon, 1913), 158–59.
[69] *A. D.*, Q–28, Articles 638–708.
[70] *A. D.*, Q–28, Articles 1152–1207; See also M. Balotte, *La baronie de Saint-Julien à travers les âges* (Dijon, 1961). The pattern of purchases, a few large, but a substantial number of small ones, was the same at Saint-Julien, five miles northwest of Arc-sur-Tille.

After 1800, the Napoleonic regime established a system of "electoral colleges" made up of local "notables," men chosen for life, who had a certain revenue and social standing in each canton and who could be relied upon to support the regime and serve as a pool of recruits for the imperial administration. The "colleges" had negligible political power, their deliberations were strictly circumscribed by the prefect.[71] If it is too much to say that these lists present the men who "won" the Revolution, they clearly include those who did rather better than survive it.

The list for the Côte d'Or includes at least five of the Saulx-Tavanes' former *fermiers*: the Rochet brothers, Calignon, Jacotot, and Marchand. All but Jacotot were among the 550 most heavily taxed people in the department in 1802. It is not altogether surprising that the ironmasters along the Tille River—Robert, the new owner of the forge at Tilchâtel, Lagnier at Tarsul, and Dubois at Diénay are also listed—were favored by a new regime that needed canon, arms, and naval supplies. Their political activity was perhaps less expected. Jean-Baptiste Rochet, despite his difficulties with the Tavanes lease, took over another forge on the Tille, and drew an income of at least 3,000 francs in 1810. His political career since 1789 was even more impressive. Rochet became vice president of the departmental directorate, president of the administration of the district, of the civil tribunal, and of the municipal government at Is-sur-Tille, member of the General Council of the department, and president of the canton. Rochet's older brother, Jean-Frédéric, was ironmaster and mayor at Bèze. Much less active politically, he was considered by the prefect, along with Robert of Tilchâtel, as among the six "most notable" ironmasters in the department in 1810. He and Robert had incomes of 10,000 and 12,000 francs respectively, and an annual production of iron valued at six times this amount. Rochet's son-in-law and partner, M. Sirodot, was cited in a prefectoral report as especially "active" and intelligent, his service in the army as an artillery officer no doubt having contributed to his knowledge of ironmaking. Clearly, the imperial government encouraged men like Robert and Rochet much more than their noble landlord did twenty years before.

In 1810 Jacotot was a *propriétaire* with 1,200 francs revenue, modest in comparison with the ironmasters, but independent. Nicolas Marchand,

---

[71] These "notables" appear as names on the electoral lists of 1802–10 and the most wealthy on the departmental lists of the *600 plus imposés* (1802–), *A. N.*, F[1] C III. See the *Bulletin des lois* XXI, 535–50 for the law establishing the electoral colleges.

négotiant and *propriétaire* became mayor of Arc-sur-Tille after Jean Calignon. Calignon himself probably died before 1810—his name disappears from the lists after 1802—but his son appears as a "notable" from Dijon. Having studied medicine before the Revolution, the young Jean Calignon served as army doctor during the war, to become a respectable surgeon in 1810 with an income of 3,000 francs. There was nothing unique about moving from the grain trade to medicine, but Calignon's long struggles with both Tavanes and the villagers of Arc-sur-Tille may have encouraged his son to take up a more secure profession in town. It is also possible that the war had made the medical profession more respectable.

A number of village notaries also advanced their careers, thanks in part to the Revolution. Jean-Baptiste Petitjean became justice of the peace at Beaumont and a member of the municipal council and hospice at Dijon, with a revenue of 4,500 francs. Jean Bartet, the notary who kept the *terrier* of Beaumont for the villagers in their contest with the duke twenty-five years earlier became *juge de paix* and one of the fourteen "notables" of the canton. Jean-Baptiste Boniard, modest *cultivateur* with only 150 livres income, became president of the municipality of Beaumont and mayor of Champagne. With the possible exception of the hospice at Dijon, these were not important offices, but now there was a place for the village notary and small owner-occupier in a more elaborate local administration.

Land surveyors (*arpenteurs*) also "survived," though perhaps less successfully than *fermiers*, notaries, and *cultivateurs*. Edme Morizot—perhaps the same *maître* Morizot the duke attempted to exile as a "troublemaker"—became justice of the peace and assistant to the mayor of Is-sur-Tille, the most important *bourg* in the district. On the other side of the department, in a village near Saulieu, the name of François Fénéon appears. He was 56 in 1810, identified as a "former commissioner of feudal rights" and manager (*régisseur*) of a private estate, with an estimated income of only 700 francs, the second lowest on a list of 21 "notables" from a completely rural canton. It is also worth noting that the name of Jacquemard does not appear on any of the electoral lists for 1810. Quite possibly, the Napoleonic prefect did not feel that Jacquemard should be recognized as a "notable."

If these few examples suggest changes in social mobility, the release of certain entrepreneurial energies, and the arrival of "new men" in the local

191

government, there were continuities as well. At least nine former councilors of Parlement and four magistrates of the old Chamber of Accounts appear on the list, with incomes ranging from five to 20,000 francs. Louis Maulbon, former *Trésorier de France* and erstwhile helpful acquaintance of the first duke, is listed as *propriétaire* with 6,500 francs revenue. He was a member of the General Council of the department in 1810. Near the end of the list of the 550 "most heavily taxed" for the year 1802—but not among the "notables" of 1810—was Charles Saulx-Tavanes, *propriétaire* at Lux.[72]

* *

Although Fénéon stopped keeping the estate accounts at the end of 1793, he did not cease his efforts on behalf of the Saulx-Tavanes. His report to the duchess in 1818 makes this clear. Accusing Calignon of not honoring verbal agreements regarding wood sales, Fénéon sought out one of the tenant's factors in order to obtain written receipts that he could later use in court. He found one of these intermediaries on his deathbed, only to learn that he had transferred all the bills of sale and the money to Calignon. But the agent did not give up hope of recovering written evidence from other buyers.[73]

More important than Fénéon's pursuit of old tenants was his effort to repurchase at least a few pieces of the duke's land. There is no evidence that the duke left either instructions or the means for Fénéon to serve as a straw man to repurchase large portions of the estate. But Fénéon was able to buy scattered pieces, totalling 80 acres of grainland and meadow worth over 100,000 francs and to resell some, making a profit of 40,000 in the process.[74] His greatest service, however, consisted of liquidating family debts, presumably in assignats, at a considerable discount. In January, 1792, at the death of the first duke, the debts had attained the spectacular figure of 1,622,553 livres, with annual interest charges of 84,160 livres, not including obligations to artisans, merchants, and suppliers of all kinds.[75] But after 1793, there were few creditors of the family who believed they

---

[72] *A. N.*, F¹ C III (Côte d'Or), (3), (4). For the ironmasters, see *A. N.*, F¹²937, *Liste des fabricants les plus notables des départements (1810).*

[73] *A. D.*, E–1744, Letter of February 11, 1818.

[74] *A. D.*, E–1728, *Etat des affaires faites pour Mme la duchesse de Saulx-Tavanes*, November 18, 1818.

[75] *A. D.*, E–1727, *Etat général des créances*, January 1, 1792.

would ever hear of the duke again, much less collect their money. Fénéon apparently chose the winter 1796–97, the height of the post-Thermidorian inflation, to begin liquidation.[76] A portion of Fénéon's report will give an idea of the type of operation he was conducting:

Credit of M. Guershal	23,500 livres
and five years' interest——	28,200 livres (27,851 francs)*
liquidated for 16,669 fr.	Profit ....11,182 francs
Credit of Petitor	4,600 livres
and five years' interest——	5,520 livres (5,451 francs)
liquidated for 4,590 fr.	Profit ....861 francs
Credit of Villière	19,000 livres
and five years' interest——	22,800 livres (22,518 francs)
liquidated for 18,765 fr.	Profit ....3,753 francs
Credit of Duleu	8,000 livres
and five years' interest——	9,600 livres (9,481 francs)
liquidated for 3,600 fr.	Profit ....5,881 francs

* The account indicates that the franc was slightly stronger than the livre.

Fénéon later claimed that he had saved the family 86,359 livres by his "acquisitions and negotiations" at Dijon and Paris.[77] Even after the return of the duke and duchess, Fénéon was able to continue liquidating the family debts at substantial discounts. But where did he obtain the capital to pay off creditors in the 1790s? Was he in contact with the second duke after all? In any event, it is not surprising that after his return from abroad in 1799, the second duke continued to employ his father's agent. Fénéon was still useful.

If defense lawyers in 1801 spoke of the "poor vestiges of an opulent succession," the Tavanes properties were not all lost beyond recall. A great deal had been sold, but some 5,000 acres of woodland was in government hands and still unsold. Fortunately for the duke and duchess, the suggestion of the Department of Water and Forest that the Tavanes tracts be declared permanent national property or "Imperial Wood" was not followed through.[78] If this forest could be restituted intact, the

[76] A. D., E–1728, *Etat*, November 18, 1818. The precise date is not given. Fénéon's accounts refer to five years' interest in every case. I have identified one of the loans, originally contracted in December, 1791.

[77] *Ibid.*

[78] A. D., Q–1118, *Restitutions, An XII–1821.*

second duke could still hope to enjoy a landed income of near 30,000 francs, a third of the income in 1789, but a sum worth having.

Unfortunately, the estate was now endangered not by direct public confiscation or sale, but by the inheritance claims of the duke's two sisters and his uncle. They were not unaware of recent changes in the laws of inheritance. As early as April, 1793, before the sale of the properties in Burgundy, the countesses Castellane and Kercado renounced their rights under the new inheritance law to an equal share in the fortune of their father. Instead, they submitted claims to the full payment of their dowries to which they were entitled under a new decree in 1794. They thereby became privileged creditors of the inheritance of the amount of 200,000 livres each.[79] Dangerous enough to a shrinking estate, the sisters were joined by their uncle, younger brother of the first duke, who claimed another 100,000 livres by his marriage contract in 1771.[80] If family charges had been a threat before the Revolution, they were now a catastrophe. The entire estate was not worth much more than 500,000 livres in 1800.

The action of these close relatives is an interesting commentary on the breakdown of family solidarity during the Revolutionary decade. No doubt the second duke's brother-in-law, Comte de Kercado, had his own family interests to consider and exerted pressure on his wife to assert her dowry claims. But the reputation of the two sisters as "Saulx-Républicaines" was not entirely unearned.[81] For one thing, the Comtesse de Castellane had taken advantage of the new divorce law. For another, the sisters had not waited for the return of their brother from Russia to take matters into their own hands. In the summer of 1799, they had begun action in the courts of Dijon, and by the spring of 1800, they had surveyed and divided the wood into two lots of about 2,000 acres each.[82] The second duke's uncle, Charles-Dominique-Sulpice, was not far behind. By the fall of 1800, he had submitted a claim to 600 acres of wood at Arc-sur-Tille.[83] In older aristocratic circles at least, such rapid conformity to the new laws of inheritance—indeed improving on equal divi-

---

[79] A. D., Q–1118, *Liquidation des créances, 1793–An VIII*; A. D., E–1727, *Deliberation à Paris, 15 Messidor, An IX* (August, 1801).

[80] A. D., Q–1118, *Liquidation des créances*, Claim of 3 Nivôse, An. VIII.

[81] Duchesse de Saulx-Tavanes, *Mémoires*, p. 154n.

[82] A. D., Q–1118. The surveyor was one Jacques Fénéon of Saulieu.

[83] *Ibid.*

sion by claiming strict enforcement of the marriage contract—smacked of Republicanism. Was it simply a case of every man for himself? The young Duchess de Saulx expressed it this way.

> More than others we have suffered the consequences of the emigration. At the very moment their brother returned, my sisters-in-law took possession of the wood he owned in Burgundy, the only property that had not been sold. Already, because of the consequences of revolutionary law and the cupidity of one of the sisters, the rich inheritance of M. de Montrevel escaped us. This dissension in the family and the countless negotiations either with business people or at the offices examining *émigré* claims caused a great deal of trouble after our return to France.[84]

Though only twenty-eight in 1800, the duchess was not defenseless. More determined and intelligent than her husband, she had learned a great deal about money in her seven years abroad. But the negotiations were long. Although one sister-in-law proved reasonable, the other held out for full payment of her dowry and one third of her mother's inheritance.

> Our arrangements over money have ended with Madame de Castellane, the eldest of my sisters-in-law. Her sentiments were perfectly noble, and although subjected to many privations, she resisted the temptation to take possession of her brother's land. Madame de Kercado, the younger sister, imposed conditions that scarcity of money made impossible to accept.[85]

It was not until 1809 that an "arrangement" was made with Comtesse de Kercado. The duke and duchess had to pay her 290,000 francs in order to regain the forests and the remains of the maternal inheritance.[86] The family accounts, memoranda, and legal briefs in these years make it plain how long and difficult these negotiations were. Even after a sum had been agreed upon, the schedule of payments provided fresh problems for a much reduced income. Every possible resource had to be mustered.

Fénéon was again in the family employ. This time his services were not limited to Burgundy. In 1803 he went to Caen in Normandy to regain whatever properties had not been sold. The prefect proved cooperative and Fénéon regained 250 acres of wood that was sold a few years later to General Grouchy for 58,000 francs. He also tracked down a number of

---

[84] Duchesse de Saulx-Tavanes, *Mémoires*, p. 154.
[85] *Ibid.*, p. 172.
[86] *A. D.*, E–1728, Fénéon to Duchesse, February 6, 1809; Accounts 1806–1818.

purchasers of the duke's land in 1789, though it is not clear that he gained more than a promise to pay. Returning to Dijon, he had more success. He regained 400 acres of unsold woodland and some 80 acres of grain and meadow land.[87] All this was not painless. In 1806, the second duke's uncle was still cutting wood on the estate and had to be stopped by a court order.[88] It was not until 1811 that the state gave up its last claim to 500 acres of forest "withheld" in 1800.[89] Nevertheless, a domain had been reconstituted. It consisted almost entirely of forest—5,000 acres of it. The wood was sold in much the same manner as before the Revolution, that is, as firewood for Dijon, as fuel for the ironmasters of the region, and as lumber for the navy. The new canal of Burgundy now made it possible to float logs from Dijon as well as from the river ports on the Saône.[90] By 1812, Fénéon could promise the duchess important revenues from his wood contracts with local ironmasters who were now working for the war effort.[91] Thanks to these contracts, Fénéon could assure his employer that the "affaire" with Madame de Kercado could be terminated.[92]

In 1810, the duke gave his wife full power to administer all the property and business of the family by a special procuration.[93] It had been clear for some time that the duchess was the financial manager of the family. Since her return to France, the duchess had used her influence with Talleyrand's circle to regain favor. She had not failed to cultivate such parvenus as Madame Bonaparte and even Fouché when necessary. But she was equally adept at the long, wearing financial negotiations with her in-laws and at poring over estate accounts. Her signature appears on a consignment of lumber from her wood at Arc-sur-Tille to the royal navy.[94] Fénéon addressed his letters to the duchess rather than to

[87] A. D., E–1728, *Etat*, November 18, 1818.

[88] A. D., E–1727, Petition to halt Charles-Dominique-Sulpice de Saulx from cutting wood, by ten creditors of the Tavanes estate, An XIV (1806).

[89] A. D., Q–1118, *Prélèvement du 2 floréal An VIII* (1800); Restitution of January 8, 1811.

[90] A. D., E–1771, Sale of wood at Arc-sur-Tille *"par port flottable de Dijon via le canal"*—41 oaks for the royal navy, 1820.

[91] H. Drouot et J. Calmette, *Histoire de Bourgogne* (Paris, 1928), p. 365.

[92] A. D., E–1728, Letter of February 6, 1809.

[93] A. D., Q–1118, Procuration of June 2, 1810.

[94] See note 90 above.

the duke even before the official act of 1810. Moreover, the very absence of comment about him from any contemporary source suggests that the second duke was not a forceful personality. His five years of silence in the House of Peers after 1815 seems to confirm this impression.

In 1820, at the age of only fifty-one, the second duke died. The duchess was to outlive her husband by forty-one years. Her long life marks the last generation of the house of Tavanes. Her memoirs, written after 1830, trace a life of declining expectations, disappointments, and the final alienation from a society that was no longer hers. With due allowance for her peculiar inclination to romantic nostalgia, the impressions of the duchess in these last years suggest something of a more general significance—the sense of being left behind by a new society.

This is especially interesting since the duchess had demonstrated much greater will and adaptability than her husband on behalf of a family name that was hers by marriage only. In the first decades of the new century, she was still optimistic. Her return to Burgundy after the emigration made her feel that the old rural society was still there.

> We left for Burgundy. I was so happy to see this province again. Tokens of affection preceded our arrival and even the Revolution had not destroyed those sentiments of which M. de Saulx continually received proof. ... *The old ideas still had great power.* One spoke with pride of the old Estates of the province and one often recalled M. de Tavanes who governed here for forty years and whose authority was equally approved by the court and by the people of all classes. At this time [ca. 1805] the idea of seigneurial power was still associated with the fall of revolutionary principles in the countryside. Men were proud to have held offices of seigneurial justice, and association with our family was remembered as a title of honor.[95]

That the local peasantry were making the best of the situation seems likely. Indeed, their alleged respect for the seigneurial system was pure hypocrisy. But the attitude, the wishful thinking of the duchess, was not feigned. She was touched by the poor sharecropper who saved the family three acres of land, by the "old race of the woodcutters," and by the dialect of the modest villagers. She indulged a taste for gardening that she had "learned in a foreign land," supervised the needed repairs of château and farm buildings, and interested herself "even in agriculture."

[95] Duchesse de Saulx-Tavanes, *Mémoires*, p. 173. (Italics mine.)

> We were still young, and our efforts seemed to promise long years of happiness. The birth of our son fulfilled our deepest wishes.[96]

The struggle to reconstitute the family estate was time-consuming, but effort was slowly rewarded, at least in material terms. Fénéon was busy again, and there was much traveling between Paris and the château of Lux. By 1809, the receipts for six months exceeded 17,000 francs, and the duchess, at the age of thirty-seven, could afford a few *folies* in Paris—a set of porcelain china, a fur piece, and three elastic corsets.[97] The daughters could go to school in the capital and meet the right people. The Napoleonic regime, "checkered" though it might have seemed, had not been unkind to the duke and duchess.

The Restoration opened up even brighter prospects. Louis XVIII named the father of the duchess minister of State and peer of France. Equally loyal, if less accomplished aristocrats were not forgotten either. Duc de Saulx-Tavanes was given a seat in the House of Peers and a pension of 12,500 francs.[98] And the reestablishment of the Bourbon government promised even more in the form of indemnification of the *émigrés*. But like others of her class, the duchess had to wait ten years for legislation and four more for payment. Tenaciously, she carried on the correspondence necessary to substantiate her claims under the Indemnity Law of 1825. Shrewdly, she drew up the estimates of income in 1790 that served as the basis for indemnification. The seigneurial rights, so substantial in 1789, were now minimized, since they were excluded from the provisions of the new law. And since debts had to be deducted from the final claim, they too had to be played down.[99]

The duchess soon found herself dealing with one of the most tight-fisted accountants in France, Comte de Villèle.[100] Her efforts to maxi-

---

[96] *Ibid.*

[97] *A. D.*, E–1728, *Mémoires, 1806–1818.*

[98] The pension was revoked in December, 1819, by the Decazes ministry. I wish to thank Mr. Gordon Anderson of Hamilton, Scotland, now doing research in France on the Restoration peerage, for drawing my attention to this information. See *A. N.*, 51.AP.5. Papiers Gabriel Deville, Pensions of Peers. See also F. Ponteil, *Les institutions de la France de 1814 à 1870* (Paris, 1966), pp. 20–21, 147–48.

[99] *A. D.*, Q–1118, *Etat général des revenus pour biens-fonds aliénés*, December 26, 1827.

[100] J. Fourcassié, *Villèle* (Paris, 1954). Villèle was a *gentilhomme campagnard* from Toulouse; his frugality was legend. For him, the simplest domestic furnishings were *fantaisies.*

mize the claim did not pass the eyes of the alerted Ministry of Finance. The duchess could not have appreciated the following dispatch:

> The Secretary-General of Finances observes that the debits applicable to M. Charles-Marie-Casimir Saulx-Tavanes must include 288,019 francs in addition to the debts already communicated.[101]

In February, 1828, the government suspended liquidation of the Saulx-Tavanes indemnity. But the duchess did not give way. How could a Tavanes *née* Choiseul surrender to a Villèle! For the next two years she persisted in writing to the prefect, protesting the interminable delay in payment. Her technical competence was reflected in the following passage:

> I shall reiterate what I said in my letter of November 28, in which I requested that a distinction be made between the principal of each debt and the interest on capital and the *rentes*. My purpose is to oppose the deduction of these interests from the amount of the indemnity.[102]

It should be added that the prefect was one Marquis d'Arbaud, and that the duchess always employed his noble title rather than his official one. Her references to correspondence with the prefect's brother in Madrid were also helpful. But it was probably the change in ministers in Paris that aided the duchess most. In January, 1830, not six months before the July Revolution, the Polignac government awarded an indemnity of 279,194 francs to the Saulx-Tavanes, 120,000 francs more than the estimate of the Villèle ministry.[103]

What did the duchess do with this capital? Recall that the indemnity was paid in government bonds at three per cent and that the market for bonds had fallen since 1825. There was a temptation to hold them for the income. Moreover, the indemnity had to be divided among all the children under the provisions of the Napoleonic Code. The duchess, as

---

[101] *A. D.*, Q–1118, Letter from the Ministry of Finance, December 1, 1827.

[102] *A. D.*, Q–1118, Duchesse de Saulx to Prefect, March 16, 1826.

[103] *A. D.*, Q–1118, *Indemnisation*, 1825–29. The revenues of the lost properties in 1790 were estimated at 50,652 livres and the interest charges at 37,002 livres, leaving a net income of 13,650 livres. This figure was then multiplied by 18 to arrive at an indemnification of 245,700 livres. This was subsequently adjusted upward to 279,194 livres. But it was the deduction of debts that was such a serious blow to families like the Tavanes. See A. Gain, *La Restauration et les biens des émigrés* (Nancy, 1929), II, 249–50. "The administration assumed a clear position against the *émigrés* and in favor of their creditors." *Ibid.*, II, 253.

guardian of her son, could claim only half of the sum.[104] Two married daughters claimed the other half. The third daughter had forfeited her claim because of her marriage to a foreigner. Furthermore, the indemnity represented a final land settlement that reassured the Revolutionary buyers and made them less willing to sell out to the old owners. Land was still in great demand; population pressure in the department did not begin to recede much before 1830, and the new proprietors would hold on if possible.[105] There is only one example of a purchase of land by the duchess. In 1826 she bought 53 acres of grain and meadow land near Beaumont for 25,000 francs in coin. The seller is identified as M. Bureau of Bèze, almost certainly the ironmaster and tenant at Tilchâtel in 1790, since then retired as *propriétaire*.[106] That the duchess was interested in improving the estate is indicated by a royal ordinance in May, 1829, authorizing her to establish a blast furnace for smelting iron on the Bèze River near one of her mills.[107] This was six months before the indemnity was awarded.

But if the duchess was unable to use the indemnity to buy much land, she nevertheless felt that the house of Tavanes still stood, its continuity assured by a son who would one day occupy Lux. Roger-Gaspard-Sidoine, third duke of Saulx-Tavanes, could scarcely have known his father. Born in 1806, he was educated by his mother. His sojourn in Vienna in 1823 and the marriage of his sister in Madrid to a diplomat supports the possibility that he was being groomed for a diplomatic career.[108] Unfortunately, whatever hopes the duchess had placed in her son were not

---

[104] *A. D.*, Q–1118. The indemnity reads that the young duke "is designated by the wish of his father for one-fourth and by the law for one-third of the remaining three-quarters." Thus the new inheritance law struck the family fortune again.

[105] During the Restoration, the birth rate in the department was 26 and the death rate 30; by 1870, it had fallen to 24 and the mortality rate to 26. Rural depopulation was not marked until after 1850. G. Martin et P. Martenet, *La Côte d'Or: étude d'économie rurale* (Dijon, 1909), pp. 30–34, 112n. Modern demographers may rectify these estimates somewhat, but it is doubtful that the demand for land lessened before mid-century.

[106] *A. D.*, E–1795, Contract of November 3, 1826.

[107] *Bulletin des Lois*, 8e Série, T. II, 39. Ordinance of May 28, 1829.

[108] *Ibid.* The land purchase of 1826 was made in the name of the young duke still in his minority and living in Vienna; *A. D.*, Q–1118, Letter of August 12, 1825, "Madame de Greppy married a foreigner after April 1, 1814 and by this marriage lost her French nationality."

to be fulfilled. What little we know about the third duke points to an unstable and sickly boy, *faible d'esprit* according to one authority, of a "bizarre character" according to another, and "melancholy" according to still another. Perhaps it is enough to know that he never married and that he committed suicide in 1845, at the age of thirty-nine.[109] With him ended the long line of Saulx-Tavanes.

The duchess was to live for another twenty-six years. She died in 1861, at the age of eighty-nine. The Marquis de Valous tells us that, at the end of the last century, the old people of Lux still spoke of the dowager Duchesse de Saulx, who passed the *belle saison* at the old château. She could be remembered, dressed in white, meditating for long hours by the steps of the château or strolling along the paths of the park. As the years passed, she spent more time at Lux, attended by a small household staff and two lady companions.[110] It was here that she wrote her memoirs. Most of her reflections on these last years have not been published. All we have are the following lines.

> I lack strength to retrace the years which followed the happy moment of my return to Burgundy. If there have been happy times, there have also been troubles provoked by powerful interests which gave rise to watchfulness and even alarm. . . .
> I have known the illusion of hope for those whom I loved. . . . It has slipped away and nothing will replace it. All the ties which hold me to life have been successively broken. Only a few traces of what I have known remain. Ideas, opinions, mores have changed; and like the daughters of Jerusalem, I mourn the miseries of Zion in a strange land. . . .[111]

The allusion to fearfulness gives some substance to an anecdote allegedly told by the old woodcutters of the forest of Velours. The second duke, husband of the duchess, was said to have seduced his intendant's wife, who bore him an illegitimate child. In revenge, the agent defrauded the dowager duchess by falsifying the accounts, especially those relating to the woodcutters' cottages in the forest of Velours. The anecdote would have us believe that the agent's efforts were so successful

---

[109] N. Garnier, *Arc-sur-Tille; Les familles seigneuriales*, 243n; Marquis de Valous, Introduction to *Mémoires* of the Duchesse de Saulx-Tavanes, 18–19; *Dictionnaire Parlementaire* V, 272. For the suicide, see A. Révérend, *Titres, anoblissements, et paires de la Restauration, 1814–1830* (Paris, 1906), VI, 214.

[110] Duchesse de Saulx-Tavanes *Mémoires*, 19–20.

[111] Ibid., 174–75.

that, they led to the division and sale of the Forest of Velours in 1853.[112] The accuracy of the story is not important. But as a reflection of the local attitude toward an old noble family, the tale has significance. The tone is that of retributory justice if not spiteful revenge. If this was the way old aristocratic families were regarded in the nineteenth century, the "broken ties" about which the duchess spoke may not have been purely subjective, a sign of old age. What did the loyal and conscientious Fénéon mean at the end of his final report to the family in 1818 when he wrote that the duchess "will no longer be bothered hearing about me"?[113] After thirty-seven years of service, had even Fénéon turned against the family? Between 1820 and 1860, the *beau nom* of Saulx-Tavanes lost its luster.

[112] S. de Montenay, "Comment la maison de Saulx-Tavanes fut ruinée en dernier lieu par son homme d'affaires", *Pays de Bourgogne*, No. 45 (1964). The cottages still stand (1964) at "Etoile de la Duchesse," a curious little hamlet in the middle of the Forest of Velours about three miles east of Lux.

[113] After submitting a bill for 28,218 francs based on his services to the family since the Revolution, Fénéon wrote: *"Elle [the duchess] ne sera plus fatiguée d'entendre parler de moi. Dijon, 19 novembre, 1818."*

CONCLUSION

The "story" of the house of Saulx-Tavanes ends here. But a short analytical conclusion is perhaps in order. Let us return to the broad questions posed in the preface.

The rewards of Paris and the court that induced this noble family to leave an estate in Burgundy were considerable: opportunities for life-time, even hereditary, pensions; possibility of good marriages promising fortune, influence, and *éclat*; and a national money market to negotiate loans and make investments. To these benefits must be added the incomparable satisfactions of a Parisian style of life, not limited to an address on the Rue du Bacq, but including all the pleasures and pomp of salon, theater, court ceremonial, distinguished company, and fastidious dress.

In securing these rewards, an old military family had a number of assets with which to begin. A venerable aristocratic name that evoked great military services to the crown in the past could more than make up for a limited competence in provincial administration, church, army, and royal household. The "alliances" of court circles with high royal administration appeared well established, with the distinct understanding on the part of ministers, secretaries of state, and intendants that a family like Saulx-Tavanes would always receive special consideration. Wayward younger sons, distant cousins, presumptuous creditors, and pleading "clients" could be contained or kept at a distance with the help of friends in high places. Moreover, once having arrived at court, it was not too difficult to remain there for generations, barring a political indiscretion such as visiting the Choiseuls at Chanteloup after the minister's fall from grace.

At the same time, Paris was expensive, and apparently increasingly so after 1774. The court of Marie Antoinette set very demanding standards of expenditure. For anyone who has studied the income and spending habits of provincial nobles, it seems incredible that a single family could spend between 150,000 and 200,000 livres per annum: yet it was true. By the 1780s, the Tavanes could consume at least 60,000 livres on current "needs," much of it on luxury goods. Even more prodigious was the expenditure of almost 120,000 livres—three-fourths of the annual income in 1788—to *service* family debts. Such large disbursements point to the cost of prestige, the burden of status at Paris. Adornment, equipage, servants, table, and legal fees were demanding enough, but the cost of children— not their education or supervision, but their dowries and portions—constituted the greatest single burden on family resources. No study of the upper nobility can be complete without an investigation of the Paris marriage market. Of course, some families harvested much larger dowries for their sons than they spent on the marriages of their daughters. Yet the very young marriages contracted in the French peerage as a whole suggest that aristocratic families were anxious to secure dowries early. This practice threatened each family with the clustering of generations and the consequent cost of simultaneously maintaining two and three generations on a single income. Moreover, unlike their Italian counterparts, Parisian aristocrats were not inclined to have several generations living under the same roof and thus economize on household expenses. The clustering of generations also meant that fresh dowries had to be raised before those in the previous generation had been liquidated. The two financial "crises" in the Tavanes family after 1750 can be ascribed to family charges and the clustering of generations rather than to conspicuous consumption, though the two factors are obviously related.

Closely associated with the serious game of dowries was the management of inheritances. The local customary law did not invariably favor eldest sons. The *Customs of Paris*, for example, prescribed equal division of property among all the children. It was, therefore, wise to have at least part of the family fortune in more distant provinces, where the *coûtumes* favored eldest sons, thus protecting the property from fragmentation in each generation. Hence, a fortuitous legal situation almost forced Parisian nobles to be absentee landlords.

The complex arrangement of dowries, portions, and inheritances assumed greater importance in Parisian aristocratic circles than it did in the provinces. To be sure, noble families at Toulouse, Dijon, or Rennes bargained and wrangled over portions and dowries, but usually with other local nobles. Paris was a national marriage market, the stakes were much higher, and the prejudices against *mésalliances* much less. The marriage history of the Tavanes demonstrates a consistent policy of attracting robe and even banking fortunes without any apparent loss of prestige. With the prospect of finding an heiress, a Parisian noble could hardly be expected to worry about meticulous provincial domain-building—the acre by acre accretion so evident around Toulouse, Dijon, or La Rochelle—when he bargained for entire seigneuries and marquisats at each marriage. The problem was rather to accumulate new domains before the overall indebtedness on old ones forced their sales. This veritable race to rescue old fortunes with new acquisitions, made the Parisian noble regard the land more as a transitory, negotiable commodity, to be mortgaged or sold in case of need, than as a basis of family continuity and local ties. True, the oldest family lands were the last to be alienated, but coupled with nonresidence, the attitude of a Parisian aristocrat to the land was quite different from that of a provincial *gentilhomme* who knew every acre, every seigneurial right, every sharecropper. It should be added that this emphasis on marriages and inheritances multiplied law cases which were not only costly, but may have given Parisian nobles an exaggerated respect for the legal instrument as opposed to verbal contracts and implicit understandings. Certainly, they spent much more time in litigations over inheritances than they did visiting their lands.

There is also evidence that it was becoming more difficult for a "great family" to borrow money in the 1780s than it had been only twenty years before. Commercial practices were changing; even shopkeepers and suppliers charged interest on credit extended. Shifting from a few large to numerous small loans, the Tavanes borrowed more and more money on short-term notarized bills at five and even six per cent, rather than by constituted *rentes* which had always favored the debtor. Credit was tight for everyone in those last years of the Old Regime, but it is also possible that creditors as a group had less tolerance for the aristocratic borrower. Why should he not pay interest and submit to the same terms of reimbursement as other debtors in the category of high risk? But whatever the reasons, financial pressures—from clustering generations, increasing consumption, higher prices, or harsher terms of borrowing—had important consequences for estate management.

How did the absentee noble landlord manage his estate from Paris? It is usually assumed that an absentee landlord is a more careless land-lord, and hence, by default, a more generous one than the tight-fisted, economy-minded resident proprietor. But the truth is that an absentee noble landlord like Saulx-Tavanes could administer his land tightly and efficiently. Furthermore, he had no difficulty reconciling the virtues of economy on the revenue side of the ledger with the need for lavish liv-ing at Paris on the expenditure side. The estate administration was neither elaborate nor highly paid, consisting essentially of an intendant in Paris and an agent on each domain. Simplicity of administration was facilitated by the fact that much of the estate was in forest, an increas-ingly important part of landed revenue, and probably typical of the estates of Parisian aristocrats. A half-dozen forest guards surveyed thou-sands of acres of woodland, backed by a seigneurial judge and his clerk, all at very modest wages. As for the arable land and pasture, excessively fragmented, it was leased to three or four substantial tenants (*fermiers principaux*) who paid a money rent and sublet to those who worked the land for a rent in kind, a portion of the harvest. There is no need to review the entire estate organization of the Saulx-Tavanes (Chapter II), except to insist on the attentiveness of the absentee landlord and the sub-stantial amount of paper work devoted to accounts, reports, and memo-randa, all directed toward minimizing estate expenses and maximizing the net receipts sent to Paris. Parisian nobles did not spend all their time sipping tea *à l'Anglaise*. There was always a study where they dictated letters to estate agents and reviewed long summaries of receipts, ex-penses, and estimated returns on every item, from mills to chickens.

What role did the absentee landlord play in agricultural improvement? Do estate accounts have a greater survival capacity than projects for agricultural innovation? One might argue quite the contrary, given the normal tendency of proprietors to keep their balances to themselves. But more than negative evidence, the correspondence between landlord and agent indicates that projects for improvement, or even current repairs, were discouraged at every turn by the lease terms and by explicit re-fusals to implement a tenant's project. The estate agent, so different from his English counterpart, understood his role to be that of a book-keeper and negotiator of leases, not that of entrepreneur or farm im-prover, and he saw to it that the tenants followed his example. Exactitude and surveillance were the watchwords, supplemented in the 1770s by the

injunction to raise rents at each lease renewal. It appears that noble landlords at Paris compared their rents and none wanted to be left behind
by his peers.

The exact assessment of tenants' income, the detachment of wood from
the leasehold, and a dramatic rise in rents were developments of the last
twenty years of the Old Regime, though on some estates they began
earlier. Sometimes prompted by the accession of a new head of the
family, the upward revision of rents was general and steady, despite the
fall in grain prices after 1778. It might be ascribed to a widely held conviction among proprietors that the land was not yielding its "full value."
This meant not that the land should be more productive, but that the
tenant's profits were too large in the eyes of landlords in Paris. The
negative response of Tavanes's agent to a tenant's proposal for improvements is significant: "Rents will rise anyway." The relationship of landlord, agent, and tenant was not of a kind to encourage mutual confidence in a common enterprise.

What were the effects of this kind of management on the local rural
community? The "seigneurial reaction," which was very real, appears as
the culmination of a larger policy of tighter estate management. Periodic
reform of the *terriers* can be traced to the Renaissance, but the Tavanes
example makes clear that the assertion of seigneurial claims in the 1780s
was much more comprehensive and thorough. Whereas, for reasons already explained, the tenant (*fermier*) suffered most from the rise in
rents, the seigneurial offensive affected much larger sections of the rural
population. Nor were its effects only material, though the enforcement of
the *dîme* and the incursions on the communal wood were onerous
enough. The replacement of the land agent with a *feudiste*, the irritation and loss of confidence involved in drawing up the new *terriers*, the
apparatus of a ducal *bailliage* complete with itinerant judges and *grands
jours* did not create new bonds of confidence between seigneur and "vassal." Moreover, the village community, in northern Burgundy at least,
was not totally disarmed in the face of this new legal challenge.

The Revolution on the Tavanes estate suggests a number of questions
about the nature of the rural revolution in France. Historians have perhaps overestimated the importance of bread prices and rising taxes as the
twin ingredients of open resistance to the old establishment. Something
should also be said about the sense of dignity of the village *habitant*,

especially in regions where he could appeal to a still active and organized local village community. In retrospect, it is clear that the Revolution in Burgundy witnessed the last counter-offensive of the village community against the *seigneurie*, the outcome of which was that both ultimately went down under the weight of the centralized state.

First, the villages as corporate bodies owned substantial amounts of woodland, enough to sell some wood on the market and provide enough money to hire lawyers, go to court, print *mémoires* and petitions at Dijon, and organize meetings of village representatives on a regional basis in 1788 and 1789. Second, the villagers were not hopelessly ignorant and poor; the distribution of income in three villages on the estate (Document IX, below) includes a large complement of poor people, but it also suggests a graduated scale and a large "middle group" of *laboureurs* and artisans who had enough income, energy, and time to worry about slights to their dignity as well as incursions on their revenues. In this case, it is also relevant to note that at the very moment the duke was renewing his *terriers* in the early 1780s, the villages had gained permission to reassess their royal taxes with the participation of a cross-section of citizens. To be treated simultaneously as "vassal" and "citizen" could not have gone unnoticed, and must have affected the self-esteem of more than one villager. The later appearance of an equalitarian vocabulary in village *cahiers* and petitions was not imposed entirely from "outside."

At no point did the rural revolution in these dozen villages result in any deaths. The *jacquerie* or *Grande Peur* of 1789 missed this region, though not by a wide margin. But the refusal to pay the seigneurial *dîmes*, the claims to and seizure of the lord's wood, the reassessment of taxes to include the "former seigneur," and the willingness to buy Tavanes's château furnishings and his land indicates, if not bitter hostility, at least the absence of any positive loyalties or "ties" to the seigneur. Moreover, the agent Fénéon's correspondence makes it clear that the villagers did not hesitate to put pressure on the new tribunals and threaten direct action if he did not give way. The change was not sudden; yet, by 1790, the villagers had certainly become "indocile," and the duke's agent could no longer ascribe his difficulties to "outside troublemakers." The remark of one of the villagers about the news of legislation from Paris, that it was "intended especially for us," indicates a slow awakening to a new sense of importance.

Who "won" the Revolution on the Tavanes estate? In terms of the redistribution of property, the conclusions of Marcel Marion for the Bordelais seem appropriate here. True, the tenants (*fermiers*) and a certain number of outsiders from Dijon (*forains*) bought the largest pieces—perhaps twenty per cent of the total—but the rest went in small pieces to local residents, including *laboureurs*, artisans, winegrowers, and even a few day laborers. Small and medium property (of less than 100 acres) was reinforced; large property lost, as the sales of other *emigré* lands at Dijon also show. But the Tavanes, like other owners of forest, did not lose everything. After 1800, despite some resistance by the Department of Water and Forests, sequestered woodland was returned to the original owners.

The issue of "winning" or "losing" a rural revolution is not only a matter of incomes and acreages. New offices from village and *bourg* to district and department were filled by local people, primarily by notaries and *fermiers*, at least in the more important posts. It is significant that *fermiers* as well as notaries and curés were frequently elected as mayors during the revolutionary decade. By 1800, the more radical rural leaders were less in evidence, but a new "notability" was forming, made up of "*proprietaires*" apparently more "medium" than "large" in the Dijonnais.

But whether regarded from the perspective of land sales, access to public office, or a new individual dignity, there is no question that the mystique of individual farm ownership swept all before it. If the vitality and cohesion of the village community would ebb away after 1800, the attachment to a larger, vaguer, rural community of individual farmers, each master of his own house, came into its own. In such a *milieu*, the tenant (*fermier*) who had joined the Revolution in the hope, no doubt, of liberating himself from the restrictions of the rent contract as well as from seigneurialism would be sadly disappointed. His economic goals, his entrepreneurial skills, had to be satisfied on his own plot and not on rented land.

The years 1800 and especially 1815 raised hopes for the *emigré* aristocracy that the Old Regime would be restored. But the tenacious duchess slowly learned that the Tavanes could not recapture their previous "rank" and influence in society. If the forest was returned, almost every scrap of arable and pasture land had been sold. A lone château in the midst of tracts of forest was not the same as a "duchy" with plowed fields and, above all, with seigneurial officials, tenants, ironmasters, sharecroppers, artisans, millers, and all those villagers who were once "vassals" of the

Saulx-Tavanes. The court with all its rewards would never return; the Restoration monarchy, perhaps typified by the ministry of Comte de Villèle and the *gentilhomme* prefect, was not the world of Versailles or even of the Estates of Burgundy. Equally distressing were family disagreements over property, now encouraged by a new equalitarian inheritance law that not even a noble majority in the Chamber of Deputies would change. The duchess waited thirty years for compensation for her lost lands and received her indemnity in bonds, all family debts deducted. She was unable or unwilling to invest much of this capital in the land. If the duchess wrote in her memoirs of "disappointments" and of a new world that she scarcely understood, there were good reasons for it.

Not all Parisian nobles faded into the countryside as *rentiers* or *non-actifs*, as the tax-officials would label them. For example, the Broglie family produced deputies and ministers in the nineteenth century and an atomic physicist in the twentieth. But the burden of past habit and style of life weighed heavily on this "society" of families, making it difficult for them to develop other skills than those of courtier, army officer, or *châtelain*. Of the several hundred families of court nobility before 1789, how many followed the example of the Broglie family and how many followed that of the Saulx-Tavanes, slipping into undistinguished obscurity during the course of the nineteenth century?

Perhaps there is a pattern here that tells us something about the rise and fall of great families. Three centuries from the reign of Francis I to the last Bourbon king mark the life-cycle of the Saulx-Tavanes. Biologically, they lasted longer than the actuary tables of aristocratic families would allow. Socially, they represented a "class" whose longevity depended on a capacity to transform the hot-blooded martial talents of Renaissance soldiers into the refined manners and careful calculations of eighteenth-century courtiers. For eight generations—from Marshal Gaspard to the first Duke—they met every turn of fortune, every fresh challenge with a successful parry. Then, near the end of the eighteenth century, the pace changed, the demands of status accelerated, while apparent triumphs of prestige proved too costly. In 1789, a whole world of *duchés* and vassals, of *terriers* and *feudistes*, of royal favors and brilliant marriages, of influential friends and deferential relations was shaken to the foundations. For the Saulx-Tavanes, decline—political, economic, social— was irreversible. Partly the result of economic blows, new legislation, and

210

less sympathetic governments, this decline was characterized by the atrophy of favors from above, of respect from below, and of family solidarity from within.

It would be tempting to draw a moral lesson. In those last years before the Revolution, the Tavanes had taken their court connection too much for granted, had relied to heavily on *beau nom* and too little on *capacité*. At the same time, they had undermined the vestiges of local ties and loyalties by preferring titular honors to public service, immediate returns to agricultural improvements, and seigneurial preeminence to local paternalism. Yet it is difficult to see how these "sins" could have been avoided. For more was involved than short-sighted cupidity in the service of status. The Saulx-Tavanes were reacting to the imperatives of a special *milieu*. Beneath the glittering surface of Versailles and Paris with endless receptions and court ceremonial, there was the more prosaic world of government *bureau*, solicitor's office, and even townhouse study, where one negotiated marriage contracts and bills of exchange, fought interminable lawsuits, and perused an intendant's balance-sheet or a *feudiste*'s new atlas. Here in Paris was the professional organization a court noble was expected to employ. Here was the expertise that made it possible for a *grand seigneur* to manage his affairs. The traditional "*désinvolture*"—aristocratic disdain for detail—had probably always been a mask. In the late eighteenth century, it was surely one. The Saulx-Tavanes did not fail to make use of these ready-made instruments to uphold their outward style of life. And to a large extent, these instruments—professional estate administrators, seigneurial experts, and legal councillors—functioned according to their own rules of procedure which owed little to the varying dispositions of individual noblemen. Such professional organization became itself a kind of pressure group for the rationalization of estate management. This, a nobleman was informed, was how it was done. In addition, there were the exigencies of social pressure. If a Tavanes heard that a Choiseul-Gouffier was raising his rents, why should he be left behind? Fashion, as well as need, might prompt action, beginning with the appointment of a general estate manager, a *chargé d'affaires*.

Given this *milieu* with such instruments and habits, how could one reasonably expect these court families to foresee that this professionalism could falter or, more accurately, be turned to other uses and serve other masters. How disconcerting to see the same lawyers and *procureurs*, the

211

same petty royal officials, the same estate agents, tenants, and even country notaries working for someone else after 1789! Professionalism and bureaucracy had a life of their own. If the Saulx-Tavanes had not understood this, how disarmed they must have been in the face of a revolution of ordinary villagers who seemed to be discarding their "natural docility." The aura of a great name was fading, and the family could not acquire the values and skills of this newer world. For the Tavanes, decline proceeded apace. In one generation—albeit a long one led by a lady of strong will—the House of Saulx-Tavanes slipped from ducal splendor to provincial obscurity.

ANALYSIS OF DOCUMENTS

These documents are meant to be more than a few *pièces justificatives* or simple appendices. They are elaborations of several themes whose incorporation into the body of the book would have encumbered the "story." They remain, however, an integral part of the book as a "study."

Using a particular source as a starting point, each section which follows pursues an issue already treated—the creation of the "duchy," the administration of the land, the treatment of tenants, the distribution of village income—with the intent of keeping the reader in close touch with the evidence, so that, while appreciating the problems and ambiguities of the sources, he will see the bases of the author's conclusions.

DOCUMENT I: CREATION OF THE DUCHY OF SAULX-TAVANES

ROYAL LETTERS RAISING THE COMTÉ OF LUX AND THE BARONIE OF
BEAUMONT TO THE TITLE OF HEREDITARY DUCHY OF SAULX-TAVANES

Louis, by the Grace of God, King of France and of Navarre: To all, present and future, Our greetings. Our Royal Predecessors have always considered the rank of Duke one of the highest rewards they could bestow on those who, by their brilliant birth, by the illustrious alliances contracted at various times by their family, by the merit of their personal services and those of their ancestors, and by their constant loyalty, have stood out among the rest of their subjects. We have noted with statisfaction that these advantages are united in the person of CHARLES-FRANÇOIS-CASIMIR DE SAULX, COMTE DE TAVANES, marshal of Our camps and armies, chevalier of Our orders, Our first lieutenant-general in Burgundy, governor of the Château du Taureau in Brittany, *chevalier d'honneur* of the Queen, Our beloved Spouse and Companion, and formerly *Menin* of the late, beloved Dauphin, Our Father.

The venerable age of the house of Saulx-Tavanes is very well known, as are [known] its alliances with Royal Houses, and with those of Vienne, Beaufremont, de Grammont, de Rye, de Crux, de Vergy, de Joyeuse, de la Baume Montrevel, de Rochechouart, de Chabot, de Gouffier, de Choiseul, de Mailly, de Grimaldy, de Tessé, de Lévis, de Rieux, the distinguished services this house has rendered the state under several of Our Royal Predecessors, the dignities it has enjoyed under various reigns, and the great seigneuries it has owned and still owns in the Duchy of Burgundy, having in very early times held the comté of Langres, which was then part of Burgundy. Already enjoying great renown at the end of the tenth century, the distinction of this house increased during the eleventh century; and Gui de Saulx, at the beginning of the reign of Philip I, bore the title of comte de Saulx and seigneur of Grancy, both of which places are near Dijon. This house has existed ever since, continued from father to son without interruption. In an exchange of the year twelve hundred and ninety-nine, Guilleaume de Saulx ceded to King Philipe le Bel the château of Saulx and its dependencies, which to this day are part of the Royal Domains. Jean de Saulx, under the reign of Louis XII married Marguerite de Tavanes, of the ancient Scottish house of that name. Vernier de Tavanes had come to Switzerland with a princess Berthe, daughter of the King of Scotland to whom he was related. Jean de Tavanes, brother of Marguerite, brought the black bands of lansquenets from Switzerland into France, and at their head performed important services to the state under Louis XII. The house of Tavanes having ended with his person, the King, in recognition of his services, permitted his nephew Gaspard de Saulx to add the name of Tavanes to his own. Guilleaume de Saulx, invested with a number of offices under François I, obtained that of lieutenant-general of the government of Burgundy from Henri II in fifteen hundred and fifty-six, an office which has remained in the house of Saulx ever since. When Gaspard de Saulx, who had inherited the valor of his ancestors, had made the decisive move that gave victory to Henri II at the battle of Renti, the King took from his own neck the chain of his Orders and decorated Gaspard with it, also embracing him in front of his army. Gaspard having also distinguished himself at the battle of Jarnac and Montconcour, King Charles IX, in the year fifteen hundred and ninety, created in his favor a fifth place of marshal of France, which was to be only temporary, until such time when he could be given one of the four that then existed. Guilleaume de Saulx, son of marshal de Tavanes, was made chevalier of the Order of Saint Esprit under Henri III in fifteen hundred and eighty-five. In Burgundy, he supported the party of Henri IV with such zeal and ability that in fifteen hundred and ninety-six the whole Province was entirely pacified. Jacques de Saulx, comte de Tavanes, his son, who held great offices under Louis XIII, has left useful memoirs on the wars of sixteen hundred and fifty and sixteen hundred and fifty-three. Charles-Marie de Saulx-Tavanes was lieutenant-general of the Autunois, the Auxois, and the Auxerrois under Louis XIV. Under Louis XV, the house of Saulx-Tavanes, in addition to the military services it rendered and the eminent ranks it held in the army, was invested with the highest commissions of the Court. Henri-Charles de Saulx, comte de Tavanes, lieutenant-general of the armies of the King and chevalier of his Orders, commanded for thirty years in Burgundy, where he twice held the Assembly of Provincial Estates in the name of the King. Cardinal de Tavanes, his brother, was Grand Almoner of France, having first been Grand Almoner of the Queen; he was also commander of the Order of Saint Esprit and presided three times at the Assembly of the Clergy of France. Comte de Saulx, son of the afore mentioned comte de Tavanes, having first been *Menin* of M. le Dauphin, Our late, beloved Father, became *chevalier d'honneur* of the Queen, Our late, beloved Grandmother, also chevalier of the King's Orders, lieutenant-general of his armies, lieutenant-general in Burgundy, and governor of the Château du Taureau in Brittany. Comtesse de Saulx, his spouse, was lady-in-waiting to the Queen.

Charles-François-Casimir de Saulx, comte de Tavanes, their son, in whose favor We wish to create a hereditary duchy, has served Us with the same zeal as his ancestors and possesses, as they did, the highest military ranks in Our armies, the highest offices, and the most eminent honors in Our kingdom and at Our Court. Born on the eleventh day of August, seventeen hundred and thirty-nine, he entered Our service in seventeen hundred and fifty-four as musketeer in the first company. From then on, he passed through the different military ranks in the King's Infantry Regiment as well as in the Regiment of Vienne and the Cavalry Regiment of M. le Dauphin. During the Westphalian campaign he was present at the battle

215

of Hastenbeck, at the seizure of Hameln, at the conquest of the electorate of Hanover, at the capitulation of Closterreven, and at the seizure of Halberstadt in seventeen hundred and fifty-seven; and, in seventeen hundred and fifty-eight at the battle of Crevelen, at the defense of Landvert, and during the retreat to Neurs, where he formed the rear-guard of the army under enemy fire. During this campaign, his father, comte de Saulx, *Menin* of the Dauphin, Our late, beloved Father, having been named *chevalier d'honneur* of the Queen, Our late, beloved Grandmother, comte de Tavanes was given the afore mentioned post of *Menin*, the functions of which he assumed after the campaign in seventeen hundred and fifty-nine. He participated at the battle of Minden and at the retreat to Kassel, having been named colonel in the Grenadiers of France. During the campaign of seventeen hundred and sixty-one, he was colonel second-in-command in the Royal Grenadiers of Cambis, and was present at all the military engagements in which that regiment took part. At the end of that campaign, he was in charge of fortifying and guarding the town of Retz, near Wesel on the Rhine, in order to protect the encampment of the army. In seventeen hundred and sixty-two, he was attached to the corps of the Grenadiers of France, where he commanded a brigade throughout the German campaign. He took part in the engagement at Williamstadt, and in the attack on the Forest, from which he alone, the third of eight colonels attached to that corps, returned; all the others and more than thirty officers, as well as two of four brigadiers, having been killed, wounded, or taken prisoner. He and his brigade formed the rear-guard of the reserve of comte de Stainville during the retreat to Kassel under continuous enemy fire. During the retreat from Hesse, he also participated in the attack on the fortified castle which was taken by assault by the same reserve. Subsequently, he went with that same unit to protect the junction of the army of Prince de Soubise with that of Prince de Condé. He and his brigade manned the heights of the salines of Friedberg at the moment when the army of the hereditary Prince of Brunswick advanced to attack the army of Prince de Condé, and he was partly responsible for the victory won in that engagement.

Peace having been concluded toward the end of that same year seventeen hundred and sixty-two and King Louis XV, Our most honored Lord and Grandfather, wishing to give comte de Tavanes some mark of his satisfaction with his military services, he named him lieutenant-colonel in the Queen's Infantry Regiment. He was made *brigadier* of the King's Armies on January twenty-second, seventeen hundred and sixty-nine and named chevalier of the Royal and Military Order of Saint Louis on June twenty-second, seventeen hundred and seventy. In seventeen hundred and seventy-one, on May thirteenth, King Louis XV, our most honored Lord and Grandfather, taking into consideration the services rendered by the family of the afore mentioned comte de Saulx in the various charges it had held at Court, and his personal services as *Menin* of the Dauphin, Our late, beloved Father, named him *chevalier d'honneur* of Madame la Dauphine,

216

subsequently Queen of France, Our beloved Spouse and Companion, *en survivance* of comte de Saulx, his father, who was given permission to carry out his functions in his absence. He became titulary of this charge in seventeen hundred and seventy-eight, upon the retirement of comte de Saulx. We have also created him marshal of Our camps and armies on March first, seventeen hundred and eighty. Wishing to give him further marks of Our benevolence, We have named him chevalier of Our Order of Pentecost of the year seventeen hundred and eighty-three, and We have received him on the first day of the following year, seventeen hundred and eighty-four. In that same year, as a reward for his military services, We have named him, on February fifth, to the governorship of the Château du Taureau, which had become vacant through the death of comte de Saulx, his father; and, desiring to perpetuate in his house the charge of lieutenant-general of Burgundy in the bailliages of Dijon, the comtés of Auxonne, Châtillon, and Bar-sur-Seine, in which comte de Saulx had succeeded his ancestors, We have granted him the title to it on February seventh, seventeen hundred and eighty-four.

We are informed, furthermore, that the afore mentioned Sr. comte de Tavanes owns in Our Province and Duchy of Burgundy several large and beautiful estates which have long been in his family, and most of which are entailed in favor of males. Outstanding among them are those of Beaumont and Lux, which are considerable by virtue of their great nobility, the number of vassals, and the importance of the rights attached to them. In the last-mentioned domain, there is a magnificent château, perfectly suited to become the seat of a domain of high rank. The comté of Beaumont is composed of five parishes, Beaumont, Champagne, Blagny— all of which carry the right of high, middle, and low justice, the *droit d'indire*, the *taille aux quatre cas*, banalities of oven and mill, *guet et garde*, the right of *banvin*, and a number of other excellent rights, remunerative and honorific—, Renêve-l'Eglise and Renêve-le-Châtel, parishes with middle and low justice, and the very extensive seigneurie of Bessey, to which very good seigneurial rights are attached. [We are also informed] that the said comté de Beaumont has been created in favor of Claude de Saulx, direct ancestor of comte de Tavanes four generations ago, by Letters Patent of the month of October, sixteen hundred and eighteen, registered at the Parlement and at the *Chambre des Comptes* of Dijon on December twenty-first of the same year. [We are informed] that the seigneurie and domain of Lux have borne the title of baronie from time immemorial, and that it has been recognized as such by acts of *reprise de fief* and by *aveux* submitted to the *Chambres des Comptes* in Dijon. [We are informed] that it is composed of the domains, fiefs, seigneuries and parishes of Lux, Spoy, Orville, Fley, and of a fief at Gemeaux, all having justice high, middle, and low, called Le Clos de Gemeaux. At the said place of Lux, there is a grand and handsome château, flanked by towers and surrounded by a water-filled moat, with extensive and beautiful dependencies, all of them

217

carrying rights of high, middle, and low justice, in addition to *dîmes, champart, taille seigneuriale, cens, banalités* of oven and mill, *guet et garde,* rights on hunting, fishing, weights, and measures, *banvin, droit d'indire, taille aux quatre cas,* and other excellent rights, remunerative and honorific. [We are informed] that the afore mentioned comté de Beaumont and baronie of Lux are *mouvances* directly held from Us as Lords of Our Duchy of Burgundy, and are within the competence of Our Parlement of Dijon, with the exception of some small parts of the said domain of Lux which fall within the competence of Our Parlements of Paris and Besançon, namely about half of the *finage* of Orville whose jurisdiction falls within the *bailliage* of Gray in Franche-Comté, and the village and territory of Fley, whose jurisdiction falls within the *bailliage* of Langres, even though the said territories are *mouvances* of Our said Duchy of Burgundy in the same manner as the rest of the said domain of Lux. These domains of Beaumont and Lux, united into a single *corps de fief* would have enough importance and revenue to create and maintain the rank, title, and quality of a duchy. Moved by THESE REASONS, and other considerations, We, in a special act of grace, power, and royal authority, have decided that by the present letters, signed by Our own hand, the said comté of Beaumont and baronie of Lux with all their fiefs, sub-fiefs, domains, seigneuries, and dependent jurisdictions, together with any domains, fiefs, and seigneuries the afore mentioned Sr. comte de Tavanes and his male heirs born in legitimate wedlock may hereafter add or annex, shall be and are herewith given the title and rank of a hereditary DUCHY under the name and designation of SAULX-TAVANES, which We wish and expect them to bear henceforth, instead of those of comté of Beaumont and baronie of Lux. Which two domains We unite and incorporate together, so that in the future they will form but one and the same *corps de seigneurie* under the title, rank, and name of DUCHY OF SAULX-TAVANES; with the proviso, however, that the afore mentioned Sr. comte de Tavanes and his successors to the duchy will hold it solely and as a full fief from Us as titularies of Our Crown, and that in a single *foy et hommage,* for which they will swear the oath of fealty in the customary manner.

We also wish the duchy of Saulx-Tavanes to be henceforth and in perpetuity within the immediate competence of Our parlementary court of Dijon, under the sole and immediate jurisdiction of which We wish to place all the appeals of the officers of the said duchy. To that effect We have separated and exempted, hereby separate and exempt, the said domains of Beaumont and Lux, their appurtenances and dependencies, from the *mouvances* of Our Duchy of Burgundy, so that they will henceforth be held directly from Our Crown. We similarly separate the jurisdictions of the said domains from the competence of the *bailliage* of Dijon, before which the appeals of the judges of these domains used to come in the past; except, however, for royal cases, which Our *bailli* in Dijon will continue to recognize. It is understood, however, that no changes will be made with respect to the right of competence of the *bailliage* of Langres over the jurisdiction in the village of Fley, nor with respect to that of the *bailliage* of Gray over the part of the *finage* of Orville within its competence; which competences will remain unchanged and be exercised in the said jurisdictions as in the past, given the small size of these jurisdictions and the difficulties that might arise when separating them from the competence of Our Parlements of Paris and Besançon and incorporating them into the competence of Our Parlement of Dijon, and given, furthermore, the assurance that the rest of the domains of Lux which remain comprised in the creation of a duchy is sufficient to assume that title. We have excepted and do except from the creation of a duchy as established by the present Letters those portions of the domain of Lux which are comprised in the said jurisdictions under the competence of the said *bailliages* of Langres and Gray. We wish the said portions of the said domain of Lux to be held directly from Us as Titularies of Our Duchy of Burgundy as in the past, and We wish to be furnished the *aveux* and *dénombrements* for them in Our *Chambre des Comptes* in Dijon. We also wish the jurisdictions of the said excepted places to be exercised henceforth by special officers, separate from those of the said duchy, which officers will render justice subject to appeal to the Royal *bailliages* of Langres and Gray.

Regarding the jurisdictions of the rest of the said domain and baronie of Lux, We have united them and do unite them by these Letters, so that they will henceforth be exercised in one and the same seat, under the title and name of Ducal *Bailliage* of the Duchy of Saulx-Tavanes. Before this court, which We wish to be established at Lux, since the château of that place is to be the seat of the duchy, before which all cases and contentions hereafter arising among the vassals and *censitaires* of the said duchy shall henceforth come in the first instance, except for royal cases; and appeals shall be made to Our said Parlement of Dijon, within whose direct competence the ducal *bailliage* of the said Sr. comte de Tavanes shall come, as has been said above. For the operation of this said ducal *bailliage* the said Sr. comte de Tavanes shall have a *bailli général*, a lieutenant, an advocate, a ducal fiscal *procureur*, a registrar, *procureurs*, *postulants*, *huissiers*, sergeants, notaries, scriveners, and, in general, all the officers needed for the functioning of the said ducal *bailliage*.

It is Our express wish that henceforth all the vassals and *censitaires* of the said domains and seigneuries which have been transformed into a duchy recognize the afore mentioned Sr. comte de Tavanes and his successors to the said duchy as dukes and render them the duties that are owed them in that quality, without, however, any augmentation in the said duties; and also that they take and render to the said château of Lux as the seat of the said duchy the *fois et hommages, aveux et dénombrements, déclarations et reconnaissances* they owe the said comté of Beaumont and

219

baronie of Lux and their annexes under the title and rank of Duchy of Saulx-Tavanes. It is Our wish that the afore mentioned Sr. comte de Ta vanes and his heirs and male descendants born in legitimate wedlock enjoy and use the title, rank, prerogatives, and all the privileges in general appertaining to a hereditary duchy in the same manner they have been and are being enjoyed by the other dukes of Our realm; but that those among his children and male descendants born in legitimate wedlock who might be engaged in Holy Orders or in any religious order can not succeed to the said duchy. In such a case the duchy will rightfully belong to him who follows in the order of primogeniture in each line and branch. It is Our wish, however, that if the only and last male descendant of the afore mentioned Sr. comte de Tavanes should be engaged in Holy Orders, he be able to succeed to the said duchy and have the right to take and bear in his arms and escutcheons the symbols, marks, and titles of ducal rank; but only on condition that in the absence of any direct male descendants born in legitimate wedlock, the domains comprising the said duchy return to their original nature, rank, and quality. However, in the absence of male heirs, neither We nor Our successors will have any rightful claim arising from reunion of property, reversion, or ownership of the said duchy, as stated in the edicts of fifteen hundred and seventy, fifteen hundred and seventy-nine, and the declarations of December, fifteen hundred and eighty-one, March, fifteen hundred and eighty-two, and fifteen hundred and eighty-seven on the creation of duchies, marquisats, and comtés, the strict provisos of which We herewith modify by virtue of Our full power and royal authority, since it is Our wish that the domains composing the said duchy shall, in the said case, be in no way considered joined with Our domain and Crown, especially since otherwise comte de Tavanes would have refused to accept and permit the gift and favor of the present creation of a duchy.

We, then, therefore, enjoin our good and faithful councillors in our court of Parlement and at the *Chambre des Comptes* of Dijon, the *bailli* of that city or his lieutenant, and all of Our other officers of justice, each in his appointed function, to have the present Letters read, published, and registered, and to grant the afore mentioned Sr. comte de Tavanes and his said heirs and successors born in legitimate wedlock the full, peaceful, and perpetual enjoyment of its contents; without, in so doing, placing before them, or permitting to be placed before them, any difficulty or obstacle whatsoever; and, in case any such obstacle should arise, to remove, lift, and restore it to its proper order, notwithstanding any ordinances given by Us or Our predecessors, nor any customs and other things apt to interfere which, to that end, we have expressly modified and do so modify by these present Letters.

FOR SUCH IS OUR PLEASURE, and so that it might be firm and stable forever, We have caused Our seal to be attached to the present Letters. GIVEN at Versailles in the month of August in the Year of Our Lord seventeen hundred and eighty-six, and the thirteenth of Our reign.

Signed: Louis

SOURCE: *A. N.*, T–109.[1-2]

COMMENT:

The Letters Patent making Charles-François-Casimir a duke are a clear example of what crown and court considered significant in the history of an "illustrious family." They demonstrate what had become the goal or self-image of the French court nobility, the epitome of aristocracy at the end of the *Ancien Régime*. Notice the attention given to the age and venerability of the house of Tavanes, its "alliances" with other old noble families. Significantly, the robe alliances—Brulart, Daguesseau, Amelot—are discreetly passed by; wealth, administrative talent, and family discipline could not quite compensate for newness of blood. Distinguished service to the crown "under several reigns" is closely associated with this venerability. Gaspard de Saulx receives his deserved recognition, but his descendants are not less praised. Even Jacques de Saulx is commended for his *Mémoires*, although his activities in the Fronde are not mentioned. Service at court is as meritorious as service on the field of battle. In fact, the cascades of honor attain a merit of their own and serve as justification for more rewards and titles. The closer a Tavanes came to the person of the king—as companion of royal grandmother, father, or wife—the more deserving he was. In this, Louis XVI seemed little different from Louis XIV, though knowing something about the two royal personalities, one wonders who was the object of manipulation.

From this document, what appears important about the land? *"Grandes et belles terres"* are not made into a *duché* because they are productive or even extensive in acreage. They are distinguished by their *beaux droits*, their number of "vassals," their entails, their justice, high, middle, and low. The revenues are also sufficiently important to sustain the new rank; the jurisdictions—not the domains—from a *corps de seigneurie* with claims to *foy et hommages, aveux et dénombrements* over many villages. The new *duché* could justify and provide its own corps of officers and replace a *bailliage court*. It was called a *fief* with a "magnificent château," flanked by towers and surrounded by a moat.

221

Little wonder the first duke had maps drawn up, showing geometric lines radiating out from his château at Lux to all of his nine villages and 480 households. Little wonder he made plans for an extended formal garden, laid out on an axis perpendicular to the *perron* at Lux. The duke did not have to live there to sense its symbolic value. Indeed, distance improved the impression of "magnificence." Lux was no Chambord after all; it was a modest manor house confined between the village and the meandering river Tille (*A. N.*, T-109).

In all of this there was an aspect of unreality, of play-acting. Yet the wording of such a document would encourage pretention, even self-delusion; clearly, it would not encourage the more mundane processes of land improvement. *Beaux droits* and numerous "vassals" counted for more than well-tilled fields and prosperous peasants: for the rank of hereditary duke was earned at Versailles, not in the apparently sleepy villages of the Dijonnais.

DOCUMENT II: POSTED BILL ADVERTISING THE AUCTION OF A LEASEHOLD

LAND AND SEIGNEURIE OF ARC-SUR-TILLE FOR LEASING

Be it known that the land and seigneurie of Arc-sur-Tille, belonging to M. LE DUC DE SAULX ... is for leasing beginning ... January 1, 1790; it consists of 700 *journaux* [560 acres] of leased land, for the most part at 9 measures per *journal*, of 800 *soitures* [640 acres] of meadow, in *Dîmes*, in a mill leased at 1,040 livres, in 30 *arpents* [30 acres] in timber aged at 18 to 20 years, in *cens, rentes,* chickens, *corvées,* fines, *épaves,* in 81 measures of wheat due by the inhabitants of Arc-sur-Tille for the Right of the Oven, *Lods* due on all the land in the *finage* [jurisdiction] of Arc-sur-Tille, *Droits de Retenue,* lodging for the *fermier* and *Herbergeages* [forage]. Those who wish to lease the said Land and Seigneurie ... for nine years, may address themselves to M. BILLARD, Advocate, Porte-au-Fermerot, who will furnish full details about the said land and will grant the lease to those who will offer an acceptable price [rent].

DIJON, January 3, 1788.

SOURCE: *A. D.,* E–1744.

COMMENT

Nine measures represented about half the gross harvest. See P. de Saint-Jacob, *Les paysans de la Bourgogne du Nord au dernier siècle de l'Ancien Régime,* (Dijon, 1960) pp. 503–6. In 1788, this meant a rent of about 36 livres per *journal,* or 25,200 livres if all 700 *journaux* had been at 9 measures. In reality, the lease was not that attractive. Fleury, the special assessor, estimated the revenues for the entire property at 25,153 livres in 1783. It leased for 23,000 livres in 1788.

DOCUMENT III: A LEASE FOR A MONEY-RENT
OCTOBER 19, 1790

(Bail à Fermage)

Sr. Jacques Fénéon, commissioner of *droits féodaux*, living at Lux, *procureur-général* of Monseigneur le Duc de Saulx-Tavanes, *chevalier d'honneur* of the Queen and *Ordres du Roi, Maréchal des Camps* in the Army of France, Governor of the Château du Taureau, and Lieutenant-General in Burgundy, hereby executes the private agreement signed at Paris, October 10, 1789, between Sr. de Saulx and Sr. Bureau, *négociant* at Paris, for a lease of nine years from January 1, 1792, until January 1, 1801, to Srs. Jean-Baptiste Bureau, *négociant*, resident of Paris, Aubin Bureau, resident at the forge of Bèze, and Jean-Louis Edme Bureau, resident of Tilchâtel, consisting of the following items:

1. The forge and furnace of Tilchâtel.
2. The revenues of the attached lands, seigneurial rights, *dîmes*, *cens*, and other obligations and dues.
3. The *métairie* of "Petite Forêt."
4. The *dîme* of one-twelfth in the jurisdiction (*finage*) of Marcilly.
5. *Rente d'Inteau.*
6. Meadow of "Clos Gemeaux," and all the revenues of the vineyard of Tilchâtel, right of *banvin*, and the toll (*péage*) of Tilchâtel.
7. Product of iron mines on the land of Tilchâtel.
8. The tenants will take and will cut 2,250 *arpents* (acres) of copse woods (*bois taillis*) at the rate of 250 *arpents* per year from the forests of Velours, Lux, and other specified areas in nine equal fellings (*coupes*).
9. In addition, to cut 180 *arpents* in the Petite Forêt of Tilchâtel at the rate of 20 *arpents* per year, retaining 20 saplings per *arpent*.

The tenants will burn their charcoal only in the customary places and build the cabins for the woodcutters in these same areas. The said Sr. de Saulx will furnish 30 hammer shafts annually in oak or cedar. The tenants are responsible for all minor repairs, excluding the wheel and the hammer of the forge. All cartage will be paid for by the tenants. The tenants will set aside 48 acres of wood to fuel the two iron ovens. There will be no change in the crop rotations. An inventory will be made of the forge and tools and any diminution in value at the end of the lease will be paid by the tenants.

The *lods et ventes* (mutation fees) above 300 livres are reserved for Sr. de Saulx. The tenants will pay the seigneurial officers. They will also be responsible for holding court sessions (*Grands Jours*) annually on the said lands of Tilchâtel. They will receive the seigneurial judges on that day, give them a decent dinner, and pay their *gages*, that is, to the *Bailli*, 30 livres; to the Lieutenant, 10 livres; and to the *procureur d'office*, 10 livres. They can claim no indemnity. The manuals [of seigneurial rights] will be expedited.

The price [rent] of this lease is 30,000 livres per annum to be paid at the château of Lux in three equal payments in coin and in no other manner. The tenants will pay 12,000 of the first year's rent in advance, that is, before January 1, 1792. They will also pay an entrance fee (*pot de vin*) of 600 livres at the signing of this lease.

Notarized (*controllé*) at Tilchâtel, October 19, 1790.

(Signatures of the Bureau brothers and Fénéon, the duke's agent, follow. Notarial fee: 85 livres, 10 sols.)

SOURCE: *A. D.*, E–1919.

COMMENT

The marquisat of Tilchâtel was the duke's most valuable property. In 1790, it was leased to the three brothers Bureau, two of whom were ironmasters in the area and the third a *négotiant* at Paris. Sr. Bureau at Paris had negotiated for this lease as early as January, 1787, five years before the previous lease to the Rochets was to expire. He succeeded in obtaining the lease, but for a rent fifty per cent higher than the previous one. All the marks of heavy competition for leases are here—the payment in advance, the entrance fee, the obligation to pay for any diminution in the capital value of the forge, and payment in silver at specified dates. The woodcutting is carefully scheduled. Conservation was in the interest of the duke. So was conservation of crop rotations in his eyes. It is curious in retrospect to see the details of ironmaking mixed with those of seigneurial administration, repairs on the forge hammer followed by reservation of mutation fees (*lods et ventes*). Here, the duke is insistent that court sessions (*Grands Jours*) be held and the seigneurial judges properly fed and paid. Notice the date is October, 1790. Two years later, the lease would no longer be valid.

DOCUMENT IV: TABLE OF TENANTS

The table of tenants is based on a reasonably complete series of leases for the eighteenth century, complemented by partial information for the seventeenth century. The purpose of the table is to shed some light on the *fermiers*, a layer of the rural hierarchy about which social historians still know too little. I have retained the French terminology on purpose in order to emphasize how imprecise certain labels were. For example, Belin, the tenant at Beaumont between 1758 and 1785, was described in the lease contracts as a *"marchand"* in 1757, a *"négotiant"* in 1765, and a *"Bourgeois"* in 1776. In all three cases, there seems little doubt that Belin was a grain merchant at the river port of Pontailler. The change in vocabulary is probably attributable to nuances of social prestige. Was Belin becoming more respectable and perhaps richer? Consider also Sr. Berault, tenant at Arc-sur-Tille in 1749. Berault is called a *"fermier-négotiant"* and *"Bourgeois* at Dijon." Here it is clear that *"Bourgeois"* does not mean *rentier* as the tax rolls would have us believe. And what should one make of Sr. Bachet, tenant at Bourberain in 1785, who is labelled a *"laboureur-marchand"*? Did Bachet push a plow as well as sell grain? It is equally curious to find Bourgeot, tenant at Arc in 1772, designated simply as a *"laboureur,"* when he paid a rent of 16,000 livres per annum. Was a *"laboureur"* in this case a kind of "agriculturalist" like Calignon, the tenant in 1790? There also seems to be a certain evolution in the use of terms. At Beaumont and Arc, the late eighteenth-century tenants are identified as *"marchands"* in most cases, while in the late seventeenth century, the term *"Bourgeois"* seems more common. It is doubtful that the tenants' functions changed in this period; more likely the designation of *"marchand"* indicates greater respectability, at least in the eyes of the law.

Turning from problems of vocabulary, notice how the tenants on the larger properties (Beaumont, Arc-sur-Tille, and Tilchâtel) usually formed partnerships either with members of their own families (wives, brothers, sons) or with other merchants or *"Bourgeois."* This is especially clear in the case of the ironmasters at Tilchâtel. Many of these men had other forges, often in Franche-Comté to the east. The Rochets contracted a partnership with a Lyon banker, and one of the Bureau brothers was a Paris merchant. Where partnerships did not exist, one often finds a *caution*, that is, a legal guarantor of the rent, who may have had a sep-

226

arate arrangement with the tenant. Wives and widows also appear as parties to rent contracts, suggesting that the *fermière* had a legal and financial status that may have placed her not only above the ordinary peasant woman but even above the noble lady in respect to her claims on her husband's estate.

Running counter to the image of a social group (the *marchands-fermiers*) growing in commercial sophistication and social respectability is the rapid turnover of tenants. Few seemed to last more than one nine-year term and many were obliged, for reasons of rent arrears, to terminate their tenancies before the full term had expired. Other sources inform us in greater detail of the bankruptcies of Rochet at Tilchâtel, Villers at Bourberain, and Huvelin at Arc-sur-Tille, but even the abbreviated leases, especially at Arc, suggest that the profits of the grain, wine, or iron trade were not always enough to meet rising rents.

Strictly speaking, the document presented here is not a sample document, but a summary of lease terms put in tabular form. The step graph in the following section is based on the same leases.

BEAUMONT

Date of Contract	Years of Lease		Rent (livres)	Description of Tenant (Fermier)
1608	1609–18	(9)	3,500	G. Rigolety, *marchand* of Auxonne.
1622	1623–29	(6)	4,100	Droucille, *procureur d'office* of comté de Champtible and Villemar, *marchand* at Beaumont.

(The gap in the leases in these middle years is undoubtedly due to the Thirty Years' War which lasted until 1659 for the French. Beaumont was literally a frontier fortress.)

1668	1669–75	(6)	5,400	Bouillaud, *Bourgeois* of Auxonne.
1674	1675–84	(9)	5,400	T. de Pierrepont, *marchand* of Auxonne and his wife, Rigolier.
1689	1689–95	(6)	5,200	Trouvé, *Bourgeois* at Champagne and wife, Aubert.
1696	1697–1703	(6)	5,200	Potier, *Bourgeois* at L'Heuilley-s-Vingeanne, son-in-law of Trouvé.
1704	1705–14	(9)	5,047	Collin, *fermier général* at Tilchâtel and wife, Salbreux. Leasor to administer the *bail à cens*.
1711	1712–18	(6)	5,047	Clesquin and Joliot, *fermiers* at Beaumont. Same conditions as lease of Collin in 1704.
1718	1719–31	(12)	5,011	Clesquin, *Bourgeois* at Beaumont, son of Clesquin above. No *billets* accepted in rent payment.

BEAUMONT (cont.)

Date of Contract	Years of Lease		Rent (livres)	Description of Tenant (Fermier)
1730	1731–40	(9)	6,000	La Foulet, marchand at Champagne; Guillaud, marchand at Blagny; Moureau, marchand at Champagne; Bouhier, marchand-fayencier at Dijon "porte caution." Manuals of seigneurial rights given to fermiers. Cens of 13th and 30 deniers per journal "in future."
1739	1740–49	(9)	7,600	Lecomte, marchand of Beaumont.
1747	1749–58	(9)	7,600	Lecomte.
1757	1758–69	(9)	8,100	Belin, marchand at Pontailler. Lease terminated in 1767.
1765	1767–76	(9)	8,100	Belin, négotiant at Pontailler and Noirot, marchand at Pontailler.
1776	1776–85	(9)	13,000	Chabeuf, wife of Noirot, marchand at Pontailler, for her husband and Belin, Bourgeois at Pontailler.
1784	1786–95	(9)	16,462	Moniotte, Blandin, Barthey, Guelaud, Relteret, Garnier, Balet, subtenants.

TILCHÂTEL

Date of Contract	Years of Lease		Rent (livres)	Description of Tenant (Fermier)
1723	1726–35	(9)	13,500 and 50 aunes of cloth	Sr. Boudouin, Directeur des Forges of Pesme (Franche–Comté), and Sr. Jourdain, procureur à la Chambre des Comptes de Dijon, caution.
1733	1733–44	(9)	200 milliers of iron delivered to Dijon.	Sr. A. Delandre.
1739	1741–50	(9)	20,000	——
1748	1750–59	(9)	20,000	H. M. d'Arbaumond, ironmaster (maître de forge).
1757	1759–68	(9)	21,500	Sr. Quillard, ironmaster at Bèze. Lease terminated in 1765.
1763	1765–74	(9)	21,100	Sr. Loquin.
——	1774–83	(9)	24,000	Sr. Rochet, ironmaster at Bèze.
1780	1783–92	(9)	30,000 and 600 pot de vin (18,000 in advance)	Sr. Rochet and son, ironmasters at Bèze in société with Sr. Courtois of Lyon.
1790	1792–1801	(9)	30,000 and 600 pot de vin (12,000 in advance)	Sr. Bureau, ironmaster at Tilchâtel; Sr. Bureau, brother, ironmaster at Bèze; Sr. Bureau, brother, négotiant at Paris.

ARC-SUR-TILLE

Date of Contract	Years of Lease		Rent (livres)	Description of Tenant (Fermier)
1684	1683–89	(6)	4,000	Jacques Goussard.
1710	1711–17	(6)	4,600	Sr. Louis Didran, *Bourgeois* at Morilly, Sr. Humbert Seignet, *Bourgeois* at Talmont.
1714	1717–29	(12)	4,700 and 50 *aunes* cloth, 2,000 tiles, 12 doz. pigeons.	Me. Charles-Marie Goussard, *Bourgeois* at Arc-sur-Tille, *marchand-fermier*. Lease terminated in 1726.
1724	1726–35	(9)	6,600 and 50 *aunes* cloth, 2 doz. pigeons.	Sr. Goussard.
1747	1747–56	(9)	8,000	Sr. Lavoignant, *Bourgeois* of Dijon; Sr. Lamy, *marchand-négotiant*. Lease terminated in 1748.
1748	1749–58	(9)	8,500	Sr. Berault, *fermier-négotiant*, *Bourgeois* at Dijon. Lease terminated in 1754.
1753	1754–63	(9)	9,600 and 400 *pot de vin*	Sr. Lecomte, *marchand* at Beaumont. Lease terminated in 1758.
1758	1758–63	(5)	7,600	Sr. Huvelin, "*interessé dans les affaires du Roi*," at Belfort and Dijon.
1759	1763–72	(9)	13,000	Sr. Huvelin, died 1765. Leasehold divided into three sub-leases.
1770	1772–81	(9)	16,190	Bourgeot, *laboureur*, living at Arc-sur-Tille and Madame Richard, widow of the *greffier-commis* at the Parlement of Dijon, *caution*.
1776	1781–90	(9)	19,000	Sr. Marchand, *fermier* at Arc.
1788	1790–99	(9)	23,360	Sr. Calignon, *marchand* at Dijon and *fermier* at Arc.

BOURBERAIN

Date of Contract	Years of Lease		Rent (livres)	Description of Tenant (Fermier)
1725	1726–35	(9)	1,800 and 40 emines grain	Jean Dumier, *marchand* at Veronnes, subtenant of Sr. Boudouin, *Directeur des Forges* and *fermier général* of the marquisat of Tilchâtel (above).
1733	1735–44	(9)	4,100	Sr. A. Delandre (included in lease of Tilchâtel).
1748	1749–58	(9)	4,350	Mossère of Tilchâtel.
1757	1758–64	(6)	5,160	Georges Villers, *fermier* of Chazeuil. Bankrupt. Personal property sold at auction to pay rent arrears.
1765	1767–76	(9)	3,600	Prisset, *fermier* of Martigny-le-Comte.
1774	1776–85	(9)	4,500	Rochet brothers, ironmasters at Bèze and Tilchâtel.
1784	1785–94	(9)	5,800 and 560 *pot de vin*	Sr. E. Bachet, *laboureur-marchand* of Equilly. Carbon, *caution*.

LUX

Date of Contract	Years of Lease		Rent (livres)	Description of Tenant (Fermier)
1652	1653–62	(9)	4,000	Boussais.
1669	1670–76	(6)	4,500	Pelleret.
1690	1691–1700	(9)	3,100	Martinecourt, *marchand* at Gemeaux.
1699	1700–09	(9)	3,500	Martinecourt, *fermier*.
1708	1709–18	(9)	3,600	Benquinet, *marchand* of Fontaine-Francaise.
1723	1726–35	(9)	4,500	Sr. Y. Boudouin, *Directeur des Forges, fermier-général* of Tilchâtel.
1735	1736–45	(9)	4,300	Leuret, *marchand* of Tilchâtel.
1750	1751–60	(9)	4,000	Drapier. Lease terminated in 1757.
1756	1757–66	(9)	4,800	Moitoiret. Lease of Spoy added.
1765	1766–72	(6)	4,050	Sr. Caroillan and Priouset.
1770	1770–79	(9)	4,800	Widow Caroillan.
——	1785–	(9)	6,300	Jacotot and Mochat.

DOCUMENT V: TABLE OF RENTS

The step graph is probably the most effective way of seeing at a glance the acceleration of money rents on the Tavanes estate. The first increases cluster around 1730, after at least a half-century of stagnation. The most spectacular rise was at Arc-sur-Tille, where rents almost quadrupled between 1730 and 1790. But even at Beaumont rents rose almost three times in the same sixty years, and at Tilchâtel two and one-half times. But it was after 1765 and especially after 1780 that the greatest acceleration can be detected. This increase was not compensated by any comparable rise in the prices of wheat, wine, or iron. No doubt the *fermiers* were better "armed" with seigneurial titles in the 1780s than in the 1750s, but these were not enough to justify (from the tenants' point of view) increases of this dimension. Profit margins most surely narrowed in almost every case. The rise in rents, therefore, should not be interpreted simply as a reflex to prices of farm produce or an increasing demand for land. It was a result of the conscious policy of the counts of Tavanes in the last twenty years of the Old Regime.

231

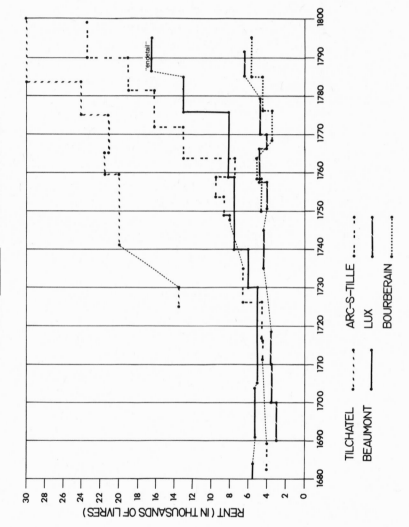

MONEY RENTS (FERMAGE) OF THE SAULX-TAVANES

RENT (IN THOUSANDS OF LIVRES)

"en detail"

TILCHATEL · · · · · · · ·
ARC-S-TILLE · · · — · · ·
BEAUMONT —————
LUX · · · · ·
BOURBERAIN · · · · · · ·

DOCUMENT VI: THE INCOME OF A TENANT

The estimation of the revenues of the barony of Bourberain was made by one of the count's special agents in order to determine the revenues of his tenants and adjust the rents accordingly. The diversity of sources of revenue indicates the need for a single rent-collector, namely the principal tenant (*fermier principal*), M. Rochet, ironmaster at nearby Tilchâtel. All but three *arpents* of wood had been detached from this lease and assigned to the forge in a separate contract. Over half of the total revenues here come from a *champart* on 2,160 acres of land. Only about one-sixth of the revenues came from arable domain land, which was sublet to a *laboureur* who worked the land, paying one-third of the harvest to Rochet. Subletting at one-third the harvest was common practice in the Dijonnais. Meadowland, by contrast, was almost always leased for a money rent, often in small pieces.

Rochet was, therefore, a grain merchant as well as an ironmaster, marketing about 100 *emines* (1,455 bushels) of grain annually. He was in a position to stock (note the grain magazines) his grain and wait for a favorable market in which to sell. But such careful surveys as this made the margin of profit narrow and forced men like Rochet to take risks, hold the grain off the market for long periods of time, thereby increasing the hostility of the grain consumer. Rochet's rent in 1780 was 4,500 livres; in 1785, it was raised to 5,800 livres. It is doubtful that the sub-tenant Faille had much grain left to market after he paid the expenses of the farm, including all the seed. On the other hand, he was less exposed to increases in his produce rent, tied as it was to a customary formula—one-third for rent, one-third for farm expenses, one-third for the *laboureur*. In short, it was not easy for a Rochet to pass on his increasing rent burden to his subtenants.

STATE OF THE REVENUES OF BOURBERAIN, MAY, 1783

1. Four small grain magazines, tenant's lodging (three rooms and one on the second floor which can be used to store grain).
2. Arable land: 168 *journaux* (134.4 acres) planted as follows:
   56 in wheat
   56 in barley or oats
   56 fallow

M. Rochet, ironmaster and principal tenant, sublets to Faille, *laboureur*, for one-third of the grain, taken on the spot by Rochet at the harvest. It is estimated that the *journal* produces 18 measures of grain in a common year. Therefore, 6 measures of wheat and 6 measures of oats belong to the said Rochet. At 31 measures to the *emine* [14.55 bushels] this amounts to 336 measures or 10¾ *emines* of each kind of grain.

The *emine* of wheat sells between 55 and 65 livres,
average 60 or . . . .   645 livres
The *emine* of oats sells at 25 livres or   266

                                                            Total   911 livres

It is true that the lands of the local inhabitants and the non-residents are leased at only 4 measures per *journal*, but they are charged with the twelfth sheaf, while the lands of the Seigneur's domain are exempt. Consequently, the Seigneur's land returns more per *journal*.

3. By a survey of 1782, 63 *soitures* [50.4 acres] of meadow:

60 at 20 livres . . . .   1,200 livres
 3 at 22 livres   66

                                                          Total: 1,266 livres

4. Ponds—29 *journaux* [23.2 acres] . . . .   200 livres
5. Oven and 3 *arpents* [3 acres] of wood sublet to Faille . .   300 livres
6. *Dîme* on wine at the rate of 1/16 or 10 *muids* [602 gallons]
   at 20 . . . .   200 livres
7. Seigneurial rents in grain (a *champart*) at the rate of one-twelfth on the lands of Bourberain by a survey in 1782. 2,700 *journaux* (2,160 acres) producing 71 *emines* of grain in the following manner:

26 of winter wheat at 60 liv . . . .   1,560 livres
 9 of rye   at 36 liv   324
30 of oats   at 25 liv   750
 6 of barley   at 36 liv   216

                                                            Total   2,850 livres

8. One chicken per resident—75 at 8 sols . . . .   30 livres
9. A *taille* on the community   30
10. A *cens* on the *métairie* of Mendinet   40

                              Grand Total: 5,735 livres
                              Rent (1783):   — 4,500

                              Profit (before taxes):   1,235 livres

SOURCE: *A. D.*, E–1818.

234

DOCUMENT VII: COMPOSITION OF THE TAVANES PROPERTIES OF BEAUMONT, BOURBERAIN, ARC-SUR-TILLE, AND LUX

It is extremely difficult to discover the precise areas and composition of properties of nobles. Fiscal records, even private fiscal records, seldom reveal the amount of land in question, and notarial documents—wills, marriage contracts, death inventories, and even the division of an inheritance (*partage*)—identify only the names of seigneuries and domains without specifying areas. The composition of the land was kept a well-guarded secret not only from the royal tax authorities, but also from most members of the family. Among a hundred bundles of Tavanes papers, many of them full of copious accounts, I have located four examples of the composition of the land, drawn up primarily for the purpose of enforcing seigneurial rights. About 1783 the *feudiste* of the duke made a simple table of each seigneurial jurisdiction, indicating if the land was arable, meadow, vine, or woodland, and separating the "domain," land owned directly by the seigneur, from the *mouvances*, that is, the land of the *habitants* subject to seigneurial dues, the *dîme* in particular. These tables, together with "observations," provide a comparative picture of the amount and kind of land held by the seigneur and local villagers, and reveal the full extent (in area) of seigneurial claims.

The *comté* of Beaumont consisted of five parishes in addition to the "lands of Bessey" and five ponds which were apparently drained and cultivated. The seigneurial jurisdiction extended over more than 10,000 acres of which 1,500 acres belonged directly to the Count of Tavanes. Considering the area as a whole, the Tavanes owned only 7.5 per cent of the arable land, but 21.0 per cent of the meadow, and 40.3 per cent of the woodland. No more need be said about the preference for wood among absentee seigneurs. The substantial share of meadowland along the Vingeanne River gave the Tavanes an important hold on local pasturage, essential for cultivation of the arable land. The Tavanes owned no vineyard, no doubt because it necessitated close supervision. All of the domain lands, except the forest, were fragmented to the extreme, indistinguishable in size from the peasant plots.

On the other hand, the local *habitants* owned 87.0 per cent of the soil, an average of 20 acres per household, excluding the wood. Nor was this a purely abstract "average." The land was very widely distributed (see

Document IX). And there was no doubt about the "ownership"; the seigneur's agent referred to the *habitants* as *propriétaires et cultivateurs*. Moreover, each of the five communities owned substantial quantities of forest land (from 40 to 400 acres each), which could be used even by the poorest villager to pasture his livestock or gather his firewood. Fortunately for the villagers, the duke's *feudiste* had been unable to "discover" any seigneurial rights of usage other than nominal "justice" on these thousand acres of communal wood. This is not a picture of abject rural poverty. Perhaps this security, however modest, made the shock of the seigneurial reaction in this instance all the more severe.

The situation at Bourberain suggests similar conclusions. Although the Tavanes owned 75 per cent of the woodland, there was still 960 acres remaining for the three villages as communal property. The "average" plot (and here it must remain a mathematical abstraction) of arable land, meadow, and vineyard at the parish of Bourberain was 25 acres. The seigneur owned only 3.7 per cent of the arable land, i.e., 130 acres compared with holdings of the local inhabitants of 3,383 acres. It was perhaps to compensate for this small proportion of arable land that the duke was especially anxious to enforce his *champarts* and *dîmes* both in the parish of Bourberain and at Velours.

The enforcement of seigneurial dues was the principal motive for making these tables. At Bourberain, Tavanes claimed the 12th sheaf on the entire 3,500 acres of arable land. The revenues of course varied with the harvest and the price of grain. It is significant, however, that the lease for the *dîme* of Velours rose regularly in the fifty years before the Revolution.

1735–44	800 livres
1754	1,000 livres
1772	1,200 livres
1788	1,827 livres

The rise in rent until 1772 could be at least partially justified by the rise in grain prices from 1755 to 1772. But the rent rise in the 1780s is unrelated to any price rise and must be attributed to greater efficiency of enforcement. This efficiency might have come from a more exact supervision of the collection per acre or from an extension of the total area owing the *dîme*. At Beaumont, a detailed *terrier* was to spell out each *cens*, but the claim to a *dîme* of one-thirteenth on 1,300 acres at Bessey and Renêve was clearly the most remunerative in the eyes of the duke's agent.

The four domains (see summary table below) within these seigneurial jurisdictions account for seven-eighths of the Tavanes estate in Burgundy in 1788. The duke owned one-quarter of the land in thirteen parishes, two-fifths of the meadow and two-thirds of the wood, though only eight per cent of the arable. Meadow and wood were not only easy to manage, but also indispensable for local forage, heating, and construction. Did the duke have a virtual monopoly on this land and consequently a "hold" on the livestock, the principal farm capital? Although the communities envied the duke his extensive holdings and resisted his claims to their own communal lands, it can not be said that they were deprived of these resources. There were 1,700 acres of meadow and 2,500 acres of wood in these thirteen communities that did *not* belong to the duke, most of the wood communal property. Furthermore, the pressure of population on the land does not appear desperately "Malthusian." A thousand households living on 30,000 acres, two-thirds of it arable, is not an excessive density, even with a productivity of 10 bushels an acre. Each household owned an "average" of 20.0 acres at Beaumont (5 parishes), 25.0 acres at Bourberain (1 parish), 15.5 acres at Arc-sur-Tille (1 parish), and 25.5 acres at Lux (4 parishes), excluding woodland.

On the other hand, the duke enforced seigneurial rights on at least 20,000 acres. His *feudiste* claimed the *dîme* on no less than 13,000 acres. This meant that the peasant occupant (*tenancier*) paid from 10 to 20 per cent of his *net* harvest for the *dîme* alone, as collection became more efficient. To stress the monetary side of the seigneurial reaction is not to forget the less measurable aspect of the *complexe féodal*, the insistent legal jargon of the *feudiste*, the registers, *aveux, reconnaissances*, atlases, tables, and *états* of which these documents are examples. The economic aspect can not be separated from the social impact of the elaborate apparatus, a new kind of seigneurial agent "armed" with venerable parchment, copious accounts and fine legalistic distinctions before which the average *habitant* of Beaumont or Renêve was surely perplexed, skeptical, and finally frustrated and irritated. Little wonder that the nineteenth-century peasant viewed any legal document, especially where a signature or cross was required, with implacable suspicion.

Comté de Beaumont (ca. 1783)

Parish	Households	Property of	Arable*	Meadow*	Vine*	Wood*	Total*	%	Total*
Beaumont	80	Seigneur	250	50	—	688	988	33.8	2,922
		Inhabit.	1,450	144	40	300	1,934	66.2	
Dampierre	30	Seigneur	52	2½	—	95	149	16.2	917
		Inhabit.	600	88	30	50	768	83.8	
"5-Etangs"	—	Seigneur	150	—	—	—	150	—	150
Métairie Bessey	1	Seigneur	108	16	—	—	124	—	124
Land of Bessey worked by Inhabit. of Beaumont, Dampierre, Fontenelle			1,077	—	—	—	1,077	—	1,077
Blagny	45	Seigneur	108	66½	—	—	174½	9.0	1,933½
		Inhabit.	1,500	100	12	147	1,759	91.0	
Champagne	112	Seigneur	53	33½	—	24	110½	3.6	3,069
		Inhabit.	2,518	211	—	230	2,959	96.4	
Renêve	153	Seigneur	12	17	—	29	49	2.0	2,409
		Inhabit.	1,640	200	20	500	2,360	98.0	
Luelley-en-Comte		Seigneur	—	11½	—	—	11½	—	11½
Dixme at Change		Inhabit.	264	—	—	—	264	—	264
Total for Comté de Beaumont	421	Seigneur	733	% 7.5	197	% 21.0 —	% 0.0	827	% 40.3	1,756	% 13.0	12,877 (10,945 acres)
		Inhabit.	9,049	92.5	743	79.0	102	100.0	1,227	59.7	11,121	87.0	
5 Parishes		Total:	9,782	100.0	940	100.0	102	100.0	2,054	100.0	12,877	100.0	

* All areas are measured in *journaux* (*journal* = 0.85 acres).

Observations [on the *Comté* of Beaumont]

On the 9,049 *journaux* of arable land of which the inhabitants of the five parishes of the Comté de Beaumont are *propriétaires* and *cultivateurs*, the seigneur, comte de Beaumont has the Right of *Dîme* of the thirteenth sheaf. That is:

1) on 1,077 *journaux* of the lands of Bessey and 20 deniers per *journal*
2) on 500 *journaux* at Renêve divided with seigneur d'Oisilly as follows:

$$\left. \begin{array}{l} \text{Tavanes } 7 \\ \text{d'Oisilly } 2 \end{array} \right\} \text{ of each 9 sheafs}$$

3) on 260 *journaux* divided among

$$\left. \begin{array}{l} \text{Seigneur de Beaufremont} \quad 1 \\ \text{M. Anguartan} \quad 1 \\ \text{Comte de Tavanes} \quad 5 \end{array} \right\} \text{ of each 7 sheafs}$$

All the rest of the arable land and the vineyard of the Comté are subject to the *dîme* of MM. les curés at 2 sheafs per *journal*, except at Renêve where the *dîme* belongs to the seigneurs, at the rate of one thirteenth, without "justice," making a total of 7,212 *journaux*.

On part of these 7,212 *journaux* as well as on a number of vineyards and houses, a *cens* is due to M. le comte de Tavanes.

As for the wood belonging to the five communities [1,227 *arpents*], until this moment, no rights (*droits*) have been discovered other than those of complete justice, fines, and confiscations, with the exception of Renêve, on which M. de Beaufremont has the Right of High Justice and M. le Comte de Tavanes Middle and Low Justice and the fines to a maximum of 60 sols tournois....

SOURCE: *A. D.*, E–1768. Although there is no date given, the table and comments were undoubtedly made by the *feudiste*, Fénéon, about 1783. The table for Bourberain makes this clear.

BARONIE DE BOURBERAIN (ca. 1783)

Parish	Households	Property of	Arable*	Meadow*	Vine*	Wood*	Total*	%	Total*
Bourberain	87	Seigneur	153	115	—	3,400	3,668	56.9	6,445
		Inhabit.	2,400	107	35	235	2,777	43.1	
Métairie of Mandinet	1	Inhabit.	80	106	—	—	186	—	186
Lands of Velours worked by the Inhabit. of Chaseul, dependency of Bourberain			1,500	—	—	—	1,500	—	1,500
Chaseul		Inhabit.	—	—	—	300	300	—	300
Fontaine-Franc.		Inhabit.	—	—	—	600	600	—	600
				%	%	%	%	%	%
Total for Baronie of Bourberain	88	Seigneur 153	3.7	115 35.0	— 0.0	3,400 75.0	3,668	40.6	
		Inhabit. 3,980	96.3	213 65.0	35 100.0	1,135 25.0	5,363	59.4	9,031
3 Parishes		Total: 4,133	100.0	328 100.0	35 100.0	4,535 100.0	9,031	100.0	(7,676 acres)

* All areas are measured in *journeaux* (1 *journal* = 0.85 acres).

OBSERVATIONS [ON THE *Baronie* OF BOURBERAIN]

The Seigneur is due only a general right of the twelfth sheaf on all the arable land in the jurisdiction (*finage*) of Bourberain and the sixteenth basket of grapes in the vineyards.

MM. Fénéon can dispense with calculating the areas owned by each individual proprietor; the General Plan of all the land is sufficient.

MM. Fénéon estimate the wood of the Baronie of Bourberain, including the forest of Velours en Champagne, at about 5,000 arpents [4,250 acres].

SOURCE: *A. D.*, E–1818 (ca. 1783).

THE MARQUISAT D'ARC-SUR-TILLE (ca. 1783)

Parish	Households	Property of	Arable*		Meadow*		Vine*	Wood*		Total*		Total*
				%		%			%		%	
Arc-sur-tille	167	Seigneur	690	25.7	845	58.6	——	641	91.4	2,176	45.0	4,834
		Inhabit.	2,000	74.3	598	41.4	——	60	8.6	2,658	55.0	
1 Parish		Total:	2,690	100.0	1,443	100.0	——	701	100.0	4,834	100.0	(4,109 acres)

* All areas are measured in *journeaux* (1 journal = 0.85 acres).

THE BARONIE DE LUX (ca. 1783)

Parish	Households	Property of	Arable*	Meadow*	Vine*	Wood*	Total*		Total*
								%	
Lux	120	Seigneur	180	70	10	970	1,230	26.1	4,705
		Inhabit.	3,000	35	40	400	3,475	73.9	
Spoy	65	Seigneur	66	16	——	43	125	4.9	2,530
		Inhabit.	2,000	300	25	80	2,405	95.1	
Orville	60	Seigneur	——	——	——	——	——		805
		Inhabit.	680	100	25	——	805	——	
Fley	12	Seigneur	40	9	——	16	65	14.1	460
		Inhabit.	320	30	12	33	395	85.9	
Gemeaux	"fief"	Seigneur	——	14	——	——	14	0.9	1,514
		Inhabit.	1,500	——	——	——	1,500	99.1	
			%	%	%	%		%	
Total for Baronie of Lux	257	Seigneur	286 3.7	109 19.0	10 8.9	1,029 66.7	1,434	14.2	10,014
		Inhabit.	7,500 96.3	465 81.0	102 91.1	513 33.7	8,580	85.8	
4 parishes		Total:	7,786 100.0	574 100.0	112 100.0	1,542 100.0	10,014	100.0	(8,512 acres)

* All areas are measured in *journeaux* (1 journal = 0.85 acres).

OBSERVATIONS [ON THE *Marquisat* OF ARC-SUR-TILLE]

All the arable lands are charged with a general right of the thirteenth sheaf and a *cens* of 2 sols per *journal* (0.85 acre). The meadows owe 2 sols 6 deniers per *soiture* (0.85 acre). There is also a *cens* due on each house at Arc-sur-Tille. In the seigneurie there is a general right to *lods et ventes* on all houses, lands, and meadows exchanged or sold.

All the arable, meadow, and pasture composing the said marquisat charged with a *cens* of 2 sols, and 2 sols, 6 deniers per *journal* or *soiture*, must be surveyed and marked on the *General Geometrical Plan* which will be made of this land in order to collect the *cens*. The present tenants (*fermiers*) do not collect anything close to what is due the seigneur by the proprietors, who have not submitted honest declarations.

240

A survey of the seigneur's property [*domaine*] is indispensable. It consists of 681 *journaux* of arable in 56 pieces, of 819 *soitures* of meadow in 26 pieces, and of 641 *arpents* of wood in four pieces.

MM. Fénéon have established the jurisdiction (*finage*) of Arc-sur-Tille at 10,000 *journaux* [8,500 acres]. It is at least half this size. They estimate the dues at 300 articles. There could well be this number.

There is also the matter of adjusting the right to the *dîme* of the curé of Arc-sur-Tille. Under the present arrangement he collects one-fifth of the total *dîmes* at Arc-sur-Tille.

SOURCE: *A. N.*, T–109.[1-2]

SUMMARY OF FOUR SEIGNEURIAL JURISDICTIONS (ca. 1783)

Jurisdiction	Households	Property of	Arable*	%	Meadow*	%	Vine*	%	Wood*	%	Total*	%
ARC-SUR-TILLE (*marquisat*) 1 parish	167	Seigneur	690	25.7	845	58.6	——	——	641	91.4	2,176	45.0
		Inhabit.	2,000	74.3	598	41.4	——	——	60	8.6	2,658	55.0
		Total:	2,690	100.0	1,443	100.0	——	——	701	100.0	4,834	100.0
LUX (*baronie*) 4 parishes	257	Seigneur	286	3.7	109	19.0	10	8.9	1,029	66.7	1,434	14.2
		Inhabit.	7,500	96.3	465	81.0	102	91.1	513	33.3	8,580	85.0
		Total:	7,786	100.0	574	100.0	112	100.0	1,542	100.0	10,014	100.0
BEAUMONT (*comté*) 5 parishes	421	Seigneur	733	7.5	197	21.0	——	——	827	40.3	1,756	13.0
		Inhabit.	9,049	92.5	743	79.0	102	100.0	1,227	59.7	11,121	87.0
		Total:	9,782	100.0	940	100.0	102	100.0	2,054	100.0	12,877	100.0
BOURBERAIN (*baronie*) 3 parishes	88	Seigneur	153	3.7	115	35.0	——	——	3,400	75.0	3,668	40.6
		Inhabit.	3,980	96.3	213	65.0	35	100.0	1,135	25.0	5,363	59.4
		Total:	4,133	100.0	328	100.0	35	100.0	4,535	100.0	9,031	100.0
Total of 4 Seigneurial Jurisdictions (13 parishes)	933	Seigneur	1,862	7.6	1,266	38.5	10	4.0	5,897	66.8	9,035	24.6
		Inhabit.	22,529	92.4	2,019	61.5	239	96.0	2,935	33.2	27,722	75.4
		Total:	24,391	100.0	3,285	100.0	249	100.0	8,832	100.0	36,757	100.0

* All areas are measured in *journeaux* (1 *journal* = 0.85 acres).
Area of the Seigneurial Jurisdiction: 36,757 *journaux* = 31,243 English acres or 12,649 French hectares.
Area of the Seigneurial Domain: 9,035 *journaux* = 7,680 English acres or 3,109 French hectares.

DOCUMENT VIII: SECTIONAL MAP OF LUX

This is but a section of a larger map of the Barony of Lux drawn up by Fénéon, the *feudiste*, about 1786. The shaded areas—the original is in beautiful color—represent the domain lands of the Duc de Saulx-Tavanes. The jurisdiction or *finage* of Lux extended over 3,400 *journaux* (2,720 acres), not including the wood, of which 383 (306 acres) belonged in full property to the duke. These 383 *journaux* were divided into 91 pieces, the largest of which are shown here. Piece number 62, the largest, measured 28 *journaux* (22.4 acres) and piece number 77 was 5.6 *journaux* (4.4 acres). Notice also the "slivers" of land, pieces 36,37,38 or 42,43,46, for example. They are all less than one *journal* (0.85 acre). The "sliver" pattern is even more characteristic of the adjoining jurisdiction of Spoy where 153 *journaux* were divided into 81 pieces. Such a pattern lent itself to subletting and to fixed rents in kind per *journal*. Single plots were larger at Bourberain—237 *journaux* divided into only 13 pieces—and at Arc-sur-Tille where 1,500 *journaux* of arable and meadow were divided into 82 pieces. In both cases this is an average of 18 *journaux* (14.4 acres) per piece. At Arc-sur-Tille it was possible to employ some day-labor in the fields (see Document IX). The forest, of course, was held in large tracts. Notice the château of Lux in the center of the village. There was little space for an elaborate park.

SOURCE: *A. N.*, T-109.[1-2]

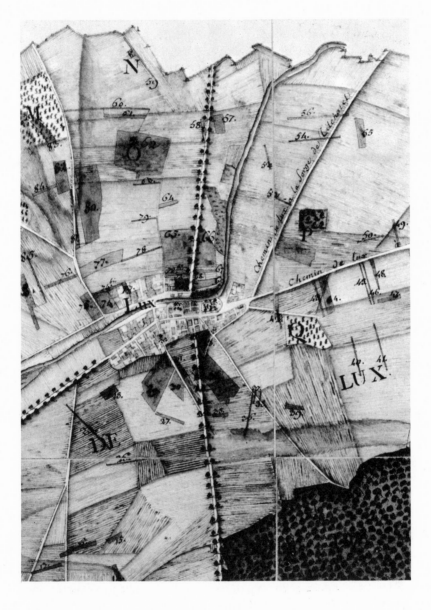

DOCUMENT IX: DISTRIBUTION OF INCOME AT BEAUMONT, LUX, AND ARC-SUR-TILLE 1781, 1779, 1772

These three tables are based on the reformed *taille* rolls established in the villages of the Dijonnais during the two decades preceding 1789. As Jean Loutchtsky discovered seventy-five years ago, these *nouveaux pieds des tailles* or reassessments of income are extremely precious sources for determining the standard of living and income distribution at the level of the rural village. The authenticity and value of these documents is supported by the descriptions given of the procedure and manner in which the reassessments were made.

In January of 1781, forty-six inhabitants of Beaumont—more than half of the households—petitioned the Estates of Burgundy for a new assessment to "correct abuses" and reapportion the taxes in a more equitable manner so that the "poor will no longer be overtaxed as they have been heretofore in order to favor the rich." Contrary to expectations, the petition was approved; three months later, a general assembly of inhabitants named four men from among the local residents to act as a committee of assessors. They were M. Philibert Petitjean of Macilly, *Bourgeois*; Pierre Minard, the elder, a *laboureur-rentier*; François Le Jour, the elder, a wine-grower; and François Mariotte, an illiterate *manouvrier*: a remarkably representative group. They were instructed to "fix the value" of the land, commerce, and *industrie* and then determine the tax rate. Here are the results:

1. Without distinction of quality of land, the *journal* (0.85 acres) returns 9 livres for the proprietor-cultivator and in the case of leasing, half this sum. In the first instance the tax will be 9 sous (one-twentieth) and in the second case, the proprietor will pay 4 sous, 6 deniers and the leasee (*reteneur*) 4 sous, 6 deniers.
2. For leases at one-third, the tax will claim one-twentieth of the total product in a common year to a maximum of 300 livres rent, one-twenty-fifth for rents between 300 and 600 livres, and one-thirtieth for rents above 600 livres. Leases in money rents will follow the same rate.
3. For meadowland, one-twentieth of the rent in money from the proprietor and one-fortieth from the non-owner who harvests the hay.
4. For *rentes* and pensions, one-thirtieth of the revenue to 300 livres, one-twenty-fifth from 300 to 600 livres and one-twentieth above 600 livres.

[Note that for *rentes* the tax was "progressive," but for leases of land it was "regressive." Perhaps this suggests something about rural attitudes toward *rentes*. *Rentes* here presumably refer to mortgage loans (*rentes foncières*). Few were declared.]

5. The vineyards will be taxed in three categories:

"good"——4 sols per *ouvrée* (0.1 acre)
"mediocre"——3 sols
"bad"——2 sols

6. All other kinds of land will be taxed at one-twentieth the estimated income.
7. Houses: one-thirtieth of the rent, expenses deducted.
8. Livestock: For owners: Cows——3 sols
Sheep——1 sol
For owners leasing out: Cows——1 sol, 6 deniers
Sheep——6 deniers.
9. Revenue from the work (*industrie*) of merchants, artisans, and *autres états*. One-twentieth for tax.
10. For the impositions on *manouvriers*, winegrowers, more or less fully employed, there will be five classes:

1. ——12 livres
2. —— 9
3. —— 7
4. —— 5
5. —— 3

This rate is independent of any property they may own. Widows will pay at half this rate.
11. For the aged, ill, and families with numerous young children, all their expenses should be deducted before any tax is levied.
12. If the resulting tax money, following the above rates, is insufficient, the deficit will be divided by adding a supplement to each tax-payer on a pro-rata basis (*au marc la livre*). If there is a surplus, each tax-payer will receive a diminution in the same manner.

[The new tax schedule was signed by the three literate members of the committee and by two commissioners from the Estates of Burgundy in Dijon.]

The procedure of reassessment followed the same pattern at Lux. The assessment of revenues was more sophisticated, especially for land leased at one-third, but the resulting estimates of income were almost the same as at Beaumont. And so were the tax rates—almost invariably 5 per cent of income. As at Beaumont, the tax on money-leases was regressive, the *fermier* paying a diminishing rate as his rent increased. No doubt the *fermiers'* opinions could not be ignored in the discussions of the assessment committees. Furthermore, a higher rent did not necessarily mean a higher revenue for the *fermier* by 1781.

One obvious conclusion emerges from the tax assessments. The vocabulary chosen to describe the local social groups, *états*, *métiers*, or occupations was not an altogether happy one, even for contemporaries. Each rubric encompassed numerous functions. A substantial part of this book has been concerned with various breeds of *fermiers*. The term *laboureur* is equally elusive. There were *laboureurs-propriétaires*, *laboureurs-rentiers*, *laboureurs-marchands*, *demi-laboureurs*, and even *ci-devant laboureurs*. Since most *laboureurs* at Beaumont both owned and rented land, both grew grain and sold it, they fulfilled many economic roles. There is no doubt, however, that the phrase *laboureur-propriétaire* carried the most prestige, while *laboureur-rentier* in this case meant renting the land of another (*pour autruy*). Consider the case of Pierre Minard, the wealthiest of the *laboureurs* at Beaumont:

Pierre Minard, *laboureur-rentier*, proprietor of:

2 houses
30 *journaux* of land in many pieces
   one-half *soiture* of meadow
18 *ouvrées* vineyard
 3 cows, 10 sheep

rents and cultivates:

75 *journaux* of land of M. St.-Pierre
 5 *soitures* of meadow
75 *journaux* of land of Madame Tesand
 5 *soitures* of meadow

Now contrast Minard with François Boudrot, also called a *laboureur-rentier* by the local assessors. Boudrot owned nothing but one cow and two sheep. If we did not know that he leased 60 acres, he would appear as a poor *journalier*, potential victim of Marc Bloch's "*individualisme agraire.*" But Boudrot rented:

17 *journaux* of land of Mlle d'Autrey
20 *journaux* of M. le Curé de Dampierre
30 *journaux* of the lease of Beaumont (Noirot, principal tenant, hence a sublease)
1 *journal* of M. Bodin
5 *soitures* of meadow
3 *ouvrées* of good vineyard

---

ca. 73 *journaux* (58.4 acres)

Clearly, neither Minard nor Boudrot could work all this land alone. They must have employed some of the *manouvriers*, winegrowers, and artisans that appear elsewhere on the tax roll. Moreover, they may have subleased other parcels, though the tax assessment gives no evidence of it. In any case, the Barrèsian portrait of the *laboureur* as a self-sufficient owner-occupier does not fit. The *laboureurs* at Beaumont and Lux were small *fermiers*.

The case of Joseph Moniotte demonstrates the elasticity of subletting and the full complexity of landholding in the Old Regime. Moniotte was the subtenant (*sous-fermier*) at Beaumont. He leased a part of M. Noirot's larger lease from the counts of Tavanes for 2,002 livres. This sublease included 300 *journaux* of land of which Moniotte worked 116 *journaux*, presumably with day-labor, and sublet the other 184 *journaux*. In other words, he sublet part of a sublease, now three times removed from the original owner, Tavanes. Moniotte was an intermediary, a farm manager, a grain merchant, a subleasor of *dîmes*, ovens, gardens, as well as an owner of 18 *journaux* of grainland, 29 *ouvrées* of vineyard, and 13 *quartiers* of meadow. As if this were not enough, he also ran the local *cabaret*. He must have lent money too. In common parlance, Moniotte was a "hustler," *un homme à tout faire*. That he somehow managed to keep control of his multifarious operations and make them pay seems confirmed by his capacity to buy 64 acres of the duke's domain and his mill when they were placed on the market in 1794, the largest single purchase at Beaumont.

Turning to the other end of the social scale, the term *manouvrier* seems scarcely more suitable for social analysis than *laboureur* or *sousfermier*. At Beaumont, half of the *manouvriers* owned some land and all owned some livestock. Eight of the fifteen *manouvriers* at Lux owned land. This does not mean they were all contented landlords, but it is hard to conceive of them as a uniformly rootless class of landless day-

---

med to prosper or at least make ends meet. That is one for every fif-
families, clearly too many to rely on a local clientele alone. At Lux,
re was only one tavern keeper, and he was also the baker. At Beau-
nt, there was only one—Moniotte, the *fermier*. Arc-sur-Tille was ap-
ently a stop-over for travellers in the Saône Valley. Recent work in
glish agrarian history of the early nineteenth century has also drawn
ntion to the role of the "beer-house keepers" as village radicals; what
the French *cabaretier*?[1] Simply as a meeting-place, the *cabaret* may be
portant in the spread of unrest.

Tables are always interpreted in different ways. Some readers will be
re impressed by the 28 to 45 per cent of households that fall below
livres per annum, the "poverty level" in my estimation. Others will
struck by the 50 to 65 per cent in the "middle group," earning be-
en 200 and 1,000 livres. Still others will immediately point to the
ster of *Bourgeois*, *fermiers*, and *laboureurs* at the top of the tables,
elling them *coqs de village* or "rural bourgeoisie." Three villages can
ve as little more than illustrative examples, but there is reason to be-
ve that the other village communities of this region, already sampled
Loutchitsky, will reveal a similar income distribution.[2]

CODE FOR TABLES

French	English Equivalent
Bourgeois	"Bourgeois"
Notaire	Notary
Proprietaire	Proprietor
Fermier	Tenant-farmer (paying a rent in money)
Meunier	Miller (paying a rent in money)
Forain	Non-resident
Laboureur	Farmer (with plow-team)
Laboureur-proprietaire	Farmer who owns more than he rents
Laboureur-rentier	Farmer who rents more than he owns

See E. J. Hobsbawm and G. Rudé, *Captain Swing* (London, 1969).
See J. Loutchitsky, "De la petite propriété en France avant la Revolution et de
vente des biens nationaux," *Revue historique*, LIX (1895), 80–92.

laborers. In any case, there do not appear to have been many of them. In fact, the winegrowers and artisans outnumber the *manouvriers* two to one at Beaumont and four to one at Lux. But this should not lead us to the opposite conclusion that few villagers engaged in day-labor. A rapid glance at all three categories—*manouvriers, vignerons,* and *artisans*—indicates a great deal of similarity of occupational functions, ownership, style of life, and probably of outlook. *Manouvriers* owned some vineyards and livestock, *vignerons* almost always worked as day-laborers, artisans worked side by side with both other groups—if indeed they can be called "groups." True, the artisans tended to own larger plots of land, but not much larger. At Lux, among forty-one *artisans,* there were eight "weavers" and ten "stonecutters," whose occupations and landholdings made them scarcely distinguishable from the *manouvriers.* In short, one has the impression of a merging of these three categories, not in the sense of complete equality of income, but in the sense of a cluster of interests, habits, and aspirations.

It is difficult to see any economic basis for proletarian class-consciousness here, which is not to deny the existence of a rural proletariat elsewhere in France in these years. If one is looking for potentialities for social conflict in these villages, it would be more likely to erupt between the *laboureur-rentier* on the one side and the artisan, winegrower and *manouvrier* on the other. Such potential conflict would turn on the availability of land to buy or lease, opportunities for work, and the "hoarding" of grain or forage, rather than a struggle between rich and poor. More impressive are the cohesive elements in this village society. Recall the long-standing importance of communal rights, communal harvesting, and communal ownership, especially of woodland. Add to this the wide distribution of property, the absence of extreme deprivation (the seven beggars at Lux were taxed), and a graduated income distribution. Even the two extremes of the scale should be modified. The income estimate for the *sous-fermiers* is based largely on their money-leases which is not all the same thing as their net incomes. They are therefore overestimated even with a coefficient of thirty instead of twenty times the tax. On the other end of the income scale, the revenues of the widows have been underestimated, since they were taxed at only half the regular five per cent rate for their day labor.

The community of Arc-sur-Tille presents a somewhat different picture. A village of 172 households and 4,000 acres in the parish, Arc-sur-Tille

had the marks of a more specialized commerci a third of the community consisted of meadow. O ing land, much of it reclaimed from the marshes frequently held in substantial blocks, three piece each. The local residents owned 266 cows, leased 2 hundreds of sheep. There were no winegrowers ir artisans than at Lux. There were more carters an sible indication of commercialization. Even the ara mented than at Beaumont or Lux. There were a 40 acres and one of eighty. It was surely less nec same extent as in the other two parishes. There enough to make employment of day-labor (*faire-v* MM. Jacquemard and Devienne, *Bourgeois,* work acres in this fashion. Many of the *laboureurs* as w to plow alone. They sublet some and used day-lab altogether surprising, therefore, to discover a s *manouvriers* at Arc, 37 per cent of the househol per cent at Beaumont and only 11 per cent at Lux 64 day laborers, only three of whom owned any l owned some livestock, and 32 owned their own About two thirds of them rented a few acres a for at least 200 days during the year. Twenty othe ing a living," as the tax roll phrased it.

Did this mean a less cohesive community at Beaumont? The actions of Arc during the early y would not lead one to think so. In fact, the inha even more united in their protest against the n *d'indire,* and the duke's claims to the communal v ants of Beaumont. To be sure, there were political in the village, but no evidence of social tensions c nomic function or disparities of wealth. The thirt the backbone of the "middle group," and it is pro *vriers* followed their political initiative. Economic when combined with a common physical effort in meals at harvest time, does not necessarily lead Moreover, there was Fénéon, to serve as an out frustrations in the village after 1780.

Finally, there were eleven *cabaret*-owners at Arc-s

L–A	*Laboureur-pour-Autruy*	Farmer who rents more than he owns
Vig.	*Vigneron*	Winegrower
A	*Artisan*	Artisan (carpenters, wheelwrights, blacksmiths, weavers, stonecutters, etc.)
Man.	*Manouvrier*	Day-laborer
Vev.	*Veuve*	Widow
Dom.	*Domestique*	Servant, or hired man
Pat.	*Pâtre*	Shepherd
Jar.	*Jardinier*	Gardener
G-B	*Garde-Bois*	Forest Guard
R.E.	*Recteur d'Ecole*	Schoolteacher
Ser.	*Sergent*	Policeman
Gre.	*Greffier*	Clerk
Md.	*Mendiant*	Beggar (not *vagabond*)
Fille	*Fille*	Spinster
Cab.	*Cabaretier*	Tavern keeper
Aub.	*Aubergiste*	Innkeeper
Mar.	*Marchand*	Merchant (retail)

THE DISTRIBUTION OF INCOME AT BEAUMONT IN 1781

Taille 1/20	Est. Rev.	B	For.	F, Me	L–R	Vig.	Man.	A	Vev.	Dom.	Fille	Total	
200–49	4000–			1 (F)								1	
150–99	3000–												
100–49	2000–	1										1	
90–99	1800–				1							1	6–7.2% well-to-do
80–89	1600–				1							1	
70–79	1400–												
60–69	1200–				1							1	
50–59	1000–				1							1	
40–49	800–	2	1		3							6	
30–39	600–				3		1					5	54–65.1% middling
20–29	400–	1		1 (Me)	4	2	1	4	1			13	
15–19	300–		1		1	3	2	4	1			12	
10–14	200–					5	6	6	1			18	
5– 9	100–		8				5		1	2	1	17	23–27.7% poor
1– 4	20–		2						4			6	
Total		4	12	2	15	10	15	14	8	2	1	83	
%		4.8	14.5	2.4	18.1	12.0	18.1	16.9	9.6	2.4	1.2	100.0	

SOURCE: *A. D.*, C-5927.

251

THE DISTRIBUTION OF INCOME AT LUX IN 1779

Taille 1/20	Est. Rev.	B, N	F, Me.	L	A	Vig.	Man.	Vev.	Dom.	R.E. Mar.	Md.	Total	
200–49	4000–		1 (F)									1	
150–99	3000–			1								1	
100–49	2000–												11–8.1% well-to-do
90–99	1800–			1								1	
80–89	1600–			1								1	
70–79	1400–			2								2	
60–69	1200–	1 (N)	1 (Me)									2	
50–59	1000–			3								3	
40–49	800–			3								3	
30–39	600–			6	5							11	84–61.8% middling
20–29	400–	1 (B)		5	10	2	1	1				20	
15–19	300–			3	6	3	1	2		2		17	
10–14	200–			1	14	8	5	5				33	
5– 9	100–			1	6	6	7	9	1			30	41–30.1% poor
1– 4	20–						1	3			7	11	
Total		2	2	27	41	19	15	20	1	2	7	136	
%		1.4	1.4	19.9	30.1	14.1	11.0	14.7	0.7	1.4	5.2	100.0	

SOURCE: *A. D.*, C–6018.

THE DISTRIBUTION OF INCOME AT ARC-SUR-TILLE IN 1772

Taille 1/20	Est. Rev.	B,N,P	F, Me.	L–P	L–A	A	Cab.	Man.	Vev.	Pat. Jar. G–B	R.E. Ser.	Md.	Total	
200–49	4000–													
150–99	3000–	1 (P)	1 (F)										2	
100–49	2000–	1 (N)	1 (F)										2	
90–99	1800–													9–5.2% well-to-do
80–89	1600–			1									1	
70–79	1400–													
60–69	1200–	2 (B)				1							3	
50–59	1000–			1									1	
40–49	800–			1	2								3	
30–39	600–			2	6		3						11	
20–29	400–	1 (B)	1 (Me)		10	4		1			1 (RE)		18	86–50.0% middling
15–19	300–				3	9	2	6					20	
10–14	200–				5	5	4	13	4	3			34	
5– 9	100–					9	1	36	1	5	1 (Ser)		53	77–44.8% poor
1– 4	20–					3		8	9	1		3	24	
Total		5	3	5	26	30	11	64	14	9	2	3	172	
%		2.8	1.7	2.8	15.1	17.4	6.4	37.0	8.1	5.2	1.2	1.7	100.0	

SOURCE: *A. D.*, C–5916.

DOCUMENT X: THE PRICE OF WHEAT IN BURGUNDY

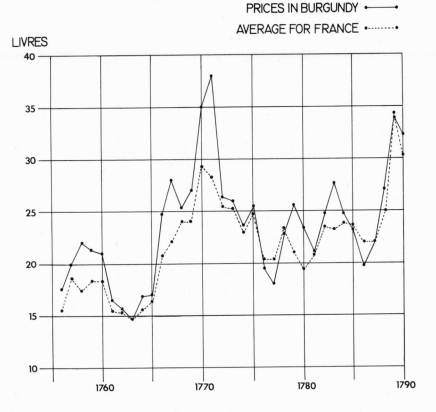

THE PRICE OF WHEAT IN BURGUNDY

PRICES IN BURGUNDY •——————•
AVERAGE FOR FRANCE •·········•

NOTE: Price per setier de Paris (240 livres).
SOURCE: C. E. Labrousse, *Esquisse du mouvement des prix et des revenus en France au XVIIIe siècle*, I, 104, 107.

BIBLIOGRAPHY

PRIMARY SOURCES

A. Unpublished

The principal sources of this book can be found in the Departmental Archives of the Côte d'Or in Dijon, France. The *Fonds Saulx-Tavanes* (Series E–1661 to E–2023) consists of 362 bundles of family papers, the vast majority of which concern the eighteenth century. Rather than list each bundle here, the author has attempted to summarize the contents of each bundle as it is used in the footnotes. The family papers have been supplemented by relevant materials in Series Q (*émigré* property), Series C (administration of the province, including the *taille* rolls), and Series L (Revolution).

Additional source material concerning the Saulx-Tavanes and the villages on their estates can be found in the National Archives in Paris. These include Series H (local administration-Burgundy), Series O^1 (*Maison du Roi*), Series T (sequestered papers), Series F^I C-III (Côte d'Or) for the electoral lists of 1810, and F^3-II (communal administration). Each of these series contains hundreds of bundles; the precise call number will be indicated in the footnotes.

B. Published

Aguesseau, Henri-François d'. *Lettres inédites du chancelier d' Aguesseau*, ed. D. B. Rives. 2 vols. Paris, 1823.
———. *Oeuvres complètes du chancelier d'Aguesseau*, ed. M. Pardessus. 16 vols. Paris, 1819.
Almanac Royal, 1730–1790.

255

Anselme de Sainte Marie, Père. *Histoire généalogique de la maison royale de France, des grands officiers de la couronne....* 9 vols. Paris, 1733.

Archives Parlementaires. 2nd Series. Paris, 1888–1908.

Argenson, René-Louis Voyer, marquis d'. *Journal et mémoires du marquis d'Argenson, publiés...pour la Société d'histoire de France,* ed. E. J. B. Rathery. 7 vols. Paris, 1859–67.

Aubert de la Chesnaye des Bois, F. A. *Dictionnaire généalogique et historique, contenant l'état actuel des premières maisons de France...de l'Europe ...les familles nobles du royaume....* 7 vols. Paris, 1757–65.

Bernis, Armand-Louis de Gontaud, duc de Lauzun. *Memoirs of the Duc de Lauzun,* trans. C. K. Moncrieff. London, 1928.

———. *Mémoires,* ed. F. Barrière. Paris, 1862.

Bernis, Cardinal de. *Mémoires et lettres,* ed. F. Mason. Vol. I. Paris, 1903.

———. *Memoirs and Letters,* transl. K. P. Wormley. 2 vols. Boston, 1901.

Besenval, Baron de. *Mémoires.* Paris, 1821.

Boncerf, P. F. *Les Inconvéniens des droits féodaux* (London, 1776).

Bouhier, M. *Les coutûmiers du duché de Bourgogne avec les anciennes coutûmes et les observations de M. Bouhier, président à mortier.* 2 vols. Dijon, 1742–46.

Brosses, C. de. *Lettres du Président de Brosses,* ed. Y. Bézard. 2 vols. Paris, 1929.

———. *Lettres familières sur l'Italie publiées d'après les manuscrits,* ed. Y. Bézard. 2 vols. Paris, 1931.

Campan, Madame J. H. *Mémoires sur la vie privée de Marie-Antoinette, reine de France et de Navarre,* ed. F. Barrière. 2 vols. Paris, 1849.

———. *Journal anecdotique de Madame Campan, ou souvenirs recueillis dans ses entretiens par M. Maigne.* Paris, 1824.

———. *Memoirs of the Court of Marie-Antoinette.* Vol. I. London, 1850.

Choiseul, E. F., duc de. *Mémoires du Duc de Choiseul, 1719–1785,* ed. F. Calmette. Paris, 1904.

Claudon, F., ed. "Journal de la réunion des trois ordres du bailliage de Dijon, tenue à Dijon (mars–avril, 1789)," in *Enquêtes sur la Révolution en Côte d'Or.* Dijon, 1913.

Code Napoléon, ed. Collin. Paris, 1807.

Créquy, R. de Froulay, marquise de. *Souvenirs de la marquise de Créquy.* Paris, 1840. [These *Souvenirs* are considered apocryphal, the work of their purported editor, Maurice Cousin, comte de Courchamps.]

Croÿ, duc de. *Journal inédit du Duc de Croÿ, 1718–1784,* ed. Viconte de Grouchy and P. Cottin. 4 vols. Paris, 1906.

Dangeau, P., marquis de. *Journal de la cour de Louis XIV,* ed. A. de Montaiglon. 19 vols. Paris, 1857–60.

Duclos, C. P. *Considérations sur les moeurs de ce siècle.* London, 1769.

———. *Oeuvres complètes.* 10 vols. Paris, 1806.

Du Deffand, M. de Vichy-Chamrond, marquise. *Correspondance complète de Madame Du Deffand avec la duchesse de Choiseul, l'abbé Barthélemy et M. Craufurt,* ed. Marquis de Saint-Aulaire. 3 vols. Paris, 1866.

Dufort de Cheverny, comte J. N. *Mémoires sur les règnes de Louis XV et Louis XVI et sur la Révolution,* ed. R. de Crèvecoeur. 2 vols. Paris, 1909.

Duvergier, J. B., ed. *Collection complète des lois, decrêts, ordonnances, règlements, avis du conseil d'état.* Paris, 1834.

Echerolles, Alexandrine des. *Mémoires.* Paris, 1879.

———. *Une famille noble sous la Terreur. Paris,* 1879.

Entrée à Rouen du Cardinal de Saulx-Tavanes, ed. J. de Beaurepaire. Rouen, 1903.

Ephémérides du citoyen, ou bibliothèque raisonnée des sciences morales et politiques. Vol. V (1766), pp. 163 ff.

Genlis, S-F., Ducrest de Saint Aubin, marquise de Sillery, comtesse de. *Mémoires inédites de Madame la comtesse de Genlis sur le XVIIIe siècle et la Révolution française depuis 1756 jusqu'à nos jours.* 10 vols. Paris, 1825.

———. *Les soupers de la maréchale de Luxembourg.* Paris, 1928.

Kent, N. *Hints to Gentlemen of Landed Property.* London, 1775.

La Tour du Pin, marquise de. *Journal d'une femme de cinquante ans.* 2 vols. Paris, 1914.

Lauzun (Biron-Gontaut), duc de. *Mémoires,* ed. F. Barrière. Paris, 1862.

Lespinasse, J. de. *Correspondence entre Mademoiselle de Lespinasse et le comte de Guibert,* ed. comte de Villeneuve-Guibert. Paris, 1906.

Lévis, G. P. duc de. *Souvenirs et portraits, 1780–1789.* Paris and London, 1813.

Ligne, C. J., Prince de. *Memoirs, Letters, Miscellaneous Papers,* trans. K. P. Wormley. 2 vols. London, 1899.

Luynes, C. P. d'Albert, duc de. *Mémoires sur la cour de Louis XV (1735–58),* ed. L. Dussieux and E. Soulie. 17 vols. Paris, 1860–65.

Marais, M. *Journal et mémoires de Mathieu Marais sur le règne de Louis XIV et le règne de Louis XV, 1715–1737,* ed. M. de Lescure. 4 vols. Paris, 1863.

Mercier, L. S. *Tableau de Paris.* 12 vols. Amsterdam, 1782–89.

Monluc, B. de. *Commentaire et lettres de Blaise de Monluc,* ed. A. de Ruble. 5 vols. Paris, 1864–72.

Montlozier, F. D. de Reynand, comte de. *Souvenirs d'un émigré, 1791–1798,* ed. Comte de Larouzière and E. d'Hauterive. Paris, 1951.

257

Moréri, L. *Le grand dictionnaire historique, ou le mélange curieux d'histoire sacrée et profane....* 5 vols. Paris, 1713.

Pothier, R. J. *Traité du contrat de constitution de rente.* Paris, 1763.

Richelieu, Maréchal, duc de. *Mémoires du maréchal| duc de Richelieu,* ed. F. Barrière. 2 vols. Paris, 1868.

Saint Simon, duc de. *Mémoires,* ed. A. de Boislisle. 42 vols. Paris, 1930.

Saulx, Gaspard de. *Mémoires de très noble et très illustre Gaspard de Saulx, Seigneur de Tavanes, Maréchal de France, Amiral des Mers du Levant, Conseiller du Roy et Capitaine de Cent Hommes d'Armes.* Lyon, 1657.

Saulx, Jacques de. *Mémoires de Jacques de Saulx, comte de Tavanes,* ed. C. Moreau. Paris, 1858.

Saulx-Tavanes, M. A., duchesse de. *Mémoires, 1791–1806,* ed. Marquis de Valous. Paris, 1934.

Saulx-Tavanes. *Correspondence des Saulx-Tavanes au XVIe siècle,* ed. L. Pingaud. Paris, 1877.

Ségur, L. P., comte de. *Mémoires, souvenirs, anecdotes,* ed. F. Barrière. Paris, 1859.

Turgot, A. R. J. *Oeuvres,* ed. E. Daire. 2 vols. Paris, 1844.

Vaillant, M. *Statistique du Département de la Côte d'Or.* Paris, An IX.

Villèle, J., comte de. *Mémoires et correspondence.* 5 vols. Paris, 1888–90.

Walpole, H. *Horace Walpole Correspondence,* ed. W. S. Lewis and W. H. Smith. New Haven, 1939——.

Young, A. *Travels in France.* Dublin, 1793.

SECONDARY SOURCES

The bibliography which follows makes no claim to be exhaustive. For an excellent bibliography on the French nobility in the eighteenth century, see J. Meyer, *La noblesse bretonne au XVIIIme siècle,* vol. I (Paris, 1966). For the peasantry and agrarian history region by region, see the bibliography of G. Walter, *Histoire des paysans de France* (Paris, 1963). For France in the Ancien Régime, the most recent bibliography is R. Mandrou, *La France aux XVIIe et XVIIIe siècles* in the "Nouvelle Clio" series (Paris, 1967). The indispensable "classics" on the social and economic history of Burgundy during the Ancien Régime are those by Gaston Roupnel and Pierre de Saint-Jacob. The books and articles listed below were used in preparation for this study.

Ariès, P. *Centuries of Childhood,* trans. R. Baldick. London, 1962.

Babeau, A. *La vie militaire sous l'Ancien Régime.* 2 vols. Paris, 1890.

——. *Le village sous l'Ancien Régime.* Paris, 1879.

Balotte, M. *La baronie de Saint-Julien à travers les âges.* Dijon, 1961.

Balteau, J.; Baroux, M.; Prévis, M.; et al., eds. *Dictionnaire de biographie française*. Paris, 1932——. [Unfortunately completed only through "D". See the standard *Biographie universelle*.]

Baudrillart, H. J. *Histoire du luxe privé et public depuis l'antiquité jusqu'à nos jours*. Paris, 1878–80.

Behrens, B. "Nobles, Privileges, and Taxes in France at the End of the Ancien Régime," *Economic History Review*, Second Series, vol XV, no. 3 (1963).

Black, C. E. *The Dynamics of Modernization*. New York, 1966.

Bloch, M. *Les caractères originaux de l'histoire rurale française*. Paris, 1952, 1954.

——. "La lutte pour l'individualisme agraire dans la France du XVIIIe siècle," *Annales d'histoire économique et sociale*, II (1930).

——. "Sur le passé de la noblesse française, quelques jalons de recherche," *Annales d'histoire économique et sociale*, VIII (1936).

Blum, A. *Les modes aux XVIIe et XVIIIe siècles*. Paris, 1928.

Bluche, F. *Les Honneurs de la Cour*. Paris, 1957.

——. *Les magistrats du Parlement de Paris au XVIIIe siècle, 1715–1771*. Paris, 1960.

Bois, P. *Paysans de l'Ouest*. Le Mans, 1960.

Bourde, A. *Agronomie et agronomes en France au XVIIIe siècle*. 2 vols. Paris, 1968.

Bourgin, G. *Le partage des biens communaux*. Paris, 1908.

Braudel F. *Ecrits sur l'histoire*. Paris, 1969.

Braudel, F., and Labrousse, E., eds. *Histoire économique et sociale de la France*. Vol. II (1660–1789). Paris, 1970.

Brette, A. ed. *La France au milieu du XVIIIe siècle (1747–1757) d'après le journal du marquis d'Argenson*. Paris, 1898.

Brissaud, J. *A History of French Private Law*. Boston, 1912.

Buffenoir, H. *La maréchale de Luxembourg*. Paris, 1924.

Carré, H. *La fin des parlements*. Paris, 1912.

——. *La noblesse de France et l'opinion publique au XVIIIe siècle*. Paris, 1920.

Castries, duc de. *Le testament de la monarchie. Vol. III, Les emigrés, 1789–1814*. Paris, 1963.

Chambers, J. D. and Mingay, G. E. *The Agricultural Revolution, 1750–1880*. New York, 1966.

Chaussinand-Nogaret, G. *Les financiers de Languedoc au XVIIIe siècle*. Paris, 1970.

Clark, C., and Haswell, M. *The Economics of Subsistence Agriculture*. New York, 1966.

Cobban, A. *A Social Interpretation of the French Revolution*. Cambridge, 1965.

Colombet, A. *Les parlementaires bourguignons à la fin du XVIIIe siècle*. Dijon, 1937.

Corvisier, A. *L'armée française de la fin du XVIIe siècle au ministère de Choiseul*. Paris, 1964.

————. "Les généraux de Louis XIV et leur origine sociale," *XVIIe Siècle*. Vol. 42 (1959).

Courtépée, M. *Description générale et particulière du Duché de Bourgogne*. 4 vols. Dijon, 1847.

Crouzet, F. "Agriculture et Révolution industrielle: Quelques réflexions," *Cahiers d'Histoire*, no. 13. Paris, 1967.

Darnton, R. *Mesmerism and the End of the Enlightenment in France*. Cambridge, Mass., 1968.

Daumard, A. and Furet, F. "Structures et relations sociales à Paris au XVIIIe siècle," *Cahiers des Annales*, no. 18. Paris, 1961.

Davenport, M. *The Book of Costume*. New York, 1956.

Delaby, R. "La survivance des dîmes et des droits féodaux en Côte d'Or pendant la Révolution," *La Révolution en Côte d'Or*. Dijon, 1926.

Delbeke, F. *L'action politique et sociale des avocats au XVIIIe siècle*. Louvain, 1927.

Destrey, P. "Un village de mainmortables bourguignons au XVIIIe siècle," *La Révolution française* (1914).

Devèze, M. *Histoire des forêts*. Paris, 1965.

Drouot, H. *Mayenne et la Bourgogne: Etude sur la Ligue*. 2 vols. Paris, 1939.

Drouot, H., and Calmette, J. *Histoire de Bourgogne*. Paris, 1928.

Du Puy de Clinchamps, P. *La Noblesse*. Paris, 1959.

Faucher, D. *La vie rurale vue par un géographe*. Toulouse, 1962.

————. *Géographie agraire, types de culture*. Paris, 1949.

Favier, J. *Les Archives*. Paris, 1965.

Febvre, L. *La terre et l'évolution humaine*. Paris, 1970.

Festy. O. *L'agriculture pendant la Révolution française: Les conditions de production et de récolte des céréales*. Paris, 1947.

Flammermont, J. "Lettres inédites de Marie-Antoinette: la banqueroute Rohan-Guéménée," *La Révolution française*, XXXIV (1898).

Flinn, M. W. "Timber and the Advance of Technology: A Reconsideration," *Annals of Science*, vol. 15, no. 2 (June, 1959).

Fohlen, C. "La décadence des forges comtoises," *Mélanges d'histoire économique et sociale en hommage au Professeur Antony Babel* (Geneva, 1963).

Ford, F. *Robe and Sword: The Regrouping of the French Aristocracy after Louis XIV*. Cambridge, Mass., 1953.

Forster, G. *Briefe und Tagebücher*, ed. A. Leitzman. Halle, 1893.

Forster, R. *The Nobility of Toulouse in the Eighteenth Century: A Social and Economic Study*. Baltimore, 1960.

——. "The Provincial Noble: A Reappraisal," *American Historical Review* (April, 1963), 681–91.

——. "The Survival of the Nobility during the French Revolution," *Past and Present* (July, 1967). "Rejoinder." (April, 1968).

——. "Obstacles to Agricultural Growth in Eighteenth-Century France," *American Historical Review* LXXV, no. 6 (Oct., 1970).

Fourcassié, J. *Villèle*. Paris, 1954.

Gain, A. *La Restauration et les biens des emigrés*. 2 vols. Nancy, 1929.

Garaud, M. *Histoire générale du droit privé français: la Révolution et la propriété foncière*. Paris, 1958.

Garnier, N. *Arc-sur-Tille: les familles seigneuriales et quelques familles bourgeoises*. Arc-sur-Tille, 1913.

——. *Arc-sur-Tille: La Révolution, 1789–1802*. Dijon, 1913.

Gaston-Martin, H. *Nantes au XVIIIe siècle: L'ère des négriers, 1715–1771*. Paris, 1931.

Gille, B. *Les origines de la grande industrie métallurgique en France*. Paris, 1950.

——. *Les forges françaises en 1772*. Paris, 1960.

Gillot-Voisin, J. "La communauté des habitants de Givry au XVIIIe siècle," *Etudes sur la vie rurale dans la France de l'Est*. Dijon, 1966.

Girod, P. "Les subsistances en Bourgogne et particulièrement à Dijon à la fin du XVIIIe siècle." *Revue Bourguignonne*, XVI, no. 4 (1906).

Glass, D. V. and Eversley, D. E. C., eds., *Population in History*. London, 1965.

Glotz, M. *Salons au XVIIIe siècle*. Paris, 1949.

Godechot, J. *Les institutions de la France sous la Révolution et l'Empire*. Paris, 1951; 2nd ed. 1965.

——. *La Contre-révolution: doctrine et action*. Paris, 1961.

Goncourt, E. and J. *The Woman of the Eighteenth Century*, trans. Le Clercq and Roeder. New York, 1927.

Gooch, P. *Louis XV: The Monarchy in Decline*. London, 1956.

Gottschalk, L. *Lafayette Comes to America*. Chicago, 1959.

Gottschalk, L. and McDonald, J., eds. "Letters on the Management of an Estate during the Old Regime," *Journal of Modern History*, VIII (1936).

Goubert, P. *Les Danses et les Motte de Beauvais, familles marchandes sous l'Ancien Régime*. Paris, 1959.

————. *L'Ancien Régime, I, La société*. Paris, 1969.

Grigg, D. B. "A Note on Agricultural Rent and Expenditure in Nineteenth-Century England," *Agricultural History* (1965).

Habakkuk, H. J. "Economic Functions of English Landowners in the Seventeenth and Eighteenth Centuries," in W. E. Minchinton, ed., *Essays in Agricultural History*. Plymouth, 1968.

Herbert, S. *The Fall of Feudalism in France*. London, 1921.

Hobsbawm, E. J. and Rudé, G. *Captain Swing*. London, 1969.

Hufton, O. *Bayeux in the Late Eighteenth Century: A Social Study*. Oxford, 1967.

Hyslop, B. *L'Apanage de Philippe-Egalité, Duc d'Orléans, 1785–91*. Paris, 1965.

Labrousse, C. E. *Esquisse du mouvement des prix et des revenus en France au XVIIIe siècle*. 2 vols. Paris, 1933.

————. *La crise de l'économie française à la fin de l'Ancien Régime et au début de la Révolution française*. Paris, 1944.

Landes, D. "The Statistical Study of French Crises," *Journal of Economic History*, X (1950).

Lane, F. C. *Andrea Barbarigo: Merchant of Venice, 1418–1449*. Baltimore, 1944.

————. *Venice and History*. Baltimore, 1966.

Laurent, R. *L'agriculture en Côte d'Or pendant la première moitié du XIXe siècle*. Dijon, 1931.

Lefebvre, G. "Les recherches relatives à la repartition de la propriété foncière à la fin de l'Ancien Régime," *Revue d'histoire moderne*, III (1928).

————."La place de la Révolution dans l'histoire agraire de la France," *Annales d'histoire économique et sociale*, IV (1929).

————. *La Grande Peur*. Paris, 1932.

————. *Questions agraires au temps de la terreur*. La Roche-sur-Yon, 1954.

Lefranc, R. "Les propriétés privées de Charles X dans la Vienne," *Bulletin de la Société des Antiquaires de l'Ouest*, VII (1964).

L'Héritier, M. "La Révolution municipale: point de départ de la Révolution française," *Révolution française*, XVIII (1939).

Lemarchand, G. "Les troubles de subsistance dans la généralité de Rouen," *Annales historiques de la Révolution française* (Oct.–Dec., 1963).

Léonard, E. G. *L'armée et ses problèmes au XVIIIe siècle*. Paris, 1958.

————. "La question sociale dans l'armée française au XVIIIe siècle," *Anales: E.S.C.*, III (1948).

Lerner, A. *Everybody's Business*. East Lansing, 1961.

Le Roy Ladurie, E. *Les paysans de Languedoc*. 2 vols. Paris, 1966.

262

Letaconnoux, J. "Les transports en France au XVIIIe siècle," *Revue d'histoire moderne et contemporaine*, IX (1908–1909).

Levron, J. *La vie quotidienne à la cour de Versailles au XVIIe et XVIIIe siècles*. Paris, 1965.

Lévy, C., and Henry, L. "Ducs et pairs sous l'Ancien Regime: Caractéristiques démographiques d'une caste," *Population* (1960).

Lévy-Bruhl, H. "La noblesse de France et le commerce à la fin de l'Ancien Régime," *Revue d'histoire moderne et contemporaine*, VIII (1933).

Loutchitsky, J. "De la petite propriété en France avant la Révolution et de la vente des biens nationaux," *Revue historique*, LIX (1895).

———. *L'état des classes agricoles en France à la veille de la Révolution*. Paris, 1911.

———. *La propriété paysanne en France à la veille de la Révolution*. Paris, 1912.

Luethy, H. *La banque protestante en France*. 2 vols. Paris, 1960 and 1961.

Mandrou, R. *Introduction à la France moderne: essai de psychologie historique, 1500–1640*. Paris, 1961.

———. *La France aux XVIIe et XVIIIe siècles*. "Nouvelle Clio." Paris, 1967.

Marion, M. "Etats des classes rurales au XVIIIe siècle dans le généralité de Bordeaux," *Revue des études historiques* (1902).

———. *Histoire financière de la France depuis 1715*. 6 vols. Paris, 1914–26.

———. *Les impôts directs sous l'Ancien Régime*. Paris, 1914.

———. "Les rôles de vingtième et les statistiques de la propriété territoriale sous l'Ancien Régime," *Revue d'historie moderne et contemporaine*, XIV (1914).

———. *Dictionnaire des institutions de la France aux XVIIe et XVIIIe siècles*. Paris, 1923, 1968.

Martin G., and Martenet, P. *La Côte d'Or: étude d'économiee rurale*. Dijon, 1909.

Martin, H. *La dîme ecclésiastique en France au XVIIIe siècle et sa suppression*. Bordeaux, 1912.

Maugras, G. *The Duc de Lauzun and the Court of Louis XV*. London, 1895.

———. *The Duc de Lauzun and the Court of Marie-Antoinette*. London, 1896.

———. *La disgrâce du duc et de la duchesse de Choiseul*. Paris, 1903.

———. *Le Duc et la Duchesse de Choiseul*. Paris, 1924.

Mendras, H. *Sociologie de la campagne française*. Paris, 1965.

Mendras, H., and Tavernier, V. *Terres, paysans et politique*. Paris, 1969.

Merle, L. *La métairie et la révolution agraire de la Gâtine poitevine de la fin du Moyen Age à la Révolution*. Paris, 1958.

Meyer, J. *La noblesse bretonne au XVIIIe siècle.* 2 vols. Paris, 1966.

Minchinton, W. E., ed. *Essays in Agricultural History.* Plymouth, 1968.

Monnier, F. *La chancellier d'Aguesseau, sa conduite et ses idées politiques.* Paris, 1863.

Montenay, S. de. "Comment la maison de Saulx-Tavanes fut ruinée en dernier lieu par son homme d'affaires," *Pays de Bourgogne,* no. 45 (1964).

———. "L'établissement d'une manufacture à Bèze sous la Révolution," *Annales de Bourgogne* (1966).

Moore, B. *Social Origins of Dictatorship and Democracy.* Boston, 1966.

Morineau, M. "Y-a-t-il eu une révolution agricole en France au XVIIIe siècle?" *Revue historique,* CCXXXIX (1968).

Mousnier, R. ed. *Problèmes de stratification sociale.* Actes du colloque international, 1966. Paris, 1968.

———. *Les hierarchies sociales de 1450 à nos jours.* Paris, 1969.

———. *La plume, la faucille, et le marteau: institutions et société en France de Moyen Age à la Révolution.* Paris, 1970.

Ormancey, J. "L'affaire du fauteuil, 1744," *Annales de Bourgogne,* XXXVIII (1966).

Pariset, E., ed. *Bordeaux au XVIIIe siècle.* Bordeaux, 1968. [The chapter by F. Crouzet on the commerce of Bordeaux is excellent.]

Picard, E. "Le commerce du bois de chauffage et du charbon de bois à Dijon au XVIIIe siècle," *Mémoires de l'Académie des Sciences, Arts, et Belles Lettres de Dijon,* vol. V (1896).

Pingaud, L. *Les Saulx-Tavanes.* Paris, 1876.

———. *Choiseul-Gouffier: La France en Orient sous Louis XVI.* Paris, 1887.

Ponteil, F. *Les institutions de la France de 1814 à 1870.* Paris, 1966.

Postan, M. "Investment in Medieval Agriculture," *Journal of Economic History,* XXVII (Dec., 1967).

Postan, M. and Habakkuk, H., eds. *The Cambridge Economic History,* 2nd ed. Cambridge, 1966, VI.

Ranum, O. *Richelieu and the Councillors of Louis XIII.* Oxford, 1963.

Redfield, A. *Peasant Society and Culture.* Chicago, 1956.

Révérend, A. *Titres, anoblissements et paires de la Restauration, 1814–1830,* VI, 213–14. Paris, 1906.

Richard, J. *Histoire de la Bourgogne.* Paris, 1957.

Robert, H. *Les traffics coloniaux du port de La Rochelle au XVIIIe siècle.* Poitiers, 1960.

Roche, D. "Aperçus sur la fortune et les revenus des princes de Condé à l'aube du XVIIIe siècle," *Revue d'histoire moderne et contemporaine,* XIV (1967).

————. "Recherches sur la noblesse parisienne au milieu du XVIIIe siècle: la noblesse du Marais," *Actes du 86e congrès national des Sociétés Savantes, Montpellier, 1961*. Paris, 1962.

Roover, R. de. *L'évolution de la lettre de change du XIVe au XVIIIe siècle*. Paris, 1953.

Roupnel, G. *Histoire de la campagne française*. Paris, 1932.

————. *La ville et la campagne au XVIIe siècle: étude sur les populations du pays dijonnais*. Paris, 1922; 2nd ed. 1955.

Sagnac, P., *La législation civile de la Révolution française, 1789–1804*. Paris, 1898.

————. "Les comités des droits féodaux et de législation, et l'abolition du régime seigneurial," *La Révolution francaise* (1905).

Saint-Jacob, P. de. "Etude sur l'ancienne communauté rurale en Bourgogne." *Annales de Bourgogne* (1941, 1943, 1946, 1953).

————. *Les paysans de la Bourgogne du Nord au dernier siècle de l'Ancien Régime*. Dijon, 1960. [Excellent Bibliography.]

————. *Documents relatifs à la communauté villageoise en Bourgogne du XVIIe siècle à la Révolution*. Dijon, 1962.

Sée, H. *Histoire économique de la France*, ed. R. Schnerb. 2 vols. Paris, 1951.

————. *La France économique et sociale au XVIIIe siècle*. Paris, 1967.

Slicher van Bath, B. H. *The Agrarian History of Western Europe, A. D. 500–1850*. New York, 1963.

Soboul, A. "The French Rural Community in the Eighteenth and Nineteenth Centuries," *Past and Present*, X (1956).

————. "De la pratique des terriers à la veille de la Révolution," *Annales, E.S.C.* (1964).

————. *Paysans, jacobins, et sans-culottes*. Paris, 1966.

————. "La Révolution française et la féodalité," *Annales historiques de la Révolution française* (1968).

Sombart, W. *Luxury and Capitalism*. Ann Arbor, 1967.

Sourdillat, J.-M. *Géographie agricole de la France*. Paris, 1969.

Spring, D. "A Great Agricultural Estate: Netherby under Sir James Graham, 1820–45," *Agricultural History* (April, 1955).

————. *The English Landed Estate in the Nineteenth Century: Its Administration*. Baltimore, 1963.

Taylor, G. V. "The Paris Bourse on the Eve of the Revolution, 1781–1789," *American Historical Review* (July, 1962).

————. "Types of Capitalism in Eighteenth-Century France," *English Historical Review* (July, 1964).

Tilly, C. *The Vendée*. Cambridge, Mass., 1964.

Tuetey, L. *Les officiers de l'Ancien Régime: nobles et routuriers*. Paris, 1908.

Vaughan, R. *John the Fearless*. London, 1966.

Venard, M. *Bourgeois et paysans au XVIIe siècle: recherches sur le rôle des bourgeois parisiens dans la vie agricole au sud de Paris au XVIIe siècle.* Paris, 1957.

Vermale, F. "Le retour de l'émigré," *Annales révolutionnaires*, VIII (1914).

Vidalenc, J. *Les emigrés français, 1789–1825*. Caen, 1963.

———. *La société française de 1815 à 1848: le peuple des campagnes*. Paris, 1969.

Vovelle, M. "Sade et Mirabeau," *Provence historique* (1967).

Walter, G. *Histoire des paysans de France*. Paris, 1963.

Waugh, N. *Corsets and Crinolins: A History of Women's Underwear*. London, 1954.

Weiner, H. *The French Exiles, 1789–1815*. London, 1960.

Wiley, W. L. *The Gentlemen of Renaissance France*. Cambridge, Mass., 1954.

Wolf, J. B. *Louis XIV*. New York, 1968.

INDEX

THE JOHNS HOPKINS PRESS

Designed by the Johns Hopkins Press Staff

Composed in Granjon text and display
by Monotype Composition Company

Printed on 60-lb. Sebago, MF, Offset Regular
by Universal Lithographers, Inc.

Bound in Columbia Bayside Vellum
by L. H. Jenkins, Inc.

HIGHSMITH   #LO-45220